Child Abuse and Neglect

Also by David Howe:

Social Workers and their Practice in Welfare Bureaucracies
An Introduction to Socal Work Theory
The Consumers' View of Family Therapy
Half a Million Women: Mothers Who Lose their Children by Adoption (with P. Sawbridge and D. Hinings)
On Being a Client: Understanding the Process of Counselling and Psychotherapy
*Attachment Theory for Social Work Practice**
Attachment and Loss in Child and Family Social Work
Adopters on Adoption: Reflections on Parenthood and Children
Patterns of Adoption: Nature, Nurture and Psychosocial Development
*Attachment Theory, Child Maltreatment and Family Support** (with M. Brandon, D. Hinings and G. Schofield)
Adoption, Search and Reunion (with J. Feast)
The Adoption Reunion Handbook (with L. Trinder and J. Feast)
Contact in Adoption and Permanent Foster Care (with E. Neil)

* Also published by Palgrave Macmillan

Child Abuse and Neglect

Attachment, Development and Intervention

David Howe

palgrave
macmillan

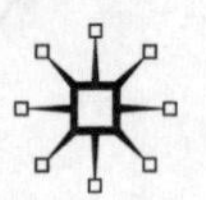

First published 2005 by
PALGRAVE MACMILLAN
Houndmills, Basingstoke, Hampshire RG21 6XS and
175 Fifth Avenue, New York, N.Y. 10010
Companies and representatives throughout the world

Reprinted 2005

PALGRAVE MACMILLAN is the global academic imprint of the Palgrave Macmillan division of St. Martin's Press, LLC and of Palgrave Macmillan Ltd. Macmillan® is a registered trademark in the United States, United Kingdom and other countries. Palgrave is a registered trademark in the European Union and other countries.

ISBN-13: 978 1–4039–4825–0 hardback
ISBN-10: 1–4039–4825–9 hardback
ISBN-13: 978 1–4039–4826–7 paperback
ISBN-10: 1–4039–4826–7 paperback

This book is printed on paper suitable for recycling and made from fully managed and sustained forest sources.

A catalogue record for this book is available from the British Library.

A catalog record for this book is available from the Library of Congress.

Library of Congress Catalog Card Number: 2005045732

11 10 9 8 7 6 5 4 3
14 13 12 11 10 09 08 07 06

Printed by Creative Print and Design (Wales), Ebbw Vale

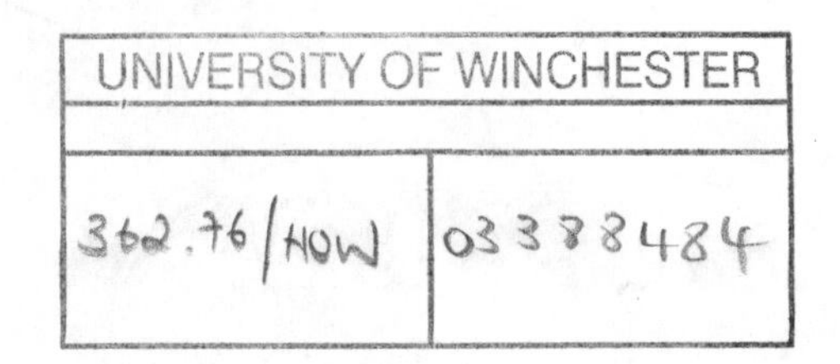

This book is dedicated to the memory of my mother and father

Contents

Preface

Social and psychological scientists have always been intrigued by the part that early life experiences might play in human growth and behaviour. Early explorations of the subject inevitably raised theories of one kind or another and those who promoted them tended to attack and dismiss their rivals. There were those who felt that the role of genes and nature deserved more prominence. Others saw human personality as entirely the product of nurture. Radical behavioural psychologists argued that the environment is the only force capable of objectively shaping behaviour and development. In contrast, psychodynamic perspectives recognized an interior world of human experience; there were minds at play and behaviour needed to be understood at the subjective level. The second half of the twentieth century was dominated by cognitive psychology. Here thought and 'information processing' were affected by perception, memory and mental schemata. Cognitive psychologists recognized a mind at work but one that processes, in a computer-like fashion, environmental inputs.

John Bowlby, a child psychiatrist, was also absorbed by the possible impact that social and environmental events might have on children's development. Some of his earliest thoughts were triggered by his work with children in residential care, many of whom had suffered family adversity. As his clinical experience grew, he became more and more impressed with the relationship between children's experiences of early loss and trauma and the risk of later maladjustment, behavioural difficulties and impaired mental health. For example, in 1944, he published 'Forty-four juvenile thieves: their characters and home lives' as a journal paper. In 1945, after army service, Bowlby became head of the children's department at the Tavistock Clinic. His work on maternal loss and separation continued, and he was commissioned by the World Health Organisation to write a report on the fate of the thousands of homeless children in post-war Europe. This was published in 1951 under the title of *Maternal Care and Mental Health.*

Anxious to understand the psychological mechanisms that might link early adversity with later problem behaviours, he soon realized that most mainstream schools of thought, including psychoanalytic thinking, were not up to the job of explaining his clinical and research observations. From the outset Bowlby was willing to consider a wide range of ideas from a variety of disciplines to help him understand children's early development. Systems theory, control theory, ethology, evolutionary theory and most of developmental psychology influenced his thinking.

Of particular importance in the genesis of attachment theory was Bowlby's recognition of the value of ethology and evolutionary theory in trying to make sense of parent–child relationships. Ethologists observe and study animals in their natural habitat. Using the principles of evolutionary theory, they examine how instinctive behaviours contribute to adaptation and actual survival. Although these behaviours are not learned, they are shaped by the social environment. Applying this type of thinking to human behaviour and development, Bowlby opened up a radically different way of thinking about children's development. Given the vulnerability and dependency of human infants, it would seem reasonable to expect that they arrive in the world with a range of inbuilt behaviours likely to increase their survival. One of these is attachment behaviour, activated at times of perceived threat or danger. The goal of the behaviour is protection, gained by seeking proximity to the caregiver.

Now of course there are many other instinctive behavioural systems present in humans, some active at birth, others programmed to become prominent later on in childhood.

'Adult relationships typically have multiple determinants,' write George and West (1999: 286), which 'arise from and serve the needs of more than one motivational system'. For example, 'the affiliative system motivates the individual to establish friendships and other forms of social support; the sexual system motivates the individual to engage in behaviour related directly to reproduction. Ultimately all behavioural systems support survival and reproductive fitness, but they are not identical to attachment' (George and West 1999: 287). Nevertheless, developmentally, there is something fundamental about the attachment system. Not only does it act to increase survival, it also requires engagement with others of the species and thus involves relationships. Although attachment behaviour and an attachment bond are not one and the same thing, bonds of attachment or 'affectional ties' do generally, though not necessarily, begin to develop between children and their attachment figures. In the context of the relationship with caregivers, other developmentally interesting things are set in train.

Bowlby observed that 'Many of the most intense emotions arise during the formation, maintenance, the disruption, and the renewal of attachment relationships' (1979: 130). Postive emotions are experienced in making and maintaining attachments (feeling safe, falling in love), while negative emotions are felt when attachments are unavailable or lost (fear when alone, anger when abandoned, sadness when bereaved). Many modern definitions describe attachment theory as a theory of emotional regulation. Secure mothers continuously regulate their baby's levels of arousal and therefore their emotional states. Biologically speaking, attachment, by promoting feelings of safety, protection and care, is also a way of controlling anxiety. In helping young children regulate their arousal, caregivers also begin to introduce their infants to the world of feelings, subjective mental states, and the importance of relationships and other people. As other people are the most potent source of both emotional arousal and regulation, attachment theory has always taken a great interest in intersubjectivity, family systems and the conduct of social relationships.

With increasing maturation and continued experience of the relationship between the self and others, children also begin to develop cognitive understandings of their psychosocial environment. Bowlby was certainly interested in cognitive information theory. He recognized that the organization of the attachment behavioural system involved cognitive components. Children develop mental representations, or internal working models, of the self, other people, and how relationships seem to work. These representations are based on actual experience. Children whose parents are available and loving develop very different cognitive models of the self and others compared with children whose carers are hostile and rejecting. With these mental representations acting as guides about what to expect of the self and others in relationships, children and adults with different attachment experiences begin to behave in predictably different ways in complex and emotionally challenging situations.

This very brief outline of some of the origins of attachment theory indicates its ability to absorb, be influenced by, and integrate elements of most of the major schools of developmental thinking. Attachment *behaviour* is shaped by the character of the caregiving environment. It was Bowlby's view that the ethologists offered the strongest paradigm for understanding human growth and behaviour. Their thinking was grounded in evolutionary biology. Attachment theory is concerned with the emotions, their expression, regulation and the part they play in mental health. And attachment theory, in its use of mental representations and the way they affect feelings and behaviour, is fully compatible with cognitive theory. Out of these highly interactive, socially embedded, complex developmental processes, the psychological self emerges (Fonagy et al. 2002). Modern developmental attachment theory continues to remain open to change and new ideas as it seeks to understand the engines of human development.

There is no better illustration of this than the significant part that the developmental neurosciences are playing in helping us to understand the psychosocial self. Neurobiologists recognize the relevance of the ethological and evolutionary sciences in helping them understand brain growth and development. They have also explored the deep significance of attachment, affect regulation, and the quality of early parent–child relationships to the way the brain processes information and experience, particularly emotional experience in the context of attachment relationships, and how its hard-wiring, biochemistry and neurological organization is shaped by those very experiences. The influence of the neurosciences is proving to be especially useful in helping us make sense of the behaviours, personalities and mental health problems of children who have suffered severe abuse, neglect and trauma.

In Part I, the book attempts to capture some of the excitement and integrative outlook that currently characterizes developmental attachment theory, and to apply it to our understanding of child abuse and neglect. Armed with an understanding of attachment, emotional regulation and the defence mechanisms, Parts II, III and IV provide a framework for organizing much of what we know about the causes, character and consequences of maltreatment. In particular, these sections seek to understand the origins of problematic caregiving and how they affect children's psychological development, mental health and social behaviour. Although the complex nature of child protection is fully recognized, including the overlap between many of the main categories of maltreatment, different types of child abuse and neglect are examined separately in Parts II and III respectively. Part IV then considers what happens in cases where abuse and neglect, including sexual abuse, occur together.

Research and theory tend to run ahead of treatment. However, there is now a growing body of evidence-based practice and clinical wisdom emerging to help professionals support and treat some of society's most hurt families and individuals. Part V of the book reviews a number of these attachment-based interventions as they apply to infants, toddlers, school-age children, adults and parents. True to the integrative nature of developmental attachment theory, these interventions make comfortable use of behavioural, emotional, cognitive and systems-based approaches.

To help illustrate the behaviour of caregivers and children, case examples are used throughout the book based on the author's research work. The material has been made anonymous, and where conflation does not upset the point being made, some examples are the result of merging elements of similar cases together.

Clearly no one theory, no single approach can claim exclusive authority over its subject matter, particularly in an area so subtle and hermeneutically fraught as human behaviour and experience. It is my belief that attachment theory offers an interesting and practical perspective on familiar material. In throwing its own particular light on an emotionally and scientifically difficult subject, the hope is that the field of vision is cast a little brighter, a little sharper.

Part I

Emotions, Attachment and the Psychological Self

The interconnectedness of many of the major fields of developmental psychology and their links with attachment make the subjects of the self, personality and relationships increasingly fascinating but more complex. As a scene setter for the current conceptual landscape, Part I reviews a number of key ideas that are enriching our understanding of parent–infant relationships and children's psychosocial development. In fact it is proving more and more difficult, indeed inappropriate to disentangle talk of the biological and evolutionary basis of human behaviour from discussion of the emotions, the regulation of affect, models of stress and coping, attachment, psychological defence mechanisms, and brain growth and development. Attachment is examined in the context of this busy and buzzing field of research, theory and ideas. Increasing attention is being given to the neurological, emotional, psychological and social development of children who have suffered abuse and neglect. And as the goal of attachment behaviour is protection and the regulation of anxiety, it has a key role in these debates.

By taking a multi-disciplinary perspective on development and attachment, it is possible to offer further refinements to the traditional ways of classifying child abuse and neglect. Part I therefore ends by outlining a classification of types of child maltreatment based on patterns of attachment using caregiver states of mind, affect regulation, coping and survival strategies, and defence mechanisms.

1

Developing Minds in the Context of Close Relationships

Introduction

Although extremely vulnerable and dependent, newborn human infants arrive in the world equipped with a sophisticated array of inbuilt behaviours designed to maximize their survival. Two of these behaviours, and the systems that underpin them, require particular mention. One is able powerfully to draw people to the baby at times of need and distress. This is *attachment behaviour*. The other urges the infant to look outwards and engage with, and make sense of, the world, particularly the world of other people. This is *exploratory behaviour*, including the infant's encounters with intersubjectivity – the self in relationship with other human beings and their minds. Infants are born with an instinct to relate with other selves. They arrive with a biological need to feel understood (Fonagy et al. 1995).

There are close links between these behaviours and predispositions. Both involve intimate dealings with adults who value the child's survival and sponsor his or her development. For most children these people are likely, though not certain, to be their mother and father. They are caregivers, and they are destined to become the child's primary attachment figures as well as their psychological, social and cultural guides.

The function of attachment is to protect the young and vulnerable of the species from danger (and annihilation). When infants feel safe, they are free to find out, investigate and explore. The more secure children feel, the more time, energy and inclination they have to seek understanding and make sense. 'Whereas fear constricts, safety expands the range of exploration' (Fosha 2003: 227). This is why the social, emotional and cognitive development of abused and neglected children is so heavily compromised. They don't feel safe; they rarely relax. Fear for these children can be so endemic that exploration is weak, anxious and sporadic. Most maltreated children's psychological efforts are concentrated on survival and safety.

However, something else of exquisite fascination takes place in the relationship between children and their caregivers. The child's mind forms. It is the birthplace of the psychological self. In the words of Schore (2001a), 'young minds form in the context of close relationships'. The self is forged as the young brain purposefully engages with other minds where it begins to experience itself as a burgeoning psychosocial entity: 'the development of the self is tantamount to the aggregation of experiences of the self in relationships' (Fonagy et al. 2002: 40). Gerhardt (2004: 18) sums all this up neatly, noting that 'the baby is an interactive project not a self-powered one'.

The infant's brain is programmed to make sense of experience. But it needs exposure to the experiences of which it needs to make sense. This is true of learning to see and learning to speak, but it is also true of learning to recognize, understand and make sense of the mind and the psychological nature of both the self and others (Fonagy et al. 2002). The major source of psychological experience takes place in the interactions between babies and their carers. Psychological experience is particularly heightened at times of anxiety, fear and distress. In other words, the intensity of mental state experiences is greatest whenever the attachment system is activated and the child exhibits careseeking behaviour. This is why the quality of caregiving is critical, not just to the child's feelings of safety, but also to the quality and character of the mind and psychological self which form. And just to complete the cycle of self-formation between the generations, the thing which lies behind the way carers nurture and protect the child is their mind and the character of their adult psychological self.

Of course, there are many other factors that influence our personalities and the way our minds form. Genes and biology determine much of our temperamental make-up. Whether we are shy or forceful, irritable or good-natured, optimistic or pessimistic, cautious or adventurous is largely governed by our inherited nature. Temperament can also have a long-term impact on our development, including the emergence of antisocial behaviour if caregiving is also poor (Saltaris 2002). Our physiologies affect our moods, self-image, behaviour and abilities. The birth order also seems to have some influence on whether we are more likely to be conforming or rebellious, systematic or creative (Sulloway 1996). Moreover, attachment is just one of a number of proximity-seeking behavioural systems including affiliation, sexuality, caregiving, subordination/submission and dominance. And there are broad differences between the sexes, with men on average more likely to be spatially competent and inclined to systematize information, and women on average more inclined to be verbally proficient, empathic and relationship-oriented (Baron-Cohen 2003).

But the basic force that brings about and helps shape our mental landscape is the brain's programmed urge to interact with others. It is in this process that the self emerges. And like many processes of nature, the characteristics of the interacting elements govern the final, unique, individual outcome. Streams rushing down from high mountains of granite gouge steep valleys that have a very different profile from the gentle vales of shale and clay along which rivers meander after springing from soft limestone hills. The young mind which forms in relationship with an over-stressed parent who suffered severe abuse in his or her own childhood is likely to be very different from the mind that is shaped in relationship with a relaxed and confident parent able to reflect objectively on her own loving experiences. This brings us to the central theme of this book.

It is parents and carers, not abstract systems or physical environments per se, who maltreat their children, not just physically but psychologically and emotionally. Their actions and behaviours are the product of mental states and psychological processes that may well be adversely affected by harsh environments. It is these mental states that provide us with major clues about why some parents assault their children, others fail to respond at times of need, and yet others reject, wishing their children had never been born. However, parents who maltreat do not begin their caregiving career intending to harm or neglect their children. They have the same hopes and aspirations as other parents; perhaps even more so given their own often unhappy childhoods. They plan to right the wrongs they suffered. But somewhere along the line, things begin to break down. They might lack support. It is likely that they are living under stress. In fact, it is one of the perverse ironies in child protection work that those with the least psychological resources to cope with stress tend to have the highest levels of stress with which to deal.

Of course, it is absolutely right that we tackle poverty, poor housing and other environmental stressors. To live with little money and a violent partner in a damp, high-rise flat is stressful. However, accepting the primacy of political and economic solutions, I want to argue that at the end of the ecological line is the mind of the maltreating carer, and what goes on within it has to remain the centre of interest for front-line practitioners if they are to keep their bearings in emotionally difficult and demanding situations.

Maltreating Minds

Our subject matter is child maltreatment, or more specifically maltreating minds. We shall look at minds that maltreat and minds that are maltreated. We examine the experiences of children who have been abused, neglected and rejected. There are many excellent books that address the issue of children who are harmed (for example, Corby 2000; Wilson and James 2001; Miller-Perrin and Perrin 1999; Myers et al. 2002; Wolfe 1999). Where this one differs is in its deliberate emphasis on the state of mind of the parents and carers who abuse and neglect their children.

Whatever the context, in most cases maltreatment boils down to the actions and behaviours of carers, and these are driven by minds and what goes on inside them. It is one of the features of maltreatment that when the child's attachment system is activated, the parent's attachment system also becomes activated, triggering a range of fragile defensive mental processes, which when breached lead to highly dysregulated caregiving responses. Faced with a needy, vulnerable or distressed child, the maltreating parent feels disorganized, out-of-control, and without a strategy to deal with his or her own emotional arousal, or that of his or her child. The result is abuse, neglect or both.

Unless the child has bruises or broken bones, it is generally difficult to find any direct evidence of maltreatment. Emotional neglect, rejection and psychological maltreatment often have to be established by indirect means, including the recognition of the developmental and emotional, behavioural and social signs of abuse and neglect. This also requires practitioners to understand how maltreating carers mentally process information about their child's need for safety, recognition and hunger to understand.

The psychological processes of parents who maltreat are those that get triggered whenever the self feels anxious, helpless, under siege, under threat or under stress. The demands made by others in social relationships tend to be the most frequently met and potent of these triggers. Of the different types of social relationship, that between parent and child is perhaps the most emotionally demanding. All of us under challenge are at risk of operating less functionally, less reasonably. More primitive, survival-oriented behaviours get activated whenever we feel vulnerable and exposed. Reactions to such threats might result in attack and agitated attempts to suppress the cause of the distress; avoidance or dismissal of the object (rejection); or a helpless preoccupation with our own anxieties so that we neglect the needs of others. These various behaviours and reactions generate different types of caregiving environment.

By focusing on the mind, attachment, the development of the psychological self, and the underlying psychology of caregiving, I want to highlight a number of key features in working with and understanding child maltreatment:

- It is minds that mediate between what is perceived to be taking place in the environment, and the individual's behaviour and response to that environment. At the centre of any ecological model is the carer's mind and information-processing style.
- The carer's mind, therefore, can be viewed as a mediating variable. Depending on the characteristics of the parent's 'mind', children's behaviour and the context in which it takes places will be (i) perceived, (ii) cognitively represented, (iii) interpreted, and (iv) dealt with in a particular way, ranging from benign and supportive to hostile and rejecting.
- The minds of carers process attachment information relevant to the care and protection of their children.
- Caregivers process their child's careseeking and exploratory demands through their own mental states and interpretative biases, distortions, and defences.
- Minds form as young, vulnerable, dependent children interact, relate with and try to make sense of themselves and their social environment. The psychological self therefore emerges as the infant's subjective state interacts with the subjective states of others, particularly attachment figures.

- The characteristics of the young mind which forms depends on the child's particular genetic make-up (as it might affect temperament for example), constitutional condition (for instance, autism or blindness), and the quality of the social environment in which the child finds himself or herself (accepting or rejecting, friendly or hostile, thoughtful or neglectful).
- Minds are possessed of thoughts and feelings, perceptions and memories, interpretations and beliefs.
- Feeling states are fundamental. The need to understand and regulate emotions is central to survival and the ability to function as a competent social and interpersonal being.
- Infants learn to regulate their arousal (and their behaviour), and make sense of their emotions as they relate intersubjectively with their caregivers.
- In time, young minds become old minds, which in their turn become the minds of future caregivers who have to deal with the stresses and strains of their world. Thus, a new generation of carers creates the social environments with which their children have to interact, and in which their young minds form, and so on.

The Mental Processing of Social Information

Minds, then, form over time, and some of their main operating and processing styles are forged in childhood. This is why assessments need to be interested in the parent's own relationship history. It gives us important clues and insights into the possible information-processing characteristics being used by parents in the present, particularly when they have to deal with events that they experience as stressful. Caring for children, especially young children, is inherently demanding, and most parents experience stress and challenge in their caregiving role. Maltreating parents, however, find dealing with the child's attachment behaviour particularly difficult. It appears to activate old unresolved attachment issues from their own childhood to do with fear and danger, loss and rejection, causing them such difficulties in the caregiving role. Research has established that maltreating parents are vulnerable to stress (cognitively they are not good problem solvers), and poor at relationships, tending towards withdrawal and/or conflict whenever faced with the emotional demands of others (Pianta, Egeland and Erikson 1989).

Perhaps the most useful way to understand child maltreatment is to examine the psychological and behavioural *transactions* that take place between parents and children. A transactional model developed by Cicchetti and Lynch (1993) considers the interactions and transactions that take place between parental characteristics and attitudes, child characteristics (for example, learning difficulty, physical disability, fractious and difficult temperament), and environmental factors (for example, poor housing, lack of social support).

Research suggests that maltreating parents seem to process social information (social cognition) in ways that appear deficient, disfigured or disturbed. What they see and take note of seems both distorted and biased (for instance, abuse), or absent (for instance, neglect). More than most, maltreating parents lack understanding of the emotional and social subtleties and complexity of relationships, especially the parent–child relationship. In particular, carers have problems seeing things in an age-appropriate and developmental way, and from their child's point of view.

> Maltreating parents tend to think in global, all-or-nothing terms rather than see the shades of gray that more realistically capture human behavior ... Aber and Zigler (1981) pointed to the importance of the parents' own developmental level as a determinant of how they think and behave in regard to their children. Parental development reflects the parents' own history of care, their struggles with issues of dependence and autonomy, and their level of cognitive functioning. Parents with unresolved issues of trust, dependency, and autonomy are more likely to suffer difficulty understanding and meeting the demands of their children and may seek to meet their own needs through the parent–child relationship.
>
> (Erickson and Egeland 2002: 13)

Although I shall be concentrating on how parental minds which maltreat are themselves the product of impaired and traumatic developmental experiences, and how under the stress of attachment relationships, old anxieties and aggressions surface, the approach can be seen as part of a wider 'social information processing' perspective. Milner (2003) in particular has sought to explain child maltreatment using social cognitive behavioural approaches. The carers' cognitive activities are seen to mediate between how they perceive their child's behaviour and the way they react.

The social information-processing model has four stages, based on the individual's pre-existing cognitive schemata (Milner 2003; also see Crittenden 1997).

Pre-Existing Cognitive Schemata

These include beliefs about children, how they 'work' and how they should be raised and treated. These cognitive schemata (very similar to Bowlby's 1969 idea of an 'internal working model') influence and guide the way parents perceive their child and his or her behaviour.

> Specifically, high-risk and abusive, compared to nonabusive and low-risk, parents are believed to have more inaccurate and biased pre-existing cognitive schemata involving beliefs and values that impact the way they perceive, evaluate, integrate, and respond to information related to children.
>
> (Milner 2003: 9).

For example, physically abusive parents might believe that their children are likely to dominate them unless they show them who is boss. Emotions (affective components) also enter the schemata. If feelings of anger or irritation have been experienced in the past around issues of need, vulnerability, compliance or defiance, either as a child or as a parent, these same feelings are likely to be aroused whenever the parent feels that similar issues are being raised by their child as he or she seeks care and protection.

Emotions also affect memory, and so the evocation of certain feelings might trigger particular memories leading to behaviours associated with those memories. In other words, at-risk carers are less likely to see a new emotionally charged situation in a fresh, rounded way. The more stressful the situation and the more negative the affect, the more likely it is that a maltreating parent will employ old schemata to process information about the current situation, irrespective of the actual characteristics of the new situation.

Stage 1: Perceptions

Although individuals might perceive a situation in a relatively accurate and objective way, the more emotionally challenging the circumstance, the more likely it is that it will be seen through existing assumptions, schemata, memories and prejudices. Maltreating carers tend to have more deficits, distortions, biases, and errors in their perceptions of children's behaviours. They might be less attentive. For example, neglectful parents might fail to see, perceive or hear their children's distress and attachment needs. Abusive parents might only see the negative things in their child's behaviour, failing to note instances when the child complies or behaves well. Abusive parents readily perceive and identify noncompliant behaviour. It has also been observed that abusive carers, though likely to notice that their child has an emotional expression on his or her face, are much more likely to misidentify it – an error of coding. This is particularly true if the expression is conveyed at low intensity. For example, a look of surprise might be perceived as a look of dissatisfaction, which is much more likely to trigger a hostile response than one of reassurance.

Stage 2: Interpretations and Evaluations

High-risk parents tend to interpret negative behaviour in children as more serious, wrong and culpable than low-risk parents. They are also more inclined to see these 'hostile' behaviours as wilful and deliberate, warranting a heavy disciplinary response.

Stage 3: Information Integration and Response Selection

Maltreating parents are less likely to take mitigating or situational factors into account when interpreting a child's behaviour. For example, if the family dog knocks into a three-year-old who has just made a drink, and the drink spills on the carpet, the child is accused of being careless and annoying.

Stage 4: Response Implementation and Monitoring

High-risk parents tend to be rather rigid and inflexible in their parenting techniques, including behavioural control and discipline. Their ability to monitor, reflect on and explore the meaning and purpose of a child's behaviour is limited. They employ the same understandings and techniques in most situations, failing to adapt or develop their responses to the particular situation or circumstances.

Maltreating parents are likely to process a range of different parent–child interactions using the same assumptions, understandings and cognitive schemata. This is known as ***automatic processing***. The effect of using the same model or cognitive schema to explain a variety of behaviours is a failure to see or think about the particularities of the situation. Reactions are unreflective and quick. An injured child, an ill child, and a tired child might all be seen as conditions demanding a response, the effect of which is to annoy the parent. The distressed child is immediately told off and disciplined. In contrast, controlled processing acknowledges and is interested in the particular circumstances surrounding the behaviour, and the response is tailored to that situation.

Abusive and neglectful parents see their child's personality as fixed and their behaviour as independent of circumstance or situation:

> That little shit is always messing around and breaking things, which he knows really annoys me. There's something about him that is deliberately irritating. He knows exactly how to wind me up but if he thinks he's going to get the better of me, he's got another think coming.

Although a cognitive perspective informs the 'social information processing' model, it is the feelings generated by perception and thought that have the most powerful effect on the resulting behaviour. This is particularly important when we consider child maltreatment. Emotions and their regulation, though more subterranean in character, nevertheless demand close attention, and so it is to these that we now turn.

2

Emotions and Mind-Mindedness

Emotions and their Importance in Development, Social Competence and Mental Health

Historically, the emotions and their importance in human affairs have been under-researched. However, more recently there have been a spate of major scientific advances, as well as popular books on the subject ranging from affects and their regulation to the part that emotional intelligence plays in everyday life.

Emotions refer to the way our bodies, brains and minds react when aroused by meaningful events. Our subjective experience of the state of our nervous system gives rise to emotions that can be felt as either good or bad, leading to approach or avoidance behaviours in specific situations. The nervous and hormonal systems are affected, giving rise to physical and psychological experiences. Emotions are manifested bodily, particularly in the form of facial expressions. They can also be expressed in terms of bodily movements. *Feelings* refer to the subjective experience of these psychological, physiological and neurological states. *Affects* refer to the combination of emotions and feelings (Taylor, Bagby and Parker 1997).

Emotions are rooted as much in the body as they are in the mind. We talk of feeling 'hot and bothered' or 'sick with worry'. Fear is experienced both physically (skin feels cold as the blood gets diverted to muscles for flight or fight, the heart beats faster to increase blood flow, the senses become hyper-alert), and psychologically (feelings of alarm and danger as one's existence feels under threat). The 'language' in which emotional experience is understood lies outside the realm of rational, linear, logical thought and speech. Emotions are body-focused, experiential, and based in the senses (Fosha 2003). The infant brain, not yet geared up to model the world cognitively and reflect on it, is much better at recognizing, processing and remembering emotional states, including recognizing the affective content of other people's facial expressions, voice tone and body language, than it is at dealing with more logical, reflective material. This remains true up until the child's third year, and before full language acquisition.

Emotions are experienced in relationship to the organism's unconscious appraisal of the internal and external environment. As the infant's senses monitor these environments, so emotional states arise. Events can be appraised as beneficial or harmful. Emotions give us fast, unconscious responses to the unexpected. They are a guide to action: to approach or avoid (Gerhardt 2004). A potentially dangerous feature of the environment (a snarling dog, a menacing parent) commands a young child's total attention. Negative emotions such as fear, anxiety and disgust generally trigger actions designed to avoid, escape or suppress the upsetting event. More positive emotions, say the pleasure of play, help children approach and persist with activities that help in their exploration of the world.

The complexities involved in being a social animal seem to make emotions a particularly important part of our psychological make-up. Our emotions provide us with outline scripts for social interactions. They help us appraise and understand the subtleties of relationships, when to approach, when to back off, when to soothe, how to cooperate, how to survive in competition.

> Emotions arise largely with problems to be solved. So for recurring problems like escaping from predators, responding to strangers, meeting aggressive threats, caring for infants, falling in love, and so on, we are equipped with genetically based mechanisms that provide outline scripts for behavior that has been successful in the past, and has therefore been selected. Each kind of emotional pattern is triggered by distinctive cues. Each makes ready patterns of action appropriate to solving the problem that has arisen.
>
> (Oatley and Jenkins 1996: 82)

In individual development, emotions function to help us adapt to and coordinate with other people. Emotions therefore help us to manage action. They operate 'as a central organising process within the brain' (Siegel 1999: 4). Emotions give our memories and thoughts colour, meaning and value. Our moods influence what we see and note. Fear alerts us to danger. Joy encourages us to relax, play, learn and approach others. We tend to remember emotionally charged events much better than routine experiences. Being hit by a van makes that particular day's car journey vivid and memorable, while countless other uneventful trips are forgotten. When similar emotionally charged situations are experienced, old feelings are evoked and old reactions get triggered. Any strong emotional arousal increases the chance of an event being remembered so that it is either avoided or approached if met again sometime in the future. Much of this can take place at an unconscious level, both somatically and psychologically.

Emotions are remembered in a part of the brain that can be directly affected by the senses and which can short-circuit the cortex, conscious memory and reflective processing. A mild rebuke by a lover might activate ancient memories of being ridiculed by your father for never being good enough. Old ways of trying defensively to survive the pain of maternal rejection by becoming subdued and emotionally disengaged suddenly punctuate the present relationship, in which the other is perceived to be helpless or vulnerable. Although we deal with each other in the here-and-now, in a profound psychosomatic sense, our emotional history saturates present social encounters. Emotions are triggered whenever important things happen to us. And our strongest emotions are felt in relationship to other people – the joy of love, the pain of rejection, the sadness of loss, the anger of unfulfilled need, the fear of being abandoned.

Emotions easily override thought and cognition. A woman feels extreme anxiety at the prospect of giving a public talk. A man's sadness at the recent death of his father keeps interfering with his ability to concentrate at work. An adolescent taunted by his peers becomes angry to the point of violence. However, whereas emotions can easily outbid thought, it is much more difficult for thoughts to displace feelings. Simply wishing that you didn't feel anxious or depressed is not easy. Emotions:

> are things that happen to us rather than things we will to occur .... We have little direct control over our emotional reactions. Anyone who has tried to fake an emotion, or who has been in receipt of a faked one, knows all too well the futility of the attempt. While conscious control over emotions is weak, emotions can flood consciousness.
>
> (LeDoux 1998: 19)

Emotions influence what we see and how we see it. They motivate or inhibit our behaviour. The study of the emotions, or *affect theory*, involves the examination of how we are personally 'affected' by events. It also looks at how we evaluate and give meaning and significance to experience. Feelings therefore influence such things as attention, perceptions, appraisal, reactions, defences, relationships and communications. We constantly monitor our own and other people's affective states. Emotions, when recognized, understood and reflected upon by the individual, offer useful information about the self in relationship to others and the environment, providing feedback which helps the affect system to regulate itself (Taylor, Bagby and Parker 1997: 15). Goleman (1996) has called this reflective, cognitive skill to monitor and self-regulate affect *emotional intelligence*. People with this skill tend to show high levels of empathy and social fluency.

Children who begin to recognize how emotions affect their own and other people's behaviour quickly get the hang of social life and how it works. They become socially competent. They are at low risk of developing behavioural and mental health problems. When they have children of their own, they are likely to be 'good enough' parents.

In contrast, children who suffer abuse and neglect are at serious risk of not being able to understand their own or other people's emotional make-up. They are poor at managing their arousal. As a result, they don't deal competently with social relationships. If and when they do have children, their parenting is likely to be anxious, uncertain and distressed.

Affect Regulation

Emotions and their regulation are a key element of infant experience.

> Emotion regulation refers to the ability to modulate or control the intensity and expression of feelings and impulses, especially intense ones, in an adaptive manner ... Emotions serve as important internal monitoring and guidance systems designed to appraise events as beneficial or dangerous and provide motivation for action.
>
> (Wolfe 1999: 43)

Those who find it difficult to recognize and regulate their emotions rapidly get into social difficulty. Anger provoking aggression, shame leading to avoidance, and sadness precipitating depression can begin to affect people's ability to function acceptably or effectively. Mental health is based on the ability to recognize, understand and regulate emotions. The breakdown of emotional order leads to poor mental health. Affect dysregulation is a major risk factor in psychopathology. It can also cause physical illnesses and be involved in many psychosomatic problems including eating disorders, panic attacks and substance abuse.

Recent developments in attachment theory have concentrated on how carers help, or fail to help, infants and young children to regulate their emotions. How does a mother or father respond when a baby becomes distressed? What are the developmental consequences for children who are left unattended for long periods in states of high arousal? What does it do to a young mind to be hurt and frightened by a hostile and abusive attachment figure?

Children learn about and begin to regulate their emotions in relationship with their primary caregivers. In effect, carers help shape their infants early coping strategies. Moreover, this external regulation between a mother and her baby becomes neurologically internalized and hard-wired in the infant's fast maturing brain (Schore 2001a). Indeed, 'the brain is hardwired to take in signals from the social environment to alter its own internal states. Our minds emerge from this interdependence of the brain and interpersonal relationships' (Siegel 2003: 7).

Even more intriguingly, infants and parents share and are strongly affected by each other's emotions. This indicates to the child that feeling states can be understood, handled and contained. *Co-regulation of affect* between carer and child is extremely important if maturing infants are to develop emotional intelligence and social competence. Carers who are poor readers of their infant's emotional cues compromise the child's healthy psychosocial development. In such relationships, children remain poor at understanding and regulating their arousal and distress. Children who find it difficult to manage their emotions find social relationships problematic. Certainly it appears that parents who explain and reflect on their own and the child's emotional state help children develop strong mentalizing capacities in which emotions are understood and skilfully regulated. Fonagy et al. (2002) refer to this as 'mentalisation' or 'reflective function'. All of this marks the beginning of emotional self-regulation.

> None of us is born with the capacity to regulate our own emotional reactions. A dyadic regulatory system evolves where the infant's signals of moment-to-moment changes in his state are understood and responded to by the caregiver, thereby achieving regulation. The infant learns that the arousal in the presence of the caregiver will not lead to disorganization beyond his coping capabilities. The caregiver will be there to reestablish equilibrium.
>
> (Fonagy et al. 2002: 37)

Thus, in relationship with their primary caregivers, infants begin to tolerate increasingly high levels of stress. Having been helped to make sense of their own and other people's mental states, children also tend to be more empathic, socially oriented and popular. Indeed, children who have been encouraged by their parents to think about situations in terms of their own and other people's mental states have been found to be more secure, empathic, and flexible in their use of behavioural options (Fonagy et al. 1991). Story telling and verbal explanations of psychologically complex situations help children to see links between their thoughts and feelings.

In contrast, parents who cause great fear and distress in their children, and then fail to regulate the ensuing emotional turmoil, do their children particular psychological harm. Their children have few insights into the nature of their distress and arousal, and even less ability to contain and regulate their feelings. This means that the demands of social relationships can easily become confusing and upsetting, leading to behaviour that is either inappropriate or aggressive.

Sensitive Caregiving, Intersubjectivity and Mentalization

Newborn babies are unable to regulate their own arousal. Secure mothers intuitively and continuously regulate their baby's shifting arousal levels and therefore their emotional states. Sensitive and attuned parents recognize, or at least try to understand, what is causing their baby's distress. They then seek to do something about it – they attempt to soothe and regulate their child's affect. For the very young child, arousal states feel global and undifferentiated. It is a matter of feeling either contentment or distress, comfort or discomfort. These states suffuse and saturate the child's whole being and experience. A loud noise, feeling hungry, or suffering tummy ache is unpleasant and distressing. Babies express feelings of discomfort behaviourally and non-intentionally, which is to say, crying and yelling is just what very young human infants do when they are upset. In itself, the crying is not directed at anyone and not for any particular intentional purpose. Crying is an example of attachment behaviour – even though it is not intentionally expressed, in evolutionary terms, it is a distress signal designed to get the caregiver involved. Children cared for by sensitive parents gradually learn that their arousal can be managed; it does not lead to disorganization or abandonment. To experience arousal does not always portend danger. Distress does not necessarily imply abandonment.

When competent caregivers interact with their distressed baby, a number of important transactions take place between parent and child. It is out of these repeated transactions that infants begin to recognize and understand the nature of emotions in themselves and in other people, and how feelings, thoughts and behaviour affect each other. In trying to comfort their baby or meet their needs, good-enough parents attempt to understand their child's mental state. Is this distress the result of anger or pain, frustration or fear? Does my baby need feeding or is she feeling cold and uncomfortable?

As well as instinctive attachment behaviours designed to attract parental attention, at times of distress newborn babies also seem naturally attuned ***and responsive*** to the emotional expressions of other people, particularly their caregivers. As others interact with babies, they respond expressively. Parents engage with their babies with rhythm. A 'musical' quality is heard in their voice. Concern, interest and understanding might be seen in parental eyes and faces. Containment and safety are felt through babies' bodies, as carers gently stroke and rhythmically rock them in order to calm, soothe and reassure. When we talk with babies ('motherese' or 'infant directed speech'), our voice pitch tends to rise; tonal range is accentuated as well as being slow, sing-song like and rhythmical; pauses are relatively long; and there are fewer syllables per phrase. And according to Trevarthen and Aitkin (2001: 8), infants prefer approving rather than disapproving intonation. This psychological and social interest and responsivity shown by babies is referred to as 'purposeful intersubjectivity'.

Failures of intersubjectivity compromise psychosocial development – abuse and deprivation disturb the affective patterns between parent–child interaction. Being naturally sociable, infants seem peculiarly receptive to other people's emotional and subjective states.

> Researchers found that as early as 2 months, infants and mothers, while they were looking at and listening to each other, were mutually regulating one another's interests and feelings in intricate, rhythmic patterns, exchanging multimodal signals and imitations of vocal, facial and gestural expressions .... Mothers and fathers were behaving in an intensely sympathetic and highly expressive way that absorbed the attention of the infants and led to intricate, mutually regulated interchanges with turns of displaying and attending. The infant was thus proved to possess an active and immediately responsive conscious appreciation of the adult's communicative intentions. This is what was called ***primary intersubjectivity***.
>
> (Trevarthen and Aitkin 2001: 5)

Infants show intense interest in the human face, particularly the eyes and their ability to express emotions. The baby's gaze, in turn, stimulates the mother's gaze, and at this point of mutual eye contact, a potent, highly arousing line of communication and sharing of internal mental state information opens.

> By synchronising with the child's attentive states, mothers structure playful interactions, regulate infant attention, facilitate the development of verbal dialogue, and promote the infant's capacity for self-regulation ... mutual synchrony exists when both partners simultaneously adjust their attention and stimulation in response to the partner's signals.
>
> (Feldman et al. 1996: 349)

In her interactions with the baby, the caregiver initially tunes into the arousal. Sensitive carers look out for and follow their infant's lead. In this way, infant–parent affective behaviour becomes synchronized (Schore 1994). The mother's voice, facial expression and body movements will mimic those of the baby's presumed mental state and the type of emotional arousal that such a state might trigger (fear, anger, pain, sadness). She is representing and thereby communicating to the child that she knows and understands what is the matter:

> Who's looking sad? Can't you find your teddy, is that why you're feeling sad? Oh, you're feeling all hot and cross under those heavy blankets, aren't you?

In doing this, she is also indicating that, although the distress feels all consuming to the baby, it is in fact manageable, it can be contained, it will not overwhelm the baby. This is confirmed almost immediately as the parent begins to 'regulate' the child's arousal. The voice, which initially mimics and is tuned into the baby's level of distress, quickly adopts a gradually slower pace, a calmer tone, a lower pitch. At the same time, the parent might gently rock the child or softly stroke his or her head. These soothing gestures aim to calm and comfort the aroused infant.

All of this verbal, visual and physical 'regulation' might accompany the more practical actions of preparing a feed or changing a nappy. If all goes well, the end result is that the infant's distressed emotional state becomes 'regulated'. The child then experiences feelings of well-being, contentment, comfort and safety.

> Oh, look who's cross with mummy! I think you're hungry and you think mummy's forgotten you! Come on. There, there. Oh dear, your tummy's all empty and that's not nice, is it? I think you want some milk, is that what you want? Come on, have some milk. That's right; that's better. Oh yes, you were a hungry little girl. Aah, that's nice, isn't it? Oh yes. You're all happy now, aren't you? Yes you are. Yes you are. Who's got a big smile on her face? You snuggle in ...

In experiencing all of this, the baby learns a number of important things. Arousal, although distressing, need not be all-consuming. States of fear or anger can be recognized by others and managed; they can be contained. Other people can be trusted to help; they are available at times of need. The attuned responses of caregivers suggest that there is a relationship between how one feels and how one behaves, and that feelings do cause distress but things can be done to meet needs, calm upset, recover feelings of safety and well-being. As these cycles of arousal, distress, recognition, understanding, identification, comfort and regulation are repeated many times every day, the maturing infant begins to develop an understanding of how he or she works emotionally and psychologically, behaviourally and physiologically. And just as important, the child begins to understand that other people also operate along similar psychological lines.

Trust and understanding therefore mark the beginning of young children's ability to recognize and regulate their emotions. The ability to make sense of yourself as an emotional being means that you can handle yourself, albeit crudely at first, when arousal begins to escalate. The fear that feelings of great distress can completely overwhelm, consume and annihilate you begins to be contained and self-regulated.

Emotional understanding and interpersonal awareness also develop as carers and babies interact and play for pleasure, companionship and stimulation. Most games have strong emotional content in which the parent might adopt a 'mock' feeling of, say, anger or fear or surprise, which is then resolved into one of mutual recognition, laughter and joy. 'Peek-a-boo', 'pat-a-cake', hand clapping, bouncing, chasing, playing at tigers – all of these 'games' build up mutual perspective-taking in which the basic emotions of (pretend) surprise, fear and anger feature strongly. Many also rely on being rhythmical, repetitious, and highly predictable in the sense that the climax might be exciting, arousing and even a little frightening, but it is immediately followed by a 'safe' and 'fun' resolution in which the infant is cuddled or father stops being a tiger and is a warm, friendly daddy again. In all of these games, the parent is monitoring and regulating the baby's mental state, keeping arousal within a manageable range.

> Affect regulation is not just the reduction of affective intensity, the dampening of negative emotion. It also involves an amplification, an intensification of positive emotion .... Attachment is not just the establishment of security after a dysregulating experience and a stressful negative state, it is also the interactive amplification of positive affects, as in play states. Regulated affective interactions with a familiar, predictable primary caregiver create not only a sense of safety, but also a positively charged curiosity that fuels the burgeoning self's exploration of novel socio-emotional and physical environments. This ability is a marker of adaptive infant mental health.
>
> (Schore 2001a: 21)

Emotional intelligence and social competence therefore appear as an outcome of secure attachments. Such intelligence gives the maturing child the 'ability to interpret others' behaviour in terms of mental states (thoughts, intentions, desires and beliefs), to interact both in complex social groups and in close relationships, to empathise with others' states of mind, and to predict how others will feel, think, and act' (Baron-Cohen et al. 2000: 355).

In all these ways, secure caregivers are willing and able to interact with their young children as psychological partners. Crucially, they relate with their infant as if the child had a mind and what goes on in that mind is worth knowing (Fonagy 2000). They also share and explain their own state of mind to their young children as they discuss how the world of people, relationships and social behaviour works. Competent parents constantly explain what is going on to young children in terms of psychology, how feelings affect behaviour, and how someone else's behaviour affects other people's feelings. In short, without consciously realizing it, parents train their children to be psychologists, astute observers and interpreters of the social scene.

Mind-Mindedness

Dennett (1987) said that human beings try to make sense of each other in terms of mental states. What goes on in other people's minds in terms of thoughts, feelings, beliefs and desires is the key to understanding their actions and behaviour, and the character of their relationship with us and other people. The social world can make sense. By age three or four, most children develop 'a theory of mind' which recognizes that what people think, feel and believe is a good predictor of behaviour. Most four-year-olds realize that someone can have a false belief and that this false belief will also predict their behaviour.

For example, if a boy knows that a girl deliberately left her crayon on the table so that she could draw when she got back from playing in the garden, he assumes that she will first look for the crayon on the table when she returns even though her older sister has, in fact, borrowed it and replaced it in another room. Upon returning from the garden, the little girl has a mistaken (false) belief that the crayon is on the table; that is where she left it, that is where she will expect to find it, and so that is where she will look. It requires the observer of the story to be able to see the world from the little girl's point of view. Only then can we predict her behaviour, based on knowing that she has a false belief about the whereabouts of her crayon. This capacity for 'social understanding' based on the ability to see how things might look and feel from someone else's perspective is the basis of empathy, relationship skills and moral behaviour. It also supports children's imagination and their ability to pretend and play.

Empathy and mutual mind-mindedness is at the heart of both sound psychological development and social competence. Meins (1997, 1999; also see Harris 1999: 317) argues that caregivers who are 'mind-minded' with their children are good at translating psychological experiences into an active, coherent dialogue which not only helps achieve security of attachment, it also facilitates emotional understanding. Parents who focus on their children's subjective experiences help them understand their psychological states and so promote mental well-being. This lays the foundations for affect regulation. It marks the beginning of sound mental health and social competence. Maternal mind-mindedness with babies also seems to predict strong performance on Theory of Mind tasks when they reach around four years of age (Meins et al. 2002). Meins et al. (2002) suggest that mothers who routinely offer mentalistic comments on their infants' behaviour provide children with the 'opportunity to integrate their own behaviour with an external comment that makes reference to the mental states underlying that behaviour' (p. 1724).

In Meins' model, which she believes remains true to Ainsworth et al.'s (1978) original notion of sensitive parenting, sensitivity involves responding appropriately to children's cues and state of mind: 'Such sensitive responsivity goes beyond the ability to respond promptly to the infant's behaviour, and involves a degree of interpretation on the caregiver's part in order to calculate what a given behaviour means' (Meins 1999: 329).

As a result, the caregiving becomes 'attuned' to the infant's internal mental states. Secure mothers who show this mind-mindedness have a 'proclivity to treat their infants as individuals with minds, rather than merely entities with needs that must be met' with the 'tendency to focus upon *mental* attributes, rather than physical or behavioural characteristics' (Meins 1999: 332). Mothers who make 'mind-related' comments as they interact with their babies constantly make reference to what their children are thinking and feeling. They credit their children with mental states that they believe inform their infants' actions and intentions. They are interested in their children's internal thoughts and feelings and engage with them on this basis. In short, they view their infants as sentient, thinking, intentional beings: 'Are you thinking mummy has forgotten to change your nappy, is that why you're feeling cross?' 'You're laughing at daddy because you think he's being a silly daddy, don't you?' 'I think you think it's a ball.' Other mind-minded comments might include references to the infant's emotional engagement ('I think you're feeling bored'), or comments on the child's attempts to manipulate people's beliefs ('You're just teasing me, yes you are, you're teasing your mummy').

> Repeated exposure to such comments about their activity (or lack of activity) with reference to their likely attendant mental states may ultimately help children become aware of their own and other people's mental states and processes, and how they govern behaviour.
>
> (Meins et al. 2002: 1724)

The image of the intentional infant is internalized by the child and 'constitutes the core of [his or her] mentalizing self' (Fonagy et al. 1995, p. 257). Because it gives the child a sense of his or her inner life and affective experience, the mother's capacity to enter her child's mind and give reality to the child's internal experience is probably a vital aspect of empathic and sensitive mothering. The experience of the self as real, known, and intentional is central to the experience of security.

(Slade 1999: 581)

A study by Meins et al. (2001) illustrates some of the subtle differences between secure and insecure mothers along this 'mind-minded' dimension. As part of the study, a mirror was provided. A typical interaction involved a mother showing her baby his or her reflection:

The less mind-minded mother accompanied this interaction with the following discourse: 'Who's that in there? Is that you?', in contrast to the more-minded mother asking, 'Who do you *think* that is? Who do you *think* it is? Do you *think* that might be you?

(Meins 1999: 336, emphasis original)

Meins (1999: 338) speculates that mothers of avoidant children will make comparatively few comments on their infant's mind, whereas mothers of ambivalent/resistant children may tend to make inaccurate attributions. For example, an insecure mother of an ambivalent child might try to engage her child in animated play with a toy, claiming that this is his favourite object, when in fact the child is either showing no interest because he is tired or already preoccupied doing something else. The mother's agenda and own mental state overrides that of the child. There is no mind-mindedness, and therefore no attunement, and so the child becomes frustrated and irritated.

During this phase of becoming aware of one's own and other people's minds (what Trevarthen and Hubley [1978] call *secondary intersubjectivity*), parents interact with their children in a complex variety of ways, many of which allow the child to explore and appreciate the nature of emotions and their affect on themselves and others. Through social signalling, young children increasingly provoke other people and their minds so as to reveal their motives and mental states. A child might repeatedly show an object to a parent with accompanying inquiring vocalization. The child might point at a toy or another baby who is crying, with checks to see if the parent is also looking at what interests her. Older children constantly pose the question 'why' to their parents – Why for must I put away my toys? Why are you shouting at me? Why is my sister crying? The demand is to know what the parent thinks, feels and believes and how her state of mind influences her behaviour with the child.

Thus, human intersubjectivity is conceived as a process that makes it possible for subjects to detect and change each other's minds and behaviour, by purposeful,

> narrative expressions of emotion, intention, and interest ... emotions are the essential regulatory factor in intersubjective contact, expressed emotions are fundamentally dialogic or between person.
>
> (Trevarthen and Aitkin 2001: 18)

Intriguingly, as Fonagy and Target (1997) explain, the parent's interest in their child's mind and how it works, when shared with the child, plays a critical part in helping the growing infant develop a mind, an understanding of how it functions, and a strong sense of self, personal esteem and self-efficacy. As Winnicott (1971) observed, attuned mothers give 'back to the baby the baby's own self'. These parents value the emergence of mental states and reflective processes in their children. Fonagy and Target (1997) propose that the mother acts as a kind of mirror to the child, reflecting back the infant's internal mental states.

This is particularly true of the emotions. In a process referred to as 'affect mirroring', Fonagy et al. (2002; also see Winnicott 1967 on maternal mirroring) describe how carers credit their infant with an emotional state which they believe is congruent with the child's behaviour (angry cry, surprised look, frightened yell). From the baby's point of view, this is a kind of 'psycho feedback' in which 'my carer shows me my feelings' (Gerhardt 2004: 25). The carer's exaggerated facial expressions and tone of voice feed back to the child an idea of what the child is probably feeling. Mirroring takes the infant's disorganized and distressed psychological state and organizes it for him or her. However, this is done in such a way that the infant knows that the expression on the carer's face is not her affective state but that of the child. It is the kind of sympathetic mirrored look that most of us tend put on when we are acknowledging a friend's sadness or pleasure. In these ways, the child begins to develop an understanding of his or her own psychological make-up and how he or she works emotionally. The child learns about his or her inner world. Children can begin to recognize, understand and reflect on their own and other people's mental states and how these affect behaviour.

Parents who are not interested in their infant's mental states and fail to mirror their baby's affect, impair the child's psychosocial development and the formation of a coherent psychological self.

> For affect-mirroring to serve as the basis of the development of a representational framework, the caregiver must somehow indicate that her display is not for real: it is not an indication of how the parent herself feels. We describe this characteristic of the parent's mirroring behaviour as its 'markedness'. A display that is congruent with the baby's state but lacks markedness may overwhelm the infant. It is felt to be the parent's own real emotion, making the infant's experience seem contagious, or universal, and thus more dangerous. In the short term, the infant's perception of a corresponding but realistic negative emotion is likely to

escalate rather than regulate the infant's state, leading to traumatization rather than containment.

(Fonagy et al. 2002: 9)

Parents who show no interest in what they think their infant is thinking and feeling, and who fail to 'affect mirror', deny the child information about his or her young mind and how it works. The child cannot find *his or her* psychological self in the mind of a parent who is not mind-minded. All the child gets when he or she interacts with his mother is her state of mind.

In the case of connecting with the mind of an abusive carer, the child finds hostility towards his or her very existence. In the mind of a neglectful carer, the child finds only the thinnest of mental representations of the self and its needs – a virtual blank.

> If maternal care is not good enough, then the infant does not really come into existence, since there is no continuity of being; instead, the personality becomes built on the basis of reactions to environmental impingement.
>
> (Winnicott 1960: 54)

Thus, the only information about how to experience the self is the parent's own thoughts and feelings towards the infant. The child therefore begins to internalize and represent this 'alien', non-mirrored view of self as a core part of him or herself. However, this 'alien' self bears no relation to the child's own affect and cognitive states, and so is extremely unhelpful in terms of building up a coherent, coordinated sense of a psychological self (Fonagy et al. 2002: 11). So children of abusive carers internalize a hostile, persecutory self. Those of severely neglectful parents internalize a hollow, empty, abandoned self. These fractured, disorganized states are difficult to live with. Children (and adults) try to cope by projecting many of their distressed feelings on to others and then try to control the other, often in an aggressive way.

> We believe that what is most important for the development of mentalising self-organization is the exploration of the mental state of the sensitive caregiver, which enables the child to find in the caregiver's mind (that is, in the hypothetical representation of her mind that he constructs to explain her behavior toward him) an image of himself as motivated by beliefs, feelings, and intentions. *In contrast, what the disorganized child is scanning for so intently is not the representation of his own mental states in the mind of the other, but the mental states of that other that threatens to undermine his own self.* They can constitute within the child's self-representation an alien presence that is so unbearable that his attachment behaviour becomes organized around reexternalising these parts of the self onto attachment figures, rather than around the internalization of a capacity for containment of affects and other intentional states.
>
> (Fonagy et al. 2002: 55, emphasis added)

In effect, maltreating caregivers either:

- fail to recognize or acknowledge what is going in the child's mind (cases of neglect in which the caregiving 'mirror' where you might see and find yourself is cloudy and dull), or
- do recognize what is going on in the child's mind but reject, feel hostile towards or contemptuous of the child's mind (cases of emotional and physical abuse in which the caregiving mirror where the child might see and find itself is distorted and refracted through the fears, hostile thoughts, and anxieties of the carer).

Secure children's growing ability to 'mentalize' and to make sense of themselves and others as psychological and intentional beings provides them with high levels of resilience. They begin to see the world of people as fathomable. Other people's feelings and behaviours are not arbitrary and random. People's behaviour is being driven by their psychological states. Interpersonal things happen for psychological reasons. The child begins to appreciate that other people have minds, and that these minds, like that of the child, are full of thoughts, feelings, beliefs and intentions. This understanding leads to the recognition that other people might have a different psychological 'view' of ostensibly the same situation to that held by the child. For example, although a child might feel unconcerned about his untidy room, the child knows his or her mother is likely to react with disgust and exasperation.

The gradual appreciation of otherness, including the realization that others hold a mental view of you, is also critical to the development of the psychological self, self-awareness and intentionality. Self-awareness is achieved in interaction with others, so long as those others engage with the child as if the child had an independent mind full of burgeoning thoughts and feelings, meanings and intentions.

In the context of loving, reciprocal, mind-minded relationships other people's behaviour becomes meaningful and predictable, not arbitrary and puzzling. 'Reflective function' gives children more behavioural effective and adaptive options in increasingly complex social situations (Fonagy and Target 1997). The ability to fire on all psychological cylinders feeds into children's social understanding and emotional intelligence. It gives rise to good self-esteem and high self-efficacy. Children learn to regulate their own arousal, and by using their increasing social understanding and emotional skills, they can also regulate other people's arousal. Secure children are good at conflict resolution in the playground. They show better than average abilities to share, negotiate and develop cooperative play. These skills mean that they are likely to have friends and keep them.

In contrast, children whose parents have not shown much interest in their children's minds or burgeoning psychological self, or failed to share with them how their own thoughts, feelings and beliefs affect what they do and say as parents, are deprived of key developmental experiences and psychological information. As we shall see, both neglectful and abusive parents in their different ways, repeatedly fail to display 'mind-mindedness' and 'mentalization' when dealing with their children. They show little or no interest in or understanding of their child's mind and emerging psychological self. These interactional deficits compromise children's ability to develop 'mind-mindedness', reflective function, and a coherent sense of their mental self.

Without the ability to understand their own and other people's mental states, affect regulation, empathy and relationship competence become increasingly difficult. And with social difficulty comes stress, which triggers further arousal, which is not easily managed. Children who cannot regulate their emotions become aggressive and hostile, helpless and confused, or withdrawn and isolated, socially anxious and interpersonally wary. They experience major problems in the parent–child relationship. They have serious difficulties making sense of and dealing with emotional arousal in themselves and others. The inability to regulate emotions is generally a precursor of mental health problems. Not surprisingly, maltreated children tend to have low self-esteem and poor peer relationships.

As Schore (2001a: 16) notes, 'severely compromised attachment histories are... associated with brain organizations that are inefficient in regulating affective states and coping with stress, and therefore engender maladaptive infant mental health'. Perry et al. (1995) are clear that early life maltreatment can adversely alter the organization, structure and density of the emotional processing parts of the brain, permanently robbing children of a normal psychosocial development (De Bellis 2001: 552). As Fonagy (2001: xv) notes, 'the average human mind is simply not equipped to assimilate or protect itself from environmental assaults beyond a certain intensity'. And he goes on to observe that by far the most intolerable of such assaults are those that occur in relationship with the very people who are biologically earmarked to protect you, your caregivers. The brains of seriously abused and neglected children have an impaired capacity to regulate impulse and emotions.

> This has implications in terms of later social behaviour. 'Both lack of critical nurturing experiences and excessive exposure to traumatic violence will alter the developing central nervous system, predisposing to a more impulsive, reactive, and violent individual' (Perry 1997: 131).... When abuse and neglect persist, so that the baby has time to create a 'wired-in' response, the more primitive (in evolutionary terms) brainstem and midbrain become under-modulated. These are areas of the brain which control immediate reactions to perceived danger, that are designed to ensure bodily survival by monitoring important environmental information ... and regulating levels of alertness. This leads to hypervigilance ... as scanning the surroundings goes on constantly and unconsciously, and to instant reactions to stimuli others might not notice.
>
> (Balbernie 2001: 245–6)

Abused and neglected children show a poverty of responses and lack of variability and flexibility when dealing with the routine demands and stresses of social relationships. There is now strong evidence that all forms of child abuse and neglect increase the risk of mental health and psychiatric problems. Whenever clinical and psychiatric populations are examined, there is an over-representation of people who have suffered maltreatment as children (Kaufman and Charney 2001). This is not to deny the presence of genetic factors. Major depression, for example, does require the individual to be genetically vulnerable, but the risk increases significantly if this is coupled with an adverse caregiving history and stressful life events (Kaufman and Charney 2001).

Conclusion

Survival requires vigilance. As Beck observed, evolution favours anxious genes and fight/flight responses. Cozolino adds:

> Because of this the conscious and unconscious management of fear and anxiety is a core component of our personalities, attachment relationships, and identities. The considerable degree of postnatal brain development and the disproportionate emphasis on early childhood experiences in the sculpting of the brain add to our vulnerability to psychological distress.
>
> (Cozolino 2002: 290)

The child, in relationship with his or her caregivers, slowly recognizes that his or her own emotional states affect what he or she does, and that these feelings also have an impact on the mind of his or her carers. This in turn affects how the carer responds. These psychosocial skills and self-regulating abilities are the psychological bedrock on which children develop relationship competence, social acceptance and sound mental health.

3

Patterns of Attachment

Introduction

We now return to attachment. As noted, Schore (2001a) reminds us that attachment theory is, in essence, a regulatory theory. Attachment can therefore be defined as the dyadic regulation of emotion. Biologically speaking, attachment is a means of survival and therefore a way of controlling anxiety. As carers help children make sense of their own and other people's behaviour by recognizing that lying behind behaviour are minds and mental states, a whole train of psychosocial benefits accrues, including emotional attunement, reflective function and emotional intelligence. (For more detailed reviews of attachment theory and patterns of attachment see Cassidy and Shaver 1999; Goldberg 1999; Howe et al. 1999.)

Attachment Behaviour

Bowlby said that it would be biological folly if nature had not furnished helpless human infants with a number of innate behaviours to increase their chances of survival (1988b: 5). At root, most behavioural systems organize and direct behavioural sequences that affect the individual's ability to survive and reproduce. As human infants are extremely vulnerable and highly dependent, it is essential that they secure the interest and availability of adults who are both 'stronger and wiser.' 'Smiling, orienting toward others, shared gaze, looking where others are looking, and imitating facial gestures and movements are all driven by instinct and serve to jumpstart processes of bonding and communication' (Cozolino 2002: 172). They help connect infants both physically and emotionally to their main carers. It is these early bonding experiences that evolve into longer-term patterns of attachment.

In the case of vulnerable infants, two things increase rates of survival: awareness of danger, and seeking protection. In attachment theory, children monitor their environment for signs of danger and threat. For human infants, separation from their primary caregiver or an unresponsive attachment figure in themselves is a sign of potential danger, which will activate attachment behaviour. If children feel frightened or distressed, their attachment system is activated, triggering attachment behaviour. The goal of the attachment system is protection, and once the goal has been achieved, the system switches off. Reunion with an attuned and sensitive caregiver reduces physiological arousal and emotional distress. For most children, the need to feel close and protected is most likely to be found in relationship with one or both parents. Attachment behaviours, therefore, are designed to get either the parent to the child (crying, yelling, and other distress signals), or the child to the parent (crawling, clinging). Once the child has captured the attention of the caregiver, other attachment behaviours, such as smiling and vocalizing, serve to keep the parent engaged.

In this sense, parents and other closely involved carers become attachment figures, defined as people whom children seek as a source of protection and comfort at times of need and distress. The person most regularly involved with issues of care and protection is generally destined to become the child's primary or selective attachment figure. For most children the activation of their attachment system is acute, sporadic and highly functional. However, for children who are maltreated, either the availability of their carer at times of need cannot be taken for granted, or the behaviour of the attachment figure himself or herself repeatedly provokes feelings of anxiety and fear. In these cases, children's attachment systems are 'in a relatively constant state of activation' (West and George 1999: 138). There are few opportunities to feel relaxed and safe, to explore and make sense.

Attachment at the Level of Mental Representation (Internal Working Models)

Up to the point when language is acquired, babies can only communicate their needs and mental states behaviourally. They cry, crawl, cling and coo. Even so, their experience of how their carers react to these behaviours and how these reactions make them feel begins to be processed by the child at an increasingly cognitive level. Internal working mental models of how the world of the self, others and relationships seem to work are gradually constructed. These *mental representations* refer to the kind of memories, experiences, outcomes, feelings and knowledge about what tends to happen in relationships, particularly with attachment figures at times of need.

For example, a secure child might develop an understanding that at times of distress, more often than not his mother is available, sensitively aware and willing to respond. His existence and well-being seem to matter to her. He is loved and valued. In contrast, an insecure child might build up a picture that at times of need, her mother is reluctant to respond, or she reacts in a resentful way. The child does not feel accepted unreservedly. Parental love seems conditional on good behaviour, or requires the child to meet the parent's own need to feel loved.

While infants react in behaviourally very direct ways, toddlers begin to develop a reflective sense of what is likely to happen if they behave this way rather than that. Social situations begin to be analysed. Behavioural options open up. Plans can be made. These increasingly sophisticated mental representations, or internal working models, contain expectations based on past experience. They predict what might happen when feelings are expressed, or needs displayed. The models guide behaviour. But more fundamental still, these cognitive representations contain the early outlines of the self and how it fits into the social landscape.

> While simple and straightforward, this is a profound idea. It means that children approach new situations with certain preconceptions, behavioural biases, and interpretive tendencies.
>
> (Sroufe at al. 1999: 5)

The main purpose of internal working models is to help regulate the negative emotions of fear, distress and anxiety triggered when the child feels insecure. The infant brain is programmed to make sense of experience, and so the way other people react to the self, particularly at times of need and distress, provides maturing infants with information about what kind of selves they are – selves that are loved or not, worthy of protection or not, effective or not. A complementary model of whether or not other people are likely to be available when needed, likely to care and love, or be interested is also laid down in these early relationship experiences.

The ability cognitively to model key aspects of the social environment (including danger and the availability of others at time of need) increases both understanding and effectiveness. An individual's working model of a particular relationship therefore includes concepts of:

- the self
- others
- expectations of the relationship, and how the self and others are likely to behave and react.

Armed with these mental models of how others are likely to behave and how the self is likely to feel, children begin to *organize* their attachment behaviour to increase the availability, proximity and responsivity of their carers and reduce negative affect. They develop strategies to recover their own feelings of security when they feel anxious or frightened. In time, these mental representations begin to guide the child's expectations, beliefs and behaviour in all important relationships. Children begin to enter into a 'goal-corrected partnership' with their carer, in which they learn to modify their own behaviour in the light of the parent's plans, intentions, beliefs and personality, and still with the ultimate goal of maximizing, over the long term, the parent's willingness to provide care and protection.

> The child now begins to rely more on mental representations of attachment than the actual presence of the attachment figure ... the goal-corrected partnership that emerges during the preschool years sets the stage for attachment across the life span. As the child grows towards adolescence and adulthood, internal working models of attachment are expected to reflect an increasing understanding of the parent's own motivations, feelings, plans, and developmental goals resulting in a relationship of mutual trust and understanding.
>
> (George 1996: 413)

Under stress, securely attached children are able to appraise reasonably accurately how the situation is affecting them and how they are affecting the situation. They develop trust in the availability of others to help contain and comfort them at times of upset and arousal. This sense of trust and security translates into ease of feeding and depth of sleep. Secure children understand how and *why* they feel the way they do as they interact with other people. They are good at accessing and reflecting on their own behaviour and feelings, as they affect both the self and other people. In the light of this rounded evaluation, they are able to draw on a range of coping strategies including modifications of their own behaviour (if they recognize that they are contributing to the problem), and the ability to elicit support, care and protection from others to help them deal with life's challenges. Out of this ability to evaluate freely and objectively their own and other people's thoughts, feelings and behaviour arises 'ego-resiliency... conceptualized as the ability to control one's impulses, emotions and desires appropriately to the situation and is a measure for adaptive behaviour especially under stress, uncertainty or conflict' (Zimmermann 1999: 299).

There are three basic types of attachment organization depending on the sensitivity and interest of the caregiver: secure, avoidant, and ambivalent. Each arises as a result of the child's attempts to maximize parental proximity, care and protection – the goals of the attachment system. As long as the representational system remains organized, children can maintain functional relationships with others (George 1996: 414). In effect, children develop strategies that help them adapt to their parent's caregiving style in order to increase parental availability and willingness to respond. So, 'as long as attachment is organized in relation to the function and goal of the attachment system, it is adaptive, that is, it facilitates and maintains "good enough" proximity and, therefore, protection' (West and George 1999:140).

The attachment relationship allows the child to recognize and regulate any intense arousal of the emotions while maintaining proximity (and therefore a feeling of safety) with the caregiver. Each pattern of attachment illustrates a different adaptive strategy in different caregiving regimes developed by children to help them stay close and connected to their attachment figure at times of intense negative arousal, whether or not they actually display that arousal in the presence of the carer. (For a fuller description of each pattern, see Howe et al. 1999.)

Secure Attachments

Children who find themselves in relationship with parents whose caregiving is sufficiently sensitive, loving, responsive, attuned, consistent, available and accepting develop *secure attachments*. Parents are interested in their infant's physical needs and states of mind. They are keen to understand their child, and to be understood by their child. This offers the prospect of a coordinated and cooperative relationship.

In empathic, sensitive parent–infant relationships, there is mutual coordination, a dance if you will, of gaze, voice, touch and bodily rhythms. Attuned parents help children feel understood and competent at making sense of and managing their own affect and arousal. Securely attached children are able to experience and express negative emotions. They also know that they have the capacity to regulate their distress, either by managing the upset themselves or by getting help from their attachment figure.

It is not that sensitive parents don't upset the parent–child relationship; they clearly do. What distinguishes them is their ability to recognize that from time to time relationship rhythms break down and become disrupted. Carers might ignore the child, misunderstand the need, or inadvertently distress the infant. Having triggered the child's distress and attachment behaviour and then recognized the disruption, the sensitive carer repairs the relationship that is temporarily under stress.

The strategies used by the carer to regulate distress gradually become internalized by the child. 'The experience of being able to repair the stress of disrupted relatedness (i.e. transform negative affects into positive affects and disconnection into reconnection), leads to the individual's confidence in his own abilities, and trust in the capacity of others to respond' (Fosha 2003: 238).

Children and adults with secure attachments are able to behave flexibly and openly within relationships. They provide the other with fresh psychological information about their own mental states (what they are feeling and thinking) without too much distortion, defence or censorship. In other words, individuals feel secure when expressing their attachment needs to another. Their communication is accurate and honest. They can reflect thoughtfully and objectively about their own and other people's thoughts, feelings and behaviour. There is an underlying expectation and confidence that attachment figures will be unconditionally available and responsive at times of need.

> *Further, the secure individual does not have to manipulate his or her attachment behavior (to heighten or dampen it) in order for the attachment figure to respond to his or her attachment needs. The result is the behavioral and psychological integration of attachment experiences, memories and affect such that the individual functions in a manner that is consistent with Bowlby's ... notion of a goal-corrected*

> ***partnership – a relationship that flexibly integrates the needs and perspectives of both the self and the partner.***
>
> (West and George 1999: 140; emphasis original)

If the child feels loved and understood, the child will develop a mental representation (internal working model) of him/her self as lovable and psychologically coherent. And in a complementary fashion, in the face of stress and challenge, secure people have a positive view of others as a potentially available resource. The richer, more consistent and open is the communication between parent and child, the more 'mental state' information the child has, with which to make sense of the self and others. This is particularly true in the case of emotions and states of arousal. Children need to recognize, understand and regulate their emotions if they are to become competent social players. Affect regulation is a major component of good mental health. With the help of their carers and an increasingly sophisticated understanding of their own psychological states, secure children remain relatively organized under stress. They show resilience. Negative feelings do not easily overwhelm or psychologically threaten them.

Not surprisingly, securely attached children develop high self-esteem. They feel confident and effective. They recognize that both their own and other people's behaviour can be explained psychologically – that is, the psychosocial world can make sense. People with the ability to 'mentalize', to be 'mind-minded', give themselves and others more behavioural options. People who are able to look at themselves objectively, and evaluate openly and without distortion their own and other people's mental states, generally show the highest levels of social competence, including the experience of satisfactory relationships with peers, partners and their own children. Children who develop good reflective function or 'metacognition' (thinking about thinking) are able to manage their thoughts and feelings. Secure individuals are least likely to have mental health problems.

Insecure and Anxious Patterns

Securely attached children know that at times of need their caregivers are willing to be available and responsive. Although secure children might experience uncertainty over the whereabouts of their caregiver, resulting in a degree of vigilance, they know that when the relationship has been recovered, they will experience feelings of safety, containment and pleasure. However this is not the case for insecurely attached children, of which there are two basic types: avoidant and ambivalent. They experience normal anxiety about the location of the caregiver at times of need, but in addition they suffer uncertainty about the type and sensitivity of the response when they reconnect. There is a lack of confidence that the attachment figure will be available to provide physical or psychological safety at times of need. Main (1990: 179) explains that insecure children are 'additionally controlled by the past behavior of the attachment figure so that for these infants likely caregiver response as well as caregiver location must be continually taken into account'. This introduces a degree of hypervigilance into the minds of insecurely attached children, particularly in the case of those who have been maltreated. Insecurely attached children, therefore, find more of their mental time and energy is spent on issues of safety, security and monitoring, leaving less time for exploration and pleasurable interaction with their caregiver.

Caregivers who are unwilling (avoidant patterns) or unable (ambivalent patterns) to respond to or satisfy a child's normally expressed attachment needs create anxiety and insecurity in the parent–child relationship. In order to increase parental responsivity, children unconsciously learn that they cannot display attachment behaviour in its full, rounded and unabridged form. Instead, they develop secondary attachment behavioural strategies. By suppressing their primary attachment strategy, children reorganize their attachment behaviour in an attempt to recover parental availability and interest. If the strategy works, the child has a way of relating to the parent, and increasing the amount of care and protection available. The child then experiences a 'secondary felt security'. The feelings and behaviour associated with that strategy also becomes the preferred state of mind in which to be, that is to say, in which the individual feels most secure.

However, these adaptive strategies come at some developmental cost to the child. Children cannot find or display their true and full psychological self to an anxious carer as this reduces availability, care and protection, particularly at times of need. By minimizing affect (in the case of avoidant strategies) or exaggerating distress (in the case of ambivalent strategies), children defensively distort elements of their own and other people's psychological make-up. As a consequence, they fail to process, learn about and make good sense of either emotions (in the case of avoidant patterns) or how thought and behaviour affects people and their feelings (in the case of ambivalent patterns).

Insecure individuals feel anxious whenever attachment-related issues and experiences arise. They are unable to use other people, including their attachment figure, to help them regulate their distress and arousal, and re-establish equilibrium. Neither are they able to reflect on and consciously explore their internal working models of attachment. In the case of secure individuals, the ability to reflect on distressing attachment experiences enables them to reorganize their mental representations of both their own and other people's mental states, to update their understanding of how the self and others work as psychological and emotional subjects. As a result, secure individuals relate openly and without defence or distortion; they interact flexibly, mind-mindedly, and with emotional intelligence.

In contrast, as we shall now see, insecure individuals defend against the feelings generated by attachment-based experiences. They fail to reflect on all aspects of difficult attachment experiences. Avoidant individuals exclude information that triggers painful feelings of perceived or expected rejection. Ambivalent individuals try not to think about the hurt and shame of being cared for by an attachment figure who puts his or her own needs first. The ambivalent personality remains unreflectively preoccupied and anxious about other people's emotional interest and availability. Such people fear emotional abandonment, and in their anxiety feel driven to make endless demands on all their relationships. They become enmeshed and entangled with others, unable to let go even though they are riven with nagging uncertainty.

Avoidant Attachments

Carers who feel anxious or even angry when their children display attachment behaviour – that is when they appear dependent, seem vulnerable, show distress, have needs, and make emotional demands – cope by distancing themselves emotionally from their infants and their signals of distress. Furthermore, rather than attempt to understand the child and his or her distressed state of mind in order to help soothe and regulate it, avoidant carers prefer to impose on the child their own views of how 'good' children should behave, and how they should perceive and even experience themselves. These imposed definitions typically see 'good' children as those who do not display attachment behaviour or make emotional demands on parents: 'Don't bother mummy with your unnecessary whining; you know it makes me cross.'

Parents who reject attachment behaviour and only 'accept' the child when he/she is behaving in an independent, self-contained and self-sufficient manner, generate a distinctive type of caregiving known as 'rejecting' or 'dismissing'. The rejection is not of the child, but of the child when he/she is being vulnerable or needy or dependent. The child has to try to understand this caregiving environment in order to adapt and maximize the care and protection available under the psychological conditions generated by the parent.

Children who develop *avoidant* attachments adapt to 'rejecting' caregiving by downplaying and inhibiting their feelings of need. They *over-regulate* their emotions. According to Crittenden (2002: 113), they 'consistently omit negative affect from mental processing and behavior'. In effect, *they deactivate their attachment behaviour* as a way of *increasing* parental proximity, acceptance, responsivity and availability. They therefore increase parental availability when they downplay attachment behaviour and conduct themselves as they believe the parent would prefer them to behave. Their anxiety is that any display of need, longing, vulnerability and emotion might drive away their caregiver.

Characteristic of avoidant children is therefore a tendency to be emotionally independent, self-sufficient, self-contained and compliant, at least in the presence of the carer. Thus the parent–child relationship, which is *predictably* and *consistently* unresponsive to displays of negative affect, makes the child feel uncomfortable whenever he/she finds him/herself in an aroused or vulnerable emotional state. There is therefore a tendency to suppress and *defensively exclude* the attachment-generated emotions of fear, need, desire, vulnerability and distress from conscious, reflective mental processing. Arousal and the negative emotions make these children feel anxious and uncomfortable. Because they do not process them at the conscious level, these emotions and the attachment-based states that underpin them are not fully explored by the child and therefore not properly understood.

> Because dismissing individuals, through deactivating defensive strategies, attempt to minimise, avoid, or neutralize difficulties related to attachment experiences, these individuals engage in little inner representational elaboration of these experiences. At the same time, however, they depict their phenomenal self as independent and strong, a depiction that underpins a capacity to act which would make them believe that they can act in an effective manner. In essence, then, dismissing individuals fail to explore their internal world of attachment but view themselves as capable of taking action.
>
> (West and George 2002: 281)

In the case of children, they therefore learn what is required to achieve proximity and stay on the right side of their carers, but do not learn how to elicit care and protection. Indeed, intimacy and emotional closeness, which in the past increased the child's fear of rejection and hurt, tend to be avoided.

Ambivalent Attachments

In contrast, carers who remain under-involved with their children are experienced as *inconsistent*. These are parents who are preoccupied with their own needs and uncertainties, and whether there is anyone available to meet them. Am I loved? Am I needed? Does anyone care? Am I recognized? Does anyone in this family appreciate me and all I do for them? There is a fear by these parents of being ignored and emotionally abandoned. There is an anxious, repeated need to know what other people think and feel about the self, resulting in anxious demands that others repeatedly declare or demonstrate their love and affection, in words or deeds. This can place great demands on the relationship, often with the ironic effect of exhausting the partner to the point where he or she leaves. These anxieties can extend to parents' dealings with their children.

In the child's mind, there is little relationship between his or her behaviour, whether or not the carer responds, and if she (or he) does respond, what type of response might follow. The carer is more sensitive to whether or not she believes her child loves and values her than she is to thinking about the child's own needs and feelings. The parent is therefore relatively insensitive to the child's internal mental states. Mentalizing and mirroring the child's affect are weak. Preoccupied with her own needs and anxieties, she is slow to notice and respond to signals of distress, including the child's attachment behaviour.

In attempts to increase parental responsivity, children increase their displays of distressed behaviour. This includes crying, fretting, whining, attention-seeking behaviour, fussing, and being provocative, fractious or very demanding. In effect, children begin to *hyperactivate their attachment behaviour* in an attempt to get noticed, break into the parent's preoccupied state, and thereby overcome the caregiver's failure to be aware and respond. This hyperactivated attachment strategy seeks to increase the parent's predictability.

The pattern associated with this attachment strategy is known as *ambivalent* because the child desires an increase in parental responsivity but also feels angry that parental care and protection cannot be taken for granted. When attention is won, the child does not trust the parent to remain involved and so resists being soothed, regulated and comforted. The pattern is therefore also referred to as a *resistant* attachment.

In this adaptation, the child's emotions remain under-regulated. There is a preoccupation with and hypersensitivity to other people's emotional availability and interest, which is perceived as uncertain and unreliable unless demands are constantly made on the relationship. One of the consequences of this preoccupation is that children find it difficult to become absorbed in play and exploration. They are quickly distressed at the prospect of being left alone either psychologically or physically. If the child, or indeed adult, feels that the other's interest is being lost or withheld, provocative, attention-seeking behaviour increases even further. Anxiety and anger remain heightened, and caregivers find it difficult to provide reassurance, as they, in turn, begin to feel increasingly anxious, uncertain, unappreciated and angry in their role as attachment figure. Preoccupied parents of ambivalent children typically complain that no one in the family, including partners and children, appreciates them and the sacrifice and effort they put into being a good parent.

If the hyperactivated attachment strategy fails, the individual experiences 'abandonment' – a lack of care and protection. Anxiety increases, and a sense of aloneness can lead to feelings of despair and depression. However, in most cases, passive despair rarely lasts long. It is usually only a matter of time before the individual precipitates some drama or crisis as he or she tries to provoke other people into noticing and making some kind of response. It is as if other people's reactions define the self, and without the constant availability of other people, the self feels empty and undefined, diffuse and without a clear edge or boundary.

Broadly, ambivalent children have poor concentration, are easily distracted, and frequently display moodiness and feelings of helplessness. By under-regulating emotional arousal, individuals feel that they can increase other people's predictability and consistency. They begin to control other people's previous unpredictability through these coercive, demanding behaviours, using in particular strong displays of emotions, including threat, anger, need, desire and seduction (Crittenden 1995). However, those on the receiving end of this under-regulated, attention-seeking and needy emotional style can soon feel drained and angry. They attempt to withdraw and even give up on the relationship, confirming the ambivalent person's fear that other people and their availability can't be trusted. They eventually let you down.

In the case of ambivalent children, attachment behaviour appears not to predict parental availability. It is difficult for the child to build up any sense or consistent picture of how his or her behaviour affects others or brings about desired change. The responsivity of the carer is governed largely by *her* needs and feelings, not those of the child. The responses of the carer appear not to be contingently connected to the child's internal mental states, anxieties or attachment behaviour. Ambivalent children, and indeed ambivalent adults, therefore have little confidence in how their own behaviour might affect the behaviour of others. Only when ambivalent individuals are in a state of heightened arousal (hyperactivated attachment) do they feel that others are likely to take notice and attend. There is an anxious need to feel recognized and loved. Relationships are therefore craved, although they provoke anxiety and anger. Inasmuch as this demanding state does increase other people's involvement, no matter whether positive or negative, it reduces the fear of feeling alone and abandoned.

Because deactivated (avoidant) and hyperactivated (ambivalent) attachment strategies increase the availability of the attachment figure, they are described as 'organized' attachment patterns. These 'organized' attachment strategies allow individuals to stay connected to and in relationship with other people, including their attachment figure. Matters are not quite so fortunate in the case of children who suffer more severe abuse, neglect and early trauma.

Disorganized Attachments

Children who are parented by carers who are either frightening or frightened, or both, experience distress (Main and Hesse 1990). Abusive and hostile carers hurt and frighten their children. Depressed, drunk or drugged parents can appear helpless, and this can also frighten children. Carers who are bedevilled by old *unresolved* losses and traumas from their own unhappy childhoods can feel confused and frightened whenever they find themselves being cast in the role of carer and protector by their child seeking safety and comfort. Their unresolved attachment traumas make it difficult for them to empathize with the needs and distress of their children. Allowing themselves to sense their children's anxious vulnerability activates these old painful, distressing and unresolved attachment concerns. Like the 'disorganized-disoriented infant, the *unresolved* adult experiences the periodic collapse of his or her predominant attachment strategy' (Atkinson and Goldberg 2004: 8). Unresolved attachment issues triggered by caring for and protecting the dependent and vulnerable child cause fear and distress in the mind of the carer.

A psychologically lost, panicky parent is also frightening for the child. Thus, if the carer reacts with fear or distress when caring for the needy infant, the child experiences the self as the source of the parent's fear. The infant begins to synchronize with the mother's dysregulated and distressed emotional state caused by her own unresolved losses, fears and traumas (Schore 2001b). In relationship with carers with unresolved and helpless/hostile states of mind with respect to attachment, the child is left feeling highly distressed for long periods of time. The child's attachment behaviour goes unterminated. If the arousal becomes too intense and unbearable, the child first becomes emotionally hyperaroused, and then may dissociate as an extreme form of defence.

In these highly distressed and arousing parent–child relationships, co-regulation is absent. The parent fails to deal with the child's distress. The child is left running in a parallel, but unconnected state of unmanageable arousal. There is no intersubjectivity. Therefore the child is unable to find or explore his or her own psychological self in relationship with the distressed and out-of-control parent. Lacking a coherent subjective sense of self, the child cannot manage emotional arousal in him/herself, or indeed in other people.

When maltreated children need parents to help them contain and regulate their escalating arousal, what they actually experience is danger and psychological abandonment. This only serves to increase feelings of intense fear and shame. Fear is experienced when the self is under threat. Shame – an emotion experienced from a very young age – is felt when one is ineffective, demeaned and not socially accepted (leaving the individual outside of the group, alone and vulnerable). Fear and shame become particularly problematic when they are triggered by the attachment figure. It is at this point, says Bowlby (1980), that psychic survival is only possible when the individual *defensively excludes* the feelings and experiences that trigger the fearful arousal.

More than any other type of parent, carers with major unresolved childhood losses and traumas show very atypical behaviours when interacting with their infants (Lyons-Ruth, Bronfman and Atwood 1999; Lyons-Ruth, Bronfman and Parsons 1999). These behaviours include:

- *Affective errors*: for example, the parent might present contradictory cues in which the child is invited to approach but the parent then disengages and distances him/herself. The carer elicits distress and invites protection, only to reject the infant's approach and attachment behaviour. Some parents fail to show any response or offer comfort when their child is distressed.
- *Disorientation*: for example, a parent might look confused, frightened or panic-stricken when the child displays attachment behaviour or needs soothing.
- *Negative-intrusive behaviour*: for example, the parent mocks or teases a child in distress, or aggressively pulls an upset child towards him or her by the wrist.

- *Compulsive caregiving* is often developed by children whose parent's own needs, vulnerabilities and dependencies take precedence over those of the child. Although not obviously abusive, it is nevertheless still frightening for children to experience their carer as helpless and frightened. The young child's distress goes unheeded. The child senses that his/her carer is unavailable at times of need, particularly those times when the child is made anxious about the carer's own helplessness and fear. Finding no attachment strategy able to increase security, children become highly aroused and their emotions go unregulated. This, of course, defines a disorganized attachment.

The caregiver's behaviour implies neglect and emotional abandonment. As a way of trying to relate to and engage with the attachment figure, children begin to 'parent the parent' in a form of role reversal. The child attends disproportionately to the parent's emotional needs and vulnerabilities. This is an example of 'parentified' behaviour, often shown by children whose parents are alcoholic, drug addicted, depressed, the victims of domestic violence, or who appear frightened and overwhelmed by old unresolved feelings of childhood loss, abuse and trauma which get triggered whenever the parent is in the caregiving role. Parents emphasize their child's *special and precocious qualities.* The child might be described as a 'little saint' or 'the only one who keeps me going with her cheery little smile'. Implicit in this belief is the feeling that the parent does not need to control, care for or protect the child (that is, does not feel the need to occupy the caregiving role) – the child appears able to do these things for himself or herself.

However, even 'though these relationships do not appear to be hostile or confrontational, the mother has still abdicated her role as caregiver; that is, she is not in the position of being the "older and wiser" figure' (Solomon and George 1999a: 19). With carers who feel helpless in the face of attachment behaviour, children learn to make few emotional demands on an essentially unavailable parent. Children who develop controlling caregiving behaviours are often solicitous, reassuring, organizing, overly cheerful and exaggeratedly bright, determinedly light-hearted, and anxious to assist and care for their carer (Barnett and Parker 1998: 147–8). Parents tend to withdraw and disinvest from their role as caregiver, although they also say they feel totally merged with or exceptionally close to the child: 'She knows my every thought. I don't even have to ask her what I want. She's thought about it even before I have.'

These children inhibit and avoid attachment-related issues in play and storytelling, and when under stress. In fact, compulsively caregiving children begin to sense that for them to be in a state of need, to activate their attachment system, causes their carer even greater distress and anxiety. For these children, being needy feels dangerous. Needs are therefore suppressed. However, they do not go away. They remain beneath the

child's parentified surface, liable to erupt, often explosively and tearfully whenever the child feels under pressure. The children are at risk of developing internalizing problem behaviours (anxiety, mood disorders). In adulthood, they may develop a 'co-dependent' personality, seeking relationships with needy partners who might be alcoholics or gamblers, drug abusers or violent. Although there seems little in these relationships for the compulsive caregiver, at least the rules of engagement are familiar, and in that perverse sense, the relationship feels secure.
- *Compulsive compliance* is seen most often in children whose carers are predictably dangerous and abusive whenever children make demands or appear helpless and vulnerable. The strategy requires children to be watchful, highly vigilant, and compliant. They have to try to anticipate the carer's moods and behaviour. An essentially avoidant strategy, children suppress their affect, attachment behaviour and feelings of dependency (Crittenden and DiLalla 1988).
- In complex caregiving environments of abuse and neglect, many children switch between one or more of these 'controlling' strategies.

Controlling strategies empower children. They help them disown representations of the self as helpless, vulnerable and needing comfort. Such strategies allow some degree of mental and behavioural coherence to be achieved. However, these strategies are fragile. They break down and control is lost whenever the attachment system is strongly activated, returning the child to highly disorganized, out-of-control mental states in which feelings of fear, danger, rage and despair once again overwhelm the young mind. Attachment relationships are not mentally represented as able to offer care and protection; indeed they imply fear and danger. Thus, whenever the attachment system is activated, feelings of deep distress and vulnerability are fired. Disorganized/controlling attachments therefore leave the individual at constant risk of losing behavioural and mental coherence and organization.

It is these same unstable and incoherent states of mind that maltreating parents also bring to their caregiving role. Under *conditions of low stress* and the relative absence of attachment-related matters, the parent might interact reasonably well with her child. This might be the case during a contact visit when the parent is free of the day-to-day pressures of looking after her children while they are with foster carers, or when a father is being viewed within the safety of a structured, highly staffed assessment centre.

However, children by their very nature need care and protection. Their dependency and vulnerability mean that they are attachment-saturated beings. It is therefore inevitable that they will regularly activate the parent's attachment system, and with it, feelings of unresolved loss and abuse, rejection and trauma. In this aroused state, parents might act defensively in a controlling, punitive and belittling way, contemptuously dismissing and *rejecting* any signs of need and attachment in the child (psychological maltreatment). Or they might become anxiously protective in a bright, brittle but essentially fragile way. Or they might feel overwhelmed, hyperaroused, and out of control, leading to *hostile* or *helpless* caregiving. As we shall see, these different types of anxious, distressed and aggressive caregiving define the various mental states that maltreating parents bring to the business of looking after children.

4

Defensive Processes, Attachment and Maltreatment

Introduction

Children whose carers are the cause of their fearful states, and children who do not have access to a sensitively attuned carer at times of distress, are left acutely and chronically dysregulated. In these situations, the brain feels overwhelmed. It therefore copes defensively. But there are psychological (and developmental) consequences when defensive strategies are over-used. In their attempt to reduce anxiety, defences distort reality and lay down partial, incomplete memories and dysfunctional behavioural sequences which become reactivated whenever similar situations are met. 'The neural connections that result in defenses shape our lives by selecting what we approach and avoid, where our attention is drawn, and the assumptions we use to organize our experiences' (Cozolino 2002: 32).

As we have seen, the defining characteristic of a disorganized attachment is the inability to find a behavioural strategy that leads to a place of safety and feelings of emotional calm. Because the attachment figure is the cause of the distress, approaching him or her only makes matters worse. The attachment system remains activated, and in this situation where both approach and avoidance responses increase fear, levels of arousal can rise to the point where the child feels overwhelmed. The whole experience of being cared for by an attachment figure who repeatedly frightens the child because of what he or she does (abuse), what he or she will not do (rejection and abandonment), or what he or she cannot do (neglect), adds up in Schore's words to an experience of 'relational trauma'. Such attachment traumas make individuals fear closeness to others; even activation of the attachment system itself engenders feelings of fear. Thus, as Allen (2001: 22) points out, 'attachment trauma damages the safety-regulating system and undermines the traumatized person's capacity to use relationships to establish feeling of security'.

Maltreating carers do not help their children recognize, understand or regulate their emotions. They fail on three counts.

- They fail to provide the child with any information about what is happening to them emotionally.

- There is no attempt to help children make sense of what is happening to them at the cognitive and behavioural level.
- And there is certainly no inclination or capacity to help children feel safe and soothed, regulated and contained. They fail to terminate children's activated attachment system, leaving them in a highly aroused and distressed condition.

So overwhelming and frightening is the experience of relational trauma, young minds have to employ a variety of defensive strategies to try to keep out of consciousness the painful thought that the attachment figure does not care, does not protect, but hurts and frightens. The type of psychological defence used depends on the particular character of the caregiving. For example, the psychological problem posed by parents who deactivate their caregiving whenever their children appear needy or vulnerable is very different from that presented by carers who sexually and violently abuse their children.

However, these psychological defences tend to be fragile and can easily break down under the stress of actual or perceived neglect, verbal abuse, rejection and aggression by the attachment figure. In other words, any significant arousal of the attachment system becomes associated with, and seems to be a precursor of, fear, intimations of danger, and the collapse into a disorganized state. In time, *any* activation of the attachment system can lead to a breach of the psychological defence, leaving the child being overwhelmed by feelings of alarm and panic, rage and anger, despair and helplessness. Maltreated children therefore tend to be in one or other of two mental states:

- a controlling, defensive mode (compulsive compliance, compulsive caregiving, compulsive self-reliance) with the outline of a fragile, organized but very insecure attachment strategy, or under stress
- an out-of-control, helpless/hostile mode in which organized attachment behaviour completely breaks down.

Unless disorganized and controlling children enjoy relationships later on in life that help them develop a more trusting, reflective and less defended state of mind, they are likely to carry these mental states (controlling/out of control) with respect to attachment into all future relationships. In particular, these two states are likely to be most easily roused and activated when the adult is in relationship with a sexual partner, a young care-seeking child, or indeed a childcare professional whose very involvement might imply attachment-related issues of control, vulnerability, criticism, failure, anxiety, power, fear and danger.

Our present interest lies in what happens to young developing minds when they find themselves in relationship with primary selective attachment figures whose mental states with respect to attachment shift between defence on the one hand, and fearful, chaotic disorganization on the other. It is in these parent–child relationships we find minds that maltreat, and minds that are maltreated. More subtly, each defensive strategy and the direction of its breakdown leads to different types and combinations of maltreatment, ranging from physical abuse to depressed neglect.

Stress

According to Lazarus and Folkman (1984), a state of stress exists when there is a discrepancy between the *perceived* demands on an organism and its *perceived* or *felt* ability to cope. We feel stressed when the world around us makes demands with which we feel we cannot cope: 'stress is a particular relationship between the person and the environment that is appraised by the person as taxing or exceeding his or her resources and endangering his or her wellbeing' (Lazarus and Folkman 1984). Stressful events are not necessarily objectively defined – what one person finds stressful (for example, a competitive environment) might be experienced as exciting by another.

For the young, vulnerable infant many stimuli signal potential danger, leading to feelings of stress (and attachment behaviour). Hunger, cold, pain, overstimulation, a loud noise or an unresponsive caregiver all might distress a baby. During the early weeks of life, the primary attachment figure is the person who helps the infant cope with these various environmental, physiological and psychological stresses. She is the one to acknowledge, manage and regulate the child's emotional upset. In this sense, the attachment figure acts as the first line of defence for the baby.

Once the infant has formed a clear bond with the attachment figure, her absence, loss, unresponsiveness or hostility also begin to be experienced as stressful – the first line of defence is lost, and the baby is left feeling exposed and vulnerable. Indeed, in cases of abuse, the defence has actually turned into attack, and this is experienced as particularly traumatic. Thus the physical or emotional loss of the attachment figure requires the child to develop his own defensive strategy to deal with the stress of feeling vulnerable, frightened and in danger.

Defensive Exclusion

However, when there is nothing that the infant can do behaviourally to increase feelings of safety and reduce feelings of stress, the only resort is psychologically to defend against the rising level of arousal that threatens to overwhelm the young mind. When the individual feels under threat and unable to do anything about it, situations and information that lead to the anxiety become defensively excluded from conscious processing. 'When attachment behaviors such as searching, calling and crying persistently fail to regain [the attachment] figure, the child is forced to marshal defensive strategies that exclude this painful information from consciousness' (Solomon and George 1999a: 6). If the unresponsivity, insensitivity, unavailability or hostility of the attachment figure is chronic, or episodically very acute, the child begins to associate any activation of the attachment system as a precursor of distress necessitating a defensive psychological response.

Bowlby (1998b: 45) referred to these adaptive strategies as 'defensive exclusion'. They take place largely outside conscious awareness. Reder and Duncan note that if abused or neglected children are not helped to make sense of highly dysregulating experiences or feel 'contained', they are unable to acknowledge the hurt or believe they can survive the pain. They therefore 'resort to defences which leave the conflicts unresolved and liable to re-emerge in later life as psychological or psychiatric disturbance' (Reder and Duncan 2000: 39).

The information that is most likely to be defensively excluded from consciousness is that which when accepted for conscious processing in the past has led to fear, distress and emotional overload – that is, the attachment figure has been experienced as unavailable, unpredictable or hostile, leading to activation of the attachment system. In time, any strong activation of the attachment system can lead to the defensive exclusion of attachment-related information. Attachment-related information triggered by any stressful attachment-related experience is held in parallel, unconscious and unintegrated mental systems, and therefore remains unavailable for conscious, reflective processing. Defensive exclusion is a mechanism that allows the individual to live with and psychologically survive, at least in the immediate short term, experiences of severe attachment threat and anxiety. The defence also distorts the individual's perception of other people's needs. For example, parents may perceive a crying baby as deliberately trying to annoy them.

Carers whose own histories are blighted by loss and trauma, rejection and hurt are not always able to deal optimally with their child's distress and attachment needs. The very vulnerability and neediness of the child activates anxiety and distress in the parent, who copes by disengaging emotionally. Thus the child begins to feel that his/her own arousal makes matters worse. Any sudden or increased arousal (which might include unexpected physiological stimulation or psychological alarm), feels scary and dangerous. In the past such arousal has been associated with attack or emotional abandonment.

Three types of defensive exclusion of attachment are recognized:

- cognitive disconnection
- deactivation of attachment behaviour
- segregated mental systems/dissociation.

When carried forward into parenthood, different elements and combinations of these defensive mental states, and their frequent breakdown under the relational stress of looking after an infant, underlie most forms of child abuse, neglect and rejection.

Cognitive Disconnection (Associated with Ambivalent, Dependent and Preoccupied Attachment Patterns)

Children who experience unpredictable, inconsistent and unreliable care find it difficult to build up and trust any cognitive model of how the self or other 'works'. There is no regular and contingent relationship between what is said and done. It is the inconsistency of parental availability, sensitivity, attention, perception and effectiveness that means that the child finds it difficult to establish how one person's psychological state might affect another. And when the parent does interact, the engagement seems to be governed by the carer's mental state and psychological needs, and not those of the child. This makes the caregiving feel insensitive and unreflective. This pattern is typical of 'preoccupied' adults whose caregiving is poorly attuned and 'uncertain', and whose children's attachment is most likely to be classified ambivalent/resistant.

The parent might *intrude* her thoughts and needs into the mind, interests and behaviour of the child. Her own mental states and anxious preoccupations interfere with her ability to be 'mind-minded'. She does not read or perceive her child's mental states. The result is marked insensitivity and poor attunement. For example, the child might be playing quite happily with a toy, only for the parent to take it away and introduce another that interests her and not the baby. Or she might suddenly pick up the infant who is happily playing with a ball and cuddle him boisterously 'because mummy wants a big hug now'. It is also equally likely that a child's attachment needs might trigger feelings of despair and disappointment, leading the parent to become lost in her own memories and thoughts of an emotionally uncertain and depriving childhood. The parent–child relationship lacks synchrony, and this is both confusing and distressing for babies.

Anxious to engage with the child, but poor at seeing the child's internal mental state and point of view, the parent's desire to interact and feel effective with and valued by the infant means that her involvement ends up being driven by her own anxious need to be wanted and loved. The result is repeated misperceptions, experienced by the child as insensitivity:

> That is, the parent would try to be connected, but in a way that was not contingent to the child's communication.... The issue is that with parents with a preoccupied stance, their responses ... to their children's behavior are dominated by their entanglements with their own past. Their responses to the external world are shaped intermittently by their internal mental processes, which are independent of the signals sent by their children.
>
> (Siegel 1999: 100–1)

If the carer's responses are actually being governed by her needs and uncertainties, from the child's point of view his mind, his mental state, his psychological self are not actually in the mind of the carer. She lacks mind-mindedness. There is little mental connection. The child is not being perceived directly; only through the lens of the carer's own anxious uncertainties about the need to feel loved, valued and effective. The child's attachment behaviour triggers old anxieties in the parent around issues of uncertainty, unlovability, disapproval and ineffectiveness. It is these feelings that then drive the carer's interactions with her child, resulting in involvement (or lack of involvement) that, from the child's point of view, feels inappropriate, insensitive and unpredictable. Faced with attachment behaviour, uncertain parents might suddenly feel the anxious need to love and be loved.

Not to be accurately represented in the mind of your carer is distressing. You feel alone. To be misperceived, or not perceived at all, can be frightening. Is there anybody there to meet my needs? To be out-of-mind – not because of any parental hostility, but simply because your carer's needs override yours – is to feel emotionally abandoned and personally without value. The need to be recognized and loved can become overwhelming.

To the infant, it feels as if his interaction with the carer is being governed arbitrarily by whatever happens to be going on in the head of the parent, and this has little to do with what the child is thinking or feeling. This makes it difficult to develop cognitive understanding of the 'cause and effect' nature of human interaction. Thus whenever the child feels in need or distressed and the attachment system is activated, anxiety is further heightened by knowing that the self is unable to control if, when and how the caregiver will respond. The only thing that increases the chance of triggering a parental response is to remain in an agitated, hyperactivated attachment state, sending out high-volume distress signals in the hope that they get through to an otherwise insensitive, poorly attuned carer. This is the basis of an ambivalent attachment, in which the infant hyperactivates his attachment behaviour, knowing that sooner or later the caregiver will react one way or another.

In time, any strong activation of the attachment system causes the worrying thought that no one is actually interested, no one is attending, no one is noticing, no one cares, no one is available, no one is thinking about you or has you in mind. This distressing thought is dealt with by the defence of cognitive disconnection. With the anxious thought cast out of mind, the child (or the adult) remains in his or her own emotionally aroused present. The individual remains non-reflectively preoccupied with the pressing immediacy of his or her needs and feelings and other people's emotional availability. Thus, no overall picture is established of how the self or the other operates on a behavioural cause-and-effect basis. Relationships are handled with an immediate 'here and now' quality. Whatever the behaviour, it craves attention – now.

Cognitive disconnection, because it inhibits a mental overview of how other people operate and vary over time, leads to a split between a reflective appraisal of the situation, and the immediate feelings it engenders. At different times, based entirely on whether the other happens to be perceived as emotionally available or not, he or she is either loved or hated.

Defensive activities seem:

> to be playing a diversionary role; and this is probably what they do. For the more completely a person's attention, time and energy are concentrated on one activity and on the information concerning it the more completely can information concerning another activity be excluded.
>
> (Bowlby 1998b/1980: 66)

> Preoccupied individuals are unable to separate themselves from their attachment experiences, and the topic of attachment (including all the details and emotions that accompany it) is open for discussion. As a result, they risk being chronically overwhelmed by attachment. It has been shown that preoccupied individuals attempt to defend against this risk through the use of cognitive disconnection, a defensive strategy that attempts to disconnect affect, experience, and detail from its source ... Attachment experiences of preoccupied individuals are never fully integrated into their own representations of attachment, leaving them to continually 'worry the wound'. That is, they turn again and again to the microscopic details of attachment experiences and feelings in a futile and frustrating attempt to achieve a coherent identity. Because of an undeveloped sense of identity, preoccupied individuals are left unable to explore their internal world of attachment and they behave with little conviction that they can make things happen.
>
> (West and George 2002: 281–2)

The *thought* that the attachment figure is preoccupied with his/her own anxieties and needs, and does not actually have a very clear sense of, or interest in, your infantile mental state is, from the child's point of view, disturbing information. It is the sense that the attachment figure is unavailable and not 'mindful' of your needs and wishes that is painful. It is this painful *thought* that is cognitively 'disconnected' from awareness, a thought therefore which is not actively and consciously monitored or reflected on. The attachment system is left activated, but neither the cause nor the effect of its activation is actively processed and consciously thought about. The mind is emotionally aroused but cognitively disengaged. The individual fails to monitor or control his or her thoughts and feelings, which spill out unreflectively as and when they enter consciousness. Thinking about whether the self is valued, loved, or worthy of interest is just too uncomfortable. Feelings of anger, anxiety and desire for the caregiver remain highly active, but they erupt without reflection and simply pour out unmonitored. This results in demanding behaviours and anxious, needy feelings, the origins of which the child or adult remains unaware.

Because the experience that triggered the feeling of anxiety or despair, anger or need is not brought into conscious awareness, highly aroused affective states suffuse the individual's dealings with all those around, producing behaviour which seems unreasonable, inexplicable and somewhat distressed:

> We are so used to regarding our thoughts, feeling and behaviour as being linked more or less directly to the circumstances in which we find ourselves that it may seem strange that the link may sometimes be missing.... This cognitive disconnection of a response from the interpersonal situation that elicited it I believe to play an enormous role in psychopathology.
>
> (Bowlby 1998b/1980: 67)

As a result, children who cannot build up a consistent, predictable working model of what guides the parent's behaviour (because the carer is not actively reflecting on her own thoughts, feelings and behaviour) learn to rely only on the immediacy of what happens when they get aroused and distressed. It is the child's own affective arousal that seems to bring about some kind of response from the carer, and not some mentally represented model which helps the child trust how the carer psychologically works and how she can be accessed at times of need. Children therefore rely more on episodic memories of how their exaggerated aroused states forced a reaction from their otherwise unreliable parent. They don't think through how thoughts, feelings and behaviours, whether in the self or the other, might be used to negotiate and meet their own needs in relationship to those of others.

The overall effect of cognitively disconnecting the situation that caused the feeling from the feeling itself is to leave the individual preoccupied and adrift with the feeling and not its cause. Slade, in her description of Rose, a patient, gives a graphic picture of someone who is preoccupied in relation to attachment, an individual swamped and overwhelmed by her internal experiences:

> Continuing to this day, Rose routinely demands advice, guidance, and support from me .... 'Just tell me what to do!'... Rose's daily life ... was absolutely frenetic and disorganized. Even now ... although to a somewhat lesser extent, tasks, errands, and commitments pile up and clamor at her ... . Rose's chronic affective dysregulation is exemplified not only in her experience of life, but also in the fragmented, incoherent, and inchoate nature of her mentation. In sessions, she jumps from subject to subject, worry to worry, often without a clear path from one to the next.... What is most striking is ... her absolute avoidance and rejection of reflection. She quite simply never reflects, never wonders, never pauses.
>
> (Slade 2004: 193–5)

Although the defence of cognitive disconnection to a degree characterizes all ambivalent, preoccupied attachments, only when it becomes particularly pronounced and endemic does it brush the outer margins of child maltreatment. Carers who remain entangled with their own anxious thoughts about whether they feel loved, valued or effective are rarely aggressively hostile to their children. However, they *neglect* to think about their child's mind. The child is judged in terms of how he/she makes the parent feel. The life of the ambivalent person looks like one long search for acceptance and approval. The result is a preoccupation with relationships. There is an anxious need to be noticed and loved, which places heavy demands on relationships, with the risk that the other feels emotionally trapped, exhausted and will want out. 'Similar to the ambivalent-resistant infant,' write Atkinson and Goldberg (2004: 8), 'the preoccupied adult is engrossed in attachment relationships, but cannot modulate stress through them'.

Crittenden (1996) usefully describes the family life generated by anxious and very preoccupied parents as 'disorganized neglect', and we shall meet this again in Chapter 7. In the following extract Natalie, now with a young family of her own, reveals a 'passive' state of mind, one which is not monitoring what she is saying as she gets thoroughly lost in her angry and hurt thoughts and feelings about her unavailable and unloving mother. This was part of a very long answer to a question about how did she get on with her mother now:

> As long as I remember I have felt rejected, yeah, like she [her mother] never wanted me. So I cried a lot. I still do. My eyes can suddenly well up and off I go, blubbing all over and I can't stop. When me mum phones me and has a go, I can't hold it back even if I haven't done nothing wrong. I never learn, like, 'cos when Alan [partner] put a knife to my throat and I ask her for help and just asked her to look after the kids 'cos I was having enough of being beaten up, I said 'Mum, can you have the kids for a few days' and I was getting depressed and not sleeping and she said she wouldn't and that I was being stupid and that she'd got her own problems so I phoned the social worker and told her to take the kids into care 'cos otherwise I felt like topping myself or I'd end up killing them so she better come and take them. When she did come, all she did was talk and asked me to sleep on it overnight and if I felt the same way, then she'd help, so that was no use, so I got my friend Yvonne to have them overnight but she only lives in a flat and she said only one night and that helped. She's a great mate, the absolute best, not like some. If she hadn't have helped, God knows what would have happened, I mean, who knows what I'd have done, not that my mother would have cared 'cos she would have blamed it on me even though she wouldn't help me herself even though my head was spinning and I needed the break 'cos I was going mad, you know what I mean. I couldn't see any way out. The kids was playing up and they were so bloody awkward and ungrateful and all I needed was time to think but my mum didn't and she never has even when I was a little girl, she's never been there which was like when my boy Chaz was being difficult and I was doing the tea and Alan came in and lost his temper and hit Chaz and told me I was useless and punched me and Chaz ran off to his granny's and she came round and she said I looked a mess and told Alan he was a waste of space. She said all couples have fights but they shouldn't take it out on the kids, but it wasn't my fault but to listen to her, it's always my fault. Not that her marriage – it's her second – is anything to write home about. She's always slagging off Eric which he deserves I must say, but she's only interested in herself and always has been. When I was little she used to treat herself every week to a box of chocolates. She said it was her treat 'cos she's worked hard all week and she

deserved them and she wasn't going to share them with kids because they were expensive ones and not the sort that kids liked she said so we never got any which is not how I'd treat my kids because if I had a box of chocolates I'd share it with them, all of them.

Natalie's son Chaz, aged eight, was described by his teachers as a 'naughty' boy who was easily distracted, messed around a great deal in class, and was getting into increasing amounts of trouble, both at school and in the neighbourhood. His mother has told her social worker that Chaz won't listen to her any more. She says she sacrifices herself to her family, 'not that they care. They take me for granted.' Natalie is losing heart and gets depressed. 'I mean Chaz has his loving side, don't get me wrong, we can give each other great big cuddles and I love it then, but he keeps telling me I'm useless, so I don't know why I bother.'

Deactivation of Attachment Behaviour (Associated with Avoidant and Dismissing Patterns)

In this defence, fear and distress, need and arousal, indeed any emotional state that would normally activate the attachment system, are excluded from conscious processing. This defence is most often used by children whose carers reject or dismiss attachment behaviour. Children experience rejection whenever they present themselves in a state of need. However when they inhibit negative emotional states and deactivate attachment behaviour, thereby reducing demands on the parent's caregiving capacities, children are more likely to feel accepted, or at least not actively rejected.

With continued exposure to the pain of emotional rejection and dismissal of attachment behaviour, any event, relationship or feeling that might activate attachment behaviour or emotional arousal is defensively excluded from consciousness. The result is avoidant attachment behaviour, emotional detachment, and a general downplaying of dependence and weakness of any kind, in others as well as the self.

Children whose parents deal with their own anxieties around issues of attachment by avoiding becoming emotionally involved, learn that any display of vulnerability, dependence and need decreases the availability of the carer. It is distressing to realize that when you most need care and protection, your attachment figure is least likely to respond. As the goal of the attachment system is care and protection, its activation (which appears to distress and distance the carer) increases feelings of anxiety in the child. For the child to allow him/herself to feel in a state of need is dangerous because it predicts the decreasing availability of the carer. Any situation or feeling that is linked to activation of the attachment system and its associated feelings of anxiety is therefore excluded from consciousness. In effect, attachment-related concerns are deactivated. This shields the self from having to contemplate the upsetting possibility that protection and care-seeking behaviour perversely decrease the carer's ability to meet these needs.

Defensively, there is denial that one feels bothered by rejection, hurt or setback. There is a dismissing, even contemptuous attitude towards anyone, including the self, who is foolish enough to become dependent or vulnerable. The defensive strategy mentally represents others as unavailable and rejecting at times of need. It is therefore best not to need others. Intimacy and proximity-seeking behaviours are minimized, and expectations of others are reduced.

> The infant, being unable to conceal well, suppresses feeling internally in order to minimize them externally. He becomes disconnected from his feelings and comes to believe that his needs are minimal. The adult counterpart of this strategy is found in the dismissing speaker ... feelings of need and hurt are minimized, memory for childhood is scant, and the importance of attachments is questioned. An important part of controlling the expression of need is to keep it from consciousness. If it is not known consciously, it does not exist. To the extent it is known, it is devalued. (Sroufe 2003: 411)

In parents, more extreme states of mind that attempt to limit the influence of attachment-related relationships and experiences can result in certain types of maltreatment. These might include emotional neglect and rejection, and some forms of psychological maltreatment. Deactivation of attachment (leading to deactivation of the caregiving response) is often a strong theme in physical abuse, although here the fragile nature of the defence leads to its repeated breakdown under the stress of dealing with demanding, dependent children. Any strong activation of the attachment system might mean that the defence fails and the conscious mind becomes flooded with distress and dysregulation. It is at such times that young, vulnerable children are most at risk of physical harm.

However, under slightly less stressful conditions, including dealing with professionals as well as children, dismissing adults cope by simply deactivating attachment-related concerns. The three ways in which this might be achieved are by:

- Dismissing the importance or impact of negative feelings on the self, presenting the self as strong and unaffected by emotional experiences.
- Dismissing negative attachment-related experiences with a tendency to idealize or talk rather vaguely about relationships, particularly one's own experiences of being parented as a child, even though examples of being rejected at time of need are known to have occurred.
- Devaluing, often in a contemptuous and derogatory way, attachment figures, attachment-related experience, displays of emotion, or anyone who appears vulnerable and needy, including one's children or indeed one's self.

It is these defensive states of mind with respect to attachment that are often implicated in cold, critical, resentful forms of caregiving so often found in cases of emotional and physical abuse. The caregiving environment feels tense, threatening and very stressful.

Segregated Representational Systems and Dissociation (Associated with Unresolved and Helpless/Hostile States of Mind, and Disorganized, Out-of-Control and Dissociated Patterns)

Frightening and fearful carers who repeatedly activate but fail to terminate their child's attachment needs subject the infant to extreme states of fear that overwhelm his or her capacity for flexible defence, affect regulation and adaptation (Solomon and George 1999a, Goldberg et al. 2003). As the parent shifts unpredictably from hostility and over-control to helplessness and under-control, the child is left in a hyper-aroused, extremely distressed state.

Children who experience particularly traumatic parenting, including abuse, abandonment and loss through death, are faced with trying to process extremely painful and psychologically difficult information about the self (not worth protecting), and the attachment figure (unavailable, unprotective and hostile). These mental representations of the self and others are too dysregulating to keep in routine consciousness. The self would be left in a constant state of fear and distress. Such a mental state would be unsustainable. The extreme defensive result is that such mental representations of the self and others are excluded from immediate awareness. They are segregated in representational systems not accessible to consciousness (Bowlby 1998b/1980). The hated self and the hating mother, the abandoned self and the abandoning father, the angry self and the unavailable carer each exist in ***separate, unintegrated, multiple*** and ***incoherent*** (sometimes described as dissociated) mental representational systems.

Dissociative symptoms refer to disruptions in the usually integrated functions of consciousness, including memory, identity and perception of the environment. Under secure conditions, the self seeks meaning, linkage and coherence as it experiences even the most stressful events. Much of this integration is achieved with the sensitive help of the emotionally regulating carer as she understands and explains how feelings affect behaviour, memories trigger thoughts, thoughts create feelings, feelings colour perception, and so on. However, early-onset relational trauma means that interconnections among experiences cannot be made. This compromises the integrity and coherence of the developing self. Thus, trauma without emotional support increases the risk of dissociation. However, as a concept, it has been noted that dissociation lacks clarity. Allen (2001: 162) usefully recognizes two facets of dissociation: detachment (for example, feeling 'spaced out', in a trance-like state), and compartmentalization (which is similar to the defence of segregated representational systems of the self and others, leading to rapid switches of behaviour and personality in stressful relationship situation). Three main categories of behaviour identify dissociation:

- *Amnesia*: performing actions for which the individual has no memory.
- *Absorption*: becoming engrossed in an activity to the point of losing awareness of one's surroundings, sometimes appearing to be in a trance-like condition or a state of self-hypnosis.
- *Depersonalization*: experiencing events, including what is happening to the self (for instance, physical and/or sexual abuse) as if they were happening to someone else; the self being disconnected from body and feelings; the self as an emotionally uninvolved observer.

'Maltreated children,' report Macfie, Cicchetti and Toth (2001: 249), 'who are more likely to have disorganized patterns of attachment to their caregivers in infancy, and deviant self-development, develop an increasingly incoherent dissociated self during the preschool period.' Body sensations, feelings and thoughts that cause anxiety are disowned and put out of awareness. Frightened, abused and traumatized infants are not capable of self-regulating extreme arousal. Recovering an organized state requires a dyadic relationship, but if the cause of the distress is the behaviour of the other in that relationship, the child is left emotionally overwhelmed.

In these dissociative processes, contradictory mental representations of both the self and the other (I am loved/she loves me; I am hated/she hates me; I am frightened/she frightens me; I feel sad/there is no one there, and so on) are 'maintained in parallel organizations that are not well integrated with one another' (Lyons-Ruth, Bronfman and Atwood 1999: 34). In each particular mode, the child is unable to make connections with any of the other representational states.

Depending on the nature of the particular attachment cue, the individual can employ a range of contradictory behavioural strategies that to the observer seem sudden, arbitrary and confusing. It is as if the child (or adult) can flip suddenly between very different types of personality and behaviours – solicitous care and love one minute, total rage the next, only to be followed by despairing sadness and even talk of suicide. A foster carer described her recently placed six-year-old child as 'like Jekyll and Hyde, like he has different sides to him and you never know which one is going to appear next'. Individuals, including children, who have been traumatized when very young can therefore show rapid and 'inexplicable' shifts in affect, suffer discontinuities of thought, and sudden and odd change in facial appearance, speech and mannerisms (Schore 2001b).

Steele et al. (2003) offer a clear account of how these segregated representational systems arise. Maltreating parents are rarely abusive and neglectful all the time. Under conditions of low stress, maltreating parents are capable of being available and loving. Maltreated children who suffer love and loss, abuse and rejection, neglect and abandonment, or indeed experience a large number of carers in their early years, develop many different representations of caregiving: It is very difficult for maltreated children to establish a consistent, integrated idea of how caregivers 'work'. Caregivers cannot be trusted to react in any predictable way. This is because the parents' reactions to the child are being governed by their own unresolved, unintegrated mental states with respect to attachment, which makes their behaviour almost impossible to predict for the child.

Unpredictable behaviour, particularly if it includes hostility which is not subject to any kind of influence or control, is particularly traumatizing. When a carer with unresolved losses and traumas with respect to attachment is faced with the attachment needs of the child, he/she may feel helpless or hostile, distressed or confused, fearful or frightening, panicky or blank (a state of dissociation). Children cannot predict which of their needs or behaviours has actually triggered the carer's particular representational or dissociated state with respect to attachment. In effect, at the very time the child is aroused and dysregulated and needs his or her carer, he/she is not only unavailable and cannot be trusted, but the carer's behaviour adds further to the child's fear and confusion. The child, mirroring the carer's multiple and segregated states, will therefore develop multiple representations of caregiving at times of distress which, without the regulating response of a sensitive and available carer, remain in separate, dissociated mental systems. Young children (particularly under three years of age) who experience trauma without the benefit of mind-minded, emotionally regulating caregiving are most at risk of developing dissociated mental states under stress. The lack of emotional support in traumatized pre-schoolers mediates adult proneness to dissociation.

Therefore, unlike securely attached and organized insecurely attached children (ambivalent and avoidant) who do develop singular and coherent representational models of attachment figures, maltreated, traumatized and institutionalized children:

> may have conflicting representations of the same caregiver behaving in contradictory ways, i.e. nurturing at times, hurtful at others, or sometimes not seeming to have them in mind at all. As Bowlby (1980) commented, these various representations form multiple models in the child's mind which require more psychic energy than a singular well functioning internal world made up of coherent representations. It could also be that for some of these children, they may suffer from having multiple models from two different sources. Multiple models may, for example, arise as Bowlby postulated from experiences of a caregiver who behaves in markedly contradictory ways, i.e. at times nurturing and at times abusive. Yet another source of multiple models may be seen to arise within the internal world of the child who has the experience of being perpetually in transition. Their representational worlds may contain elements including a range of diverse and possibly conflicting representations from many and often abrupt changes of caregivers, often occurring in a context of confusion and fear.
>
> (Steele et al. 2003: 14)

In these traumatic parent–child relationships, Liotti (1999) recognizes three basic unintegrated representations of the self (and other):

- victim
- persecutor
- rescuer.

Each mental representation is generated under powerful but highly dysregulated states of emotional arousal. Each representation of the attachment figure (and the complementary representation of the self) is incompatible with each of the others. In fact, explain Ogawa et al.: 'Liotti hypothesized that an infant with multiple, incompatible models of self and others would rapidly switch back and forth between models when confronted by a stressful situation involving the parent' (1997: 858).

When children feel frightened and helpless, the self-representation is that of victim. When the child is either out of control or unmanageable, or unwittingly activates old unresolved feelings of helplessness and anger in the carer, the child feels that he or she is the cause of the other's fear and distress. In this case the self is experienced and represented as a fear-inducing persecutor – powerful and bad, hostile and punitive. And when the child has to comfort a frightened, helpless or needy parent (for example, when the parent is depressed, drunk or dysregulated by unresolved traumas), the self-representation is that of rescuer or compulsive caregiver who is responsible for the other's safety. As we have seen, it is also often the case that an abused and neglected child can sometimes experience their attachment figure as loving and available, and this might set up yet another segregated mental representation of the self as loved and loving. Depending on the environmental cues as perceived by the child, he or she might interact with others using any one of these segregated mental representations of the self and the other. 'Being so strongly contradictorily and reciprocally incompatible, these constructions of self-with-others are likely to hamper seriously the mental synthesis of a unitary sense of self' (Liotti 1999: 300).

> According to this theory, when the pain associated with certain kinds of attachment experiences is so great that the memories and feelings associated with these experiences threaten to undermine the individual's ability to function, mental material related to attachment must literally be 'housed' elsewhere. Defensive exclusion in its most complete and active form encodes trauma-related attachment memories and emotions in a separate representational model that is kept, as completely as possible, inaccessible to consciousness. Segregated systems, therefore keep attachment-related information from being integrated into the thoughts and feelings that predominantly influence the individual.
>
> (George, West and Pettem 1999: 320)

Under relatively low-stress conditions, the conscious model of the self is one of independence, self-containment and strength, as the child attempts to disown representations of the self as vulnerable, helpless and in need of care and protection from an attachment figure who is actually dangerous, unresponsive or absent. However, whenever severely maltreated children experience the stress of attachment-related issues, the extreme and anxious arousal triggered by the event activates one of their unintegrated mental representations of what to expect from a caregiver at times of need. Anything in the relationship that seems like an attachment-related issue, or any unexpected strong stimulation or arousal, can cause one of these segregated representational systems (or dissociated states) to burst suddenly into consciousness. One moment the child might be exaggeratedly loving, the next aggressive, half an hour later frightened and sad, before collapsing into a state of despairing helplessness.

> At any one point, *a personality is dominant that is most useful to the situation*, and the others often are protected from awareness of what is occurring. No one personality has full control of the psyche.
>
> (Sroufe 2003: 411, emphasis added)

Objectively, it may not be clear to the other person what has precipitated the particular reaction or mental representation/personality (victim, persecutor, rescuer). A minor element of the encounter might unconsciously have suggested an echo of some previous experience at the hands of an unpredictable, frightening and rejecting caregiver. A playful tease might be perceived by the child as a precursor to some kind of physical attack. A moment's neglect or failure to be instantly available might precipitate a whole range of fears around rejection and abandonment, resulting in either sad and frightened behaviour, or an aggressive, complaining withdrawal. To be on the receiving end of such unpredictable, and often punitive, aggressive behaviours can be bewildering.

These dissociative states of mind, therefore, reveal themselves at times of stress when the defence breaks down and children are swamped by feelings of imminent danger and utter helplessness (Macfie, Cicchetti and Toth 2001). There is a traumatic sensory overload. Dysregulation leads to a sudden and overwhelming flood of emotions, leading to mental and behaviour disintegration and helplessness (George and West 1999: 296). Disruptions in memory might be observed, for example, when a child suddenly introduces traumatic, catastrophic memories into an otherwise innocuous situation – a door is found to be locked and the child screams that he is not going to let anyone beat him up. Disruptions in identity might be suspected when a child unaccountably switches between behaviours: a girl strokes her mother tenderly then bites her viciously; or a boy laughs derisively when his sister cuts herself.

A form of dissociation is detected when children act grandiosely. They present themselves as far bigger and more dangerous and powerful than they actually are. A six-year-old boy might claim he has beaten up several larger and older boys, or that he isn't afraid of his violent stepfather. The level of emotional arousal in such situations is often so high that children 'cut out' and dissociate from the immediacy of what is happening. They cease to take in or monitor what is taking place and appear to 'blank out'. This is an extreme defensive act in which the only way to survive psychologically is to shut down all major sensory processing systems. To the observer the child or adult appears momentarily to go into a trance-like, hypnotic or frozen state. However, we might note Allen's (2001: 172) useful distinction between freezing behaviour and dissociation as two very different reactions to a traumatic event. Whereas dissociation entails a radical psychological disengagement from the situation, producing a dazed, not-with-it, spaced-out, non-registering state, freezing is associated with heightened attention and hypervigilance of the threat, as the individual dare hardly move or send out any signal that might bring the self to the attention of the dangerous other. This is part of a primitive survival strategy based on 'not being seen', a feigning of death in the hope of being ignored and bypassed by those who wish you harm.

It therefore seems that 'this form of defensive exclusion fails at those moments when the individual needs defenses the most, that is, when the individual experiences certain internal or external events that are appraised as threatening' (George, West and Pettem 1999: 321). Children who have defensively responded to early trauma by dissociating will continue to use this response whenever they are faced with what they perceive to be a stressful, difficult or disturbing stimuli. (Objectively many of these stimuli are neutral, but by some association they trigger old memories of danger and fear, pain and hurt.) In effect, under stress, children and adults with early histories of unresolved trauma and abuse stop dealing with the situation using their normal cognitive and emotional reflective processes. The perceived stressor precipitates a disconnection between the arriving sensory information (other people's words, actions, looks, behaviour) and the individual's normal psychological capacities, leaving him or her in a highly distressed, dissociated state and unable to cope.

For the maltreated child or adult with a history of unresolved loss and trauma, powerful emotions remain unprocessed, unmetabolised and therefore untamed, destined to return again and again as fresh as the day they were born. Not until such intense emotions can be linked to events, memories and conscious awareness can they be reflected upon, processed and contained. Without such integration, identity remains diffuse. Cause-and-effect thinking, in which behaviour is understood to have consequences, is weak. From the child's or adult's point of view, the self feels incoherent, not quite real. Disorganized and dissociated children find it difficult to experience themselves as mentally together, which is both confusing and frightening. Maltreated and traumatized children (and their adult counterparts) therefore might suffer a range of dissociative experiences, including amnesia, depersonalization, derealization and a diffuse sense of self. Whereas moderate levels of arousal enhance memory, traumatic levels impair memory.

In summary, the child or adult switches unpredictably between:

- Organized *controlling* strategies in which the individual seeks to control and dominate all attachment-related interactions (whether with parents, children, partners or professionals), using compulsive self-reliance, compulsively compliance, role-reversed compulsive caregiving, or combinations of two or more of these. This increases feelings of control and represents the self as less helpless.
- Disorganized, out-of-control behaviour as the individual is overwhelmed by feelings of fear and danger, anger and despair. Current attachment experiences activate old, traumatic attachment experiences that readily overcome the fragile controlling strategy. The mind becomes flooded with ancient, unresolved feelings of fear and danger originally experienced in relationship with abusive or neglectful caregivers. Hyperarousal and the complete loss of emotional control produce wild, catastrophic, frightening and frightened behaviour. These are times when the other is perceived or experienced as hostile, rejecting, dangerous, depriving or abandoning.

Types of Maltreatment

The different ways in which carers mentally process information about their children's attachment behaviours offer a method of thinking about and classifying child maltreatment. When faced with their child's vulnerability, needs and attachment behaviour, parental states of mind around unresolved issues of loss and trauma are activated (Lyons-Ruth, Bronfman and Atwood 1999). Each parental defensive strategy affects what is seen and not seen, what is felt and not felt, and what is done and not done. Each one leads to particular failures of the caregiving system, leading to abuse (hostile things seen and hostile things done), neglect (things not seen and things not done), or combinations of the two. In extreme cases of severe neglect and deprivation where there is no regular care or carer (for example, impoverished institutional care, highly inconsistent care in situations of depressed poverty, multiple placements), children might not even have the opportunity to develop a selective attachment relationship. The absence of an attachment figure of any kind, the lack of a mind with which the child might engage and 'find his/her psychological self', is perhaps the most damaging of all developmental experiences.

The three major caregiving defences and states of mind with respect to attachment (which lies behind them) give us a way of thinking about the different types of maltreatment and their developmental implications. If we then add the extreme cases of severe neglect in which children have no opportunity to form selective attachments, we can generate a simple classification of different types of child maltreatment. Each one is governed by the way carers defensively process information about care, need, attachment, control, vulnerability, danger, dependence, rejection and anxiety.

This classification will be used to organize the presentation and analysis of the main types of child maltreatment:

Abuse: (i) physical abuse, and (ii) psychological maltreatment (emotional abuse).
Neglect: (i) disorganized neglect, (ii) depressed and passive neglect, and (iii) severe deprivation and chronic neglect, including institutionalized care.
Abuse and Neglect: (i) physical abuse and neglect, (ii) drugs, depression and domestic violence, (iii) sexual abuse.

In an attempt to understand how young minds form in the context of each type of maltreatment, assessments will be considered in terms of:

- The characteristics of the caregiver and the caregiving environment.
- Children's development and behaviour within each caregiving regime.
- Children's development and behaviour understood in terms of an adaptive, coping and survival strategy in the context of the maltreating environment. The psychological self and mental states which form are outlined in terms of (i) mental representations of the self, (ii) mental representations of others, and (iii) mental representations of relationships.

Conclusion

In practice, these basic types of maltreatment tend to be much more complicated. This is a reminder that practitioners in this field need to be very case-specific in their thinking and analysis. Complex and compound types are the norm. Caregiving environments also change over time. A mother might begin her parenting career as a drug addict, and then meet a violent partner, before suffering major depression. Her first child will have experienced the mother in all these states. A younger sibling might have known his mother only in her profoundly depressed condition. Each child's unique caregiving history will therefore lead to distinctive attachment behaviours, coping strategies, mental states, relationship styles and psychopathology.

The broad thrust of the book sees the three basic types of maltreatment – abuse, neglect, abuse *and* neglect – as generally indicating three different states of mind with respect to attachment, and the way each deals with stress and arousal in the context of the parent–child relationship. Each type and its associated caregiving will be elaborated as we consider a range of issues including substance abuse, depression, domestic violence, and parents whose own childhoods were scarred by abuse and neglect. Sexual abuse features in the lives of many children and their parents. Such abuse is capable of generating very complex and difficult caregiving environments. Although we shall briefly look at sexual abuse as a separate category, it can occur as an element within any one of the main types of abuse and neglect.

In a loose sense, we might see each of the three basic forms of maltreatment as a 'category type', with many cases being made up of more than one type. In practice, the expression of each type will be unique and idiosyncratic. It is in the context of a particular caregiving environment that the child seeks to survive and increase parental care and protection by developing a range of attachment strategies.

Part II

Abuse

Although mindful of the interconnectedness and overlap of different types of maltreatment, in this section we concentrate on abuse, including physical abuse, emotional abuse, and the fabrication and induction of illness in children. It is also worth remembering that emotional abuse, described here as psychological maltreatment, appears to pervade most forms of abuse and neglect.

Abusive carers have problems coping with need, dependence and vulnerability in themselves and others. Painful memories from their own childhoods often mean that they experience distress, even fear, whenever they are faced with attachment behaviour and emotional dependency. They deal with these anxieties by defensively excluding negative emotions from conscious mental processing by the deactivation of attachment and caregiving related concerns. This can be achieved by:

- ignoring children in states of need
- punishing displays of need
- being contemptuous and dismissive of need and vulnerability
- controlling the child's mental states in a hostile manner
- physically avoiding relationships where need is present.

These anxiety-reducing strategies can mean that abusive carers can be relatively warm and accepting when the child is being independent and not showing attachment behaviour. Under low-stress conditions, abusive carers can impress professionals with their genuine caregiving competences. However young children, by their very nature, are vulnerable and saturated with attachment behaviours. It is therefore inevitable that children will constantly make their carers feel tense and anxious, feelings that are dealt with unconsciously by the defensive exclusion of attachment-related material, including protective and caregiving responses. Indeed, under any type of stress, whether caused by children's careseeking behaviour, poverty, or domestic conflict or overcrowding, carers are liable to become anxious, dismissive and hostile.

In such potentially dangerous environments, children develop a range of adaptive strategies around avoidance, compliance, emotional inhibition and aggression. Children sense that their parents' 'mental representations' of them are negative and potentially hostile. As children form a psychological understanding of themselves as they interact with their parents, they are faced with the disturbing experience of being cared for by an attachment figure who can wish them harm or might even appear to regret their very existence. The person who should be a source of comfort and protection is actually a figure capable of threat and hurt.

Nevertheless, abused children have to try to survive in these physically and emotionally hazardous environments. They therefore tend to be highly alert to other people's moods and behaviour. For example, children who live with physically abusive parents learn to look to the adult for direction before they act. On the other hand, when there is no strong adult presence, abused children can be conflictual and aggressive.

Children who have been abused and rejected adapt to the harshness of their caregiving relationship by downplaying their needs. Under stress, they first try to 'autoregulate' by inhibiting the expression of emotions and needs. They assume that other people are not available as a source of safety and love. Survival is best achieved by being self-contained and self-reliant. Children psychologically defend themselves against the frightening thought that their attachment figure is least available when most needed by deactivating their attachment behaviour. In essence, this is an extreme avoidant attachment strategy.

Emerging out of these early hostile experiences, avoidant children view the self as alone and isolated. They experience anxiety when faced with the normal demands of any close relationship, and feel unworthy of care and protection. These children have learned to defend themselves against the hurt and pain of abuse and rejection by defensively excluding attachment-related information. This includes not showing distress, never allowing the self to be needy and vulnerable, and downplaying the desire to be in a close relationship, whether with caregivers or others. When in a state of fear or distress, abused children fail to signal their anxiety. They neither seek nor know how to get care and protection, help and support. Within this perspective we shall consider physical abuse and psychological maltreatment.

5
Physical Child Abuse

Introduction

To reason and negotiate with your unruly or upset child might be the civilized thing to do, but many parents, from time to time, find themselves resorting to more primitive techniques based on size, strength and power as, in exasperation, they attempt to control and discipline their wayward offspring. Many cultures accept such practices as normal, appropriate and understandable. However, there is a point along the disciplinary spectrum at which reasonable chastisement turns into unreasonable aggression. There is, of course, a debate about whether any kind of physical punishment is ever warranted, but in this chapter we shall be dealing with parenting practices that are brutal, frightening, and dangerous to mind as well as body.

Physical abuse describes physical injuries to a child caused by punches or kicks, shakes or smacks, burns or scalds, drowning or suffocating, bites or poisons. Bruises may appear. Bones may be broken. Cuts are caused. Illnesses arise. Even before they are born, some children are exposed to damaging levels of alcohol or drugs.

All aggression by others causes those who are attacked to feel threatened, aroused and distressed. The younger and therefore more helpless the child, the more fear and agitation are suffered. This is a reminder that physical abuse is not just a body blow; it is also an assault on one's psychological integrity.

Historically, the physical abuse of children by their parents was one of the first categories of maltreatment formally to be recognized, even though it had been acknowledged since time immemorial. In the early 1960s, Kempe and his colleagues (1962) observed that many young children presenting at hospitals with physical injuries, including broken bones, were not the sufferers of unfortunate accidents, but rather the victims of deliberate mistreatment by their parents. At the time, the diagnosis was often described evocatively as 'battered baby syndrome' along with the more prosaic 'non-accidental injury'.

Current definitions have expanded the category so that it now includes a wide range of harsh, punitive, controlling and aggressive styles of parenting. Hitting, shaking, throwing, poisoning, burning, scalding, drowning, suffocating and punching cover some of the hostile parenting styles now identified (for example, Department of Health 2000: 5). Typically, many parents are slow to seek medical help, especially when their children are in obvious pain following a fractured rib or a serious burn. When carers do present their child at hospital, explanations of the injury may be implausible, vague or inconsistent.

About half of all deaths caused by child maltreatment are the result of physical abuse. The death may be either the product of one extremely violent act or the accumulation of regular assaults and beatings. Head injuries are the main cause of death, usually explained by parents as the result of the child falling off the sofa, down the stairs or out of a cot. Not surprisingly, the children most likely to die after such attacks are the young, particularly those under five. In fact, of all those who die this way, about a third are babies under 12 months old. This, of course, does not mean that older children are not physically abused. Far from it. It simply suggests that they are less likely to be seriously injured or killed by hostile and angry carers.

Other groups of children who are at slightly increased risk of being physically abused include those with physical disabilities, learning disabilities, visual and hearing impairments, low birth weights, and physical health problems. Also in danger are those born prematurely, and children who suffer chronic ill health. In other words, children who for one reason or another place psychologically vulnerable parents under stress levels over and above those normally experienced by carers are most at risk. Knutson suggests that children with disabling conditions can increase parental stress because:

> disabling conditions can result in children who are difficult to manage, who evidence significant cognitive impairments, who are communicatively limited, or who are limited in mobility, disabling conditions can be conceptualised as a chronic stressor for child care providers.
>
> (Knutson 1995: 412)

As a result children with a variety of disabilities or behavioural problems such as attention deficit hyperactivity disorder (ADHD), particularly if parented by insecure caregivers suffering other environmental stressors, can find themselves at increased risk of abuse and neglect.

It also has to be born in mind that some disabilities (for example, deafness or poorly healed fractures) can themselves be the result of abuse, and that some chronic illnesses are caused by neglect. Roberts (1988) pithily characterizes the children who are most vulnerable to abuse as those who are:

- born too soon
- born underweight
- born sick
- born with a disability
- born different
- born unwanted, and after birth remain unwanted.

Babies who are separated soon after birth from mothers who suffered violence and abuse in their own childhoods are also at increased risk of parental neglect, rejection and aggression. Midwives often notice that these mothers interact in a reluctant, unresponsive or rough fashion with their babies. These early signs suggest that the intense demands that babies make on their carers cause high levels of anxiety, distress and agitation. However, although these factors do increase the risk of maltreatment, in the general population these increases are relatively small. The vast majority of babies born premature, with a disability or unwell do not suffer maltreatment. The risk only increases significantly when a number of risk factors begin transactionally to interact, particularly negative parental attitudes, anxious states of mind, poverty and poor social support (Rutter 1979; Sidebotham et al. 2003). In other words, it is rarely the child per se who increases the risk, but the parent's perception of the child's particular characteristics and the stresses they induce in the carer. For example, Haskett et al. (2003) found that mothers most likely to physically abuse their children had a greater propensity to view their children's behaviours as both negative and wilful, but only if the parent felt under situational stress, which included being in the parenting role. Particularly at risk were children whose parents believed that the child's behaviour showed poor adjustment and general impairment:

> Parents who held unrealistically high expectations for children's developmental abilities ... were likely to view their children as having many behavioral problems and to believe their children misbehaved specifically to annoy them.
>
> (Haskett et al. 2003: 678)

Although parents appear to be the main perpetrators of aggression, it is certainly the case that in many violent families older siblings – sisters as well as brothers – can also physically and sexually abuse younger children. And more generally, large families, particularly those living in relative poverty and deprivation, place younger children at increased risk of physical abuse. This is a reminder that those with the weakest psychological resources typically have to deal with the highest levels of stress. Parents of large families on low incomes, living in poor housing, who find themselves looking after a new baby and his/her fractious older siblings, are likely to feel under considerable pressure and tension. They are often socially isolated and without family or community support. It is under stress that people's ability to cope decreases. Parents are more likely to fight and argue. All of this means that children in such families can find themselves in a world where tempers rise sharply, violence erupts without warning, and conflict is never far away.

These are frightening environments in which children also suffer emotional abuse (psychological maltreatment). In a study by Claussen and Crittenden (1991), 90 per cent of physically abused and neglected children also suffered psychological maltreatment. In fact there is a good argument that although physical abuse is dangerous to life and limb, for most children the real injury is psychological: 'Damage comes when the injuries inflicted by those to whom one looks for love and protection and there is no relief from trauma' (Steele 1986: 284). Therefore this chapter should be read in conjunction with the following one on psychological maltreatment.

Characteristics of the Caregiving Environment

Low socio-economic status and high social stress are strongly linked with physical abuse. The educational achievements of parents are typically poor. Physical abusers of very young children are more likely to be female, while abusers of older children are predominantly, though not exclusively, male. However, as Corby (2000: 105) points out, there is a tendency to overestimate maternal abuse and underestimate paternal or male abuse. Most child deaths, whatever the age of the child, are the result of male violence.

Parents who suffer depression and a personality disorder, and abuse either drugs or alcohol, are at increased risk of physically harming their children. Indeed the more severe the alcoholism, the more likely violence is to occur. And while sexually abused mothers appear more likely to react to their child's distress by withdrawing, mothers who were physically abused in childhood are more likely to react to vulnerability and need with aggression.

In the households of physically abused children, love feels in short supply. The caregivers of physically abused children tend to reject those whom they perceive to be in a needy state. Attachment behaviour is dismissed. Negative emotional demands are dealt with critically. Parental levels of anxiety and distress mount as children's careseeking increases. Under stress, carers are liable to react aggressively, both in word and deed. Parents attempt to 'wean their babies on to solids when only a few weeks old, as though wishing them to be older than they were' (Reder and Duncan 1999: 64). However, when children are emotionally self-contained or behaving in a competent, independent fashion, parental acceptance and interest can be secured. Under conditions of low stress, carers can function reasonably well.

Lyons-Ruth et al. recognize that carers whose interactional style tends to be hostile might be attempting to:

> master unbearable feelings of vulnerability by denying their own feelings of fear and helplessness. This denial may be accomplished through suppression of conscious experience of vulnerable emotions and through consistently controlling others in relationships.
>
> (Lyons-Ruth et al. 2004: 79)

Many carers with personal histories of abuse and rejection suppress their emotional life and present themselves as tough and invulnerable.

There is intriguing evidence that many physically abusive carers have a heightened sensitivity to all child-related stimuli (Frodi and Lamb 1980). Compared with non-abusive mothers, physically abusive mothers show high levels of arousal when faced with a distressed, crying baby displaying ordinary attachment behaviours. Toileting accidents, messy nappy changes, inconsolable crying, vomiting, or food refusal (interpreted as defiance or rejection), or just spilling a drink can all increase parental aggression and assault (Reder and Duncan 1999; Krugman 1985).

Distressed caregiving might be further exacerbated if the child has a constitutionally difficult temperament, that is, the child tends by nature to be fretful and fractious. In such cases the mother's heart rate increases, blood pressure rises, and skin conductance levels become high. Under pressure and stress, abusive mothers also perform less well than non-abusive mothers on problem-solving tasks and show reduced cognitive flexibility. Parental arousal in these situations can be heightened further as past memories of their own abuse in childhood disturb and distort the way they perceive and interpret their child's behaviour and presumed negative intent. The mother's anger is attached as much to past fears and hurts as it is to present stresses and frustrations.

Anxiety is dealt with by emotional disengagement and dismissal of attachment-related issues. For example, pregnant mothers are slow to register for or attend antenatal classes. Some expose their unborn child to drugs or alcohol. They are more likely to discharge themselves early, and against advice, from maternity hospital. Many abusive families fail to keep appointments with their health visitor or doctor so that developmental checks are not made and immunisations are missed. They avoid home visits and appointments made by health and social workers (Armstrong and Wood 1991).

It is perhaps not surprising to learn that the childhoods of many physically abusive parents turn out to have been harsh and loveless. Crimmins et al. (1997) observed that many women who had either killed their children or murdered other people had suffered maternal rejection or abandonment during their childhoods. Their parents, many of whom had alcohol and mental health problems, had typically subjected them to prolonged physical abuse and neglect. Lyons-Ruth and Block (1996) found that parents who suffered family conflict, witnessed domestic violence, physical abuse, lack of warmth, severe punishment, and parental mental health problems were at increased risk of being hostile and intrusive with their own children. And Crittenden, reviewing 35 years of research in the field of physical abuse, concluded 'that parents at the dangerous extremes of otherwise common child-rearing practices are those who live in the most dangerous circumstances and have themselves experienced the most danger in the past' (Crittenden 1998: 16).

Although by no means all physically abused children become physically abusive carers, the majority of physically abusive carers were themselves physically abused and felt rejected as children. Abused parents who do not go on to abuse their children are more likely to have had support from their partner, had a positive relationship with an adult (for example, a teacher or a relative) during childhood, or received some form of therapy during adolescence.

The majority of abusive mothers report being severely assaulted in childhood by their own mother, while about half say their father attacked them. For many, violence, particularly by male partners, continues to be a feature of their lives. Moreover, children who witness violence between their carers are more likely to become aggressive and difficult to manage. Such behaviour merely adds to the mother's stress and inclination to deal with her children intemperately.

If abused children become parents at a relatively young age, their ability to remain available and responsive under the stresses and strains of looking after their own children is limited. For example, Coohey and Braun (1997) found that physically abusive mothers were exposed to more stressors and less emotional support in the previous year compared with mothers who had not physically abused their children. They concluded that a 'review of theoretical approaches shows that an abusive parent's own abusive childhood is believed to be a more important factor for predicting child physical abuse than aggressive models outside the parent's personal network' (Coohey and Braun 1997: 1082). Coohey and Braun's findings are interesting in that they were able to weight which experiences of violence are best able to predict whether a mother is likely to abuse her children:

> We found that assaults by three types of prominent network members (her own mother, a previous partner, and current partner) increased the probability that a mother would physically abuse her children. Being abused by one's own mother dominated the effects of all other predictors ... The second most important probability effect was a current abusive partner.
>
> (Coohey and Braun 1997: 1090)

Egeland, Jacobvitz and Papatola (1987: 271) found that parents who were abused and rejected by their parents tended to be more socially isolated, withdrawn, and prone to disengage emotionally in close relationships. Underneath the abuser's often intimidating exterior is someone who has low self-esteem, might be depressed, and is likely to abuse alcohol or drugs as a way of trying to escape the feelings of being lonely and emotionally unconnected. It is often while under the influence or drink or drugs that the parent's most aggressive assaults occur. 'In general,' found Pianta, Egeland and Erikson (1989: 2250), 'mothers in the abusive group were younger, less educated, and less prepared for pregnancy.' They were also thought to be less able to understand and tune into their child's needs. Maltreating mothers were prone to suffer anxiety, aggression and defensiveness:

> as well as being less well aware of the difficulties and demands of parenting. These high stressed mothers who maltreated their children appeared to cope with stress

> in an angry and ineffective fashion. The stressful life events appeared to permeate every aspect of their lives and were not isolated to specific situations.
>
> (Pianta, Egeland and Erikson 1989: 225)

The psychological effect on parents raised in a climate of violence and rejection is that there is little faith that other people will be available at times of need. Making demands on others is expected to lead to rejection or even attack. Relationships, they believe, are guided by the expectation that other people only relate with you to get what they want, using their power and dominance. If you attempt to assert your own needs, rejection is the likely outcome.

Typically, many physically abusive carers do not trust expressions of love and warmth, care and responsivity in others. It has been their experience that when you get close and dependent on another person, rejection and hurt is likely to follow. Being in an emotionally dependent relationship, including being in a caregiving role with one's own children, therefore increases feelings of anxiety and vulnerability. These are feelings to be avoided or defended against. Rejecting closeness and avoiding intimacy means that abusive parents lack empathy. The family relationship style is one of emotional disengagement. Members of abusive families interact less frequently with each other than matched controls. Spontaneous displays of genuine affection are few.

However, violent behaviour can be covered by a laugh and a falsely pleasant manner (Crittenden 1996). Crittenden (1995) found that hostility and aggression often lay beneath an abuser's smile, affectionate behaviour and playful reactions. From the child's point of view this is all very misleading. The signals of love and warmth (smiles and affection) are communicated in acts of aggression and even violence. The only lesson to be learned in all of this is not to trust emotional signals and affective information.

As part of their anxiety, parents of physically abused children are also prone to attribute negative intent to other people's neutral or even benign behaviours (for example, Dadds et al. 2003). They expect and see hostility in others. The three-year-old daughter who spills her drink does it deliberately to annoy her mother and 'wind her up'. The teacher who arranges a free lunch for a student arriving at school without any food is accused of impugning the parent's good character and nurturing capacities, and a complaint is made. When children are fussy, difficult or misbehaving, the perception is not that they are tired or frustrated, but 'bad'. These hostile biases represent a form of cognitive distortion. It is inevitable that young children will make demands, make mistakes and suffer mishaps. These allegedly 'wilful' behaviours trigger irritation and coercive, rigid styles of parenting.

The whole business of being a parent and bringing up children often seems a huge chore to carers who are physically abusive. They seem to resent having to feed, protect and care for their children. The more independent and emotionally self-contained are their children, the more relaxed they feel. But of course children, particularly very young children, are not capable of total self-containment and self-reliance. Inevitably they will disappoint, disturb and irritate their parents. Children's natural careseeking tendencies cause parents to feel anxious and tense. Attachment behaviours have to be discouraged, dismissed or punished. 'It's only a scratch. Don't bother me at the moment; can't you see I'm busy?' The defence against having one's old fears and anxieties aroused is to deactivate all attachment-related matters, including deactivation of caregiving at times when the careseeker most needs it.

In an extension of their 'hostile attributional bias', parents also typically have 'age-inappropriate expectations' of their children. A toddler, says a mother, deliberately refuses to become potty trained simply to annoy her. A father might expect a four-year-old to remain quiet up in her bedroom for a whole afternoon. A five-year-old is required to make his own breakfast, and get himself ready for school to which he has to make his own way along a maze of busy city streets. Failure to carry out such tasks can lead to anger and the charge that the child is being deliberately slow or incompetent. The child is then invited to define himself as a 'bad child' because bad children, he is repeatedly told, are those who annoy their parents and make them angry. The logic of this argument is that the child who fails to meet the carer's age inappropriate expectations is both bad *and* responsible for the parent's anger. From the young child's point of view, this logic is both tough and inescapable. He seems constantly to be 'winding up' his parents, and therefore must be innately bad. Abused children are forever being reminded that they are 'a waste of space' or 'a real pain – I wish you'd never been born'. Abusive carers are inclined to see misbehaviour in situations where the neutral observer sees little that is untoward.

This parenting style is mentally 'intrusive'. The carer repeatedly interferes with the child's understanding and perception of his or her own views and experiences. The child is told what he or she should do and think in order to be a good child. 'Play quietly because if you make a noise it will make me cross which is what wicked children make their parents feel.' There are also lots of commands. Children are constantly directed what to do and not do in a voice that can be impatient and aggressive. 'Pick up that pen or else I'll smack you very hard.' 'If you don't turn off the TV when I tell you, I'll throw you right through that bleeding door, you little sod.' Praise is rare. Cooperative discussion is largely absent. There is little mutuality. Disagreements are resolved by the parents asserting their power and strength. Aggressive parents believe that strict, harsh punishment is not only acceptable, but is the best and only way to deal with a misbehaving child. They believe that the harsh discipline they received in their own childhood is appropriate for their own children. Gary, for example, who punished his daughters by holding their heads under water or tying their hands to an iron bar above their heads, reflects:

> I still think that kids need a bit of discipline. Children who are brought up soft, you know, have everything they want and never get told off or checked for being cheeky

> or disobedient, like, they grow up hopeless. They can't do anything for themselves. They can't look after themselves or be independent or tough or anything. They don't seem able to cope with situations or they get stressed, whereas people who have been brought up a bit harder, with a bit of discipline, not getting away with things, not getting their way all the time, they get on with things. Me, for example, I just deal with things. I get over things and don't let them get to me. I don't need no anti-depressants and don't go pleading to everyone or feel hard done by. I just get on with things. I don't want my kids ever being weak or moaning or anything, you know.

In general, for abusive parents, anger is the first response when faced with a problem (Miller-Perrin and Perrin 1999: 73). When the world of things and people seems in its place and in order, stress is low, and the child is safe. However, when matters appear to be unravelling, fear and anger are quick to mount. There is therefore something rigid in the make-up of the abusive carer's psychology. The parent not only copes badly with the normal vicissitudes and waywardness of everyday life, he is much more likely to perceive breakdown, ill discipline and threat in the behaviour of those around him. In response to the anxiety and fear triggered by such perceived challenges, the parent seeks to regain order and control by the use of power and aggression. But, when the parent feels in a weak or uncertain position, say with a violent partner or new authority figure (social worker or paediatrician), he or she may behave in a compliant, submissive manner, at least for a while. The parent is only a bully when he or she feels the stronger partner in the relationship.

Although exploratory behaviours, including play, are valued and encouraged, the child is expected to carry out these without parental involvement. There is unwillingness, even irritation, when abusive and rejecting carers are invited to play with their children. They berate their children's need for comfort and protection. They are contemptuous of dependence, which is seen as weakness and not worthy of a caregiving response.

Thus, parents who have been exposed to aggression in both childhood and adulthood, and who find themselves trying to cope with the stresses of poverty, poor housing, domestic conflict, social isolation, a lack of emotional support and needy young children, are most at risk of physically abusing their children. The combination of felt stress, isolation from family and friends, a rigid and intimidatory style of relating to others, the deployment of exacting standards and unrealistic expectations of their children and others, and a generally hostile attitude, mark out the majority of physically abusive carers.

Children's Behaviour and Development

At the gross physical level, abused children are at high risk of being bruised, burnt and injured. Babies are at greatest risk. Typical of their hurts are head injuries, bruising and broken bones. As children grow older they can be burnt, scalded and beaten. They can suffer bone fractures and abdominal injuries by being punched, kicked and thrown against walls, down stairs and through doors.

Oddly, in spite of being the victims of so much parental violence and aggression, abused children often say that they deserved to be punished. It was their fault that their father got so angry and gave them a beating. Children who make their parents mad are bad children, they say, and must expect to be severely chastised.

Although abused children show the usual range of attachment behaviours during their first year of life, particularly anger at the lack of response of a rejecting caregiver, thereafter they begin to inhibit their needy states. Displays of attachment behaviour are increasingly avoided. Whereas normal expressions of distress are displayed in early infancy, by toddlerhood children become increasingly compliant, cooperative and careful in their dealings with parents (Crittenden 1992).

An early study by Milling Kinard (1980) found that physically abused children had problems with their self-concept. They were aggressive, poorly socialized and unable to establish trust with others. Abused children were often sad and unhappy, unpopular and poorly behaved, withdrawn and morose. There was also evidence that their sense of identity was more diffuse than that of non-abused children. Moreover, just as they have been the victims of parental aggression, in turn they become increasingly aggressive with their peers. Children who show early signs of conduct disorders coupled with violence and aggression are most at risk of displaying violent and aggressive behaviour as adults (Lundy, Pfohl and Kuperman 1993).

Cognitively, physically abused children can show a variety of deficits, including low motivation, reluctance to initiate action, poor problem-solving capacity, and poor academic performance. Their play can lack imagination with a tendency to be repetitive.

Language development can also be delayed. Many have what Beeghly and Cicchetti (1994) call a poor internal state lexicon: that is, they rarely talk about their feelings or psychological states. An understanding of emotion, in oneself and others, is required if empathy, social understanding or indeed humour is to be achieved. Abused children are aggressively uncomfortable with humour and teasing. Without good social understanding, the ability to see the other's perspective means that abused children lack social competence. Failure to understand what is happening leads to either sulky withdrawal or puzzled anger and aggression. Smiles and other positive emotional displays, self-mockery and a sense of the absurd are largely absent.

Disagreements are resolved by violence and not reason. Physically abused children are less likely than non-maltreated children (but more likely than neglected children) to offer help and comfort when children of the same age are in distress, although they can sometimes respond with aggression (Klimes-

Dougan and Kistner 1990; Macfie et al.1999). Brothers and sisters as well as peers can be the victims of their violence. Abused children are often bullies; hence their unpopularity with peers. And as their experience of adults is not good, they also avoid grown-ups, making few demands on them.

Like their parents, they too begin to develop a 'hostile attribution bias' – the propensity to see negative intent in other people's behaviour, even when no such intent is present. More specifically, abused children are prone to (i) display hostile attributional biases, then (ii) select a hostile response, before finally (iii) acting aggressively. 'What are you staring at?' said with menace and aggression when a classmate just happens to make fleeting eye contact. An accidental bump into the physically abused child can trigger a rapid outburst of aggression. Many children who display hostile social cognitions also perceive their mothers as controlling (Gomez et al. 2001).

Under stress, the predominant emotion of abused children is one of anger. This can lead to fights, defiance and other anti-social behaviours. With age, some abused children begin to commit crimes against both property and the person. One of the signature features of children who have experienced physical violence compared with those who have suffered neglect is their tendency to act aggressively in a wide variety of challenging situations, including home life, peer groups, school, and in sexual relationships. Physically abused children are much more likely than non-abused children to commit violent offences in their teens and early adulthood. By the time they reach adolescence, physically abused children are at risk of violating rules and abusing alcohol and drugs, suffering peer isolation and becoming delinquent. Children subjected to particularly harsh and violent parenting are amongst those most likely to think about suicide.

Competent children's social fluency is a consequence of their growing empathy, emotional literacy and ability to reciprocate. Failure to achieve these developmental skills means that dealing with people is always going to be difficult. For the physically abused child, social life can be a constant strain and puzzle. 'Chronic child victims tend to show detachment, estrangement, restricted affect, thoughts that life is difficult or hard, and unhappiness. Acute victims are more likely to be anxious or agitated' (Kolko 1996: 31).

Physically abused children's vulnerability to a range of mental health and behavioural problems is captured by Flisher et al. (1997). In their study they found that compared with nonabused children, those with a history of physical abuse were about three times more likely to suffer a mood disorder, four times more likely to display a disruptive disorder, and up to four times more likely to have an anxiety disorder. In particular, compared with neglected children, physically abused children are more prone to develop depression, partly as a result of the low self-esteem caused by constant caregiver belittlement and humiliation (Bifulco and Moran 1998; Crittenden, Claussen and Sugarman 1994). Both physically abused men and women appear at greater risk of developing alcohol problems, though women are the more vulnerable. It also seems that adults who have experienced childhood physical abuse are more likely to raise families in which there is violence (Wilt and Olsen 1996).

As in most forms of maltreatment, not all victims are destined to develop the full range of symptoms, developmental impairments and social difficulties. Those exposed to less severe or short episodes of physical abuse are less at risk. Abused children who find someone to whom they can turn (an aunt, a neighbour, a teacher) and who offers them safety at times of danger also enjoy some protection. Those who receive psychotherapy, sensitive foster care or find a stable, understanding intimate partner in adolescence or early adulthood are also likely to escape some of the more extreme developmental consequences of being hurt, rejected and assaulted.

The Child's Behaviour and Mental State as an Adaptive, Coping and Survival Strategy

The caregiving environment of children who are predominantly exposed to physical abuse is to an extent predictable. Whenever they make emotional or attachment demands of their carer, they court rejection, anger and possible aggression. Their parents consistently reject displays of 'negative affect', distress, and need. When the parent feels particularly agitated by the care-seeking demands of the child, dismissal of attachment behaviour can spill over into aggression.

The parent's anxiety is quickly aroused whenever people, including their own children, make emotional demands of them. Their experience of being in a dependent or needy state is that the self is rejected, punished and even possibly attacked. All expressions of need, including attachment behaviour, therefore produce uncomfortable feelings of fear and distress in abusive parents. The only way to control them is to avoid or suppress the cause of the anxiety. Children who remain in a distressed state for any length of time, or who repeatedly make demands of their carer, are most at risk. Having said that, the level of need in the child does not have to be very high. It is the parent's perception of and sensitivity to arousal in others that is the key factor.

In such settings, children need to develop strategies to help them stay safe and cope with feelings of fear, anger and rejection. It is difficult for babies or children with neurological impairments to regulate expressions of distress, which is why they are most at risk. However, with maturation, children begin mentally to model and represent how their parent's mind 'works'. They begin to understand how a dangerous carer is likely to react when the behaviour displayed by the child is one of distress or need. In short, they learn how to increase their chances of staying safe by not going to their parent at times of need. The anxious or hurt child slowly realizes that seeking comfort or protection is unlikely to gain a warm response. The safest thing to do is make few demands on the relationship, not to cry when injured, and generally not to antagonize the parent. These children are likely to smile brightly when they feel fear, and comply when they sense parental hostility. In effect, children 'become capable of regulating displayed affect in ways which are discordant with their feelings, but concordant with both the caregivers' desires and children's protection' (Crittenden 1999b: 155). Avoidant behaviour is:

> organized cognitively (to emphasize predictable outcomes) with inhibition of negative affect (because it leads predictably to undesirable outcomes). Inhibition of negative affect (i.e. attachment behavior) is made possible when infants perceptually avoid their attachment figure and focus their attention on less arousing aspects of the environment (such as toys).
>
> (Crittenden 1997a: 42)

Many abused children also become hypervigilant. They remain alert to changes in their carer's moods, particularly those that might lead to anger and aggression. They therefore become hypersensitive to reading the minds of others, though they remain anxious and unreflective about their own emotional states. In some cases, children might seek to preempt any hostility by trying to soothe and placate the aroused parent.

However, as Crittenden (1995) points out, although abused children learn that inhibition of affect and attachment needs helps avoid hostility and rejection, they do not learn how to elicit caregiving which is warm, accepting and protective. Physically abused children are also poor at recognizing when other people are being warm, available and responsive. They therefore miss out on relationship opportunities, remaining emotionally cut-off in their avoidant, dismissing and anxiously detached world.

What abused children do sense is that their carer is most available, and they are most safe, when they are behaving in ways that the carer perceives to be compliant, undemanding and emotionally independent. In effect, they role-reverse (***compulsive compliance***) by trying to anticipate how their parent might react, knowing that asserting their own needs is likely to increase the parent's aggression, either verbally or physically (Crittenden and DiLalla 1988). This strategy also means that abused children, like emotionally rejected children, become disengaged from their own affective states. They therefore fail to understand, explore and recognize the nature of their own emotions, particularly those that are triggered in the context of close, attachment-saturated relationships. This lack of emotional understanding and 'reflective function' makes for poor social competence. Being the victims of aggression, rejection, sarcasm, belittlement, and abused and psychologically maltreated, they do not trust relationships. They invest in their own power and value things more than people. Not trusting their own vulnerability or the availability of others, they remain immune to the emotional pleas of others. Hilburn-Cobb illustrates the social dangerousness of those who have been denied love by recounting a myth from the Norse tradition:

> Alberecht, the Niebelung dwarf ... has been tantalized, spurned, and ridiculed by the silly Rhine maidens he has tried to love. In a spiteful rage, Alberecht forswears all love in order to gain the secret to power over others. He then enslaves his own kinsmen to increase his wealth. The theme here is ... complex and may be considered in three aspects: (a) Those who ridicule and reject another's love become responsible for a cascading chain of harmful events; (b) those who cannot feel themselves to be lovable will simply renounce affection at some point, in favor of survival by material gain and power and (c) those who forswear love are powerful precisely because they are not limited in their actions by the one thing that would stop others from exploitation and cruelty, that is, the valuing of human attachments.
>
> (Hilburn-Cobb 2004: 95–6)

Internal Working Model of the Self

Physically abused children develop a mental representation of the self as one unworthy of care and protection. They never presume that at times of danger or hurt there are adults available who might protect or comfort them. They suffer cuts or bruises but make no fuss. They dust themselves down and just carry on. They fall ill and take themselves off to bed with no expectation that an anxious and attentive parent will nurse them. They appear to accept and get on with their unhappy lot. On the surface, they may present a stoical, even tough image, but their self-esteem is low. Their attachment figure appears not to value their physical preservation or continued existence. Indeed the aggressive behaviour of their carer suggests that he or she even contemplates the child's destruction – the self is not experienced as worthy of being kept safe and well.

In their narrative representations of carers and themselves, physically abused children portray parents negatively (harsh, punitive, rejecting) and the self in grandiose terms (over-inflated abilities or possession of extraordinary powers, for example, the child beats up parents or several older children). Toth et al. suggest these representations 'may have emerged as a way of trying to perceive oneself as able to fend off the harm inflicted by a more powerful and frightening adult' (Toth et al. 2000: 292).

The nearest physically abused children get to parental acceptance is when they are behaving in a self-sufficient, self-reliant and self-contained manner. Children feel safest when they are being emotionally independent, and not expressing the need for care or protection. However, this does not mean that the need for love and the desire to feel safe is not present – it is simply excluded from consciousness and does not get expressed. Physically abused children, who often appear to be unaffected by distress, in fact have been found to be in a state of high physiological arousal even though it is not externally displayed. It is simply too risky for any of this fear and anxiety to be allowed to leak to the surface. Physically abused children are seething with anger that their needs are not being met, but they have learned not to show their true feelings, at least in the presence of the abusive carer.

Because the child's behaviour appears to trigger parental aggression, abused children often feel responsible for causing their carer's hostility. Abused children are told that demanding and difficult children are unworthy children who do not deserve the love, acceptance, or protection of their parents. Such children make parents angry and warrant being punished. Children who make their parents angry must therefore be unworthy children and so deserve to be chastised. If abused children are harshly disciplined by their parents, they often say that they deserved their harsh treatment. Only bad children upset their parents: 'My parent is angry with me. I am the cause of their hostile state. I must therefore be a bad child and so I deserve to be punished.' As an extension of this reasoning, physically abused children often feel responsible for regulating their carer's behaviour. It is no surprise, then, that so many physically abused children are watchful and vigilant.

Internal Working Model of Others

The experience of how abusive carers react to careseeking and attachment behaviour lays down a representational mental model of how other people are expected to react whenever the self is in a state of need or distress. Abused children expect others to be rejecting, even dangerous, threatening, and frightening if they seek comfort or protection. Children have to look after and comfort themselves. The expectation is that others will be emotionally unavailable if demands are made of them. Those who have suffered physical abuse therefore tend to relate to others in a relatively disengaged way, interacting instrumentally rather than for its own sake.

Internal Working Model of Relationships and How They Work

Crittenden (1995) says that those who have been raised in physically abusive families perceive love, attention and protection to be in short supply and allocated on the basis of power. Only the strong and aggressive get what they want from relationships. If the other is perceived to be powerful and dangerous, the best way to stay out of harm's way is to be compliant and submissive. It is safest not to antagonize those who have power and strength. In the experience of children who have been abused, upsetting those who are aggressive and strong is dangerous.

> An observational pattern among some younger physically abused children, labelled *compulsive compliance* ... refers to a child's ready and quick compliance with significant adults, which occurs in the context of the child's general state of vigilance or watchfulness for adult cues. A child's compulsively compliant behavior may be accompanied by masked facial expressions, ambiguous affect, nonverbal–verbal incongruence, and rote verbal responses.
>
> (Wolfe 1999: 43)

Although compliance is adaptive in term of increasing safety, nevertheless it becomes increasingly maladaptive as children fail to develop any understanding of reciprocity, negotiation and mutuality in everyday relationships. Their one-dimensional approach to feelings also cuts them off from gaining emotional intelligence and the ability to regulate their own states of negative arousal. Not only do abused children find it difficult to recognize and reflect on their own emotional states, they also have problems accurately reading the full range of what might be going on in other people's minds. As we have noted, the only emotions in others of which they do seem to be aware are anger and aggression. They are poor at recognizing when other people are available to love and care.

Not surprisingly, physically abused children are not very good at role-playing, humour, cooperative play and empathy. They therefore approach close and demanding relationships with a number of significant emotional deficits and poor social understanding. For example, abused children often name as best friends children who in the eyes of others appear to dislike them. They are rarely popular with peers. And although as toddlers they are compulsively compliant with their abusive carers, they are often aggressive with siblings and peers.

Abused children show greater distress and arousal when presented with difficult social situations, anger and other negative emotions. The cumulative effect of compliance, affect inhibition and poor emotional regulation is to make social relationships increasingly stressful and problematic. Anger, aggression and depression are often the result.

However, if abused children perceive themselves to be strong, then like their parents, they are able to get what they want in a relationship by the use of power. This is why physically abused children bully their siblings and weaker peers. When they believe that an adult lacks power, again they act aggressively. Teachers who lack authority or parents who appear vulnerable can be subjected to contempt and violence. It is not unusual in families where there is a lot of violence for siblings to be both bullies and bullied, with the oldest and biggest child being the one most likely to initiate and prolong the conflict. It is the experience of the physically abused child that only the strong survive. Like their parents, vulnerability triggers feeling of anxiety and danger. They therefore are contemptuous and dismissive of weakness in both others and themselves. It is a foolish state in which to be; it invites attack and hurt.

Bernard (Aged 10 Years)

Bernard is the eldest of three children. He was born in Ghana, the result of a short, violent relationship between his mother, Maria, and his father. His father was a heavy drinker and spent most of his money on beer. Maria's mother said she had no sympathy for her daughter's plight, saying, 'You have made your bed and you must lie on it.' She could expect no help from her mother. Maria had a very strict upbringing. She was beaten regularly by her mother for any perceived misdemeanour, including not carrying out domestic chores to a high enough standard, receiving a poor mark at school, and speaking when not spoken to. There was an emphasis on obedience, success and respectability. Maria left school and trained as a nurse. Having been told that her out-of-wedlock pregnancy had brought shame on her family, Maria left Ghana and went to live with an aunt in Birmingham, England. She stayed with her aunt for a few months, found a job as a nurse, and then moved into a flat, leaving Bernard with a childminder while she was at work.

A few years later, Maria met another man and had two more children, both girls: Lua, now four, and Milli, two years old. The flat is very tidy to the point of being obsessively clean. Maria provides meals for the two girls, but not Bernard. He has to make his own meals. Although she buys new clothes for Lua and Milli, she either buys Bernard's clothes from jumble sales or begs them from neighbours. For most of his childhood, Bernard has been the subject of violent discipline, either being hit with a metal-studded belt, or being hit and punched whenever he crosses his mother, which is most days. In the more recent past Maria has begun to ignore Bernard, not speaking to him for weeks at a time, expecting him to look after himself. She told him that he was being punished because he was a bad child who was always upsetting his mother, making life difficult for her. Sometimes she would lock the cupboard where food was kept and make Bernard squat and beg like a dog for something to eat. She would laugh at him and say she would unlock the cupboard just before she went to bed at around midnight, requiring her son to stay awake until late if he wanted to eat.

Maria says that Bernard has always been a problem since the day he was born. 'He is the cause of all my difficulties. He is a horrible boy who makes my life a misery. He is no child of mine. I wish he had never been born.' She tells him he is ugly, stupid and bound to end up no good. Maria has tried to send him back to Ghana, but without success, as neither her own mother or his father wanted him. From a young age he had to take himself to school, which was some two miles away.

As he got older, Maria began to forbid Bernard to be inside the house whenever she was away, either shopping or at work. She locked him out. He began to sleep in an old wooden shed that abutted the downstairs flat. This arrangement was maintained even when Maria went to work on evening shifts at the hospital. If Maria couldn't make suitable child care arrangements, she would leave the two young girls in bed, lock the door, leave Bernard outside, but tell him he was responsible and had to make sure that nothing happened until she returned home later in the evening. Maria's neighbours began to complain, about both Bernard being left outside and the girls being left alone. This resulted in police and social work involvement. Maria eventually had to give up her job. She blamed and punished Bernard for her change in fortunes. 'If you had not been seen wandering outside the house by those interfering neighbours, I wouldn't have had to give up my job.' Maria has no friends. She has gradually lost the support of her neighbours, who initially were willing to help out with childcare.

At school, Bernard's behaviour, which had always been difficult, has become increasingly problematic. He bullies other students. A teacher has been hit. The head teacher has repeatedly asked Maria to come in and discuss her son's behaviour, but she ignores all requests. More recently Bernard has committed a number of street offences, including street robbery of younger children, theft of money and wrist-watches from school, and shoplifting. Now that he is bigger, he has started to retaliate against Maria's more brutal chastisements. Two recent incidents – Bernard being found drunk in the street and being taken to hospital, and a neighbour reporting that he had been left outside all night – resulted in the young boy being placed with foster carers.

There are also concerns about the well-being of the two younger girls. However, Maria is reluctant to see either health visitors or social workers. If they do attempt to make an appointment with her, she will suggest impossible times such as one o'clock in the morning. The health visitor feels intimidated by Maria and now refuses to see her at home. Maria has forbidden the social worker to talk directly to the girls without her solicitor being present. She repeatedly makes formal complaints about the social worker to the local Director of Social Services, her councillor and Member of Parliament.

On her return to nursery school after the Christmas break, Lua, the four year old, was re-registered by her mother in the name of Gertie Gormless. The girls are very quiet in the presence of their mother. They never argue with her. Neither do they approach Maria at times of need. For example, if they fall over and scratch themselves they don't cry or seek help. Upset at Maria insisting that they call Lua by her new name of Gertie Gormless, the nursery staff contacted social services. When the social worker called to see Maria, she discovered that the family had moved. There was no forwarding address.

Fabrication or Induction of Illness (FII) in Children

More recently, it has been recognized that some parents either feign the symptoms of illness in their children (and thus expose them to unnecessary medical interventions), or deliberately cause their children to become unwell, again resulting in treatments of one kind or another (for example see Polledri 1996;

Precey 1998). This phenomenon is known as fabrication or induction of illness, 'factitious illness by proxy', or 'Munchausen by proxy syndrome'. Munchausen was a German soldier who was famous for telling exaggerating tales which earned him a great deal of attention. Munchausen Syndrome, named after the soldier, is a disorder to do with an extreme need to draw attention to the self, typically by making the self ill. When a carer transfers the syndrome to a child, the condition is then known as 'Munchausen syndrome by proxy'. Although the syndrome is real enough, by its nature recognition and diagnosis can be difficult. The idea that a parent could harm their child in this strange way feels counter-intuitive. As a result, the phenomenon leads to strong feelings and heated debates about whether or not it actually exists, and if it does, whether or not it is being over-diagnosed by over-enthusiastic paediatricians. The position taken here is that the evidence suggests that abuse of this type does occur, but by its very nature, its diagnosis will be problematic and controversial.

In his or her poorly condition, the child is presented to a health professional. Typically this results in a range of extensive and unnecessary medical investigations, or treatments, including operations. Children can spend long periods in hospital while baffled medics try to find out what is the matter. Basically, fabricated or induced illness is a form of physical abuse. Children suffer harm unnecessarily. In the extreme, they can even die as a result of their carer's actions.

Characteristics of the Caregiving Environment

Carers who abuse their children by inducing illness in them often have histories of abuse and neglect themselves. Many have had previous histories of psychiatric illness, including somatization disorder and personality disorder, particularly those who induce illness. In some cases, the loss of an emotionally significant parent or the stillbirth of a child might be a feature. It has been suggested that carers have a personality disorder with a proneness to be histrionic, dependent and antisocial. Most abusers are female. In many cases family life is stressful, and although fathers are generally present, they typically appear disengaged or passive.

'The key elements,' suggests Jones (2002: 1831), 'are parental falsification or deceit, and a triangular interaction between parent, child and health professional, in which the doctor is misled by the parent, some parental need is met, and the child harmed (directly or indirectly).' The harm may be caused by some action of the parent (for example, feeding the child poison, failure to give the child a key food or medication, suffocation), or falsifying the child's condition in some way so that the doctor believes the child is ill and needs treatment. A specimen may be contaminated; for example, a parent might add a drop of her own blood to her child's urine sample. Or symptoms may be invented, or an illness induced. As a result, the doctor may medically intervene, either unnecessarily (in the case of a fabricated illness), or necessarily (in the case of an induced illness).

Some of the more common presenting conditions include respiratory arrests due to smothering, non-accidental poisoning, bleeding from a variety of orifices, factitious epilepsy, skin rashes, gastrointestinal and renal problems. Children are brought to hospital repeatedly, though the illness typically abates once the child is under the care of health staff or substitute carers. Parents generally claim to be baffled, upset and anxious about the illness and its possible causes. There are suggestions that parents seem to enjoy the medical attention given to them and their child. Parents are usually very involved in the care of their child. They insist on being helpful – taking temperatures, measuring bodily outputs, participating in medical tests. There is an intensity to the carer's involvement that is often perceived as selfless dedication and devotion 'beyond the call of duty'.

Children's Development and Behaviour

Although relatively rare (five children in a million, though this can rise to 28 per million for those less than 12 months old), fabricated and induced illness does present children with a peculiarly distorted set of developmental experiences. Babies, who are most at risk, are likely to have feeding problems. Older children are at risk of being hyperactive or socially withdrawn. Adolescents often develop a range of somatic symptoms.

Two elements assault the child's development. The first is the distress and danger caused by the parent inducing or fabricating an illness. The second is the quality of the interaction between parent and child within such a dangerous caregiving relationship. In short, the carer not only fails to protect the child, he/she deliberately places the child in harm's way.

Jones and Bools (1999) have identified a number of problems that affect children who have suffered a fabricated illness, including:

- delayed speech and language
- development of feeding disorders, often the result of unpleasant experiences to do with food
- dislike of close physical contact and cuddling (because it recalls being smothered)
- attachment disorders
- low self-esteem, partly brought about by being constantly ill or in hospital and receiving no effective treatment
- poor peer relationships (the result of children being deprived of normal peer interaction)
- under-achievement at school because of poor school attendance
- development of abnormal attitudes to their own health.

> Other subtle but pervasive imbalances occur when the parent or partner responds to the other's needs only when they coincide with and are expressing the needs of the self. For example, the parent may respond only to behaviors that are enhancing to the parent's self-esteem, such as a child's precocious achievements, or to behaviors through which the parent's needs may be vicariously expressed, such as a child's physical symptoms requiring extensive medical visits.
>
> (Lyons-Ruth, Bronfman and Atwood 1999: 40)

FII is a subtle and tricky type of abuse to recognize and investigate. A body of knowledge is slowly developing around its detection and treatment, but the issue remains elusive, problematic and controversial.

Physical Abuse: Conclusion

Historically, physical abuse was one of the earliest forms of maltreatment to be recognized, diagnosed and understood. As a form of physical abuse, the fabricated induction of illness in children has only recently been recognized as yet another type of maltreatment, now being fought on the same contested ground that sexual and ritualized abuse went through in their day. However, whatever the type of physical abuse, permeating its conduct will be an adult who presents a hostile state of mind to the child. There is a strong argument to be made that although physical abuse is certainly capable of serious psychological damage to children, the emotional hostility lying behind acts of violence is developmentally much more disturbing. Psychological maltreatment and emotional abuse can occur on their own without the carer actually assaulting the child physically. These forms of abuse strike at much deeper levels of children's development, and it is this category of maltreatment we turn to next.

6

Psychological Maltreatment: Emotional Abuse, Neglect and Rejection

Introduction

Not feeling loved by your parent is deeply painful. Your attachment figure is the person to whom you instinctively turn at times of need, but all you find is indifference, or in more extreme cases loathing. Children are seen by their parents as worthless, irritating, bothersome, flawed, unwanted and inconvenient. But of course it is not just hurtful to feel that your well-being and safety are not uppermost in the mind of your carer, it is also frightening. If a parent rejects you, particularly when you are in a state of need or distress, then where might you find comfort and understanding? For the young child, there is nowhere else to go other than inwards with the anxiety and hurt. The developmental consequences of rejection are often severe. Self-esteem is assaulted. Emotional intelligence is damaged. Even growth can be affected when children experience severe emotional stress. This is dramatically seen in cases of psychosocial and hyperphagic short stature syndrome.

Elements of psychological maltreatment are present in most forms of abuse and neglect, although it can occur on its own. When it does occur discretely it is less likely to be reported or come to the attention of the child welfare authorities, certainly in cases of younger age children. Incidents of emotional abuse and neglect that do come to the notice of the authorities increase with age, not because the abuse does not occur in early childhood, but rather because its damaging psychological consequences accumulate over the years, until a critical point is reached when the child is drawn to the attention of a schoolteacher, neighbour or health worker. Indeed, even then it tends to be the presence of some other feature of abuse or neglect (bruising or hunger) that first alerts the child health and welfare services.

Emotional abuse, rejection and neglect are all captured by the more generic term 'psychological maltreatment'. In this chapter, the focus is on parents who perceive distress in their child but either fail, wilfully or defensively, to respond to it, or react in a hostile, dismissing way. Carers who fundamentally damage their children's self-worth are guilty of such maltreatment. Within the context of the caregiving relationship, children feel unloved and unwanted. Their only value is the extent to which they meet other people's needs – to fetch and carry, to allow carers to be eligible for social security benefits, to make the parent feel worthy (Hart, Brassard and Karlson 1996: 73).

Hart, Brassard and Karlson (1996) see psychological maltreatment as the absence of most, if not all of a child's basic developmental needs:

> It is readily seen that ... psychological maltreatment ... is in direct opposition to the fulfilment of basic needs as described by Maslow: physiological needs, safety needs, love and belonging needs, and esteem needs. By virtue of its opposition to these basic needs, psychological maltreatment has the power to produce maladaptive deviances.

Iwaniec (1995: 14) defines emotional abuse as:

> hostile or indifferent behaviour which damages a child's self esteem, degrades a sense of achievement, diminishes a sense of belonging, prevents healthy and vigorous development, and takes away a child's well being.

In milder forms, carers might interpret their children's expression of need or upset as exaggerated or unnecessary. It certainly does not warrant a response, implying children should care, soothe or protect themselves, even if they are very young. To respond to a distressed child might 'spoil' them, so an agitated baby is ignored. There is a sense that these parents feel uncomfortable with emotions, with the implication that children should learn to contain their arousal. Beyond rejection, but closely linked to it in the psychology of the hostile carer, is physical abuse. Indeed, it has been estimated that psychological maltreatment occurs in over 90 per cent of cases of physical abuse (Claussen and Crittenden 1991). The distress engendered by a demanding child leads not just to a rejection of attachment behaviour, but its active suppression. Much of what is to be considered in this chapter therefore feeds into the previous one on child physical abuse.

The content of this chapter makes for bleak reading. The family landscape is cold. It is a place of suffused tension. Warmth and spontaneous expressions of love and delight are rare. There is wariness. But lurking beneath the taut surface of every day relationship dealings, there is also anger. Under increased stress, anger can suddenly erupt without warning into violence.

Characteristics of the Caregiving Environment

Parents who psychologically maltreat their children typically suffered emotionally harsh childhoods themselves. However they are rarely inclined to tell professionals much about their history and background. The tendency is to keep authority figures at a distance. Indeed, the parents' tense and hostile dealings with those whom they see interfering gives the professional a sense of what family life might possibly feel like for young children.

Often polite, but wary and distant at first, carers either become disengaged from professional help, or react aggressively, threateningly and with intimidation. They avoid doctors and health visitors, fail to visit antenatal clinics when pregnant, and often leave hospital early with their babies in spite of medical and midwifery advice to the contrary. When social workers or health workers make home visits, parents tend to be out, miss appointments, ignore treatment advice, fail to give medication (saying it is not necessary), and move without leaving any forwarding address. Socially, parents appear isolated. Some suffer depression. Contact with the outside world is reduced. Curtains are drawn, children are not allowed to play outside, and young children stop attending nursery or school (Reder, Duncan and Gray 1993: 99). The frequent failure to attend school might be explained by an increasing and unlikely list of illnesses and injuries – diarrhoea, migraine, pulled muscle, cycle accident. Professionals are diverted from seeing the child. There is therefore a danger that an 'at risk' child is not actually seen for months at a time – he or she is said to be 'asleep upstairs', 'staying with their granny', 'playing outside'. Fathers, if they are on the scene at all, remain shadowy and under-involved in family life. Reder and Duncan (1999:18; Reder, Duncan and Gray 1993) call these types of behaviour 'closure' and 'flight':

> when the family shut themselves away from contact with the outside world and with members of the professional network by refusing to open their front door to them, failing to keep appointments and keeping the child away from school or nursery.... Another way in which families closed off from the outside world was through 'flight', in which they moved home repeatedly, often at short notice and without notifying anyone.

These behaviours are the result of psychologically maltreating parents feeling anxious and agitated whenever they have to deal with their children's attachment behaviours (upset, need, fear, distress). Defensively, they deal with their anxiety by 'deactivating' their caregiving. They therefore fail to provide care and protection at the very moment their child needs it. Deactivation of caregiving can be achieved in a number of ways:

- Whenever the child makes demands on the carer, the parent becomes emotionally unavailable, unresponsive and cold. Caregiving is withdrawn when it is required. The parent might even walk away from the child at such times.
- Alternatively, the parent might insist that the child is removed and isolated. Children in need and distress might be locked in their bedrooms for long

periods, shut outside or left with other adults. When the child is not in sight, he/she can be kept out of mind. In this way, carers can avoid activating their caregiving system and thus avoid feeling distressed and agitated. Of course, this action leaves the child alone and frightened, but without the presence of an attachment figure, their arousal goes unregulated. Reder, Duncan and Gray (1993: 107) recognize a similar phenomenon and call it a 'not existing' pattern, in which the child is allegedly 'upstairs asleep' or 'ill' and therefore cannot be seen by the professional.

- Another way of trying to suppress a child's attachment behaviour is to treat any need or upset as contemptible. Good children should not display hurt or fear; they certainly should not make demands on their parents. A child who does appeal for safety or comfort is dismissed as weak, pathetic and unworthy of attention.
- In extreme cases, some parents become so averse to responding to the normal demands and upsets of children that they terrorize them into a state of subdued, fearful silence. They might achieve this by threatening to harm them or their pets in some brutal way.
- Subtler are carers who give out strong signals that they resent ever having become parents. They find the whole business of meeting children's needs to be dreary, irritating and a waste of time. They might tell their child that they wish he'd never been born and that his appearance was the worse thing that had ever happened to the parent.

On first meeting, many families may not strike the visitor as maltreating. It is the accumulation of a number of seemingly minor observations that might provide the first clues. Children do not risk crossing their parents. It soon becomes apparent there are rules for when and how to behave. There are jobs to be done, and everyone has a role. Spontaneous touch and cuddles are absent. There is a hint of wary formality and brittleness of behaviour. Children are rewarded with material things rather than laughter, praise and hugs. In some cases, the overall appearance – of home and children – might be one of order and ordinariness.

Little that the child does seems to please or satisfy the parents. Children, typically from a very young age, are rebuked and criticized, threatened and humiliated, dismissed and disparaged. Children are forever at fault and treated harshly. Their efforts are berated; they are constantly hassled – 'Hurry up, for God's sake!','You stupid idiot, can't you do anything right!' A three-year-old is told to go and get his own drink from the kitchen and not be so pathetic or presumptuous as to expect the parent to make it. 'What did your last slave die of?' hurled at the toddler who asks for orange juice. And when the child accidentally spills the drink on the carpet he is shouted at and accused of making the mess deliberately, simply to annoy and inconvenience the parent. (Iwaniec 1995: 34) paints a painful and vivid picture of the care received by a two-year-old twin, Wayne:

> On the edge of the room, like a stranger, stood Wayne, his posture rigid, staring fixedly.... Observations of his interactions with his mother confirmed that she never smiled at him, never picked him up, never sat him on her lap, never played with him, and never showed satisfaction when he did something praiseworthy.... She told him off for minor misdemeanours, and persistently criticised and shamed him.... When she approached him he appeared to be frightened and occasionally burst into tears. He never came to her for comfort or help.... From the time of his babyhood, Wayne was difficult to feed, cried a lot, slept badly, and was difficult to comfort and to distract.... As time went on, she formed the opinion that his behaviour was deliberately calculated to hurt and to annoy her, and furthermore, he did not like her.

Five-year-old Ellie also experienced severe punishment and rejection:

> Ellie's mother had been working in a casino before she had her unplanned pregnancy. She told her daughter that she wished she'd never been born and that she had ruined her looks, figure and career. For much of the day Ellie was locked in her bedroom in which there was only a mattress on the floor. Whenever Ellie upset her mother, she was told to stand in a cold shower until she had learned to behave. This punishment could last up to twenty minutes. She was rarely touched by her mother, never received cuddles, and was dressed in old jumble sale clothes. At home, Ellie barely spoke. If her mother did speak to her, it was to shout at her, humiliate her, or ridicule her distress.

More generally, family life feels stressful. In some households, conflict, violence, and constant arguments generate a climate of fear, anxiety and tension. In other cases, the emotional maltreatment can be more low-key and insidious:

> When eight-year-old Connor returned from school, he saw a bonfire in his garden. As he got closer, he noticed a number of his toys in the flames. His mother said she had had enough of his clutter and that it was about time he grew up. She told him he was too old for such play. He couldn't expect her to keep the house tidy with all his mess everywhere. When Connor went to his bedroom, every last single toy and game he owned was gone. He cried. His mother told him to 'grow up' and 'stop being such a baby'.

Psychological maltreatment is a complex phenomenon capable of a wide variety of expressions. Bifulco et al. (1994), for example, recognize two dimensions of emotional maltreatment: parental antipathy (rejection), and psychological abuse (cruel and sadistic acts). In a further elaboration, Hart, Brassard and Karlson (1996: 74; also see Glaser 1993, 2002) recognize six major subtypes, each with a number of subcategories:

1. *Spurning* which includes *hostile rejection* and degrading put-downs of children. Parents constantly belittle, shame, ridicule and humiliate their

children. This form of maltreatment is most likely to happen when the child attempts to show need, affection, distress and dependent behaviours. It is as if anyone, including children, who is so misguided as to allow him or herself to trust, love, or expect care and protection must be stupid. People who expose themselves to the imagined goodwill of others will not only be disappointed, they will be hurt. Anyone naïve enough to expect love and protection is viewed with contempt. In response to a three-year-old who has fallen over and hurt herself, a mother might shout, 'Don't expect any sympathy from me. I told you not to play on the driveway. It's your own fault, you pathetic whinger.' This same mother, reflecting on her own childhood, recalled:

> I'd had a row with my mother before I'd gone to school that morning. She said I was getting too big for my boots and if I thought I was going to get the better of her, I had better think again. When I got home from school she said she was sorry that we had argued and that she was thinking of buying me a new top to make up for it. I was gobsmacked. She said, 'Go upstairs and get that blue top that you like and let's think about something similar.' So like a fool I went up and got it and she took it off me and got the scissors and cut it up into shreds. I couldn't believe it. 'That'll teach you to get smart with me,' she said. It was my favourite top. I just felt sick and numb.

Mothers who experienced rejection by their own mothers seem to be at particular risk of rejecting their infants. Nevertheless, these parents are very reluctant to reflect on their childhoods. They tend to offer a broad, vague, even idealized description of childhood that lacks detail. Being vulnerable and dependent as a child is either denied or glossed over. Only occasionally does the carer leak that he or she felt unloved and profoundly devalued (Main and Goldwyn 1984).

2. *Terrorizing* in which the parent threatens to abandon, hurt, maim or even kill the child unless he or she behaves or stops being needy. A child might even be placed in a frightening or dangerous situation. 'Right, that's it. I've had enough. You're sleeping outside tonight and I don't care if them wild dogs come and eat you.' Some carers threaten their child with torture or violence. Here, psychological maltreatment and physical abuse are inextricably mixed. A sibling or favourite pet might be assaulted 'to teach the child a lesson' or frighten him/her into submission. For example, a child might be made to watch a father drown a puppy, a pornographic videotape, domestic violence, or a parent's attempt at suicide.
3. *Isolating the child* from other children or everyday activities, particularly if those activities might be fun. Children are denied the chance to go on school outings, the opportunity to play outside with their friends, the pleasure of beginning playgroup. They might be confined to one room all day.

4. *Exploiting* and *corrupting* parenting that encourages children to develop anti-social, self-destructive or criminal behaviours.
5. *Denying the child emotional responsiveness.* Carers who refuse to respond with warmth or pleasure, especially when their children show some success in a task, deprive children of both affection and recognition. In particular, it seems that when children are most deserving of praise, their parents are most loath to give it. A toddler's first steps might go unacknowledged, or even trigger a hostile reaction: 'Oh God, Jamie's walking! He'll be into every bloody thing. As if life wasn't bad enough without him crashing around the place.' Nothing the child achieves or accomplishes seems to bring the carer pleasure. Moans, sighs, resentment and anger greet the first clumsy attempts to draw, dress or discuss. A lack of emotional responsiveness when children are in a state of need can also be associated with under-stimulation and physical neglect, including malnutrition, untreated injuries and ignored illnesses.
6. *Failing to meet the child's medical and health needs.* Pregnant women avoid going to antenatal clinics. Mothers refuse to take their babies for postnatal health checks. Children might not be taken to be immunized against disease. When children are injured or ill, parents refuse to take them to hospital for treatment. They delay seeking medical attention, possibly until the child is very ill or even at the point of death. Health visitors and home nurses are denied entry to monitor milestones and carry out routine checks. Health professionals are typically dismissed as 'useless' or 'intrusive and interfering', liable to make matters worse. The child's health needs are underplayed or denied. These reactions are consistent with the anxiety that very avoidant parents feel when their children are in an increased state of need or distress, causing them to react aggressively, denying and dismissing both their children's dependence and need for protection.

Barnett, Manly and Cicchetil (1993), approach the matter of defining emotional abuse by looking at what a developing child should expect from a competent, caring parent. If a parent fails to recognize, respect or value these basic psychosocial and developmental needs, then some form of emotional abuse or neglect is likely to result. So, a child's very existence and right to life should be respected. His or her individuality, including personal attributes and characteristics, thoughts and feelings, should be appreciated and valued. It is in a child's nature to be dependent and vulnerable – this should not pervasively offend, irritate or anger the caregiver. And increasingly with maturation, a child should be allowed and encouraged to become a full, interactive, communicating social being. In the case of emotionally maltreating carers, one or more of these 'rights' is abused. For example, some parents seem to resent their child's actual existence. Others are irritated and angered by attachment behaviour, and displays of need and vulnerability.

More recent findings suggest that parents with high 'expressed emotion' place their children at risk of maltreatment, disorganization and dysregulation. 'Expressed emotion' refers to the strong, intrusive and regular expression of criticism, hostility and disapproval towards other family members, including children. For example, Calam et al. (2002) found that mothers particularly prone to make hostile comments about their children were most likely to maltreat them emotionally.

Moreover, parents displaying high levels of expressed emotion often have experienced unresolved childhood losses and traumas that appear to be activated during parent–child interactions (Jacobvitz and Hazen 1999; Schuengel, van IJzendoorn and Bakerman-Kranenberg 1999). While engaging with their children, parents with unresolved feelings typically shout or speak in ways that appear odd and disconcerting. They grimace; or loom suddenly, threateningly and frighteningly into their child's physical and visual space (a hand might silently and menacingly slip round the child's throat) (Green and Goldwyn 2002: 838). Or they might 'dissociate' and switch off into a trance-like state in the middle of changing their baby's nappy or as their toddler approaches them in tears with a cut finger. The child experiences all of these behaviours as odd, unpredictable and alarming, and seemingly without any obvious cause, save they often occur whenever the child displays attachment behaviour and has need of the parent.

Although emotionally abusive carers generally resist involvement with the health and social services, occasionally they may present the child as in need of treatment. The distinct message to the professional is, 'there is something wrong with this child and I want you to sort it out and fix it.' As the child is described, the tone is one of blame and irritation. However, many emotionally stressed children relax once out of the threatening environment and cease to display some of their more extreme symptoms, such as soiling, headbanging or sleep disorders. For psychologically maltreating parents, the child's 'sudden' change of behaviour is further evidence of the wilfulness of their poor, slow or difficult behaviour. The demand is that the child is returned home where he or she might expect to be treated harshly for 'showing up' the parents and getting the family involved with professional child care agents.

Underpinning the whole of this caregiving pattern is deactivation of attachment (and caregiving) as an unconscious defence whenever the parent experiences attachment-saturated events. This includes most of what children do when they are simply being children. As infants they can only communicate needs and distress behaviourally. By their nature, young children are vulnerable and dependent. And yet it is these very states that activate anxiety in emotionally harsh and disengaged carers as old, unresolved feelings of danger, fear and attachment arousal are unconsciously evoked. These attachment feelings are defensively handled by excluding them from consciousness. The carer does not reflect on them or subject them to cognitive appraisal reflection.

The effect of deactivating attachment-related information is that the carer either avoids or disengages from the child in need, or he or she dismisses, derogates or verbally punishes the child's attachment behaviour and vulnerability. Either way, by excluding attachment-related experiences from consciousness, the carer keeps the emotionally dysregulating information out of mind and so avoids becoming distressed. The problem from the young child's point of view is that it is impossible not to present the parent with attachment-related experiences. By their very nature, then, infants and young children activate the parental defence, which in a further perverse irony denies the child an opportunity to regulate and explore his/her emotionally aroused state, which causes further distress.

It is not unusual for professionals who work with parents who psychologically maltreat their children themselves to feel intimidated. Initially, while the parent is weighing up the professional, interaction might be conducted in a cool but polite fashion. The parent is keen to know the reasons for the involvement. Feeling most safe when they are on top of the rules of engagement, carers might become very knowledgeable about the legislation that underpins the practitioner's work. Woe betides the worker who does not know to the letter his or her own statutory powers.

The parent's wish is to keep childcare authorities out of his or her life. Health and welfare workers evoke caregiving and attachment issues that will be dealt with defensively using highly dismissing strategies. The professional has to justify every action. Contracts will be demanded, any breach of which will indicate incompetence. Unannounced home visits will be resisted. Only prior appointments will be tolerated. Inevitably, the parent will find some fault or failure in the professional's practice. This will result in an official complaint to a higher authority, a politician or a lawyer. The practitioner will be derided as hopeless or unprofessional. If the parent has the ability, he or she will seek a new GP, request another health visitor, refuse to see a social worker, 'sack' a lawyer for a more competent one, leave hospital prematurely and against medical advice, fail to keep health appointments, and move home without telling anyone of the new address. Most professionals feel a degree of anxiety and stress working with such difficult and intimidating parents.

Children's Behaviour and Development

The two key features of psychologically stressful, rejecting and hostile caregiving environments are (i) the very limited and conditional availability of the carer, and (ii) the severe lack of opportunity for children to explore and reflect on themselves as psychological and emotional beings with their carer. It is particularly perverse that children who experience the highest levels of emotional stress feel least safe expressing their fears, never mind reflecting on them with attachment figures. The failure of young children to explore and understand their emotions is developmentally very damaging. Emotional avoidance and inhibition cause children great difficulty in managing feelings and handling themselves in a socially competent and relaxed manner. It can also adversely affect both their physical and mental health. A history of psychological maltreatment seems to be a feature of many forms of psychopathology and problem behaviour. After an extensive meta-analysis, Loeber and Strouthamer-Loeber (1986, cited in Hart et al. 2002: 87) concluded that parental rejection and lack of emotional responsiveness were among the most powerful predictors of juvenile delinquency.

'The cumulative list of difficulties found in children subjected to emotional abuse and neglect,' writes Glaser (2002: 710) 'reads like the index of a child psychiatric textbook.' Emotionally, children are likely to feel frightened, unhappy, anxious and distressed. Their behaviour becomes increasingly oppositional and anti-social. They can appear precocious. They attempt to care and protect themselves at ages when most children would rightly be expecting their parents to make their meals, nurse their wounds and get them off to school. At school, if they manage to get there, they typically underachieve. Socially they are withdrawn, isolated or aggressive. In situations of extreme emotional fear and stress, children can show poor growth, small stature and a range of stress-related ailments.

Recent evidence from neuroscientists is revealing how many forms of abuse and neglect affect brain growth and development. The more traumatic, hostile and rejecting the caregiving, the more healthy brain development is compromised. Severe sexual abuse, terrorizing, relational trauma, rejection and emotional unresponsiveness appear to impair the developing brain's 'hard-wiring' (Joseph 1999, Schore 2001b). In particular, the traumatized child's and adult's ability to process and regulate emotional arousal is severely disturbed.

One of the main findings is that psychologically maltreated children do not seek comfort or safety when upset or frightened. Nor do they access the parent even if he or she is present. These avoidant and disorganized behaviours often indicate a disorder of attachment (Cicchetti 1989; Crittenden and Ainsworth 1989; Egeland and Sroufe 1991). In some deep-seated way, these children feel defective and ashamed. When caregivers belittle and humiliate their children, and are critical of their every effort, indeed their very existence, the self feels fundamentally unlovable and without worth (Hartt and Waller 2002, Young 1994).

School performance is typically poor. Appetite, growth, bladder and bowel control, and skin condition can all be upset. Self-esteem is likely to be low. Intimacy and dependence can cause anxiety. Trust in the availability, care and interest of others is typically absent. This means that any relationship in which there are attachment-related issues (being a peer, partner, parent or potential client) will trigger feelings of anxiety and distress. Aggression with peers is common. Many psychologically maltreated children have no friends (Hart and Brassard 1991). In the presence of distress, they become excited, unsympathetic, agitated and even violent. For example, they might attack peers who show upset and distress (Main and George 1985). In the classroom setting this can translate into disruptive behaviour.

Depression, coupled with low self-esteem, is common and can in the case of older adolescent children lead to alcohol and drug abuse, sexual promiscuity and suicide. Under stress, children are as likely to be aggressive as they are to withdraw. Many become anti-social. They steal. They can maltreat other children, including their siblings. Some can be cruel to pets and other animals.

Although there is still much debate about the nature and aetiology of failure to thrive, there continue to be a small number of cases in which children's growth potential is compromised under conditions of severe emotional stress, including hyperphagic short stature syndrome. Mothers of these children often have histories of rejection, unresolved trauma, and physical and sexual abuse. Their caregiving tends to be dismissing of dependency and attachment behaviour. This results in a paucity of physical contact, warm handling and comfort. They generate anxiety and even fear in their vulnerable children (Leonard et al., cited in Iwaniec 1995: 24). There is certainly a growing agreement that perhaps most forms of failure to thrive are the result of complex interactions between the child's characteristics, parental responses and environmental stressors (Batchelor 1999).

Extraordinary as it may seem, extreme chronic stress can affect children's growth and physiological health. Trauma, fear and stress are able to adversely affect children's endocrine system and their nervous system. In some children, highly stressful environments can compromise the production of growth hormones, leading to 'short stature'. In the more specific case of hyperphagic short stature, as the name implies, when children are removed from the stressful environment, they gorge and show very fast and high levels of catch-up growth. Emotional stress can also affect children's health. Compromised immune systems might result in frequent illnesses, poor hair and skin condition, and an overall frail, waif-like appearance.

More generally, non-organic failure to thrive in part appears to be the result of emotionally abusive, severely psychologically unavailable, and chronically rejecting caregiving. Failure to thrive refers to children whose growth and development are significantly below what you would expect for a child of that age. Organic failure to thrive, as the name indicates, involves some physiological and medical problem. In contrast, non-organic failure to thrive seems to involve negative psychosocial factors somehow adversely affecting the child's growth and development. Most straightforwardly, some parents fail to feed the child adequately through ignorance, incompetence, neglect, poverty or a lack of thought and interest. Difficult caregiving environments can also affect children psychologically, and stress, as we have seen, can affect children's growth and physiology. It is generally agreed, therefore, that there are multiple pathways to children's failure to thrive.

It is also possible that some children experience a combination of neglect, poor diet and emotional abuse that conspires to adversely affect their growth and development. Like most forms of psychological maltreatment, the carers of children diagnosed as failing to thrive tend to have childhood histories of emotional rejection. They often fail to attend antenatal classes. Some consider abortion or adoption. The parent's caregiving system appears to remain disengaged. Interest in and concern for the infant can seem limited or even entirely absent. Parents often suffer depression, poor social support and stressful home conditions.

Iwaniec et al. (1985) and Oates (1996) observed that infants who had been thought to be non-organically failing to thrive were more likely to be lethargic, anxious, fussy, demanding and unsociable. Many had an air of general unhappiness and appeared diffusely distressed. Children who fail to thrive non-organically, having suffered psychologically unavailable and rejecting parenting, are also at risk of becoming spiteful and selfish in later childhood (cited in Erickson and Egeland 2002: 8). In relationships, they can be awkward, non-compliant, rarely smiling.

The Child's Behaviour and Mental State as an Adaptive, Coping and Survival Strategy

Most psychologically maltreated children develop avoidant and/or disorganized attachments (for example, Egeland 1991), and may show symptoms of dissociated behaviour. The prevailing characteristics of their parenting include emotional rejection, belittlement, hostility, contempt, degradation, humiliation and withdrawal. This generates a highly stressful environment. Somehow children have to try to survive and function in a world in which their very existence not only seems of no great interest or value to their carers, but also periodically may even be threatened by their attachment figures.

In parent–child interaction, it is not just the achievement of a regulated state that is important; it is the manner of its achievement. It involves emotional attunement, which in turn requires the parent to seek recognition and understanding of the child's mental state. However when psychologically maltreated children display distress or make demands on the caregiver, instead of being helped to explore and regulate their arousal, they are faced with an attachment figure who appears unavailable at the very moment when the child most needs him or her. This in itself is alarming, and only adds to the child's fear and distress, experiences that would normally lead to further increases in the display of attachment behaviour. And yet it is attachment behaviour itself that appears to reduce the caregiver's emotional availability. There is therefore nowhere for the child's anxiety and arousal to go but inwards. It cannot be expressed, as this seems to make matters worse. The child is therefore left in a suppressed state of tension and stress, which cannot be leaked to the surface if further parental rejection is to be avoided.

The most straightforward way for a maturing child to adapt to caregivers who reject attachment behaviour is to develop an avoidant strategy. By deactivating attachment behaviour, the child allows the parent's caregiving system to remain deactivated. If the parent's caregiving system remains switched off because no demands are being made of it, the parent does not feel so anxious or distressed. He or she therefore does not need to reject the child, or actively avoid or suppress the child's fear and arousal.

This is why many young, psychologically maltreated children appear subdued and wary in the presence of their carer. They inhibit displays of negative feeling. By the time they reach toddlerhood they rarely cry, even if they fall over or hurt themselves. They do not seek help or comfort when anxious, frightened, ill or vulnerable. They have learned that care and protection are not unconditionally available, and that being in a state of need only seems to make matters worse. Suppressing affect reduces the risk of being rejected. It might even increase the chances of the child being able to retain safe proximity to the carer. In effect, what children are doing is inhibiting three interlinked types of feeling.

- *Inhibition of fear* engendered by the realization that their protector is not available to protect, and may even mean them harm.
- *Inhibition of desire* for adults who are not fully available in their role as caregivers.
- *Inhibition of anger* that the caregiver is not responsive to the self being in a state of need or distress.

The psychologically maltreated child has these feelings of fear, desire and anger, but cannot risk expressing them.

The other aspect of being cared for by an emotionally abusive parent is being told, repeatedly, that you should define yourself negatively, particularly if you presume to make demands of the parent in his or her caregiving role. Children who cry or whine, want comfort or cuddles, show fear or distress are told they are weak or useless, a waste of space or beneath contempt. As with physically abused children, the carer's anger and hostility, in the child's eyes, is entirely warranted: 'If my parent is angry with me, it must be my fault because I have been told that only bad children make their parents angry and liable to reject.' All of this is just another way in which dismissing and unresolved parents suppress children's attachment behaviour, allowing parents to keep their caregiving deactivated which when it is roused causes them deep anxiety and self-loathing.

Like their parents, psychologically maltreated children begin to feel that to be in a dependent state is weak and foolish. Their experience of allowing themselves to be needy or distressed is to invite parental rejection and derision. This is wounding as well as humiliating. Every time the maturing child lets down his defences and displays attachment behaviour, it is greeted with a dismissing and diminishing response by the caregiver. This is hurtful. It is humiliating. And gradually, as suggested by the carer, the child begins to feel stupid whenever he allows himself to be dependent and vulnerable. It only ever leads to pain. Accordingly, the psychologically maltreated child learns to be contemptuous of himself every time he feels needy or distressed or weak. Psychological survival, if it can achieved at all, depends on the self being strong, unaffected by feeling, independent, self-reliant, self-contained and without compassion.

More generally, this dismissing attitude of the weak self is generalized to all experiences that generate attachment-related feelings. These can include being contemptuous of other people who present themselves in a state of distress. Any event that threatens to arouse feelings of being needy or being needed forebodes pain and rejection. It is the anxiety that wells up around these experiences that leads to the derogatory dismissal of all attachment-saturated encounters.

Thus psychologically maltreated children, like physically abused children learn that inhibition of negative affect and attachment behaviour helps reduce hostility and rejection. But what they do not learn is how to elicit warm, responsive and protective caregiving. There remains a desire for intimacy but an anxiety, a fear even, that to get close, to express needs, to make demands is to court rejection, invite derision, experience the self as of no worth.

In order to survive this kind of experience, children develop a range of defensive and adaptive strategies, all of which either keep themselves or others at an emotional distance. All attachment-related experiences are played down or avoided, dismissed or derided: when in pain – physical or emotional – do not display it; just carry on. Relate to others, but do not expect any love and warmth. The world of people is a mean place and a cold place, so extract from it what you can without compassion or commitment. Be watchful, vigilant, and try to behave as you think the dismissing carer would like you to behave. Try not to be upset, or even worse, antagonize your carer. These are the controlling strategies known as ***compulsive compliance*** and ***compulsive self-reliance***.

Relationships are governed by harsh rules, breaches of which result in pain or rejection. Therefore a sense of comfort and safety is felt when the world is in order, no one is making demands or in distress, and children are being as their parents would wish them to be (self-contained, self-sufficient, and with their attachment systems deactivated). It is when rules break down, order is lost, needs surface, and attachment matters break through that the psychologically maltreated child feels vulnerable, anxious and in danger. At this point, a state of emotional dysregulation can overwhelm the previously surly, watchful, self-reliant child, leading to sudden explosions of anger and aggression. The further distress triggered by the psychological breach of adaptive and defensive strategies produces a burst of negative emotions that cascade beyond the child's control, resulting in rage and sometimes violence.

The problem with suppressing affect and states of high arousal is that there is no opportunity to reflect on either the self or others as complex emotional beings. The presence of strong feelings, in the self or others, causes unease. This is when the defences kick in, including avoidance, contempt, hostility, rigidity and in extreme cases dissociation. And although it is too risky to express feelings of fear and anxiety, physiologically these are children who are in a high state of stress and arousal. The indirect expression of this internal stress might be seen as an increase in somatic symptoms (hair loss, eczema), although illness, of course, does not lead to any increase in overt displays of attachment behaviour.

Internal Working Model of the Self

The child's view of the self is one of being unworthy of being loved or protected. Self-esteem is therefore low. Children who are belittled and derisorily dismissed whenever they show upset, make demands or show need, begin to feel contemptuous of themselves if they show weakness, display vulnerability or risk trusting another. However, if the self is to survive, it must be conceived as aggressively strong, never admitting weakness or vulnerability. Although there may be anger and resentment, it might be dangerous to express such feelings in the presence of a cool, harsh parent.

Internal Working Model of Others

Children who have rarely experienced their carers as available and emotionally responsive at times of need find it difficult to model other people as warm, interested, protective and caring. Psychologically maltreated children presume rejection if they display distress. There is guardedness in relationships that threaten to get too close. A subdued, mechanistic style characterizes their dealings with people who appear strong or hostile. In particularly stressful relationships with hostile others, children feel an increased anxiety as they try to get their behaviour right in terms of how they believe the other person would want them to be and behave. Often it is very difficult ever to get their behaviour 'good enough'. With many rejecting and critical adults, the basic message to the child is that his or her very existence is the cause of irritation and resentment. There is therefore nothing that children can do to ease their fear and tension.

However, although compliance may be the response to hostility, people who are perceived as weak are belittled. The child's maturing working model conceives weakness and vulnerability to be dangerous states in which to be, and those who allow themselves to enter them are to be dismissed with contempt. Children can be verbally abusive towards and diminishing of siblings, peers and weak adults.

Internal Working Model of Relationships and How They Work

It is not safe to become dependent on other people. Intimacy conjures feelings of rejection and hurt. It is perhaps unwise to 'let go' and trust. It is best to assume that other people are not available at times of need. Self-reliance, caution and being emotionally distant are the safest way to proceed. Children who have not learned how to elicit responsive caregiving have needs that they want met, but they have few skills available on which to draw. With age they are increasingly likely to approach others aggressively, with intimidation and without sympathy. They develop a defensively hostile and instrumental attitude to others. Reciprocity is lacking. Relationships are experienced as tense, confusing affairs best dealt with by avoidance, aggression and suspicion. If dealing with others feels uncertain and threatening, then hostile rejection, disengagement, contempt, devaluation and moving on might be the defensive manoeuvres employed.

Peter (Aged Five) and Tom (Aged Three)

Julie, Peter and Tom's mother, is a physically large woman who rarely smiles. When asked about her childhood she is reticent and vague. 'I got on like anyone else, I suppose. Not much to say really.' However, on one rare occasion when under considerable stress and on the edge of tears, she said she felt rejected as a girl; she felt 'very alone'. 'I never talk about her [mother] because as far as I'm concerned, she doesn't exist. She's dead. Not worth wasting the breath in my mouth talking about her.' Although Julie's mother is in fact alive and well, there is no contact between them.

Julie's childhood appears to have been bleak. Her father died of an alcohol-abuse-related disease when she was four. Julie and her siblings had to keep themselves and their house absolutely spotless. Food was conditional on the children being judged satisfactory each evening by their mother. Julie, in terse, short sentences, tells a brief story of how when she was about six, she cut herself on the garden gate. She was bleeding profusely. She went in to the house and drops of blood fell on the carpet. Her mother was furious, shouting at her for being clumsy. She was smacked and sent to her bedroom. Julie was not given any dinner. She remembers not daring to lie on her bed because the blood would stain the pillow and sheets, so she stood up until she eventually stopped bleeding and then slept on the floor. In the morning she was denied breakfast before being sent to school.

Julie concludes that her 'loveless' childhood has made 'me independent and able to stand on my own two feet. I don't let anyone take advantage of me. I've been there and I ain't going to be so stupid as to ever let it happen again. No one gets the better of me.'

Such details are rare. Julie's preferred style is to give the professionals involved as little personal information as possible. She tries to avoid engagement with health workers, teachers and social workers. She has no contact with her family, no friends, and says she has 'nothing to do with the neighbours – they're a nosey, interfering lot'.

For reasons that are not clear, Julie went into residential care when she was 15. When she was 16, she met and later married Kevin. He often worked away from home and she wrote him long, passionate letters in which she said she couldn't get used to someone loving her and not beating her up. However, when Kevin no longer had to work away, the reality of day-to-day life together proved too much. She told Kevin she felt depressed and talked of suicide. Without warning Julie left Kevin, leaving no address. She found a job in an office, which gave her access to the Internet where she began a correspondence with Barry. After a couple of months they met and almost immediately set up home together. Peter was born less than a year later. While pregnant, Julie neither told her doctor nor attended antenatal classes. She appeared at hospital one Sunday morning, claiming she didn't know she had been pregnant. The midwife's notes observed that Julie seemed more anxious about whether or not Barry would visit, taking little interest in baby Peter. She told the midwife she couldn't feed Peter because she felt so tired. Barry arrived in the evening, and Julie discharged herself and her baby against the midwife's advice.

The health visitor had difficulties making appointments to visit Julie and see Peter. After one tense home visit in which the health visitor said she was a little worried about Peter's weight, Julie put in a written complaint to the area's head of health visitor services, saying that the health visitor had behaved in a hostile and critical manner. Julie said she no longer wished 'the young woman, who does not have children herself and I don't think is old enough to know anything about babies' to make further visits. It was eventually agreed that Julie would take Peter to be weighed and examined by her GP. Although Peter's weight was low, it was not felt to be of concern. The GP accepted Julie's explanation that the children on her side of the family were all 'skinny'.

Two years later Julie gave birth by emergency Caesarean to Tom, six weeks premature. She felt ill throughout the pregnancy. Tom remained in intensive care for ten days. Julie was ill for a few days after Tom's birth but once she recovered she managed to visit him most days. When she returned home with Tom, a new health visitor said she found it difficult to work with Julie. The health visitor would make appointments to visit the children at home, but Julie would be out. Peter and Tom missed some of their immunisations. When Tom was nearing his first birthday, Julie wrote saying that she no longer required the services of the health visitor.

However, Julie did take Peter to the GP for his eczema and asthma. The doctor also examined Tom, and found a faint heart murmur. He referred him to the hospital for a more specialist check-up. He also noted that Tom looked pale and possibly underweight. Julie failed to take Tom to hospital for his appointment. When seen at home by the health visitor, Julie said she believed that there was nothing the matter with Tom, and according to the health visitor, threatened to 'knock her senseless' if she ever tried to visit again. The health visitor records that Tom seemed unwell, hot and flushed but she was not allowed to examine him. His mother said that he just had a cold and that she knew more about children than 'you so-called professionals'. Julie then wrote a letter of complaint about the 'unprofessional' attitude of the health visitor. She also re-registered herself with another doctor's practice in a different part of the city, less convenient.

The health visitor contacted her local social services, informing them of her concerns. She mentioned that she felt intimidated by Julie. A meeting was held between the health and social services professionals. It was decided that if Julie refused to take both Peter and Tom to hospital for examination, they would have to take out an Emergency Protection Order. Julie and Barry agreed to take the children to the hospital, but insisted that because of a number of prior commitments, it would not be possible to take the boys to see the paediatrician for at least two weeks. This delay was not accepted by social services. An Emergency Protection Order was obtained and the children were eventually taken to see the paediatrician. Although the parents accompanied the children, Barry assaulted one of the police officers during the serving of the Order.

The doctor examined both children. Peter was described as quiet, small for his age but within the normal range. Tom's weight and small stature were marginal, but the doctor concluded they were also just within the normal range. Both children were behind in their developmental milestones. There were some old bruises along Tom's arm. Julie explained that Peter could sometimes be rough with Tom when they played together, and this account was accepted. The doctor advised more stimulation for the children, suggesting that they might be taken to the local playgroup. He also requested that Julie discuss the children's diet with the health visitor. Neither of these suggestions was taken up. Tom was dressed by a nurse who omitted to put on his jumper. Julie wrote to the hospital complaining about the nursing staff's incompetence, doubting their fitness to deal with young children.

Julie then employed a solicitor who wrote to the various health and social services professionals stating that his client had felt 'abused by the system' and that she felt 'stressed and traumatized' by recent events. Julie told him that she felt persecuted. He mentioned the possibility of suing the various agencies. Meanwhile, he requested that both the health and social services workers put in writing the nature of their concerns. In the case of the health services, Julie said that she would not allow health visitor involvement although she would take her children to see their GP when she felt it necessary. Simultaneously Julie wrote the following letter to her MP and the Director of Social Services:

> Miss Ecclestone [the social worker] is ignorant and unfit to be involved with children. She doesn't have children and doesn't have the first clue about them. I have

> no confidence in her or your department. She might have been to college but I can tell you she is useless as well as rude. I will not let her into my house ever again. There is nothing wrong with my children and I won't have people poking there [sic] noses into my business where they don't belong.

Anonymous letters then began to be received by social services claiming that Julie locked Peter in his bedroom for long periods and that Tom was being neglected. 'She [Julie] leaves him out to play in the garden on his own in all weathers.' An anonymous phone call reported that Julie had been shouting at her children outside the local newsagents. She bought an ice cream but wiped it all over Tom's face, yelling, 'Any more of your bloody whining and it will be a fist in your face next time.' Peter's school had also reported worries about his behaviour. He did not play with other children. He rarely spoke. His verbal skills were poor.

This precipitated a visit by a social worker. She was denied access and told she would have to make a proper appointment through Julie's solicitor. The solicitor advised Julie that it would be best to see the social worker. When the worker expressed the concerns, Julie denied them and speculated that the anonymous referrals must have come from her neighbours: 'They've had it in for me ever since we moved here. You ought to be investigating them and their kids. Barry will sort them out, mark my words.' Throughout the visit, Peter stood watchfully in the corner. Tom wandered around aimlessly. Twice he bumped his head against the table, but did not cry or seek out his mother for comfort. When the social worker called out Tom's name, he did not respond, 'not even a look up at me'. The social worker noted that Julie's manner was 'very hostile … . She kept me standing for a long time and said as little as she could. She always makes me feel very uncomfortable. Dealing with Julie is like "walking on eggshells". You know if you say the wrong thing, she'll complain or get her solicitor on the case.'

The social worker asked Julie if she would take the children to her GP for a check-up. It was also noted that throughout the hour-long visit, neither child spoke nor did they approach their mother. Julie appeared not to make eye contact with either boy during the visit. At times during the conversation Julie made notes, saying that she liked to keep her solicitor informed of what had been said and agreed.

The GP reported that Peter behaved very compliantly throughout the examination. The little boy repeatedly looked to his mother before he spoke, 'as if seeking her permission'. The doctor felt that the relationship between Peter and his mother was 'tense' but said he 'couldn't put a finger on the reason why'.

Tom's eczema worsened. He was underweight and still small for two years of age. There was slight bruising on his legs, but again this was said to be the result of boisterous play with Peter. Julie complained that Tom was still not toilet-trained, hence his sore buttocks. She also said he had the 'appetite of a bird', was a poor sleeper, and had a 'wilful' side to him. 'If he thinks he can wind me up, he'll try it.' When asked what she did when this happened, Julie said she ignored him: 'Whenever he puts on "his" face or whines, I ignore him or give him a look and he knows not to cross me then. I can ignore him for a lot longer than he can keep the fuss up. He knows he can't win.' Julie wondered if Tom had a medical problem. She added that she had no difficulty working with professionals 'so long as they are honest and straight with me. I'll respect them if they respect me.'

Two weeks later a further anonymous referral reported that Julie had been shouting violently at her children on the way back from school, using very strong language, threatening that when she got home she would drown both of them in the bath. The school also telephoned saying that Peter had been sent to school without any packed lunch twice that week. Peter said he'd been naughty at home, and so he wasn't allowed anything to eat. The school gave him a free school dinner, but when Julie heard about it she marched off to see the head teacher saying that on no account must they feed him food. She did not trust the quality of school meals, Peter had allergies, and their actions had put his life in danger. He did not attend school for the next four days, missing a school trip. Peter's class teacher said she was worried that he seemed very distant in the classroom: 'He keeps "cutting out", you know, kind of switching off in the middle of when you're talking to him, like he's not there. It can be exasperating, but I really don't think he's taking anything in whenever I have to have a word with him.'

Another Emergency Protection Order was taken out. A paediatrician examined the children and Peter was interviewed by a social worker. In the case of Tom, the doctor diagnosed non-organic failure to thrive. His weight and body measurements were found to be well below the normal range. His hair was falling out. Julie said he twisted his hair and then pulled out chunks himself. The paediatrician concluded: 'I suspect emotional stress as the underlying cause.' Peter told the social worker that he had to spend most evenings in his bedroom in the dark because he had been naughty. He said he was very frightened because his mother said that a poltergeist might 'come and get him' while he was alone. (Peter had also seen a horror video in which a poltergeist had caused terrible injuries to people in their house.) He also described an incident in which his mother got cross with the kitten for peeing on the kitchen floor. She filled the kitchen sink and drowned the cat while Peter and Tom watched.

The two boys were placed with temporary foster carers. Although Peter was very quiet and subdued during his first few days with his new carers, Tom, according to the foster mother, 'ate and ate as if eating was going out of fashion'. His eczema also began to clear. Peter slept very poorly, waking up with 'night terrors'. He wanted his bedroom light kept on throughout the night. He ate very little and asked for small portions.

Conclusion

Children who are physically abused and psychologically maltreated sense that their carers have them 'in mind' although these representations are negative, hostile, malevolent, even murderous. For these children, there is no safe psychological place to go at times of fear and distress, which simply increases further their feelings of inescapable anxiety. A different set of psychological dilemmas exists for children who suffer neglect. As we shall see in Part III, children sense that carers who are neglectful are not thinking about them, their needs or their safety. This too is frightening, but in a way that leads to a different set of survival strategies, defence mechanisms and psychosocial consequences.

Part III

Neglect

Neglect is an insidious form of maltreatment. It starves the developing mind of stimulation. It denies the child information and interest about the self and others. In some cases 'neglect slowly and persistently eats away at children's spirits until they have little will to connect with others or explore the world' (Erickson and Egeland 2002: 3).

Many parents display what has been referred to the 'apathy–futility' syndrome. There is a pervasive sense of despair and pointlessness. As a result, parents fail to respond to their children's attachment, social and emotional needs. Relationships and interaction are minimal and perfunctory. As a consequence, neglected children tend to be passive. There is evidence that many neglectful parents have learning difficulties.

The broad characteristics of physical neglect are familiar to most childcare practitioners. Poverty, a general air of hopelessness, dirt, mess, and the ever-present smell of old food, greasy floors and poor hygiene instantly conjure run-down homes and aimless family lives. Nutrition can be poor. Clothes are old or dirty or too big. Nappies are not changed. Babies seem to suffer rashes and permanently sore bottoms. Children's hair is often lank, wispy and thin. Many are often enuretic and prone to one minor illness after another. Children who are neglected are often smelly, scruffy, and so become the easy targets of peer taunts, rejection and bullying. Bedrooms are sparsely furnished and cold. Children are left unsupervised and under stimulated. As a result, accidents and injuries are common. School attendance can be poor. Neglected children's development is often impaired, physically, educationally and emotionally. They are tired, apathetic, and suffer various skin complaints.

Over recent years, it has been increasingly recognized that child neglect has a more severe and adverse impact on children's development than abuse (Hildyard and Wolfe 2002; Trickett and McBride-Chang 1995). Ney, Fung and Wickett hauntingly described the general developmental prospects posed by childhood neglect:

> Our evidence supports the hypothesis that the most severe psychological conflicts arise from neglect. Having been deprived of the necessary ingredients in their normal development, children never seem to accept the loss of a childhood that

> could have been. They keep searching as adolescents and adults, only to find those that they search amongst are usually themselves deprived people who not only cannot provide them with what they needed as children, but also tend to abuse them, partly out of their own frustrations in encountering somebody who they thought would give to them when they are so hungry.
>
> (Ney, Fung and Wickett 1994: 711)

Looked at broadly, most types of child maltreatment involve an element of neglect. The Department of Health (2000: 6) defines neglect as:

> The persistent failure to meet a child's physical and/or emotional needs, likely to result in the serious impairment of the child's health or development. It may involve a parent or carer failing to provide adequate food, shelter and clothing, failing to protect a child from physical harm or danger, or the failure to ensure access to appropriate medical care or treatment. It may also include neglect of, or unresponsiveness to a child's basic emotional needs.

Within this wide definition, practitioners might expect to meet children who are unkempt and malnourished, without a bed on which to sleep, denied health and medical care, left alone and unsupervised, emotionally ignored or neglected, not sent to school, and left bewildered and frightened by the behaviour or condition of the parent who might be drunk, sexually disinhibited or criminally active. Failure to protect children from physical harm and danger often occurs together with failure to feed, clothe or shelter them adequately.

Male partners, if present at all, seem elusive and shadowy. They are part of the problem, but rarely around to be involved in the solution. Some mothers have mental health problems, learning disabilities, alcohol addictions or abuse substances (Berry, Charlson and Dawson 2003; Dunn et al. 2002). Social isolation is common. Stevenson also raises the notion, quite rightly, that it is not only social isolation that causes some parents to feel incompetent and unmotivated, but also mistrustful, disengaged and difficult parents are more likely to become ostracised 'which may in turn lead to anxiety and anger towards, or withdrawal from, the host community' (Stevenson 1998: 43). The lack of emotional and social support is particularly stressful. People who enjoy the interest and help of others feel connected, valued, strong and more able to cope. Take away our affective links with others and we feel vulnerable, alone and distressed. The majority of neglectful families are known to the health and welfare services.

Many neglectful parents have childhood histories of parental death, separation or divorce, a large number of family moves and a lack of family structure and supervision, which Lyons-Ruth et al. (1989, 2003) correlated with decreased involvement with their own infants. Parental neglect of children is not a unitary condition (Crittenden 1993, Hildyard and Wolfe 2002). *Physical neglect* involves failure to meet children's basic physical needs of good food, adequate housing and proper clothing. Carers also fail to protect their children from danger. Supervision is poor. Emotional neglect denies children psychological recognition and emotional understanding. Erickson and Egeland (2002) usefully see emotional neglect as a form of psychological unavailability. This is particularly pernicious while children are still very young. Their cries go unheard. Parents seem uninterested in their infant's development. Children's curiosity goes unrecognized. Children whose carers fail to respond eventually give up; psychologically they shut down and cease to engage with those around them. Neglect can shade into emotional abuse and stress-induced non-organic failure to thrive (see Chapter 6).

The above are all acts of omission – failures to meet children's (i) physical, (ii) emotional, (iii) cognitive, (iv) educational, (v) social or (vi) cultural needs. As ever, the most basic of these is children's need to feel safe; that at times of danger, the caregiver is able and willing to provide protection. Feeling unprotected is frightening, and fear is the most primitive, powerful and dysregulating of the emotions.

The link between different types of neglect is chronic parental failure to meet some developmental need, either physical or psychological. While the abused child perceives danger, the neglected child believes him/herself to be helplessly unprotected, which is alarming (Crittenden 2002: 121). Garbarino and Collins (1999: 17) go so far as to say that whether or not a child is neglected 'has little to do with money or prestige or outward appearances but, rather, has to do with parents being simply there for their kids. Being psychologically available for a child is the most coveted characteristic of a parent by a child.' In contrast to abusive parents who act angrily and aggressively under stress, neglectful parents tend to avoid, disengage and de-activate their caregiving under emotionally taxing conditions. The child 'loses' their parent at the moment he or she needs them most.

In cases of extreme neglect, when the infant or young child is left alone for long periods in states of great distress, the child's attachment system is acutely and *chronically* activated, but in the absence of the attachment figure his attachment behaviour cannot be directed anywhere, and so it cannot be terminated. The child is left without a relationship-based strategy to help him regulate his traumatic emotional arousal. This is extremely disturbing. Evidence is mounting that severe neglect places children at some of the greatest risks of long-term psychopathology. For a young, vulnerable infant, to feel totally abandoned is to feel in extreme danger. The self is alone and exposed. There is no safe place to go. There is no adult in sight. No one has you in mind. The experience can produce such high levels of emotional arousal, children eventually shut down psychologically and dissociate.

The mind of the neglectful parent has little interest in the child's thoughts and feelings. There is a lack of empathy and mind-mindedness in general, which not only applies to children, but extends to partners and friends so that relationships rarely last or endure. Although parents often look forward to having children, once they arrive, they are found to be puzzling, taxing and distressing. Mothers, for example, typically feel ineffective and incompetent. Failure to read their infant's behaviour and cues can lead to abandonment, both emotional and physical. Fathers simply opt out and fade away.

Medical neglect also tends to be a feature of many neglect cases. Through apathy rather than avoidance, children are not immunized, taken for medical help, given medication, or returned to hospital for initial or follow-up procedures and reviews. In similar vein, educational neglect in which parents fail to ensure their children's regular attendance at school is commonly met.

According to Polansky et al. (1981), many of the following characteristics are typical of neglectful parents:

- They see themselves surrounded by unsupportive people.
- They feel lonely and isolated.
- They feel apathetic and believe that their efforts are futile.
- They feel despair, detachment and alienation.
- They experience high stress because of poor coping skills.
- They tend to relocate frequently/socially distancing themselves both geographically and emotionally.
- They emotionally distance themselves from their children.
- They interact with their children infrequently and when they do, it is generally negative in character.
- They have little social and emotional support, further reducing their psychological availability for their own children.

Crittenden (1993) is particularly interesting and helpful on explaining neglect and its various manifestations. Her starting point is a consideration of the way neglectful parents mentally process attachment-related information relevant to the care and protection of children. How do they perceive, interpret and respond to their children's needs and attachment signals? Neglectful parents appear to ignore, abort or distort information that might normally activate a caregiving response in one of four ways:

1. Failures of Perception

In cases of severe neglect, parents may not even perceive their children's needs, even when levels of distress exhibited are high. Crittenden calls this ***passive*** or ***depressed neglect***. Parental care seems to lack energy. There is a climate of depression and despair. Children may not be fed. An unwell child may go unnoticed. The emotional arousal associated with attachment behaviour triggers high anxiety in the parent which he or she deal with by excluding it from consciousness. In effect, children's need for care and protection is not perceived, and so does not require psychological processing. Attention-seeking signals, such as a child's cry, simply go unheard, at least at the conscious level.

Such 'defensive exclusion' of attachment-related information originates in the caregiver's own experience of neglect and rejection. As a child, he or she felt powerless to elicit care and protection. This is a frightening experience. Such fear, triggered in the present whenever relationship and attachment-related matters arise, is defensively excluded from consciousness. Failure to perceive need, including one's own child's attachment behaviour, is therefore a way of keeping potentially disturbing information out of mind. Often the treatment focus in these cases is to meet the carer's needs because until these are addressed, there is no parental capacity to provide care and protection.

2. Misinterpretation of Attachment-Related Information

At this level of information processing, the carer hears the distress signal, but misinterprets its meaning. A whiny child is ignored on the grounds that he or she is forever fussing and so it is unlikely that there is a legitimate basis for the distress. Or, the parent overestimates the child's ability to care for and protect him or herself. A hungry three-year-old might be told to go and feed him or herself, even though such a degree of independence and self-reliance represents an inappropriate, possibly hazardous expectation of such a young child. However, the self-care instruction allows the parent to deactivate caregiving, the arousal of which causes the parent to experience unease and discomfort.

Crittenden (1993) identifies three types of childhood experience that leads to the faulty attribution that a parental response is not needed.

- It is commonly the case that many unresponsive carers were left to fend for themselves even as young children.
- Others had parents who were absorbed with their own needs and so never seemed to recognize or respond to their children's attachment behaviour. Depressed, co-dependent, alcoholic, domestically abused and traumatized parents need their children to care and protect them. This is a form of role-reversal in which children 'parent their parents'. Although parentified behaviour helps children get into a relationship with their otherwise unavailable carer, it is a relationship in which the child's own needs are not actually being met.
- In more extreme childhoods in which there was violence and fear, as children parents might not even have developed strategies of emotionally inhibited self-reliance or role reversal. Whenever they experienced unpredictable danger and out-of-control arousal, the predominant feeling was one of helplessness. Feelings of helplessness and not knowing what to do arise for these parents in most attachment-saturated relationships, including those with their own children. When children express need or display distress, helpless parents fail to respond, feeling temporarily overwhelmed and frozen by old, unresolved fears and confusions.

3. Failure to Select a Response

Some neglectful parents, for example those with learning difficulties or severe histories of neglect themselves, might recognize their child's need and distress, but have no idea how to respond. Faced with an overwrought baby, the parent might feel desperate and helpless. Although agitated, he or she fails to respond. The child experiences the caregiver as both distressed and unresponsiveness. Family life feels run down and impoverished. Children seem socially clueless, cognitively poor and emotionally flat. Children are more likely to withdraw under stress rather than seek information or try out new responses (Crittenden 1993: 40).

4. Failure to Implement a Response

Crittenden (1993) distinguishes this form of neglect from 'failure to select a response', giving the example of a parent who knows what to do, but is overwhelmed with other pressures and so never actually delivers care or protection on a consistent or predictable basis. Too many other demands – a new baby who constantly cries, too many other children competing for attention, feeling emotionally consumed by his or her own anxieties about being accepted and loved – mean that a parent's attention is forever being distracted. This type of neglect is associated with family life that appears disorganized and chaotic, distraught and confused.

When they were children, the only way neglectful parents could increase the chances of a parental response in a 'noisy' environment was to amplify their signals of distress. But although they exaggerated their own needs and intensified their attachment behaviour, the underlying feeling was one of insecurity and an uncertainty that their carer was available. These parents compete with their children for attention in chaotic, multi-problem, crisis-ridden environments.

The common experiential thread for children coping with each of these four caregiving regimes is the unresponsiveness of their parents at times of need. Signals of distress, demonstrations of need, and displays of attachment behaviour are not noticed, ignored or mishandled. Getting no contingent or predictable reaction from parents, children feel ineffective. Their efforts fail to elicit care and protection. This is disquieting and can lead to feelings of helplessness and despair.

Four Types of Neglect

Partly following Crittenden (1999a), we shall recognize four types of neglect:

- *Disorganized neglect*: in which cognition, thought and reflective reason are minimized, affect is dominant, and feelings drive behaviour and social interaction.

- *Emotional neglect and abuse*: also referred to as 'psychological maltreatment', in which affect is omitted from mental processing (considered in Chapter 6).
- *Depressed or passive neglect*: 'in which both cognition and affect are discarded as meaningless sources of information about danger and protection' (Crittenden 1999a: 51).
- *Severe deprivation*: including institutional deprivation, multiple placements, and extreme neglect in which children fail to form selective attachments and are therefore at risk of developing disorders of attachment and non-attachment.

There is a fifth, compound type in which neglect, particularly psychological maltreatment, occurs with physical abuse. We shall consider these more extreme environments of abuse, neglect and trauma in Chapter 10.

7

Disorganized Neglect

Introduction

In the 1960s, families referred to here as disorganized and neglectful were known as 'problem families'. Children of these families are rarely in danger of being physically hurt by their parents, nor are they likely to suffer severe neglect. What does characterize such family life is chaos and disruption. Children experience little consistency. The availability and responsiveness of their caregivers simply cannot be taken for granted, and this makes for anxious, demanding children. Families lurch between one crisis and another, usually making heavy, regular and long-term demands on most child welfare agencies. Fathers row with their partners and walk out in the heat of the moment, only to return again a few days later. Mothers announce despairingly to social services that they can no longer cope with their increasingly unruly children, and threaten to abandon them all at the local police station.

The main preoccupation of the children of disorganized families is the emotional availability and interest of other people. This anxiety leads to behaviour that is attention-seeking, provocative, silly and moody. These behaviours do not go down well in the classroom or peer group. To be in relationship with such a child, whether as a parent, teacher or friend, is exhausting, and finally just plain irritating. These children come to the attention of professional child welfare workers when parents dramatically abandon them at the local social security office, police officers catch them throwing stones at passing cars, their homes are disconnected from the electricity supply, or angry neighbours report them for being cheeky, foul-mouthed and threatening.

Once 'on the books' of the agency, these children and their families are likely to be active for many years, whether or not attempts are made to close the case. Parents and their families can endear as well as annoy workers. Their antics are as likely to amuse as frustrate. They are frequent visitors to the professional's clinic or office. It is usually not long before everyone in the agency knows the family. Case files quickly fatten. Only when all the children have reached the age of majority does the case eventually close, at least for that generation of parents.

Characteristics of the Caregiving Environment

Parents appear preoccupied with their own feelings and needs. This means that they are neither sensitive nor consistently responsive to their children's needs and anxieties. There is no pattern to their caregiving behaviour. A distressed child can sometimes receive a cuddle, be ignored, or shouted at. Parents can be warm, angry or indifferent as the mood takes them. It seems that the parent's own anxiety about feeling wanted and valued drives the character of the relationship with their children. It is less what they can do for their children, and more what can their children do for them in terms of making the parent feel loved, worthy and competent.

When a parent is feeling good because her partner has bought her an ornate ring and said he'd die without her, the children are showered with unsolicited kisses and treats. When the world responds and the parent feels the centre of attention, bubbliness and smiles spill into all relationships, and children will experience their carer as available. However, her availability is not a reaction to their needs or displays of attachment behaviour, but her own positive state of mind. Equally when she feels ignored or abandoned, the mother will either fail to react to her children's needs or respond with exasperation, saying 'Stop whining the lot of you! All I ever hear is "I want this. I want that." Who ever gives me anything?' Or she might provoke them into being responsive, even if they are busy doing something else.

The point here is that there is no contingent relationship between the child's needs and the response of the carer. Whether or not the parent is available depends on how he or she feels. Thus, the child can establish no cognitive understanding of how his or her (attachment) behaviour impacts on others. The child experiences the caregiver as under-involved and insensitive to his or her needs and distress. The parent seems to have no clear understanding of what is going on in the child's mind. There is little emotional attunement. The result is a caregiving relationship that lacks synchrony and coordination.

The majority of disorganized neglectful parents had childhoods in which they felt emotionally deprived and undervalued. It is not so much that they felt rejected; rather they have memories of being ignored or thoughtlessly bypassed. They craved and continue to crave attention. To be noticed is to be loved; to be ignored is to be unloved. Out of this emerges a relationship style in which there is a constant preoccupation with and anxiety over other people's emotional interest and availability. Although there is a desperate need to be in relationships, satisfaction with them tends to be low. Only when they are the centre of the other's attention, do they feel loved. When the other person attends to something or someone else, as he or she inevitably will, it feels like abandonment, and all the old childhood feelings of worthlessness, anger and frustrated need surge forward. The same basic needs and anxieties occur as the parent relates with his or her children.

Coping with babies is not too difficult. As their parent, you are the centre of their world. They are dependent; they need you. They love you and you alone. Feeling loved helps parents feel confident. However, babies turn into toddlers. With maturation, children begin to explore and assert their autonomy. They learn to say 'No' and 'Shan't'. The anxious, needy parent begins to feel that the previously devoted child is beginning to behave like everyone else the carer has ever known. The carer feels that she is no longer the centre of the baby's universe. The child's need of the parent is no longer absolute. Confidence in the caregiving role slips. Parents are not sure how to react to an angry or distressed toddler. Agitated by familiar feelings of inadequacy and abandonment, they are not always thinking about their child's care and safety. They remain unsure about when it is appropriate to intervene. The child experiences this caregiving style as uncertain. Parents have few expectations of themselves or their children. A fatalistic attitude colours all attempts to think about the future.

The parent's need to be in a relationship ensures that there is usually a partner present, although he or she might not be the parent of all the children. This relationship tends to be stormy. Jealousy and conflict are rife. Because carers cannot take their own lovability for granted, they need repeatedly to check out the other's feelings. Reassurance is constantly sought: 'You've not said you love me today – have you got another man?' 'You've got to tell me what you're thinking – I need to know.' 'Tell mummy how much you love her!'

Running through all close relationships is an anxious desire for love and approval, coupled with feelings of anger and distress that these can never be taken for granted. There is a need to be in a relationship and to feel wanted, but a pervasive anxiety means that relaxed satisfaction is rarely achieved. The result is an intense, demanding interactional style that can soon exhaust and irritate the other. Such insatiable neediness might result in the other person walking out of the relationship, confirming what was feared all along – that other people's love and availability could not be trusted. They eventually let you down. At this point the dependent personality feels despairing and empty. Once again, he or she has been emotionally abandoned.

The origins of this anxious dependence on other people's love and approval lie in the parent's own childhood experiences of inconsistent, insensitive caregiving. Indeed, strong, ambivalent and conflicted feelings still suffuse dealings with the parent's own mothers and fathers. The need to feel wanted, and anger that love is so unreliable, produce minds that are dominated by issues of love and hate. People who give are loved; people who withhold are hated. The trouble with such a mindset is that it takes very little for another person to be perceived as either good or bad. Indeed, the same person can be loved one minute because he or she is generously attentive, or hated the next because his or her interest seems to have wandered elsewhere. What the anxious, dependent personality cannot do is mentally integrate the idea that people can continue to love and value the self while also engaging warmly with other people, or indeed while not making exaggerated declarations of love all the time. If a partner (or it may be a practitioner, a therapist or friend) attends to someone or something else, it feels like abandonment. Anger, despair and feelings of anxiety and hate well up. To stop this happening, relationships have to be exclusive. They have to be possessed and clung on to. But as we have seen, to be on the receiving end of such anxious neediness that brooks no dilution is wearing, and sooner or later the relationship will end in exhaustion.

When caregivers remain angrily preoccupied about whether or not they feel loved (by parents, partners, children), the result is a family lifestyle dominated by chaos, conflict, emotional entanglement, need and denial. Everyone is competing for affection (of which there is not much available) and demanding attention. These are noisy households, with little structure and organization. Although loud, there is no order, no predictable outcome to behaviour, no guaranteed response. These are therefore confusing environments. The result is cognitive understimulation.

On making a home visit, a professional might be greeted by a dog bounding to the door, barking loudly. The entrance is cluttered with discarded toys. The television is on. Children mill around, fighting, shouting, complaining and whining. Mum, still sitting, yells at the oldest child to make some coffee. Other adults (friends? neighbours? current lovers?), never seen before, wander in and out. The maternal grandmother, who only lives a few doors away, tells her daughter that having promised to babysit over the weekend, she is now unable to help as she is going to visit her stepdaughter and her three-week-old son. Family life feels enmeshed and confusing. There are few rules. Quarrels frequently erupt. Boundaries between the generations are blurred as a father punches away on his playstation ignoring his son's request for a drink, a mother flirts with her teenage daughter's latest boyfriend, and the eleven-year-old asks his grandmother for a cigarette.

When professionals visit, there are constant interruptions, loss of focus, and distractions as children yell for attention, a fight breaks out in another room, the mobile phone rings, or the bathroom sink overflows and drips appear through the ceiling. Bills are not paid, and then there is panic when the electricity supply is cut off. Life is lived in the dramatic and immediate present. The future and how present behaviour might affect it (for example, not paying bills) is ignored. Only the most pressing matters receive frantic attention, whether it is a child crying, the arrival of a drunken partner, or the failure of a benefits cheque to arrive. This is why every day feels like a crisis day. Long-term rational planning is absent.

Disorganized neglectful families typically make great demands on health and social work agencies. They are often dubbed as 'dependent'. According to Reder, Duncan and Gray (1993: 97–8) professionals become 'unwittingly drawn into meeting more and more demands from the parents for practical and emotional support and [become] as much stuck in the process of giving as the families did in asking. Attention to the parents often [obscures] the children's needs and the parents sometimes subtly [vie] with their children to be the main focus of input and concern.'

There is pressure by families for the professional to take sides – 'if you're not for me, then you must be against me'. This, coupled with constant demands for attention, time and resources, tends to exhaust and exasperate workers and their agencies. In spite of their pouring in vast amounts of time and effort, nothing seems to change. The parents are then dismissed as 'needy and dependent' and 'not serious about dealing with their problems'. They are accused of being 'uncooperative'. Feeling frustrated and possibly punitive, many agencies are inclined to close these cases. However, 'abandoning' the parents merely increases their distress and anxiety. They deal with this by hyperactivating their attachment behaviour – that is, they make increasingly distressed, crisis-ridden demands on professionals. A dramatic event is precipitated. A mother might take an overdose. The children spiral out of control and create a disturbance in the neighbourhood. Parents march the children down to the local social benefits office and leave them with a hapless receptionist.

Solomon and George (1996) describe this style of caregiving as uncertain. Parents are preoccupied by their own needs and anxieties. They are deeply unsure about whether they are valued or loved. They feel impotent and ineffective. Their lives are ruled by fate and destiny. Little effort is put into bringing about change because they feel helpless. Abandonment, despair and failure hover over every relationship – whether with partners, parents, children or professionals. The only way to keep the other engaged is to make constant, anxious demands on him or her.

Crittenden (1993: 40) observes that anxious adults generate chaotic environments within which they demand near-constant attention. Attention can also be sought by setting up a relationship style that ensures that other people are in constant need of them:

> In other words, they create chaotic, multiproblem environments in which there is always an emerging crisis to create conditions in which others need them. From the adults' perspective, such environments provide constant reassurance of their value to others. From the perspective of their children, such environments provide precisely the sort of unpredictability combined with occasional sensitive responsiveness, that the parents experienced in their own childhood.
>
> (Crittenden 1993: 40)

As the children mature and become more demanding, attention-seeking and difficult to placate, parents feel less and less confident in their role of caregiver. Anger and helplessness lead to much shouting and drama. Children should love their parents, but their constant demands for attention, provocative behaviour and complaints feel like disappointment, disapproval and dissatisfaction. The children's unruliness feels like a rebuff. Parents feel devalued and a failure, hurt and unloved. When children make their parents feel anxious and incompetent, they are hated for how they make their caregivers feel.

In desperate attempts to control their children's ungrateful and incessantly difficult behaviour (or the dwindling availability and responsiveness of a partner), parents threaten to abandon the relationship. In their minds, withdrawal of the caregiving relationship is the most potent threat. 'If you lot don't shut up and behave, I'm walking out right now, and then you'll be sorry!' Under more extreme circumstances a parent or partner might threaten to take his or her own life as the ultimate act of withdrawal and abandonment. Suicide gestures are made, usually in a dramatic manner, designed to gain attention, care and protection:

> Mr Trumlington's wife had left him for another man a year ago. He was finding looking after his three children increasingly difficult. He was growing more and more agitated, seeking help and advice from an ever-widening circle of agencies including social services, his doctor and health visitor, the local church, and the lone parent support group. His anxiety and feeling that he could not cope came to a head when his twelve-year-old daughter began to menstruate. He felt panicky and began shouting at the children, saying that they had to go their bedrooms and not move until he said so. They began to cry and run wildly around saying that they wanted their mummy. Mr Trumlington rushed over to the local social services office demanding that the children had to be taken into foster care immediately or else he would kill himself. The social worker tried to calm him down, but he was growing more and more distraught. The social worker tried to explain that she would call round to his home later that morning to discuss the situation, at which point Mr Trumlington took out a bottle of bright green pills and washed a handful down with a can of cola. He promptly fell on the floor, wailing and writhing in agony. The social worker called an ambulance and Mr Trumlington was whisked off to the accident and emergency unit at the local hospital where his stomach was pumped.

Professional visitors are welcomed, absorbed and expected to 'side' with the family. In the early days, they might be flattered into feeling they are the best practitioner who has ever handled the case. If the professional does become distant, this implies unavailability and a withholding response. Those who withhold engender feelings of anxiety and anger, and it is at this point that the too-cool professional is in danger of being dismissed as depriving, useless and hateful. On the other hand, professionals who are seduced into being constantly available and endlessly giving begin to feel tired, let down, emotionally depleted and angry. Professionally exhausted, the strong temptation is to abandon the case.

In the face of all this attachment-related distress, the major defence is that of *cognitive disconnection*, and the prevailing attachment pattern that of ambivalence, dependence and preoccupation (see Chapter 4). It is the distressed state that is the touchstone of how to behave. Thought is not trusted. Rational arguments are treated with suspicion; you may be deceived and misled. Although operating unconsciously, there is a familiarity (secondary felt security) with being emotionally aroused. More often than not, such emotional pressure on the other does gain attention and a response of some kind. Cognition, including distressing and painful information about the other's apparent lack of interest, is therefore defensively excluded. Negative feelings about one's vulnerability in relationships are cognitively disconnected from conscious awareness (Solomon and George 1999a: 26). Rational thought is not a good guide about what to do or what to expect; feelings are.

> By disconnecting negative feeling, the mother attempts to protect herself from experiences or memories that might overwhelm her ability to provide care. The inability to integrate underlying affect and experiences into a single point of view produces uncertainty (ambivalence).
>
> (George and Solomon 1996: 201)

Using this defence, splitting their desire to be a protective and loving carer from the more negative feelings associated with having to be available and responsive to the child's needs, parents remain engaged.

> We believe that if these mothers were unable to disconnect and separate negative affect from the child, they would be forced to acknowledge their feelings of rejection. Unable to reject the child, they (and the child) ... [are] ... left feeling uncertain.
>
> (George and Solomon 1996: 211)

As a result, parents do not cognitively monitor their thoughts and feelings. This leaves them feeling angry, preoccupied, distracted, entangled, or withholding whenever they are faced with attachment-related events, including caring and interacting with their own children. It is the uncertainty felt in the caregiving role that leads to disorganized neglect.

Children's Behaviour and Development

Infants and toddlers raised in environments of disorganized neglect are fractious, irritable and not easily soothed. They whine, cling, fret and fuss longer than other children. Their demands seem incessant. By the age of three or four, these attention-seeking behaviours become even more pronounced. Children's behaviour seems designed to provoke. Most of what they feel and do seems exaggerated – laughter, tears, sadness, anger, love, and hate. There are no half measures. There is no holding back, no containment.

Whether playing at home or working at school, concentration levels are low. There is much rushing from one thing to another, and nothing ever gets finished. They are easily distracted. By the early school years, this lack of persistence begins to affect academic performance. They are unable to work independently, and regularly appeal to teachers for help: 'Pleease help me, it's too difficult. I don't know what to do.'

Children of inconsistent and under-involved parents also need constant social stimulation. The big worry is to be ignored and not to be involved. They therefore make anxious demands of friends, often wanting a close, exclusive relationship. The possessiveness and jealousy that can surround such relationships means that they are short-lived, inevitably ending in jealousy, anger and conflict. In attempts to gain attention from peers, these immature children will show off, act silly, go too far, and annoy. Although they crave to be in relationships, they are too demanding, dissatisfied and disruptive to be tolerated for long. When they are abandoned, they sulk or shout back that they never liked the friend anyway. They readily complain that they are always being picked on, and easily adopt the role of victim. Being in a state of exaggerated need or vulnerability is commonplace. Vague, ill-defined aches and pains are acted out with theatrical affect.

By late childhood and early adolescence, children of chaotically neglectful families often feel out of their parent's control. Under stress, children feel helpless. Their immaturity, impatience and impulsivity mean that they repeatedly 'go too far'. They begin to get into minor trouble with teachers and the police. There are constant arguments at home with parents, siblings and neighbours. Underpinning all their behaviour is the drive to be noticed, valued, acknowledged and recognized. In order to gain attention, they will clown around, provoke, tease, break rules, sulk, be aggressive, be needy, be seductive and be ill.

It is at this point that chaotically neglectful parents begin to feel despairingly angry and helpless. Driven by the feeling that their child is unmanageable and ungrateful, unresponsive and unloving, the parents seek to control their distress by abandoning the relationship. Their child makes them feel incompetent and without value. After a blazing row or a stormy fight, the child is packed off to live with grandmother or placed in foster care. At school, children are at risk of falling significantly behind in their learning. Their socially disruptive behaviour in the classroom may result in suspension. And out in the community, children typically join antisocial gangs where they might get into trouble with the police for vandalism, shoplifting or verbal abuse.

The Child's Behaviour and Mental State as an Adaptive, Coping and Survival Strategy

In cases of disorganized and chaotic neglect, the caregiving environment is inconsistent and unpredictably responsive. There is no contingent link between the child's behaviour and how the parents actually respond, if indeed they respond at all. Parents tend to be under-involved. They are not very good at hearing and attending to their children's needs, distresses and attachment behaviour.

Although infants find it difficult to organize their attachment behaviour, by the age of two, most children recognize that an effective strategy for increasing the awareness and responsivity of an under-involved caregiver is to increase the volume and frequency of distress signals. In other words, they hyperactivate their attachment behaviour; compete more loudly for attention. Using this strategy, children become more demanding, emphasizing affect so that emotional displays are increasingly exaggerated and dramatic. Children act as if always in a crisis (Crittenden 1999a). It becomes hard for parents to ignore children who are in highly aroused and agitated states. Some develop hypochondria as a way of trying to activate and engage the nurturing side of the otherwise unresponsive carer.

However, it also has to be remembered that attachment includes behaviours designed to keep the caregiver engaged once he or she has been drawn into making a response. Smiling, gurgling, loving, flirting, flattering, apologizing – these seductive ploys work to hold the attachment figure in the relationship that otherwise has a habit of 'switching off' and disappearing. These seductive behaviours typically have a baby-like quality that invite a nurturing, protective response from the other. Babies after all are the epitome of helplessness and vulnerability, and baby-like behaviours are powerfully seductive in capturing the attention of adults. The child, or indeed adult, might react to someone who is angry with him or her, saying in an infantile voice: 'I'm really, really sorry, honest. I promise I'll never do it again, cross my heart and hope to die. Me don't like you being cross with me.' Doe-eyed pathos of this kind can emotionally wrong-foot the other's feelings of anger and frustration.

> By about 2 years of age ... children become able to recognise the association between their displays of anger and their mother's responses. So they show more anger. This both attracts their mother's attention and also causes their mothers to be angry with them frequently. The children need a way to terminate parental anger and aggression. Coy behavior is used to do this. By alternating aggressive-threatening behavior with coy-disarming behavior, children are able to coerce their mothers into doing what they want most of the time.
>
> (Crittenden 1999a: 53–4)

A mother says to her son that she's going to hang out the washing in the garden but he protests and throws a temper. He wants to go with her, but the garden is muddy and she doesn't want him outside getting dirty. She tells him he must stay inside. He yells even louder. She pleads with him, but he thrashes around on the floor, inconsolable. She then gets angry and threatens to smack him. He puckers his face and says, with big eyes and an exaggeratedly downcast look, he would be lonely on his own without her, adding that he is sorry. She comforts him, and makes for the door, at which point he intensifies his anger and distress. And so the battle continues.

'Frequently,' says Crittenden (1999a: 54), 'mothers win these battles by outwitting their children, that is, they use their intelligence to deceive their children to get their own way.' By telling a lie, the parent hopes to outmanoeuvre the child: 'No, I'm not really going out into the garden. Promise. You play with the dog and I'll just close the door.' The mother then bolts the door and she goes outside. The child has been fooled. 'He feels angry and afraid,' observes Crittenden (1999a: 54). 'Things did not turn out as he was led to believe. What he has learned is that his mother's words and the temporal relation between events that they describe can deceive him. Cognition, in other words, is not to be trusted. Feelings and affective displays are more powerful and have more predictable effects.'

Children and adults who have experienced such caregiving always feel in danger of being manipulated by those who make promises, use words rather than deeds, and argue that causes lead to effects. They want immediate responses, otherwise they feel anxious and in danger of being misled and duped. They do not respond well to professionals who propose rational solutions based on agreements and contracts. This feels like a fobbing off, a potential deception and a possible abandonment. Everything must be 'now' otherwise it cannot be trusted.

Thus we have the basic ingredients of an adaptive strategy under conditions of insensitive, under-involved, and erratic care: (i) exaggerate need, distress and anger when the attachment figure is not responding, and (ii) behave immaturely in an over-sentimentalized and seductive manner when the caregiver is engaged and does take notice. Crittenden (1995) describes this sequence of 'capture then hold then shape' the caregiver's attention as a 'coercive' strategy. In its basic form, the child switches between threatening and coy behaviour. More pronounced versions see children, and indeed adults, alternating between aggression and appeasement. It is highly characteristic of ambivalent attachment behaviour.

Certainly by age four and five, children begin to control the attachment figure's previous unavailability and unpredictability by using these coercive behaviours based on a two-pronged affective strategy of (i) anger and threat, and (ii) need, desire, placation and seduction. Desire for the attention and approval of an inconsistently responsive other, coupled with anger and aggression that his or her availability cannot be taken for granted, defines the child's 'ambivalent' feelings. The result is a child who feels permanently anxious that the self is not of sufficient interest or value to the carer that he or she can keep the child's safety and well-being routinely in mind. From the child's point of view, this is extremely distressing. It is only the maximized display of aroused affect that appears to increase the parent's availability, if not sensitivity. It is this ambivalent strategy in which attachment behaviour is hyperactivated that begins to feel the safest and most comfortable state in which to be. Affect dominates; reflective thought is abandoned. The endless fights and provocation function to maintain parental attention and availability, thereby producing secondary feelings of safety and security.

This produces children who are demanding and yet never satisfied or reassured. Feelings and their strong expression drive behaviour. Their intensity is designed to gain other people's attention. According to Crittenden (1995), carers respond only to the most immediate and demanding signals. Thus, children learn 'to emphasise affect and minimize or discard cognitive information' (Crittenden 1999a: 53). In this world of emotional exaggeration, all needs seem urgent; all situations feel like a crisis, all happenings are dramatic. No one listens to reasoned explanations. Everyone wants immediate gratification, not trusting delay or discussion. Children have only learned to recognize the danger associated with unmodulated arousal. And arousal itself increases feelings of distress, setting up, in the words of Crittenden (1999a: 61):

> a self-generating and self-maintaining feedback loop of escalating anxiety that becomes difficult to soothe.... Thus, we observe such children to be impulsive (i.e., they act before thinking, primarily on the basis of intense and suddenly escalating feeling states).

The combination of fretful, provocative anger and sentimental, babyish behaviour looks and feels immature to the observer. And yet this strategy is effective to the extent it keeps an otherwise neglectful parent involved. This remains true even if the parent reacts negatively. What the child needs is an attachment figure who takes notice. The more frightening prospect is to have an attachment figure that does not seem to have you in mind at all. Over time, this anxiety about the availability of others generalizes to all significant relationships, including peers, partners and professionals.

Internal Working Model of the Self

The ambivalently attached child in a chaotically neglectful household has no experience of the self being an automatic source of interest or concern. It is the child who has to make the effort to bring it home to the carer that he or she needs care and protection. Hence, self-esteem is low.

Feelings of competence and self-efficacy also tend be depressed. Although carers can be provoked into responding, this turns out to be a hit and miss affair. Because the carer is consumed by her own anxieties of not feeling loved, noticed or valued, her mind is only sporadically engaged with the business of childcare and protection. When she is feeling loved, and stress levels are low, then she can be very involved and excitable. But this availability is governed by her needs and anxieties, and bears little relationship to the child's mental state and attachment behaviour. The child therefore sees no pattern between what he feels or does and the behaviour of the carer. The supply of love and interest seems random. Care and protection certainly occur, but their appearance bears no obvious relationship to the child's efforts. Children begin to model themselves as helpless, ineffective and unable to have any calculated impact on the world. Things, whether nice or bad, just seem to happen for no apparent reason. Whatever occurs seems down to luck. Fate rules. There is no point trying.

And tied up with feelings of helplessness and ineffectiveness, is a tendency to be dependent on others. In relationship with the attachment figure, the child has not developed a good understanding of how feelings and behaviour interact, both in his or her own and in other people's minds. Being able to understand one's self and other people as mental agents not only helps children develop social competence (and personal confidence), but it also allows them to become autonomous psychological beings, able to operate independently, ensuring that their needs can be met by their own efforts. Failure to develop such autonomy means that the child is likely to remain emotionally enmeshed and dependent on others in the face of pressing need, mounting stress and increasing anxiety. Reassurance and approval is sought in every relationship, denial of which triggers great feelings of distress and doubt about one's own lovability.

Internal Working Model of Others

Although there is a nagging anxiety and desire to be in close relationship with others, the others are mentally modelled as unavailable and unpredictably responsive unless you make provocative, coercive demands. Other people are approached as if they are bound to withhold interest and deny attention. The ambivalent individual is quick to perceive other people as disapproving and devaluing, even when no such judgement is being made. It leads to defensive attacks, which can puzzle and irritate those on the receiving end of such projections:

'You think my drawing is rubbish, don't you?'

'No, no I don't.'

'You do. I can tell. I can tell by the way you're looking. I'm perceptive like that. Go on, then, tell me what you really think.'

'I think it's OK.'

'Really? I bet you're just saying that. I know when you're bullshitting me. You've got that look.'

'I haven't got "that look"; you're imagining it. The drawing is good. Certainly better than I could do.'

'OK.'

'Good.'

'You see, I can tell that you're only being polite. I've got a good sixth sense for this kind of thing.'

'Look, I said I liked it. Take it or leave it. I'm off.'

This overly sensitive way of interacting with people tends to be self-fulfilling. The other person begins to feel misunderstood and cast in a mean-spirited role, which if protested only seems to make the whole encounter even tetchier. The only way out of this frustrating exchange is to abandon the relationship. The working mental model of others therefore tends to be confirmed, even though it appears self-fulfilling. Other people seem, yet again, to withhold affection, deny interest, and devalue the self.

Internal Working Model of Relationships and How They Work

Premised on the working assumption that other people's love, interest and concern are unreliable and inconsistent, and their availability at times of need cannot be taken for granted, the only way to get noticed is to heighten one's level of distress, need and desire. Other people whose love or approval or recognition is desired but who are perceived to be inattentive, are prodded and provoked into making a response. This places demands and emotional pressure on all relationships.

On the other hand, one's own emotional availability is used to try to control the other person's interest and affection. This can vary from exaggerated sulkiness to threats of leaving the relationship. Like all ambivalent strategies, withdrawal and abandonment are carried out at full emotional volume. The signals contained in such behaviours suggest distress, hurt and vulnerability, signals that invite a nurturing response from the other who up to that point had been experienced as depriving and withholding of love and attention. In others words, in threatening to leave in an emotionally wounded state, the intention is actually to coerce the other person into becoming emotionally available and reinvolved by playing on their caregiving instincts when faced with another's hurt and pain:

> You never care what's happening to me. Well, I'm not staying with you. I'm leaving. Not that you care. You're so bloody self-centred. You hurt me. I've tried and tried with our relationship, but all you do is think about yourself. I'm so miserable; I don't feel like living any more. I don't know what I'll do, but you won't care.

It is difficult to abandon someone when they seem to be in such pain and despair.

Liam (Aged Ten) and His Family

Liam is the third eldest of four children. His mother, Sandra, had been finding Liam impossible to control. For the last four months, he has been living with foster carers.

Sandra is also the third eldest of four children. She lived with her parents until they divorced when she was eight. For a while it was uncertain who was going to care for her as she switched between living with her mother, her paternal grandparents and her father. 'I felt as if I was being shoved from pillar to post. No one seemed to want me.' After about a year, it was finally settled that she stay with her mother. Her father worked away from home a great deal, and it was on one such trip that he met his new partner. There was a great deal of upset and anger felt and displayed by her mother at this time. Sandra said she was her mother's favourite and that she used 'to get away with murder'. This led to a lot of arguments with, and rivalry between, Sandra and her siblings. She also describes her mother as 'very caring, she's a good mum, but stubborn, sort of like me, and we're always arguing clashing, you know, disagreeing. She's very headstrong and when we were children she used to make life hell for everyone if things weren't going her way.'

Sandra described her father 'as a bit of a hermit, but we hardly saw him because he was at work so much'. She felt a bit jealous of one of her older brothers who seemed to get most of her father's attention and affections when he was at home. Around the time of her parents' divorce, there were many arguments, some of them violent.

When aged 12, Sandra remembers getting into a row with her stepfather that became very heated. Her mother intervened, phoned Sandra's father and asked him to look after his daughter because she had had enough and wasn't prepared to care for her any more. Sandra then went to live with her father. She felt 'traumatized' by her mother's decision, but points out that as an adult she now gets on well with her stepfather 'and I love him to bits; we have a real bond'.

Sandra left school with no qualifications. She married Eric when she was 17.

Her mother remains psychologically involved with Sandra. For example, when she had children of her own, Sandra complains that her mother 'took over'. This made Sandra feel both dependent and cross. She left key disciplinary decisions to her mother, which made her husband, Eric, angry 'which is why when he got home he beat hell out of the kids 'cos he was wound up about me mum as well as the kids'. Sandra is on the phone to her mother every day. She tells her everything she is feeling, and becomes emotionally embroiled, and then complains and is irritated with herself. She says she wishes that she could be more independent and responsible, adding that it is her loving and very giving nature ('which no one appreciates') that is her constant downfall.

Before Liam was placed with foster carers, family life had been growing more chaotic and conflictual. Even as a toddler, Sandra found Liam difficult, and in desperation she would lock him in the bathroom. Once she taped his mouth with sellotape 'to shut him up'. Sandra said that Liam was 'a lovely, cuddly little baby' but became a very demanding, insatiable toddler.

Every day there was a row between Sandra, each of her children, and their stepfather. Sandra demanded the children respect her as a parent, adding she would walk out on them unless they behaved. Once she took a small overdose of aspirin: 'I didn't know what to do. I felt everything was a mess and no one was listening. The kids were really nice to me when I had to go to hospital.'

The children argued about who was getting more than their fair share of attention, money, clothes, space, freedom. They teased each other. There was fierce rivalry and jealousy. On one occasion, Liam nailed his brother's bedroom completely shut so that he couldn't access his favourite clothes. He got so excited by what he'd done, he then nailed planks of wood across the neighbour's front door. This led to a fight between the two families. The police had to be called.

The children constantly and noisily provoked their mother. If ever they wanted anything, they would threaten to break something (the radio, the window) until their mother 'gave in' to their demand. Daily life was loud, confusing, full of drama and histrionics as the children exaggerated every slight, hurt, injury and injustice. Sandra said that there was little to enjoy in being a mother. She felt she had given her 'all' to the children but they didn't seem to appreciate it. The only time she felt any pleasure was when the children said they loved her. She just hopes that one day they will appreciate how much she has done for them. However, she remains anxious that love can never be taken for granted: 'It seems that everybody I fall in love with or who I love dies, and I'm left on my own and I can't move on, do you know what I mean. Just before my granddad died, he would tell me things he'd tell nobody else, you know because I was special and he trusted me and I became his number one, which I wasn't when I was younger. Then he died. Sad, isn't it?' It was at about this time that Eric left Sandra, running off with one of her girl friends.

The chaos of relationships is matched by the confusing character of home life. The television is always switched on but no one ever seems to watch it for more than a fleeting moment. A large, friendly mongrel dog constantly wanders around, and regularly gets a hug from Sandra who says he is the only one who 'truly loves me and appreciates me'. Photographs of the dog and the children fill one wall.

As the children grew older, they became more and more difficult to control and discipline. Sandra felt helpless as she shouted and pleaded with them to stop running all over the furniture, leaping out of bedroom windows on to a pile of mattresses they had stacked in the garden below, and fighting with each other all the time. 'It was a total nightmare.'

At school, Liam was always in trouble with the teacher for being 'silly' or 'showing off' or 'provoking the other children in the class while they were trying to work'. His teachers found him 'wearing, eager to please, easily distracted, affectionate, volatile, babyish, and easily deflated'.

At the end of her tether, Sandra asked for Liam and his siblings to be removed. They were placed with foster carers, but Sandra said that although Liam couldn't come home, she would have the other two back. Liam can't understand why she has had them back home but not him. He said he felt 'thrown away' by his parents. He gets tearful when he thinks about the 'unfairness' that he's been singled out and rejected. This quickly leads to anger, then threats that when he next sees 'the bitch' he'll beat her up.

In her attempts to control Liam, Sandra would repeatedly deceive him. She'd promise him new trainers or money if he agreed to behave or go to school, but when he kept his side of the bargain, his mother failed to keep hers. Liam would then 'explode'. Sandra worries that people will think she is a 'useless mother', adding that Liam should be back home 'in the bosom of his family'. But then she concedes she can't control him. When she visits him, all he does is demand money, and he threatens her verbally and physically if she doesn't respond. 'He manipulates me and makes me feel a useless mum unless I give him what he wants. If I do give in to him, he's all cuddles, all smiles, and tells me how much he loves me, but I haven't always got it and then he calls me tight and mean and starts to get aggressive. He says I "owe him".'

Now in foster care, Liam phones his mother anything up to six times a day, and she phones him almost as frequently. During such calls, Liam will ask what his mother is doing, tell her that he loves her, asks her to bring something from home that he wants, or plead with her to be allowed back home. Sometimes he tells her he's ill (when he is not) or he has been beaten up by a gang (when he has not), and asks her to come and see him and comfort him. Calls can switch quickly from wheedling and sentimental chat about missing home to abuse and threat when he does not get the response he wants. Most calls end with one of them slamming down the phone, only to be in touch again a few hours later. More recently, Sandra has said she found these calls too distressing and has asked the social worker to have them stopped.

Conclusion

Families operating in what feels like a permanent state of chaos and crisis, making constant demands on a wide range of health, educational and welfare agencies, easily exasperate and exhaust practitioners. But they can also evoke the protective and nurturing instincts of professionals. As Mattinson (1975) observed, clients can engender in practitioners who work with them similar states of mind to their own. In the case of families whose lives are ones of disorganized neglect, professionals often feel ambivalent, lurching from fond despair to angry withdrawal. However, neglect comes in many colours. Whereas families in states of disorganized neglect paint larger than life pictures, those who suffer depressed neglect appear lifeless and grey.

8

Depressed, Passive and Physical Neglect

Introduction

Depressed neglect is what most people tend to have in mind when cases of neglect are mentioned. Poverty is marked, both materially and emotionally. These are families in which children are dirty and smelly. They are shunned and teased by other children. They often look sad or blank. Homes feel run down. Cookers are filthy. Floors are sticky with the congealed remains of spilt juices, and dropped greasy chips and burgers. Bedding is thin, torn and goes unwashed. Urine soaked mattresses rest on the floor in the absence of a bed. Pinned-up pieces of faded material serve instead of curtains. Broken windows are patched over with paper. The hours pass in a gloom of dreary purposelessness. The days have no structure. This is how a health visitor described her first visit to the home of the Dunthorpes:

> There wasn't a surface in the house that wasn't either greasy, dirty, or sticky with spilt beer or lemonade. Cigarette stubs and ash were everywhere. There was a sickening smell of urine and stale human sweat. The kitchen ... urr, the kitchen was indescribable. Unwashed pans and dishes were piled in the filthy brown sink and draining board. The cooker was thick black with burned fat. I could see mouse droppings underneath the cupboards, and I swear there were used condoms down there too. The only food I could see was a couple of tins of spaghetti, some old fish and chip paper, and a half pint of sour milk. There was a fridge, but it was broken and only contained some mouldering processed cheese. The dustbin, with its lid missing and full of rotting stuff, blocked the door to the yard. The children's bedrooms were bare except for old, damp mattresses on the floor, a pram with only one wheel, and a portable television with its screen smashed in. Opposite the girl's bedroom was a toilet that had hardened shit both inside and outside the bowl and some on the walls. The mother said that the flush wasn't working properly so she had to get a bucket, fill it with water and swill that down the toilet to clear it. It didn't look as if she did this too often.

The run-down feeling that pervades passively neglectful families can affect the spirits of those who work with them. There is a sense of hopelessness, which coupled with the lack of any deliberate parental malice can produce a resigned passivity in both practitioners and their agencies. However, it has to be remembered that children subjected to these extremely deprived psychological environments are at risk of major developmental impairment. There is not much social or emotional information upon which the young, developing mind can feed. Starved of stimulation and reciprocity, children hardly get to the starting blocks when it comes to processing the complexities of social and emotional life. Without such processing skills, they are psychologically lost, unable to handle themselves or their peers in any way that suggests social competence.

Characteristics of the Caregiving Environment

Carers are unmindful and unresponsive to most of their children's signals of need and distress. They appear lost in an empty world of their own. Relationships are lifeless and dull. No one seems to have much interest in anything. Neither pleasure nor anger feature in parents' dealings with their children, visitors, or child welfare practitioners. Although children do not get hugs and cuddles, neither do they get smacked or shouted at. Parents don't intend to harm their children but there is no warmth or lively emotional involvement.

In terms of basic care, only the bare minimum takes place. Food appears randomly with as little effort or preparation as possible. Babies and toddlers will be left soiled and wet for hours before they are changed. There is no structure or rhythm to the day. Very little interaction takes place between parents and children. The odd tired telling-off, the occasional comment on the need to eat is the extent to which family life gets animated. Malnourishment is a real risk. Care tends to occur when the parent remembers or becomes sufficiently energized; it does not happen in response to the child's attachment signals.

One of the major characteristics of neglectful families is their lack of supervision. It is as if parents fail to keep even quite young children in mind. They appear not to worry about possible dangers. A three-year-old might be reported by a neighbour to be wandering alone near a busy road some distance from the house. Young children are expected to rummage around in the kitchen to find food. Bare electric wires are left exposed; a broken window remains unmended; rotting takeaway food is left stuffed into plastic bags in the kitchen.

The histories of passively neglectful carers are often one of severe neglect. Their own parents might have suffered depression, lived in extreme poverty, or subjected their children to traumatic physical and sexual abuse, sometimes to the point of terror. Some neglectful parents have learning difficulties. They might remain ignorant of children's expected developmental milestones; they might be unaware of children's need for cognitive stimulation and emotional availability (Iwaniec 1995: 5).

Dealing with children, handling finances, and running a home can feel complicated, difficult and stressful. Faced with such challenges, a passive helplessness is the response. There is an ill-defined feeling that making an effort is pointless because nothing will change. Whenever children or home life make heavy emotional demands on the carer, the mind copes by disengaging. Attachment behaviour is not registered, and so does not require a caregiving response. In effect, passively neglectful carers have given up both thinking and feeling. This means that they are unable to connect with others, including their children at any meaningful psychological level. Mind-to-mind communication, so important for children's psychological development, is sporadic and thin. Children's attachment needs provoke parental states of mind that feel helpless, switched-off, hopeless and depressed.

Children's Behaviour and Development

A robust, esteemed and purposeful self emerges as young brains interact with 'mind-minded' older brains. Carers who delight in their children's growing emotional and cognitive sophistication generate richly textured psychological exchanges in which a great deal of mental activity is assumed to be taking place both within and between minds. Feelings are identified, explored, played with and shared. The links between thoughts, feelings and behaviour, in the self and others are posed, investigated and considered. The child begins to understand that the world of people is fundamentally a psychological place. Programmed to make sense of the self and others, young brains feed off this psychological fare with eagerness and gusto. Indeed, without this diet of reciprocal, reflective and resonating mental activity, psychosocially competent selves have difficulty forming.

However, the lot of the depressively neglected child is to be raised in a caregiving environment in which all the emotional energy has drained out of the system. The psychological traffic between minds has all but stopped. Parents have given up being curious about themselves, their children, and people at large. There is no interest in the fascinating and puzzling business of behaviour and relationships, thoughts and feelings. Young minds, born to make psychological sense of the self and the social, are deprived of the very experiences that help them make that sense.

Children in these run-down environments are listless and incurious. They sit around, blank and vacant. Noses run and need wiping. Infants moan defeatedly as they sit in soaked nappies that hurt their already sore rashes. Although as babies they might cry and fuss in all the usual ways, they soon give up the fight. Distress leaks out as whimpers and moans rather than full throttle anger or fear. Some children can even look depressed.

At nursery or school, such children tend to be isolated and wander around aimlessly. If they do become involved in play, they often lose their bearings in the swirl of childhood pretence, imagination, laughter, reciprocation, conflict and playground banter. In the classroom, although they may not be disruptive, their concentration is poor. Academic achievements are low. They have no faith in their own abilities and hardly try. There is no belief in their powers to bring about change, so nothing is tried. Self-esteem is very low. And if they smell, neglected children are teased, stigmatized and no other children will play with them.

The Child's Behaviour and Mental State as an Adaptive, Coping and Survival Strategy

The major dilemma for children in deflated and depressed environments is that their behaviour seems to have little impact on their caregiver. Distress, discussion, emotion or thought do not appear to get through. Children need adults to acknowledge, understand, explore, explain and respond to their mental states. That is how they begin to make sense of how relationships work. But if their signals are not received, if there is no message back, there is nothing on which the young, eager-to-learn brain can purchase. It is conversation, recognition and mental interaction that help shape and form the self and the mind that underpins it. Without a reaction, displays of thought and feeling are without meaning. It is the interaction with the other that helps the child make sense of psychological information. Young children normally communicate largely through a variety of emotional expressions and signals, including crying, smiling, making eye contact and touching. Passively neglectful parents, however, fail to respond to these behaviours. Although depressively neglected babies might display their distressed state for prolonged periods, eventually they give up, sensing that there is no point. The caregiver remains passive. If the child cannot get the caregiver to tune in, a state of helplessness is experienced:

> When people, of any age, learn that their behaviour has no meaning, the human mind shuts down. It ceases to perceive or interpret information. Without thoughts and feelings that can be shared with others, humans become hollow shells. In this vacuum, parents do not perceive the occasions that call for action – so they don't act.
>
> (Crittenden 1999a: 63)

In effect, young children suffering severe psychological neglect fail to develop an attachment strategy. It seems to make little difference whether they maximize or minimize their attachment behaviour. Their carer remains unresponsive and unavailable at times of need. The result is helplessness under stress and challenge, despair in the face of need. Children, even in states of distress or difficulty, simply give up trying. Their mind becomes looped back on itself in a self-soothing, disconnected defence. This might manifest itself in slow, rhythmical rocking. Or children might daydream in trance-like fashion, with glazed, blank looks. Disengaged from others, the self finds difficulty finding shape or form. Children exist in a depersonalized state. They disengage from what is happening around them. Both children and adults appear emotionally flat. Their behaviour appears to lack focus and direction. Little is achieved that might solve a problem or meet a need.

In some cases, children might develop coping strategies around compulsively caring for the helpless/fearful carer in a form of role reversal. And in others, when flat, passive children who appear to be without an attachment strategy are removed and placed with new, responsive carers, we sometimes see children shift into a more organized, albeit insecure ambivalent pattern. It is as if they suddenly realize that at long last, distress is beginning to get a response, and so a hyperactivated attachment strategy seems a more secure state in which to be.

Internal Working Model of the Self

In a sense, the self in situations of profound and depressed neglect barely exists to be mentally modelled. There is an all-encompassing sense of helplessness; that all effort is futile because nothing responds, nothing changes. To the extent that there might be self-evaluation, esteem and efficacy are very low. To the observer, these are children who appear dull and sad. They lack the energy and will to protest. They expect little and little is given. Not being in danger of violence or abuse, it is easy to underestimate the developmental damage that these switched-off caregiving environments can cause. Certainly while they are young, although neighbours and professionals might express sorrow at their plight, they are not children who impact on others. Because as toddlers they don't display anti-social behaviour, they can be missed by the childcare authorities.

Internal Working Model of Others

In general, neglectful caregivers might fail to respond to children's attachment behaviour because they feel too agitated when emotional demands are made on them. In these cases, children can develop conforming, compliant strategies. By not making demands on their parents, they might increase their own acceptability and their carers' willingness to engage on a low-attachment agenda. In contrast, carers who are absorbed with their own needs fail to hear their children's signals of distress. In the case of preoccupied parents, children might increase the responsiveness of the carer by exaggerating their levels of distress and arousal.

Matters are far more complicated and desperate for children subjected to passive and depressed neglect. Whereas the caregivers of avoidant and ambivalent children are defensively excluding attachment-related information, which implies a mind at work, albeit a defended one, the mind of the passively neglectful parent is so weakly structured that psychological information passes straight through and hardly registers. It is a mind in a state of extreme passivity. The unconscious assumption is that there is no point in processing, either cognitively or emotionally, interpersonal information as nothing can be done about it. Children therefore have a representation of others as unavailable, uninterested and unresponsive.

Internal Working Model of Relationships and How They Work

In a sense, severely neglected children have no clear or coherent mental representations of themselves, others and the relationship between them. Starved of affective and cognitive experience, denied caregiving responses at times of need, and without any information about how feelings and behaviour interact, the child finds it difficult to develop a model of any kind. Outwardly, it might appear that the child represents others as profoundly unavailable at times of need, and the self as totally unable to elicit care and protection. However, such mental modelling suggests a degree of cognitive activity that is not actually present. Passively neglected children either never develop or shut down much of their social and emotional processing capacities. The result is inertia and severe passivity. The world simply goes on (or not) around them with little effort being exerted on the child's part to affect it in any way. As Crittenden (1999a: 64) observes, 'the failure to use either affect or cognition to organize information about reality closes the doors to both relationships and learning'.

The Ledward Family

Mrs Ledward finds few words to describe her childhood, except in vague terms. 'It seemed all right. I just got on with things ... really.... I suppose.' Her mother suffered from 'nerves', and spent some time in psychiatric hospital. There was talk of ill-health pervading much of family life, with her mother often feeling physically unwell, taking to her bed for much of Mrs Ledward's childhood. Her father is rarely mentioned, but it is known that he drank heavily. At such times, he became maudlin and felt sorry for himself, bemoaning the lack of love in his life. Neighbours who knew Mrs Ledward as a girl described her as very thin, pale and 'looking like a lost soul'. Her clothes were always unkempt and dirty. She was often ill.

When Mrs Ledward was ten years old, her mother died. Her father drank even more heavily, saying to anyone who asked that he was 'drowning his many sorrows'. For the remainder of her childhood, Mrs Ledward and her two siblings were reluctantly looked after by a variety of relatives, including their maternal grandmother and her other daughter, who also suffered poor health.

Aged 16, Mrs Ledward left school with no qualifications, and worked on a production line in a vegetable-canning factory. She married when she was 18 and immediately became pregnant, giving birth to a boy, George. By the time she reached 24 she had two more children, Jessica and Ruth. She said she had always wanted children to love, but according to the health visitor seemed 'lost and clueless' when they arrived. Her husband was 12 years older. He came from a large, extended family. The majority of his male relatives had convictions for child physical abuse, child sexual abuse or rape. In turn, several of these men and their sisters had also been victims of sexual abuse when they were children, many of them spending time with foster carers.

There had been a number of allegations that Mr Ledward had been physically abusive towards George, but either these were unproven, or the explanations that the bruises were the result of various accidents were accepted. After the birth of their third child, Mr Ledward was found guilty of a series of sexual assaults against women in the area, and was sent to prison for seven years.

The health services had long-standing concerns about the children's development and well-being. Mrs Ledward was described by one health visitor as 'lethargic, depressed looking, and barely able to go through even the slow motions of being a mother'. The home was felt to be under-furnished, dirty and smelly. A few broken toys and games were stacked in a corner of the living room. 'There is no routine or structure in this family,' noted one health visitor. 'Mrs Ledward can sit looking blankly at the TV for hours and only seems to remember that the children need feeding when she feels hungry. She feeds them biscuits or crisps. Occasionally she will put things like chips or a bought pie in the microwave.' Various home support services were put in, but after a few weeks Mrs Ledward asked them not to visit again. The children all slept on a large mattress in an undecorated, uncurtained, unheated bedroom. The smell of urine was strongest in the children's bedroom. It was felt that the children were not in any physical danger, but it was acknowledged that they lacked stimulation and a good diet. There were occasional bursts of activity by the health and welfare services, but they tended to fizzle out after a few months.

Two years ago, George was repeatedly found wandering the streets late at night. A paternal aunt said she would look after him, and he went to live with her. Jessica, now aged seven, is described as a very quiet, reserved girl. Although she is not a problem at school, she is behind most of her classmates in her studies. At home, she does most of the caring for her younger sister Ruth. She tries to keep them both clean, but there is rarely hot water or soap in the house. She now cooks them both food when she gets home from school. Most often this amounts to a plate of baked beans heated in the microwave. Jessica also seems to look after her mother. She reminds her when she is supposed to see the doctor, or when the social benefits officer is due to visit. But most of the time Jessica sits watching the television with her mother. There is little conversation, and the evening peters out with the children drifting off to bed at about ten o'clock. Although Jessica is passive most of the time, she has been known to be tearfully angry both at home and school. It is never very clear what triggers these outbursts. They are not directed at anyone. They simply involve Jessica breaking down in tears. No one has seen her laugh. She has no friends.

Ruth is now aged five. Her speech is still very poor. When the social worker visits, she is found sitting in a small child's chair close to the television screen. For a long time, her extreme passivity made people think she might be autistic, but this diagnosis has since been ruled out. Whenever any health or welfare official visits the home and tries to talk to her, she retreats to a corner of the room and stares at the ceiling. Her face is always expressionless. She does not play, and simply stares at any toy or activity put in front of her. Occasionally, if she hurts herself, say by accidentally scratching herself on a nail or by bumping into a table corner and suffering a bruise, she will cry very quietly. She does not seek out her mother, or indeed anyone else who might be present. Occasionally, Jessica might try to comfort her, but Ruth does not respond. To date, no professional worker has observed any meaningful interaction between Ruth and her mother.

The general concerns about the children's development and well-being became so pressing that both girls were placed in foster care. Neither girl displayed any distress when they were removed. Mrs Ledward said little except that life had dealt her a 'bum hand'. Ruth has now been in placement for four months. She is becoming increasingly animated. Her foster carer describes her as whiny, petulant, confusing and confused: 'She seems to want my attention, but when I give it, she gets angry and tries to hit me. Then when I move away, she grabs my dress and pulls me, not letting go, but then not calming down when I try to soothe her. For much of the time she seems to be in a state of distress, but I don't know what about. Only at bedtime does she seem to relax and let me cuddle her.' However, Ruth's speech has improved and she is putting on weight. And although still not very sure, she is beginning to play with toys.

Conclusion

Children respond to lively, interesting and interested environments. Any developing system needs energy, and growing children are no exception. If the children of psychologically tired and empty parents are to be fuelled for life, they are in urgent need not only of structure and stimulation, but also warmth and recognition. We have seen what happens when children are raised by physically present but emotionally absent parents. We now need to consider the fate of children who have not even had an opportunity to develop a selective attachment with a primary caregiver, including those who have been raised from a very young age in poor-quality institutional care.

9

Severe Deprivation and Chronic Neglect Including Institutionalized Care

Introduction

To be cared for by an abusive, hostile and rejecting parent presents its own special problems for young children and their survival. In the most extreme cases, the experiences can be traumatic. And yet however perverse it may seem, the abusive carer is also the child's attachment figure. In contrast, some children suffer extreme environments of an entirely different kind. Here there is neglect and severe deprivation. But the key difference from all other kinds of maltreatment is the absence of an attachment figure. In most forms of abuse and neglect, the way the mind of the primary caregiver processes attachment-related information is the key to understanding how the child's own mind forms. In the case of severe deprivation and sparse institutionalized care, there is not a selective attachment figure present. There is no key relationship, however disturbed, in which the child might explore his or her own and the other's mental states and psychological make-up. This major deficiency produces its own unique and peculiar train of developmental impairments.

The most graphic cases of severe neglect involve children raised in large, grossly under-resourced institutions, where they exist out of sight and forgotten by the host community. Historically, most societies at some time have shut away and raised apart, often in appalling conditions, the young of the poor, the feckless, the dead, the stigmatized, the foreign and the outcast. Recent examples include children of the Romanian poor who, under the dictatorial regime of Ceausescu, were placed in 'orphanages'. After the overthrow of Ceausescu in 1989, these babies and children were found to be severely undernourished and poorly clothed. Hundreds of children were being looked after in overcrowded, unsanitary conditions by a handful of staff in large run-down buildings. Medical care was poor, illness was rife, sensory and motor stimulation was lacking, and emotional and social relationships were minimal.

Row upon row of cots, crowded into cold dormitories, were occupied by listless babies. Older children were sometimes left naked – it was too time-consuming and costly to keep them clean and clothed. In the worst cases, interactions between adults and children were minimal. Even with the best will in the world, staff could barely keep the children fed, never mind warm, clean or stimulated. As a result the children suffered severe and global deprivation. And given the relative absence of familiar adults, they also failed to develop any selective attachments.

It is also possible that children who live with their parents can suffer severe deprivation through chronic neglect. They, too, might possibly fail to establish selective attachments. Though ostensibly cared for by their parents, they show many of the features found in neglected and institutionalized children. Tired or depressed parents or parents with serious learning difficulties might leave their babies in their cots, alone, hungry and wet, for long periods. Mothers who have a pressing drug habit might go out at night prostituting themselves for money, leaving their children to fend for themselves for whole days and nights. Some desperate parents might leave their young children with a relay of 'friends', exposing their infants to a bewildering array of new faces day after day. If the childcare authorities catch up with these children, they might be placed in short-term foster care before being returned to their contrite parent, only for the cycle of serial caregiving to repeat itself. Multiple placements in the first couple of years of life can also mean that infants fail to establish a selective attachment figure.

The three key risks in all of these cases are:

- neglect, severe deprivation and gross understimulation
- a deep, frightening sense of abandonment and being absolutely on your own
- a failure to form a selective attachment.

Characteristics of the Caregiving Environment

The caregiving environment for these children lacks many of the basic psychosocial and interpersonal opportunities that help infants develop a reflective, coherent sense of self. In the early weeks and months the distress caused by the neglect would strongly activate the child's attachment system. Hungry babies and infants who need changing would cry. But for much of the time there is no one listening. Sensitive and attuned caregiving is absent. Staff are busy and overwhelmed. Severely depressed and listless parents sit motionless, looking vacantly into space. Or the 'friends' that your mother has left you with are downstairs, high on drugs, oblivious to your crying and fearful state. There are no familiar faces. There is no one who has you and your needs in mind. There is no attachment figure to be found. In batch regimes of institutionalized care, there may be activity and noise all around, but your voice commands no special attention. Institutions offer only 'serial caregiving'.

Secure children experience and begin to understand when, how and why other people respond, and how their responses bring about feelings of safety and comfort. The baby's distress matters and concerns the sensitive parent. However, in cases of extreme neglect, the infant is essentially alone. There are the briefest of interactions. There is no time or inclination on the part of carers to explore with the child his or her state of mind. No one asks, in that inimitable way that loving parents do, why the baby is crying or frowning or laughing or looking so sad. The child is left traumatically aroused and dysregulated, affective states which go without recognition, explanation or understanding. Locked in your bedroom with only a urine-soaked mattress, your introduction to life is painful and bleak.

This combination of severe neglect and the absence of selective attachment figures is the worst of all possible worlds. Hungry and frightened, confused and alone, with no one to turn to, to soothe you, to make you feel safe and to help you make sense of all that is happening, leaves the essence of your very being as no more than a cauldron of undifferentiated fear and distress.

Children's Behaviour and Development

According to O'Connor and the ERA study team (1999), attachment disorders indicate the violation of the basic organization of the attachment behavioural system – attachment, exploration, fear, and wariness behaviours. Under conditions of severe neglect, infants lack most of the pre-attachment behaviours, including smiling, making eye contact and crying. These are critical to promoting and maintaining proximity to caregivers (Chisholm 2000: 172). The evidence is generally strong that early patterns of rearing are 'a decisive and important influence on psychopathology, with particular respect to hyperactivity and possibly unsociability' (Roy, Rutter and Pickles 2000). Many children who suffer early and global deprivation typically also develop disorders of non-attachment. Behaviours associated with this condition can include:

- impulsivity
- very poor relationships, including peer rejection
- educational problems
- hyperactivity, restlessness and attention deficits
- delayed language development
- cognitive impairments (seriously affecting their academic performance)
- aggressive and coercive behaviours
- eating problems (usually eating too much voraciously).

Parallel behaviours to those shown by severely neglected children have been observed in a variety of other species. Kraemer and Clarke (1996) describe extremely fearful behaviour alternating with out-of-control aggression displayed by infant rhesus monkeys that had been raised with their peers but without an attachment figure. The absence of an attachment figure meant that not only was it distressing to be abandoned, but also there was nowhere to turn to have the distress soothed and the emotional arousal regulated. An equally fascinating example is provided by Fischer-Mamblona (2000). She describes the attachment-disordered behaviour of a goose named Feli. Immediately after hatching, Feli spent the first ten weeks of her life in total isolation from other geese and with no goose-mother. Her subsequent behaviour and development was observed to be grossly impaired. In short, she seemed to have real social and behavioural problems in knowing how to behave as a normally functioning goose, and when she had goslings of her own, how to be a competent mother. (See Chapter 10 for a fuller description of Feli and her development.)

Some severely neglected children who have had little experience of being physically regulated via all their senses are easily and suddenly alarmed and massively aroused by new and unexpected physical stimulations. A young three-year-old girl's first visit to the beach was seen as a treat by her new foster carers. But as soon as she was placed on the wet sand, the cold, squelchy sensation between her toes triggered feelings of great fear and threat. She screamed inconsolably for several hours. Many children cannot fathom their senses. They get confused about whether they are hungry or full, thirsty or parched, hot or cold. One little boy, who had just drunk a litre of squash, returned crying to his carer saying he was 'very, very thirsty'. Children's sense of time is often poor. Their friendships are fleeting and shallow. They have a vague sense of how their bodies and senses work – children learn about the physical behaviour of their bodies and senses in the context of a loving, physical relationship with their caregiver.

One of the diagnostic features of institutionalized children who are placed with foster carers and adopters is their continued failure to develop a selective attachment. Or if they do form an attachment, they fail to show many of the separation anxieties displayed by children who are securely attached. One of more extreme effects of profound deprivation is the development of quasi-autistic impairments, lack of social awareness, and attention difficulties found in some children (O'Connor and the ERA study team 1999; Rutter et al. 1999).

Zeanah (1996: 48) discusses the two types on attachment disorder recognized in the major diagnostic manuals:

- the emotionally withdrawn (*inhibited type*)
- the indiscriminately social (*disinhibited type*).

Attachment-disordered children with *inhibition* show emotional withdrawal and general passivity. They rarely smile. They appear to have little interest or spontaneous pleasure in social interaction, exploration or eating. Their behaviour is described as listless. Some children show autistic-type behaviours. The self-soothing behaviours developed when the adult world has all but neglected them include thumb sucking, rhythmical rocking backwards and forwards, or if standing, rocking from side to side, one foot to the other. Some children bang their heads repeatedly against the cot or wall. Others scratch away at a sore or wound so that it bleeds and never heals. If distress is shown, it is not directed towards anyone. Children might wander aimlessly, whimpering, but not knowing how and where to seek comfort. There is the suggestion that this inhibited form of attachment disorder is more likely to result when there is both neglect and maltreatment, that is the persistent disregard of the child's basic needs (O'Connor/ERA 2002: 786; also see Chapter 10).

Other deprived and institutionalized infants develop attachment disorders of the ***disinhibited*** type. Indeed, O'Connor/ERA (2002: 786) suggests that 'the disinhibited form of attachment disorder appears to result *only* when there has been severely disrupted care; namely, a virtual absence of care in the early months or years of life.' These children are very attention-seeking, clingy and over-friendly. They make inappropriate approaches to unfamiliar adults, approaching them without wariness. Or they seek out any adult when they are distressed, even if their new, primary carer is present (Chisholm 1998). At times of need, they do not differentiate between or select particular adults for comfort or regulation – anyone seems to do. They violate social boundaries and conventions by interacting with strangers at very close quarters. Without hesitation, these children will sit on an unknown adult's knee, ask an excessive number of very personal questions, and fiddle with their clothing. Those on the receiving end generally feel uncomfortable with such intrusive behaviour. Nevertheless, social engagement is superficial and shallow, lacking reciprocity. The intrusive questions, the excited demands, the silly playfulness are all one-way. Many children show an alarming willingness to wander off with a total stranger with not a backward look to their main carer, including those placed with adopters (O'Connor/ERA 2000; Howe 1998: 190–6). Peer relationships tend to be poor, with a good deal of rejection by other children of the same age.

Although these children display insecure attachment behaviour, it is rarely classified as disorganized. Rather, their attachment behaviour suggests a number of very atypical features. For example, when distressed, children often do show attachment behaviour (approach, contact-maintaining), but it might as well be directed toward a stranger as the parent. Much of their behaviour in middle childhood tends to be typical of children of younger ages. They can become emotionally over-exuberant, wildly excited, silly, coy and excessive playful, both with their parents and strangers. In Ainsworth's 'strange situation test', these severely deprived children also have 'difficulty regulating or containing their excitement and arousal' (O'Connor 2003: 33).

According to Lieberman and Pawl (1988: 331), the development of severely deprived children shows major impairment in three areas: interpersonal relationships, impulse control and the regulation of aggression. There is a long-term incapacity to establish emotionally meaningful relationships. Notions of reciprocity and mutuality are lacking. As these children progress through childhood, rates of criminal behaviour, anger, interpersonal conflict, poor concentration and problems with school increase. Throughout life many of these children continue to cope best in environments that are socially and physically structured rather than those which are permissive and relaxed.

Recent research evidence that has followed the progress of Romanian 'orphanage' children placed with adoptive families has found that the most powerful predictor of developmental impairment, attachment disorder, quasi-autistic symptoms and disinhibited behaviour is early and long exposure to severely deprived institutional care (O'Connor 2002; O'Connor/ERA 2003; Chisholm 1998). Although many of these children show remarkable recovery when placed with autonomously minded adopters, those who suffered the severest deprivation from the earliest ages over the longest time were at greatest risk of impaired development and problem behaviour. There is even evidence that extreme stress and neglect can suppress the growth of the long bones, resulting in shorter than expected height – psychosocial short stature. Stress affects the neuro-endocrine system, including the production of growth hormones, lack of which can lead to inhibited growth (Gunnar et al. 2001; Johnson 2000). In general, severe deprivation, which is tantamount to being psychologically abandoned, places children at some of the highest risks of psychopathology (Gauthier et al. 1996).

The Child's Behaviour and Mental State as an Adaptive, Coping and Survival Strategy

The developmental pathways followed by chronically neglected children are still not fully understood. The two basic adaptive options, which we have already recognized, depend on the particular characteristics of the caregiver's unavailability and neglect. One pattern is the 'disinhibited' type, and the other is the 'inhibited' type. We might now attempt an explanation of the adaptive character of these two types as follows.

In institutionalized environments where there are few staff – who come and go, who are overstretched and busy, though many might be caring – the children who cry loudly and smile warmly whenever they capture someone's attention are likely to receive most notice. The adaptive pattern, in Crittenden's terms (1995), is likely to be based around a coercive strategy – behaviours that get them noticed in the crowd. In an environment where there is severe competition for what little adult attention is available, those who can first capture adult notice by maximizing displays of distressed attachment behaviour can then hold and shape the relationship by switching rapidly between endearing attachment behaviours such as chattering and smiling, and further bouts of distress immediately the carer threatens to depart. This strategy is used indiscriminately. Any attention from any adult is better than no attention. This might explain why children diagnosed with the disinhibited type of disorder of non-attachment relate so unselectively and impersonally with strangers, bombarding them with inappropriate questions, pulling and tugging at their clothes, and prattling on without focus. As a result, their behaviour is experienced as superficial and shallow. When there are so few carers available and when none of them ever reach the status of selective attachment figures (no adult is ever around long enough for this to be achieved), children learn to get what they can, while they can, from who they can.

However, many children experience environments that are even more deprived. Carers are either absent are infrequently available, or they are deeply disengaged. If carers are present, they are tired and without interest. If they do respond, it is perfunctory, without warmth or animation. To all intents and purposes, children find themselves in a non-caring, harsh world of extreme and chronic neglect. Displays of attachment behaviour have little impact – there is no one to respond. Infants soon give up trying – attachment behaviour is *inhibited*. Children lie passively in their cots or stare blankly while sitting on a wet mattress; there is no one to comfort them other than the self. As a result there is the self-soothing rhythmical rocking, self-harming and head banging so characteristic of many of these children. There is little crying, no smiling and an absence of eye contact. The attachment system appears to shut down. When there are no adults or when carers are deeply neglectful, children are unable to develop any kind of attachment strategy that might, even marginally, increase the responsivity and availability of adults.

O'Connor/ERA (2003) also suggests that under stress and challenge, institutionally and severely deprived children, having failed to develop a discriminating selective attachment, do not show the same patterns of behaviour with carers, strangers and peers that children with ambivalent (dependent), avoidant (defended), or disorganized (disoriented) attachments do. In particular, these children are quite likely to display both approach ***and*** wary behaviour with a stranger in the presence of their current carer. In this sense, the children might not be displaying insecure attachment behaviour as such, as this implies anxieties about the availability and sensitivity of the primary selective attachment figure. Rather, what we see is a more fundamental disturbance in children's ability to organize any strategy that helps them regulate distress at times of arousal, whether this is the excitement of play, the fear of being alone, or the uncertainty of new people and strange situations.

> In an environment in which a discriminating attachment relationship could not have formed, such as may be the case in a severely depriving institutional environment that lacks both continuity in personalized caregiving and interpersonal conversation, the biological and/or social mechanisms underlying the development

> of attachment may not have been established. More specifically, the lack of a consistent caregiver to provide a pattern of predictable interactions may have impaired the child's ability to develop (interaction-based) strategies for regulating his or her arousal level and for the activation and termination of attachment, exploratory, wary, and sociable behaviour.
>
> (O'Connor/EPA 2003: 34)

Internal Working Model of the Self

It can be argued that the very sense of self can only emerge out of relationships with others who trade with you in psychological information, one mind to another. Fonagy et al. (2002) describe this exchange as 'mentalisation'; Meins (1999) calls it 'mind-mindedness'. As parents interact with their babies, they constantly feed back to their children their mental and emotional states as they perceive them to be. They also report to the child his or her own psychological state, thus setting up a rich, two-way traffic of mental state information, between minds. This is how children learn who they are and how they work, psychologically speaking. In such stimulating and sensitive relationships, they also feel interesting, worthy, influential and loved.

Contrast all this with children who suffer severe deprivation and chronic neglect. Who helps them explore their own thoughts and feelings? Where do they go to understand how they tick psychologically? Not only do they have extreme feelings of fear and confusion with which to deal, but they also have the least responsive and understanding environment to help them make sense of it. The minds, which form in this environment, are going to lack integration. The formation of an objective self that can reflect on all aspects of its and other people's cognitive, emotional and behavioural make-up is going to be weak. Little wonder impulse control is poor. And maybe under these extreme conditions, the emerging ability to empathize and play around with social reality fails, producing impairments that look very similar to those suffered by children with autism.

At best, therefore, the internal working model will represent the self as unlovable and without value. At worst, the very notion of the self lacks shape and coherence. The boundaries between the self and others are diffuse. Needs, desires and wants will not be regulated by thought, reflection and social understanding. The self is helpless to change events or influence people. And the self, being without value to others, feels of no worth. As they mature, many of these children regularly put themselves in situations of danger. Busy roads will be crossed carelessly, and total strangers will be approached without guile or fear. Whereas secure children quickly appreciate from their carers what is dangerous and that they are worthy of protection from danger, chronically neglected children miss out on these twin survival experiences.

The Internal Working Model of Others and Relationships

The dominant experience of severely deprived children is that other people at times of need and distress are simply not available. Since they have had little experience of mindful care, relationships are experienced as of little value, import or significance unless as a means to an end. Relationships with others are based simply on attempts to satisfy some immediate need. Once the need has been met, the relationship has served its purpose. Children show little upset when one carer leaves and another one arrives. People are interchangeable so long as the basic needs of food, attention, money and sex are met. These children have no trust in the availability of adults, and so invest nothing in relationships – there is little point when their only experience is that people come and go, fleetingly and without care, love or warmth. In adulthood, relationships are casual and conflictual. Although some institutionalized and severely deprived children do show good developmental recovery when placed with new families, many adopters of the most severely deprived children do feel disappointment. Their children seem to lack reciprocity. At times of need, they turn to any adult who happens to be present.

Georgia

Georgia was born in poverty, the fourth child of an ill, frail mother and a father who drank heavily and was violent. Four months after she was born, Georgia's mother died. A few weeks later, the authorities found the children in the care of their drunken father, dirty, hungry and badly neglected. The older three children were farmed out to relatives, while Georgia was placed in the local institution. She received no visits from her father, siblings or relatives. For most of each day she was left in a cot in a room with 19 other babies and toddlers. Along with the other children she remained soiled and dirty for hours. Her mattress was more often than not wet with urine. Her care was infrequent, cursory and impersonal. The children were left to their own devices; there were no toys, few sources of stimulation, and in spite of the overcrowding, little interaction between the children.

Just before her third birthday, Georgia was adopted. She arrived in her new home malnourished, sore with rashes, and ill with a number of medical problems. At first she was solemn and expressionless, but soon became animated and prone to act the clown. She gained weight quickly and rapidly recovered from her illnesses. She would go to talk to anyone, and although this extreme sociability was at first endearing, its indiscriminate nature began to worry her parents. If she hurt herself or got upset, she made no demands on her adopters, preferring instead to sit under the table, rocking to and fro, making distraught but not particularly loud, whimpering sounds. If her parents tried to comfort or cuddle her, she looked around in a confused, distressed fashion, making neither eye contact nor physical responses.

As she got older, Georgia remained very attention-seeking. Her demands on adults could be experienced as wearing. She continued to respond in a very familiar fashion with all grown-ups, whether she knew them or not. With one new visitor, Georgia announced she was a baby, and then lay on the stranger's lap with her feet in the air saying she wanted a bottle. Professionals who visited the home would experience Georgia touching their face, or having their blouse buttons undone. She would look in their pockets or handbags, ask them a string of questions without ever appearing interested in the answer, and wander off with them if they attempted to leave. When drifting away, she made no reference to her parents even if she found herself in a difficult, stressful situation. Other times, she would quite happily skip off without a glance back. In parks or shopping malls, she would run off towards anything or anyone who took her interest, again without concern for her parents' whereabouts. The only solution her mother could come up with was to go out shopping on her own, leaving Georgia with her father, or if that was not possible, keep her on a lead.

At school, Georgia would insert herself into any group of peers, but usually in an inept and irritating manner. She would say she had lots of friends, but in fact she was friendless. Her ability to concentrate in class was very limited, and her teachers found it difficult to keep her quiet and still. Although for most of the time this didn't present the teachers with too difficult a problem, occasionally she would erupt into an uncontainable temper tantrum or 'switch off' as if she had gone into a trance.

As she got older, new problems emerged around Georgia's failure to keep her parents in mind. On occasions she would leave school at the end of the day and not look out for her mother by the gate, wandering off instead with other groups of parents and their children, until the mum or dad would notice they had an addition to their numbers. Although Georgia could be fun at home, and clearly enjoyed family life, her mother felt disappointed that the relationship seemed one-way. 'I really don't think I'm any more special to Georgia than the lady who serves her sweets in the local corner shop. I'm sure we'll get her through school OK, but I do worry about her now that she's on the edge of adolescence. She is naïve, socially clueless, immature, very pretty. She can throw a temper at the drop of a hat. And she is prepared to go off with anyone who shows her the slightest interest or pays her any attention.'

Conclusion

We have been examining the developmental prospects of children in situations of increasing neglect, recognizing the fundamental importance that emotionally engaged and thoughtful adult minds play in this process and what happens when they are absent. In practice, of course, many children live in complex, shifting environments in which different types of both abuse and neglect occur. Having analysed cases in terms of the presence of one, relatively uncomplicated type of maltreatment, Part IV considers what happens in compound cases where there is both abuse and neglect, including cases of sexual abuse.

Part IV

Compound Cases of Abuse *and* Neglect

There is a good case to be made that perhaps the majority of children subjected to maltreatment in fact experience a degree of both abuse and neglect. Certainly, children exposed to abuse and neglect suffer more than just the addition of the two maltreatments. To an extent, children who are either abused or neglected might be able to develop some kind of adaptive strategy, although this is less likely in the case of severe deprivation. However, infants who experience abuse *and* neglect find it extremely difficult to organize any attachment pattern that might increase their safety and their caregiver's availability. These children find themselves in environments in which there is danger and uncertainty, aggression and unpredictability, hostility and unavailability. This is the worst of both worlds. It is traumatic. It is therefore also a profound form of psychological maltreatment.

Although the child's deactivation of attachment behaviour in a dangerous relationship might increase safety, it is totally the wrong strategy to improve the responsivity of an under-involved carer. On the other hand, hyperactivation of attachment behaviour might get you noticed, but this is not necessarily a good thing if the kind of attention it triggers is likely to cause you harm. Infants in particular find it difficult to organize any attachment strategy in environments in which there is both random care and unpredictable danger. Unable to increase feelings of safety, children remain in states of unrelieved distress for long periods.

Most difficult health and child welfare cases possess these compound features. Practitioners meet parents who are violent when drunk, helpless when sober, and who live in a state of permanent family crisis. Or they encounter carers with histories of sexual and physical abuse, who perhaps suffer depression or experience great agitation and distress whenever their children make emotional demands on their caregiving. Within these environments, we meet children who suffer combinations of physical abuse, domestic violence, sexual abuse, psychological maltreatment and neglect.

Part IV

Compound Cases of Abuse and Neglect

[illegible]

10

Physical Abuse *and* Neglect

Introduction

Some children have one parent who feels helpless and depressed in their role as caregiver, while the other is prone to anger, violence and aggression. In other cases, the distress experienced in the caregiving role by just one carer leads to a range of erratic parenting behaviours including despair, out-of-control anger, collapsed helplessness, and threats of abandonment. In both cases, children are subjected to regimes of unpredictable abuse *and* neglect. Achieving psychological coherence and emotional integrity in such environments is very difficult, and as a result we can meet some behaviourally very disturbed young people. Although conceptually difficult, we are trying to understand children's development in environments where they have to deal with the fear of direct threat and danger on the one hand, and the fear of loneliness and abandonment on the other. Randomly violent, emotionally unresponsive caregiving presents children with a peculiarly difficult environment in which to survive and prosper. Allen (2001: 7) believes that *uncontrollability*, *unpredictability* and *helplessness* predict traumatic responses: there is no escape and there is nothing you can do to stop the threat.

Characteristics of the Caregiving Environment

Under stress, abusing/neglectful parents tend to feel *out of control*, reflecting the breakdown of their defensive attempts to avoid and not engage with arousing and dysregulating attachment-related experiences. Strong activation of their attachment system overwhelms their inhibitory defences and leads to either aggressive or helpless behaviour. Under conditions of low stress, parents might function tolerably well, but the normal, everyday demands and challenges made by children easily dysregulate them. In their agitated state parents might attack their children, or withdraw, leaving children to cope with their upset and disquiet on their own. Solomon and George (1999) observed that maltreating parents switched between being in rigid control of their emotions on the one hand, and feeling overwhelmed, helpless and out of control on the other. Parents seem to operate in states of both rage and fear. Not surprisingly, young children experience this as 'relational trauma'. Caregiving is experienced as both scary and unresponsive.

An air of depression descends on mothers and fathers when they attempt to describe their parenting. They present their toddlers as unmanageable, evil, wild, powerful and bad. Parents feel that their children are not only beyond control, but also beyond help. Children throw things around the room, shout, fight each other, lock parents in rooms, and tear wallpaper. The helpless parent begins to feel that the young child is actually in control of the relationship.

> Like, I can't get Michelle [aged 3] ready for nursery in the morning. She runs around screaming and yelling like a mad thing. She totally ignores me and pushes me away. This morning she put a whole toilet roll down the loo. Then she locked me in the kitchen and laughed saying she was never going to let me out. I was in tears and then I blew it and stormed out the back door and came in the front and smacked, and smacked, and smacked her.... I just can't seem to handle her.

One of the consequences of this parenting failure is that children are left in prolonged states of high arousal. This represents an abdication of two key caregiving functions: protection of children from danger, fear and over-arousal; and helping children recognize and regulate their own arousal and mental states. In other words, helpless parents fail to terminate their child's highly activated attachment system.

In many cases carers' feelings of fear and helplessness, which produce their alarming behaviour, can be the result of frightening memories associated with their own childhood experiences of abuse and trauma erupting uncontrollably into consciousness. Their experience is that whenever they find themselves in situations where attachment-related issues are taking place (upset, anxiety, need, dependence, vulnerability, behavioural breakdown, aggression), anxiety rapidly escalates. The mental processing of such attachment-relevant information disorganizes the parent and seriously dysregulates his or her caregiving (George, West and Pettem 1999: 328–9).

Thus, out-of-control and unpredictable care arises when the carer has an unresolved state of mind with respect to attachment-related issues concerning loss and trauma. This is dealt with defensively, by trying to exclude from consciousness the fear and distress associated with the unresolved material. However, under the relational stress of parent–child interaction, contrasting but unintegrated (dissociated) models of attachment-related experiences well up into consciousness, reflecting the carer's own childhood experiences of hostile and helpless care and lack of protection. In some cases, the daily routine of being a caregiver saturates the parent's mind with ancient feelings of worthlessness, abandonment and helplessness. This results in feelings of emptiness, isolation and bleak hopelessness. Carers in this state of mind appear unaware and deeply unresponsive to their child's needs.

Dissociation when displayed by the parent in the act of caregiving is particularly disturbing for children. The child's attachment behaviour triggers old feelings of unresolved loss and trauma in the carer's mind. As a result, he or she might blank out or appear to the child to go into a trance-like state, or become helpless and panic-stricken. This can also result in *constriction* – a mental state that is the product of extreme fear, leading to mental freezing, frozen panic, a total inability to act, and sudden feelings of rage or even identification with the aggressor. The carer might try to cope by obsessively attending to some detail, but forget the overall purpose of the caregiving task. A health visitor, observing a young mother with a history of physical and sexual abuse putting a clean nappy on her baby daughter, noted:

> I watched Beverley change Zee. She smiled weakly and seemed a bit absent-minded as she very slowly dressed the baby. Zee watched her mother without much animation. I noticed that on a couple of occasions, Beverley seemed to switch off and just stop what she was doing, which seemed very odd. Zee reacted with some distress. These trances lasted anything up to five to ten seconds, then Beverley would get on with dealing with Zee, but even then she seemed to move in slow motion. I don't think Beverley spoke once to Zee during the whole operation.

The child's attachment needs might therefore trigger caregiving that is variously helpless, panicky, hostile, rejecting, controlling, confused, seductive, sentimental, loving or sadistic. But whichever one it is, it bears no relationship or relevance to the child's own current state of mind. All the child senses is that any arousal of his or her attachment system appears to have a major, but unpredictable, impact on the mind and behaviour of the carer. The child therefore feels both potent (that he or she can have such dramatic effects on the carer) and frightened (that the effect is unpredictable, sometimes dangerous, and leaves him or her feeling hyperaroused, abandoned and extremely dysregulated).

Some parents attempt to explain the hopelessness and stressfulness of trying to deal with their uncontrollable children by appealing to supernatural forces. Ghosts and the spirits of dead, often violent or nasty relatives, are said to have taken over and possessed the young child, making him or her evil and bad. Or the parent might talk to the deceased relative or believe that the dead person is still an active, malign force disturbing family life. 'These images are, by definition, considered to have a dissociated quality because they reveal dissolution of the boundaries between what is real and not real, or between the living and the dead' (George, West and Pettem 1999: 328).

> Vicky says that she feels at a loss what to do with her seven-year-old daughter Lucy. 'One minute, she can't stop crying,' says her mother, 'then next she's running around in a state, throwing things and ripping the curtains.' Lucy has had problems wetting the bed and urinating on the carpets. Vicky was physically abused as a child.

> She feels her own mother rejected her. Even today, Vicky is still frightened of her mother: 'She gets into my head and screws me up. She's in there and I can't get rid of her.' Vicky uses heroin, has had a number of violent relationships, and is socially very isolated. Lucy won't go to the toilet on her own and is suffering major sleep disturbances. Vicky said the whole house was getting 'very spooky ... lights come on, you know, in the middle of the night then turn themselves off. You hear loud knocks. Things keep disappearing. See that lamp over there. The other night it just moved off the table and fell on the floor. Scared the shit out of me. I've been to see a spiritualist who says that Lucy must wear a protective charm around her neck at all times to keep the evil at bay.' Lucy is now frightened to remove the charm, fearing that she will die without it.

Although the underlying psychology is the same, at other times abusing and neglectful parents defensively sense that engaging with their distressed and needy child will lead them into an agitated, fearful and hostile state of mind. So they don't engage; they don't deal with their child's attachment needs for comfort and protection. They might walk away or psychologically 'switch off'. They might lock their child in the cellar or outside in the dark. Shutting their child away and feeling compelled to escape the parent–child relationship represent attempts by carers to maintain some kind of fragile control over their own distressed, hyperaroused, and confused behaviour for fear of what might happen next. The effort of trying psychologically to protect the self from disintegration leaves the child abandoned and in a state of fear and distress. For example, Wendy had a deeply unhappy childhood:

> Her mother was an alcoholic who told Wendy she didn't really like children, especially girls. Wendy finds it difficult to describe her childhood. When asked to talk about it, her voice trails off and she stares vacantly with a far away look in her eye. During an argument when Wendy was 14, her mother told her that her father was not in fact her real father. As a young adult, Wendy has had a series of relationships with violent, drug-abusing men. Her first child died in a cot death. She then fabricated the death of a second, nonexistent child for whom she obtained a birth and death certificate.
>
> By the time she was 23 years old she had four children, each with a different father. Will was the second eldest. One of his 'step-fathers' was particularly violent, and as a young child Will saw him beat up his mother, crash out on drugs, and on two occasions set fire to the house, necessitating rehousing each time. Throughout their early years, the children were intermittently looked after by short-term foster carers. Their lives were ones of great inconsistency and unpredictability. The family moved 15 times before Will had reached the age of five.
>
> Wendy was beginning to leave the children to fend for themselves more and more often. When interviewed about her children, she seemed to have only the vaguest notion of their likes and dislikes, their routines and needs. Her interest in them seemed almost nonexistent. During one observation session when the

assessor had brought in a range of toys, Wendy played on her own, engrossed with some of the puppets, leaving the children to amuse themselves. Whenever the children did try to engage her, she would shout, telling them to play on their own. At one point she slapped Will for interfering with her drawing.

The young ones were not toilet trained and would wander around with full nappies and urine rashes. Faeces encrusted the furniture and walls. The house was dirty, unkempt and sparsely furnished. Many of the windows were broken. Wendy's drug-dependent partners had sold all the children's toys. The children were often ill with infections. Wendy would disappear for a day or longer, leaving the children to cope on their own. The children would wander around the streets and would latch on to any neighbour who fed them and took pity. There were reports of the children seen scavenging in dustbins.

By the time Will had reached the age of eight, his behaviour was very disturbed. He was regularly setting fire to curtains, paper and other people's fences and sheds. He talked a lot about wanting to die and kill other people. When asked to make a wish, he said, 'I want to die. I always want to die. Then it won't matter any more.' At school, Will gets into fights. He steals food from other children's lunch boxes. Twice he has hit and bitten a teacher. His mother says she cannot control him. At home, he is aggressive, enuretic and 'wild'. Wendy believes that Will has a mental health problem and wonders if he is schizophrenic. The two oldest boys asked the visiting social worker if they could go into foster care because they were fed up being hungry and left alone.

If the parent must *restrict* her conscious attention to the infant's fear-related signals in order not to evoke her own unresolved fearful experiences, the parent's fluid responsiveness to the infant's attachment-related communications become disrupted. The more pervasive the failures on the part of the parent to mentalize and regulate the infant's arousal, the more the parent's need to regulate her own negative arousal takes precedence over the baby's need to be soothed and emotionally contained (Lyons-Ruth, Bronfman and Atwood 1999). The baby's attachment-related communications only serve to activate the parent's defences, leaving the child psychologically abandoned at the time when he or she most needs emotional contact and understanding. All the child can find in the mind of his carer is a mental representation of him as the source of her fear, hostility and helplessness. The only information about his emerging psychological self is that it appears to be highly negative, malevolent, and perverse in the sense that it seems to threaten, agitate and make dangerous or precipitate the loss of the very person who should be a source of protection, comfort and safety. Drugs, alcohol and domestic violence frequently fuel this distressed and hostile parenting.

Trisha has five children, ranging between the ages of 12 months and seven years. Only two of the children have the same father. Her own history was turbulent. She was physically abused by her stepfather and emotionally rejected by her mother, spending the last four years of her childhood in residential care. All Trisha's partners have been violent and abusive towards her. The children often witness these aggressive outbursts, during which Trisha is cut and bruised, doors are broken and smashed, and items hurled across rooms or through windows. She says, 'I just want to be loved. I know the guys I fall for can be bastards but they want me and I want them.' Most of the men in her life are users of drugs, including heroin and crack cocaine. Professionals visiting the home have found needles and other bits of drug-taking paraphernalia. The current home (the fifth in 12 months) is under-furnished and dirty to the point of being squalid. Trisha has considerable debts and the gas and electricity are frequently disconnected. The children's clothes are never clean. Medical checks and immunisations have all been missed. The children are frequently ill, suffering colds, diarrhoea, and upset stomachs. They appear underweight.

The incident that led to their final removal found two of the children locked in their bedroom, naked and with only an old, ripped, damp mattress as furniture. Both had severe diarrhoea that had run all over them, the floor, the bed and the walls. They had been left in this condition for two days. Trisha said she had to do this because she couldn't cope. They were taken to hospital, ill, dehydrated and undernourished. The other three children were placed with foster carers. Trisha was encouraged to visit the two children in hospital, but she never made it. She was given money for a taxi to the hospital, but used it to visit her current partner who was in prison. Two months later Trisha has not visited any of her children, saying that they don't deserve to see her because they had been so aggravating and had caused her to feel 'stressed out' and 'ill'.

Children's Behaviour and Development

The research evidence strongly indicates that abusive/neglectful carers fail to show much interest in their children's minds and mental states, thereby depriving their children of a rich two-way human relationship. Infants frightened by the helplessness, hostility and unresponsivity of their carers remain in a state of fear and attachment disorganization, with no strategy to recover equilibrium.

Maltreated babies and those classified as disorganized in their attachment behaviour show very low levels of joint attention and shared social interaction (Claussen et al. 2002). This adversely affects children's ability to develop social understanding. It also upsets children's social motivation to share and explore emotional and interpersonal experiences with others. As a result, relationships with their peers are poor. There is *fear* and *wariness*. They have problems developing symbolic thinking and sound language.

It has been observed that during infancy and early toddlerhood, severely abused and neglected children often remain in a distressed, anxious state for long periods. They might wander about aimlessly, whimpering, making no demands on the adults present. When they feel hurt or frightened, their levels of emotional arousal can be extreme. Their distress seems overwhelming. Some children become absorbed in self-soothing behaviours that might include rocking, head banging, and repeatedly scratching a scab or a wound.

However, with maturation a range of distinctive behaviours begins to appear. Most of these revolve around feelings of hostility and aggression, fear and helplessness. The need to feel in aggressive control is highly characteristic. Parents of four year olds will describe their children as 'bossy' and unmanageable, an example of an aggressive controlling/compulsively self-reliant strategy. Violent, raging arguments will erupt over minor disagreements with carers, siblings and peers. Crittenden (1992) found that in free play with siblings and peers, abused and neglected children tend to fight more, with the number of aggressive episodes increasing with higher numbers of children present. Early adverse experiences result in increased sensitivity to stress throughout life, leaving the individual vulnerable to stress-related psychiatric disorders, self-harm and dissociation (Hartt and Waller 2002). Children who have suffered abuse *and* neglect develop a range of problems in most behavioural, emotional, cognitive, social and developmental domains.

Behaviourally, they show poor impulse control, hyperactivity and restlessness. Destructiveness and aggression are not only directed at other people and property, but can also be turned against the self. Treasured possessions can be smashed in a fit of temper. Angry thoughts against close family members can erupt in play. They might appear in drawings where chaos, blood, gore, evil and violence are depicted. Some children are preoccupied with knives and other dangerous weapons. In some cases, pets and other animals can be treated with great cruelty, suggesting anxious contempt for anything or anybody, including the self, who appears small and vulnerable. Some children also show a complete disregard for their own safety and well-being, wilfully courting danger. Most lie in a blatant, 'crazy' way. Many steal. For example, an adopted child might take money from those who have become emotionally important to him, particularly adoptive mothers. Sexually abused children can also display inappropriate sexual conduct and attitudes. However, the underlying fear and insecurity of these children can manifest itself in sleep disturbance, enuresis and encopresis.

Emotionally, abused and neglected children find it difficult to regulate their affect. Inconsolable sadness and feelings of helplessness can suddenly turn into anger and rage. Inappropriate emotional responses such as laughing in public at someone else's misfortune can embarrass new carers. Children make great emotional demands on other people, who quickly feel as if they are losing their bearings in a relationship where the child switches bewilderingly between desperate need, rage, depression and indifference.

In terms of *cognitive functioning*, some abused and neglected children seem to lack cause-and-effect thinking. They fail to see how their behaviour might affect others. They do not feel responsible for their choices and actions, preferring to blame others. Some perceive themselves as unwanted, bad and helpless. Very disturbed children might cast themselves as supernaturally and powerfully dangerous, acting in a grandiose fashion, making themselves big and scary so that they can deal with fear, threat and danger: 'I beat up six older kinds at school today, and they didn't hurt me.' 'I was knifed by my uncle who has just come out of prison, but I just laughed and told him he was a head case.' Sadly, these children all too easily perceive all carers as unavailable, hostile and unloving.

Socially, many children are superficial and charming with strangers. This is particularly true in cases in which children have suffered severe neglect (see Chapter 9). Though socially uninhibited, they are socially inept. Their relationships with peers are poor. They relate to others in a manipulative, controlling and exploitative fashion (for example, they borrow things and either lose, sell or keep them). There is a lack of remorse or conscience for harm or hurt caused. They can be bossy and directive, always fighting to be in control.

As far as their *physical* welfare is concerned, some abused and neglected children display very poor personal hygiene and self-neglect. They can be confused over their own physiological states, perhaps getting mixed up about whether they feel hungry or full, hot or cold, wet or dry. In some situations they seem oblivious to pain, and yet in others they overreact to the slightest scratch. In some cases, children have abnormal eating patterns. They might gorge, steal and hoard food, or refuse to eat – particularly in the presence of other family members. Their bodies might be permanently tense. They become rigid if anyone touches them or attempts to hold or cuddle them. It is common to find that many abused and neglected children are clumsy and accident-prone.

Although it is unlikely that any one child will show all of the above behaviours, severely disturbed development is highly characteristic. Elements of these disturbances are picked up at surprisingly young ages, but their diagnostic significance is often missed. A three-year-old who is excluded from playgroup for biting other children, a drug-addicted mother who says her four-year-old is evil, schoolmates who describe a boy as 'weird', are all small clues about children's possible traumatic experiences of abuse and neglect.

Young children typically present as hyperactive, vigilant and poor sleepers. As they grow older, many remain restless, fidgety and constantly on the move, seeking and provoking reaction and stimulation. Very distressed children might wet and soil themselves, smear faeces over the wall of their bedroom, and urinate in odd places.

By the time they reach four and five, they seem oblivious to extremes of heat and cold. When ill, hurt or in pain, they rarely make demands on adults. Some children also seem unaware of danger. They wander across busy roads, climb unsafe buildings, and play dangerously with sharp knives or snappish dogs. And yet these children remain highly sensitized to stress. Even minor stresses that appear innocuous seem able to trigger very exaggerated reactions. It is as if every arousal indicates possible danger. Minor stresses can therefore lead to a cascade of arousal that very quickly feels extremely dangerous to the child. They seem to be constantly on the edge of fear, and when frightened they either attack (fight), flee (flight), or in some cases dissociate (freeze). Spilling a warm drink, being told off, suffering an accidental scratch, getting glue stuck all over fingers, or even getting over-excited with pleasure, might precipitate feelings of terror and rage out of all proportion to the incident. However, in the child's brain made highly sensitive to stimulation through chronic exposure to relational trauma, the feelings of fear and being overwhelmed are real enough.

These helpless/hostile strategies are carried forward by controlling children into their peer relationships where they lead to victim/victimiser, bullied/bully roles. It seems that these children can only play in a very imbalanced fashion – being either the passive, bullied partner, or the dominant, bullying peer. Again, the child is either emotionally out of control, becoming verbally and physically aggressive, or emotionally over-controlled, in which the child is withdrawn and uncomfortable with his or her own feelings (Jacobvitz and Hazen 1999: 146).

Children desire contact and involvement, but seem clueless about how to join in play with other children. When peer relationships are experienced as particularly stressful, some disorganized children become aggressive, fearful, or display odd, strange, annoying, disconnected, 'weird' or contradictory behaviours, as their feelings of fear disorganize and disorientate them (Jacobvitz and Hazen 1999). Thus, when flight or fight behaviours are not options for the frightened and powerless child, 'displacement' activities are the only alternative. They manifest themselves as self-stimulating but 'out of context' behaviours whenever feelings of irresolvable conflict (fear without escape) overwhelm the child. In their observations, Jacobvitz and Hazen note that:

> [T]hese behaviors included the following: (1) verbal responses that had no connection to the peer's preceding utterances; (2) quirky mannerisms ... (e.g. rolling the tongue around in the mouth ... characteristic facial distortions); (3) repeated annoying and intrusive behaviors that were unrelated to the ongoing play (e.g. repeated tugging on peer's shirt; shining a flashlight in peer's eyes); (4) odd or bizarre behaviors that were unconnected to the ongoing play (e.g. licking the wall, spinning around; making strange noises); (5) behaviors in which the affect expressed was inappropriate to the context (e.g. crying out for no apparent reason; responding with anger or fear to the peer's neutral or positive initiation); and (6) juxtaposition of extreme positive and negative affect (e.g. hugging then immediately beating a doll).
>
> (Jacobvitz and Hazen 1999: 152)

There is growing evidence that childhood abuse and neglect adversely affect brain organization, development and function (Bremner and Vermetten 2001). These neurologically based effects mean that maltreated individuals find it difficult to cope with stress, regulate emotional arousal, learn, memorize and achieve academically (Cicchetti, Toth and Hennessey 1993). Deficits in verbal memory have been found to be particularly great in patients who have suffered severe sexual abuse in childhood (Bremner and Vermetten 2001: 483).

Beeghly and Cicchetti (1994; also see Lyons-Ruth 1996) found that children who had experienced severe neglect and abuse used significantly less 'internal state language', that is they talked less about their own thoughts, feelings and actions than non-maltreated toddlers. They were also less able to differentiate between feelings (for example, they were confused between their feelings of sadness, anger and fear). And on top of this, their range of feelings also appeared limited and rather blunted. One effect of these affective deficiencies is the inability of many maltreated children to regulate their own arousal or to differentiate, label and understand emotional expressions in other people. A study by Moss, St Laurent and Parent (1999) found that mothers who were underinvolved, and had poor communication skills, were at risk of having disorganized children who had low metacognition and mind-mindedness. Many maltreated children, therefore, appear to lack empathy, and without empathy, moral behaviour is difficult. It is our ability to project ourselves into other people's feeling states, to have social imagination and understanding, that inhibits being hurtful towards other people.

Similarly, humour and joke-telling often rely on being able to see the world from other people's points of view, particularly when reality is distorted in a playful, flexible and imaginative manner. Children who are unable to make these leaps of imagination and explore the surreal have a poor sense of humour. Indeed, as with physically abused children, maltreated children are just as likely to think the joke and laughter is somehow getting at them. As a result they might react aggressively or withdraw, feeling sulky and confused. However, they do enjoy and laugh at slapstick humour in which people have accidents or get hit. This is humour based on out-of-control behaviour and not one that appreciates other people's misinformed or misguided mental states. Lacking social imagination, maltreated children are also poor at novelty seeking and pretend play (Cicchetti, Toth and Hennessey 1989).

The aggression that is often seen in quite young children grows more pronounced with the years. Fighting, pinching, and punching upset peers, annoy teachers, and make parents feel increasingly helpless. Referrals to child psychologists and psychiatrists are not unusual. Stealing, shoplifting, fire setting and robbery can appear in some cases as early as eight, nine and ten years of age. Under challenging and stressful conditions, abused and neglected children can very quickly get into hyperaroused, excited and uncontrollable states. They crash, trash and rage about in a highly destructive manner. Impulse control is extremely weak.

For many traumatized children, any number of stimuli can trigger old, unresolved memories that have been stored in the lower emotional centres of the brain, but outside consciousness. They remain unintegrated (dissociated) from the more reflective, verbal parts of the brain. In relationships that unwittingly trigger these intense feelings, the individual is dominated by feelings of 'infantile' rage, inner turmoil, dread, and out-of-control thoughts, emotions, images and behaviour. It is at this point that any semblance of collaboration and open communication break down. Indeed, it is this same dysregulated, frightened and frightening behaviour that is triggered when parents with unresolved attachment issues engage with the vulnerabilities and attachment needs of their children, leading to disorganized attachments in the second generation. Essentially the traumatic experience is stored in non-verbal, emotional memory where it remains, unprocessed, disconnected and unintegrated with other developmental experiences, but ready to be activated whenever an event feels like a precursor to the original trauma.

Beyond childhood, survivors of abuse and neglect are at increased risk of a wide range of physical and mental health problems (Kendall-Tackett 2002), from heart disease to suicide, cancer to depression, obesity to sexually transmitted diseases, post-traumatic stress disorder, and borderline personality disorder. The pathways to these greater risks are complex, involving increased likelihood of more harmful behaviours such as smoking or drug taking, proneness to end up in more violent relationships, more chance of engaging in high-risk sexual behaviour, more negative views of the self, and an increased risk of stress-related diseases and illnesses. Many people with histories of abuse suffer sleeping difficulties.

Post-traumatic stress disorder is briefly described in Chapter 12 in the context of sexual abuse, but its effects run throughout this chapter too. Allen (2001: 4 emphasis original) writes that '*the essence of trauma is feeling terrified and alone*', that it is a form of extreme stress. Those who suffer borderline personality disorder (BPD) have often suffered early and traumatic abandonment, whether physical or emotional, and abuse by their primary caregiver. Individuals with the disorder lead chaotic and highly problematic lives, which respond poorly to treatment. They exhibit dissociative behaviours and identity disturbances, switching between an idealized and a devalued presentation of the self; have relationships that are intense, exhausting and deeply unstable; behave compulsively, recklessly and destructively; and remain hypersensitive to abandonment in all their relationships. Their emotions explode in an infant-like and unregulated manner, producing powerful feelings of fear, rage, hostility and shame, triggered by events, however innocuous to the observer, that seem to echo old hurts and dangers. In relationship with others, there is lack of trust, and a lack of expectation that feelings can be regulated and contained (Gerhardt 2004: 160). One way to try to defend against such fear and despair is to not reflect, think and mentalize, because they threaten catastrophically to flood the mind with memories and feelings of hurt, emotional abandonment and incoherence. The individual with BPD cannot protect him/herself against the cauldron of emotion inside his/her head, and old unresolved traumas could easily be triggered by a casual word, a touch and an image.

The Child's Behaviour and Mental State as an Adaptive, Coping and Survival Strategy

As we observed in Chapter 3, when children experience their attachment figure as the source of both danger and safety they simultaneously experience two incompatible behavioural responses – *fear* (an avoidance response) *and attachment* (an approach response). These instinctual behavioural forces cannot be reconciled. Infants feel compelled to escape the relationship and rush towards their frightening attachment figure. Under these relationship conditions it is not possible for children to organize an attachment strategy – hence their attachments are classified as 'disorganized' (Main and Solomon 1986, 1990). In states of need or distress, toddlers might wander aimlessly about, dazed or crying, bang their heads against the wall, freeze, display confused avoidance/approach behaviours, rock rhythmically, screw their fists into their eyes, dissociate, or turn in circles, disoriented and distressed.

The fear in children caused by out-of-control parents goes 'unrepaired'. Indeed, not only do maltreating carers fail to modulate their children's arousal, they provoke even higher levels of unmanageable distress. The child therefore remains in a chronically hyperaroused and highly dysregulated emotional state. These high arousal states are well beyond the coping capacities of immature children (and their developing brains). Children therefore feel 'at the mercy of these states. Until they are brought under control, infants must devote all their regulatory resources to reorganizing them. While infants are doing that, they can do nothing else' (Tronick and Weinberg 1997: 56). In the case of children who suffer chronic relational trauma, they have little opportunity to make sense of themselves or others as socio-emotional beings.

With maturation, when distressed by the behaviour or condition of their carer (helpless or hostile), children might therefore react in one of three ways:

1. Fearfully inhibit and avoid all attachment-related cues and triggers which arouse feelings of fear, danger and *helplessness* (for example, avoid feeling needy, dependent, vulnerable).
2. Feel frightened, *hostile*, angry and out of control as their attachment system remains highly activated. They feel explosively aroused, raging and emotionally very dysregulated.
3. Alternate between these two states of helplessness and hostility, fear and aggression.

The young mind tries to find sense, consistency and meaning in relationships with others. When caregivers behave inconsistently, insensitively and frighteningly, it is not possible to build coherent, integrated mental representations of either the self or other people. At different moments, the self might be experienced as loved, worthless or bad. As a result, children can develop 'multiple', 'dissociated', conflicting and incompatible models of attachment. From the child's point of view, it appears that his or her own attachment needs and vulnerabilities can cause a range of extreme behaviours in the caregiver. Cognitively, therefore, the child begins to model the self as:

- powerful ('I can bring about major changes in other people')
- bad ('but those changes are harmful and destructive')
- frightened and sad ('my malign power leaves me abandoned, isolated, and alone without care and protection').

Under stress and at times of need, disorganized children might therefore dramatically and unpredictably activate any one of these incompatible, segregated (that is, dissociated) mental representations of the self, and one of these incompatible representations of their caregiver, giving a number of possible child–parent combinations as shown in Table 10.1 (Liotti 1999: 300).

Because of the inconsistent, confusing and unpredictable nature of the parent–child relationship, disorganized children are unable to synthesize their overall experience of these interactions with their caregiver into a cohesive and

Table 10.1 Possible child–parent combinations of mental representations

Mental representation of the self	*Mental representation of the caregiver*
Frightened, helpless, the 'victim', the subject of catastrophes and disaster and hopelessness	Frightening, the cause of the other's fear and helplessness, the aggressor, the 'persecutor', out-of-control caregiver
Frightening, the cause of the other's fear and helplessness, the aggressor, the 'persecutor', controlling-punitive toward the caregiver, the self as bad, evil, and dangerous	Frightened, helpless, the 'victim', finds the child out-of-control and unmanageable
Comforting, benevolent and loving toward the frightened and helpless other, the 'rescuer' of the vulnerable attachment figure; controlling-caregiving (role reversal)	Frightened, needy, helpless, the 'victim'
Frightened, helpless, the 'victim' of dangerous and unknown external forces	Frightened, helpless, the 'victim' of dangerous and unknown external forces

integrated model of the self, others and the way relationships work. When relationships are experienced as traumatic, Liotti (1999) believes the multiple models generated in these environments lead to dissociative experiences (trance-like states, blank spells, flashbacks, panic attacks, pervasive feelings of emptiness, disorganized thought processes). All attachment-laden, stressful and fearful experiences are capable of generating these contradictory representations of the self and the other.

When frightened and distressed, disorganized children can also 'defensively and unconsciously try to rely on inborn motivational systems different from the attachment system (for example, the sexual system, or the competitive, agonistic system)' (Liotti 1999: 308). Under relationship stress and confusion, disorganized children may therefore unconsciously, but improperly, activate another behavioural system, so the child may behave seductively or aggressively. For example, a child who is being fiercely told off by a teacher might play with his genitals, or start laughing, or become violent. So although the child is actually feeling confused and frightened, and in need of protection and containment, his or her behaviour is inappropriately and unacceptably sexual or violent. He or she displaces the arousal away from the attachment system to another one, such as the sexual system. This is another example of the defence known as 'segregated mental systems', typical of those whose psychological development lacks integration. Personalities appear incoherent. Other people experience children as bewildering, inconsistent, Jekyll and Hyde-like individuals who can be as nice as pie one minute, then violent and verbally abusive the next.

Daydreaming and staring off into space, in a trance-like manner, switching-off and blanking out, and other forms of 'de-personalized' and 'dissociated' behaviours are not unusual, particularly amongst girls who have been neglected and traumatically abused, both physically and sexually. Mollon (1996) calls it 'detachment from an unbearable situation'; Putnam (1997) 'the escape when there is no escape' (both cited in Schore 2001b: 211). And in attempts to self-regulate, children can also self-harm. They might cut their arms with a knife or dig away at a wound with a pin. The immediate physical pain feels less persecutory than the highly disorganizing psychological distress of fear, confusion and feelings of derealization.

Thus, according to Crittenden's dynamic maturational model, many abused/neglected children switch between helplessness and aggression, being punitive and seductive, and feeling paranoid and menacing (Crittenden 1997b). In cases where the caregiving is predominantly unpredictable and hostile, the child's strategy might collapse solely into being helpless and afraid. When the caregiving is predominantly one of out-of-control helplessness, the child may well become increasingly aggressive, punitive, frightening and scary. Most coercive children are preoccupied and over-involved with their attachment figures. They fail to learn constructive interactional skills. They find it difficult to be self-reliant.

Controlling Strategies

As we saw in Chapter 3, with maturation the 'disorganized' child begins to try to gain some 'control' of the people and situations that he or she experiences as frightening or confusing. The development of a 'controlling' pattern represents an attempt by the disorganized child to reduce his or her feelings of fear and helplessness when being parented by a helpless and hostile, frightened and frightening carer. Controlling strategies empower the child. They allow the child to disown mental representations of the self as helpless and needing comfort.

One of the major controlling patterns is based on the child becoming compulsively self-reliant as well as increasingly hostile, aggressive, punitive, sarcastic and belittling towards the carer. This pattern is particularly likely to occur in children whose temperament has been assessed as 'difficult' and whose attachment style in infancy was classified as 'disorganized' (Shaw et al. 1997). However, under stress and under strong activation of the attachment system, this fragile coherence achieved by adopting a controlling strategy quickly breaks down, and the child becomes rapidly disorganized, emotionally dysregulated, frightened, catastrophically full of rage and self-destructive. According to Liotti:

> This pattern of response in children who had been disorganised in their infant attachment – shifting from an organised, controlling strategy to disorganization in the context of a strong activation of the attachment system – is in keeping with the idea of a multiple, dissociated [internal working model] of attachment underpinning the seemingly unitary representation of the self as 'controlling'.
>
> (Liotti 1999: 301)

Highly characteristic of abused and neglected children is a heightened sense of needing to stay safe. With maturation, children continue to remain highly sensitive to even low levels of arousal, which they interpret as potential danger warranting a defensive, self-protective response. So objectively mild or even neutral experiences can produce highly dysregulated responses and hyperarousal in children with histories of abuse and neglect. These result in a fight, flight or freeze response, with fight being the most likely. In other words, children unnecessarily activate aggressive, self-protective and survival responses in situations that do not necessarily warrant them. 'As a consequence, the wariness that protected the children from past danger may persist, thus protecting them from enjoying the benefits of safer contexts' (Crittenden and Clausen 2000: 247). This observation explains why so many adopted and fostered children experience such difficulties in their new families, and why every issue, however minor, feels to them like a survival issue. A foster carer might switch off the television, triggering in the child's mind old unprocessed memories of a father coming home drunk, turning off the TV and beating up his son. The boy's response to the later, non-threatening stimulus might be one of extreme rage that might even lead to the television being smashed.

Abused and neglected children who develop aggressive behaviours are trying to control their own safety and well-being. If the carer is not available to offer care and protection (neglect) or is the source of danger (abuse), then survival begins to depend on the child being in charge of his or her own care and protection. It is simply too frightening and risky to remain at the mercy of an unpredictable parent. This is why these children are described as bossy, unmanageable and aggressive by their carers. In their minds, to allow a frightened or frightening carer to be in control is to be in danger, which is frightening. The *aggressive-controlling*, compulsively self-reliant strategy is a way of feeling less helpless, and less at the mercy of random acts of parental neglect and violence. However, when levels of stress become too great, or relationships become too difficult, confusing or demanding, the controlling strategy breaks down and the child is left feeling helpless and vulnerable, full or fear and rage.

Taking a slightly different tack, Crittenden (1992) suggests that abused and neglected children do show organized attachment behaviour. Their coping strategies have to be complex, rapidly flexible and even contradictory in order to deal with the shifting and unpredictable character of the caregiver behaviour. Avoidant strategies are appropriate when the carer is dangerous, while ambivalent, coercive and demanding behaviours make sense when the attachment figure is under-involved and neglectful. In their attempts to read their carer's mind and likely behaviour, children switch rapidly between provocative and demanding behaviour when they feel their carer is under-involved (ambivalent) and compliant, disengaged or role-reversed caregiving behaviour when they feel their carer is over-involved (avoidant). Some children develop *coercive* strategies that depend on whether the parent is being helpless or hostile in his or her caregiving role. When the parent is being helpless, the child reacts in a hostile, demanding and aggressive manner to provoke attention and parental compliance. When the parent threatens to abandon the relationship, the child behaves in a helpless, needy or coyly seductive fashion. These behavioural strategies are refinements of an essentially ambivalent strategy (Crittenden 1992: 583).

Fonagy (2000: 21–5) explains why he thinks that much of the social behaviour of seriously abused and neglected children is so aggressive and destructive. First, we need to remind ourselves that the defining characteristic of their caregiving is that it is both hostile and helpless. The child's ordinary careseeking behaviour appears to trigger increased distress, arousal and emotional dysregulation in the parent as old unresolved anxieties, fears and agitations are activated around issues of need and love, warmth and safety. Under stress and emotional dysregulation, the parent ceases to interact with the child as an intentional being. The parent stops mentalizing. Mind-mindedness and reflective function are necessary if the caregiver is to be sensitive. Sensitivity is a prerequisite if the child is to be helped to contain, understand and regulate his or her own arousal. Thus, parents who react with hostility and helplessness to their child's attachment behaviour frighten the child. This amplifies further the already over-aroused attachment system. The caregiver–child system then goes into a sudden and rapidly escalating state of hyperarousal, as the parent frightens the child who gets even more distressed, which increases the parent's helplessness/hostility, and so on. The child's massively overactivated attachment system is neither terminated nor repaired, as repair requires parental recognition, reflection and mentalization.

> Consequently, these children come to experience their own arousal as a danger signal for abandonment, which triggers non-mentalizing functioning; the image of the parent who withdraws from the child in a state of anxiety or rage, elicits a complementary dissociative response.
>
> (Fonagy 2000: 21)

Children sense that they have triggered the fear and hostility in their carer simply by expressing their own need for protection and containment. Children therefore experience themselves as powerful, dangerous and unmanageable, and yet alone, frightened, unprotected and unable to elicit care and safety. Their state of mind at such moments is full of fear, rage and turbulence. This image of the self undermines psychological self-organization. Children are left on the edge of mental disintegration, and a deeply incoherent, incomprehensible psychological self that lacks any mentalizing capacities and reflective function. One desperate way to try to impose a more coherent self-representation is to externalize this image of the self as frightening and unmanageable. It is just too painful to have a self-image that is unloved, hated, unworthy of protection, and actually capable of causing the attachment figure, the person who should be the source of care and safety, to turn into someone who can either attack or abandon you. Fonagy (2000: 21) suggests that the disorganized attachment behaviour in infancy may be a rudimentary attempt to blot out these destructive and alarming aspects of self-representation. With maturation, a more coherent self is achieved by behaviours that seek to try to control the parent. These are the parents who say that their out-of-control child must be 'possessed' or 'mentally deranged' or 'evil'.

By being in fierce and fearful control, children avoid being cared for and protected. Care and protection involve 'letting go' and allowing the carer to be in control, something that feels too dangerous and arousing. Intimacy of any kind implies fear and danger. These children have survived by not trusting adults. Thus, every confrontation feels like an issue over survival. This is why many abused and neglected children can never allow other people to be right, to win, or to be in control. It feels too threatening and might open the door to untold fears and dangers. For example, an adoptive father leaves some small change on the kitchen table while he hangs up his jacket. His adopted son scoops up the money and quickly heads towards the door. But his father sees him take the coins and the boy sees that his father has seen him pocket the money:

'Simon, don't take money that doesn't belong to you.'

'I didn't take it.'

'Don't be silly. You saw me see you take it. I'll give you some more pocket money if you need some, but don't steal.'

'I didn't steal your money. You must be blind. I never touched it.'

In this example, Simon would be unlikely ever to admit he stole the money. However, his 'crazy' lying is less to do with telling an untruth and more to do with remaining in control. For these children, to admit the theft is to lose control, and to lose control is to court danger and so feel anxious, frightened and hyperaroused. Every battle, whether it's over a request to tidy away a pair of shoes or to put on a coat because it's cold outside, is a battle of survival. 'Controlling' children make parents, and indeed new carers, first feel helpless, then hostile. To the parent, the child seems 'out of control'.

Internal Working Model of the Self

Because abusive and neglectful parents are not interested in or able to think about their children's needs and emotional states, their behaviour towards their children bears no relation to the children's internal mental states, including their wants, thoughts and feelings. As far as the children are concerned, not only is the parent experienced as unpredictable and unresponsive to anything children do, but also much of what the parents do is alarming, confusing or distressing. The result is a lack of contingency between what children do and the way their carer reacts. Children therefore feel powerful and bad, because they are able to distress and dysregulate their caregivers, but also ineffective and helpless, because they can feel at the mercy of random threat and dangers. Things, often scary and violent things, seem to happen out of the blue, bearing little relation to objective events. It means that there is no relationship between what children do and how others might behave. Feelings of self-efficacy are typically very low:

> Individuals whose mentalising or psychological self is poorly established may readily feel that they are not responsible for their actions. They lack a sense of agency, thus they may also lack a sense of responsibility for the consequences of their actions.
>
> (Fonagy 2000: 19)

When abused and neglected children are asked to paint, draw or enact a story with dolls, many depict scenes of chaos and violence. Dreadful things suddenly happen in the drawing or the story, resulting in mayhem, death and injury. Monsters appear and bite people's arms and heads. Fires may flare up and burn down houses and people. For these children, life is full of unexplained, dangerous and frightening things that suddenly appear. They cannot be controlled, and although the self is modelled as aggressive and occasionally able to kill off or control these dangerous and frightening forces, the feelings of respite and safety are only temporary. The monsters, the evil spirits, the earthquakes and storms appear again and again in their stories and paintings. The strange, often frightening world of many of these children is recognized in the case of seven-year-old Joe.

> Whenever Joe paints, plays or draws, his images are of death and violence. His foster carer says that he seems 'obsessed with death. All his drawings are full of dead people – some of them dead with their hands and arms and heads chopped off. Other people are dead, but still walking about attacking other people in his drawing or story. Joe gets very excited and frightened when he gets into this kind of play. I think his favourite colour when he's painting is red so he can show what happens when people's heads are shot off. Joe has regular dreams in which he is attacked and eaten by sharks.' Although Joe wakes up screaming, he says he isn't scared by what happens. He says he likes being eaten, then goes on to say 'And when I'm inside the shark, I'll eat him from the inside. Ha! Ha!' Joe constantly tries to frighten some of the younger children in the foster home, walking around with a wild, menacing robot-like stare and puffed-up, monster-like body posture, telling them that there are evil creatures and vampires in the house that will eat everyone up while they are asleep at night, and in the morning everyone in the house will be dead and there will be blood everywhere. But when Joe feels frightened and in danger of falling apart, he has to make himself feel big and menacing. Before he gets into bed each night, Joe has to make sure the window is shut and there is nothing lurking under his bed. He insists on a small night-light remaining on while he is asleep.

This graphic account gives us powerful clues what it must feel like for children whose world is randomly frightening, and in which they are essentially alone, without care and protection. Their aggressive controlling strategy works for a while (they can vanquish and keep at bay the forces of danger as they present themselves as powerful and big), but inevitably the monsters and evil forces, having been killed, once more magically rise up and return, no matter how many times they have been defeated. The stories mirror their lives. You are starved. A drunken father fumbles affectionately with you before vomiting in your face. Your mother locks you in the cellar and shouts that she hopes the rats will eat out your eyes. A stepfather twists your arm up your back until it breaks. Life is one of constant, unavoidable peril from which there is no escape, no matter what you do to try to survive. And somewhere in this fragmented self, there is a sense of being powerful and bad, as the child's attachment states seem to cause other people to lose control or become fearful.

Since they have been given little help to understand how their own mind or other people's minds work, and how thoughts and feelings affect behaviour (reflective function), 'things', including their own and other people's actions, just seem to happen. The behavioural world seems 'agent-less' – no purposeful minds appear to lie behind what takes place, including what they do and make happen. There is therefore a lack of cause-and-effect thinking. There seems to be no psychological cause or explanation behind what people do. This is why there is little point in demanding of these children that they explain why they have just done what they have done. In terms of self-monitoring and evaluation, they literally do not know. And without the ability to mentalize and see the world from other people's point of view, there is no basis for empathy, morality or remorse. Children are therefore capable of mean and violent behaviour.

A feeling of authorship for one's own actions normally emerges in relationship to responsive, reflective and interested caregiving. It is while we are developing a sense of effectiveness and agency that the very experience of the self as an autonomous, conscious and responsible being begins to form. The self begins to feel solid, bounded, permanent and worthy. One of the characteristics of abused and neglected children is their feeling of diffuse emptiness. Many talk about feeling depersonalized, unreal and incoherent.

Developmentally speaking, the absence of cause and effect thinking, particularly at the psychological level, is equivalent to infancy where actions replace thought. As Fonagy (2000: 24) reminds us, the meaning of an action for an infant is judged entirely on its observable consequences. For an older child or adolescent who has never developed full-blown mentalization, his or her psychological development may well still be infantile. The child seems to treat people as objects which, when needed or perceived as threatening, are abused, exploited or destroyed. 'The youth,' says Fonagy (2000: 24), 'functioning at this level, can only interact with other minds through physical acts'. Such aggressive behaviour is further evidence of the child's need to control other people, particularly in situations where the child or adolescent feels confused, anxious or threatened. It is at such times that the child, or indeed young adult, once again feels under tremendous fear and threat; the very self feels in danger of breaking down, as emotional hyperarousal begins to escalate and overwhelm the mind, which in developmental terms is infantile in character.

Internal Working Model of Others

Abused and neglected children expect other people to be emotionally unresponsive and unavailable at times of need and danger. They anticipate rejection if they make demands on others. Without the capacity to 'mentalize', their level of social understanding is poor. They therefore experience other people as unpredictable, threatening and possibly even dangerous. Situations that do not make sense cause us to feel watchful and nervy. Controlling children are hypervigilant. It feels unsafe to relax. For some children even going to sleep seems risky, and so they wake up early, get up repeatedly in the night, or can be found wandering outside in the small hours.

Children who have suffered abuse and rejection, neglect and trauma do not trust others. Why should they? Those who should have protected them abused them. Those who should have nurtured them starved them. Their caregivers showed little interest in what they were thinking and feeling. The people who should have provided safety, warmth, containment, interest, understanding and mutuality have abandoned these children at every psychological level. This inability to trust carers or feel safe in close relationships often extends to new carers, including foster parents and adopters.

Internal Working Model of Relationships and How They Work

Lacking a strong understanding of their own and other people's mental states, for these children social behaviour and interpersonal relationships can be a puzzle and a source of frustration. Severely deprived and traumatized children react to emotional arousal without fully understanding what has triggered it, how it affects them, and how it impacts on other people. Children desire intimacy, they want to become involved in games and play, but they are confused about how to go about it. They get it wrong. They approach peers too aggressively, or in ways that cause other children to describe them as 'weird' or 'odd'. The result is often social rejection, hurt and anger.

Fischer-Mamblona gives the intriguing example of the origins of attachment-disordered behaviour in a goose, which has clear parallels with infant development in humans. She recognizes that even attachment-disordered behaviour has 'its origins as a functionally adapted biological process' (Fischer-Mamblona 2000: 9). The example of Feli (a goose) is particularly evocative of children who have suffered severe neglect and deprivation (see Chapter 9), but her condition also has parallels with children who have experienced extreme neglect and abuse:

Feli was a white-fronted goose that, after hatching, spent the initial ten days of her life in total isolation from other geese with no goose-mother. She spent the next eight weeks in an enclosure, again deprived of contact with other geese. Other than being kept warm and fed, she received no other stimulation. Her distress signals went unheeded, and this lack of response seemed to confuse Feli. She would run about wildly in a form of escape behaviour, followed by weak greeting sounds into empty space. Although Feli's motivation to seek an attachment relationship was very powerful, it had no clear outlet. 'During the first phase of life, escape behaviour is always directed to the object of attachment ... [but] ... as Feli had no object of reference her escape behaviour had no aim' (Fischer-Mamblona 2000: 15–16). Basic trust in the availability and protective responsiveness of others was never achieved.

After the eight weeks, the young goose was given her freedom to join the rest of the flock. 'She was a bundle of anxiety.' She seemed confused and frightened when approached by other geese and would run back to her pen. Compared with the other geese her fear and 'escape' behaviour was very intense, and would be triggered by a range of innocuous and ordinary social situations. As she matured, Feli began to take more notice of her age-mates – her conspecifics. As a stranger, she would be chased away, and although she remained in a constant state of anxious arousal, she kept trying to make contact. In her conflicted state of wanting contact (attachment) and fearing the hostile response she always received (escape), she developed a number of displacement activities. These included suddenly preening herself and shaking her feathers whenever the tension became greatest. In spite of being highly inappropriate to the situation, such displacement activities are self-soothing and they help 'calm down conflicts that cannot be resolved' (Fischer-Mamblona 2000: 11). The self-soothing behaviours, including rocking and head banging, of severely abused and deprived human infants are also examples of displacement activity. These 'symptoms' typically appear at times of great stress and conflict, in which the organism experiences the simultaneous activation of the two incompatible behavioural systems of fear and attachment.

A vicious cycle set in. Feli's strong desire for social contact led to repeated rejection. This intensified her feelings of distress and escape behaviour from the social encounter – an irresolvable conflict. With further maturation, Feli was mated by a male but she became an unsuccessful mother. Her first attempts to hatch her eggs were a failure, with only one gosling emerging. She was unresponsive to the greeting sounds of her gosling. She shrank away and showed distressed escape and displacement behaviour whenever it made attachment demands of her. The conflict between the urge to care (approach) and the fear of being hassled (escape) generated high levels of stress, under which Feli expressed a kind of frozen, apathetic indifference. A day or so later, the gosling was dead.

Fischer-Mamblona (2000: 18) concludes that within many species, including human beings, in complex social situations, there is always the possibility of a tension between approach behaviours (attachment, nutrition, social affiliation, sexuality, caregiving) and escape behaviours (fear). Certainly for children who find social relationships desirable but difficult, these tensions can lead to too much approach (fight/aggression), too much escape (flight/withdrawal), apathy and dissociation (freeze), or displacement activities as the child attempts to soothe his or her hyperarousal (inappropriate laughter, sexualized behaviour, rocking). In secure caregiving environments, attachment and escape are directed towards the same person. The attachment figure is a safe haven. She helps recognize, and then regulates, the infant's arousal. She terminates the attachment system and allows the child to feel calm, safe and able to return to exploration. But for children whose carers trigger the fear/escape response, their arousal escalates, they remain in a highly dysregulated emotional state, their attachment system is not terminated, and their escape behaviour is frantic and aimless because the attachment figure is either the source of danger (abuse) or chronically unavailable (neglect).

Feli, in her attempts to interact with other geese, showed very disturbed approach-avoidance behaviours, with no secure resting point. Human sufferers, as well as geese, are torn between the longing to have their needs met and 'the fear of the consequences of doing so' (Holmes 2001: 57).

The combination of a controlling strategy, poor mentalization, weak reflective function, interpersonal confusion, social incompetence, with a tendency to become disorganized and highly dysregulated under emotional stress, means that relationships are going to be difficult and conflictual. Little things can produce big reactions. As children grow, peers and parents begin to feel increasingly wary and anxious. It is difficult to relax for long in the company of such disturbed children. They prefer to attack rather than be dominated. Aggressive control and compulsive self-reliance represent desperate ways of disowning internal working models of the self as vulnerable and helpless.

Kerry (Aged Five) and Luke (Aged Three)

Kerry's mother, Donna, was placed in permanent foster care when she was 12 years old. Before then, Donna had been in and out of foster care many times over the years. Her mother was an alcoholic who died when Donna was 13. Donna suffered neglect and abuse as a girl. The middle one of three children, Donna remembers coming home from school and regularly finding her mother drunk or in bed. Food was in short supply. She shared a bedroom with her brother and sister. Donna's teachers worried that she was underweight, mentioning that she would often arrive at school poorly dressed, dirty and smelly. At school she was described as quiet, but deceitful. She would steal other children's pens or money. She had no friends. Educationally Donna achieved little.

Her father also drank heavily. He was violent towards his children and their mother. He once chained all four of them up to a water pipe in the house and left them there until the early hours of the morning while he went out drinking.

> It was cold ... My mum kept shouting and shouting. I was frightened, yeh.... And.... And.... Yeh.... Well. So I can't lie down 'cos I'm chained to my sister.... My mum, 'cos she drank as well ... peed herself 'cos we couldn't get to the toilet, and it ran in a big puddle on the floor, everywhere ... all around me, you see ... and I'm in the middle and I can't get away.... So, it was like that....

Donna's voice trails away as she recalls the event.

Donna remembers feeling great relief whenever her father disappeared, which could be for months at a time. She didn't know where he went and she seemed without curiosity. Although she can't remember how old she was – nine? ten? – he was found by the police in a canal, dead and drowned, in a city some hundred miles away. Her mother's drinking began to worsen. The house got dirtier. Food became more erratic and makeshift. Donna retells these events in a dull, remote voice.

Before she reached the age of 22, Donna had three children by two different partners. She then met and began living with Darren. He had convictions for domestic violence and physically abusing his own daughters, for which he had received a prison sentence. At various times and at the hands of Darren, Donna suffered a broken nose, fractured ribs and facial bruising. The young children witnessed the brutality. Donna began to find her children's behaviour increasingly difficult, saying she couldn't control them. Her unpredictable lifestyle, the children's difficult behaviour (both at home and at nursery), and the mounting domestic violence, eventually resulted in the children being removed and placed with a foster carer. Although Donna was encouraged to maintain contact, her visits to see her children grew increasingly infrequent and unpredictable. She kept moving from town to town with different partners. When she met Mikey, she was introduced to a range of drugs and soon developed an addiction to crack cocaine. She was arrested repeatedly for a variety of criminal offences including shoplifting, fraud and deception. Her failure to stay in touch with her children was interpreted as abandonment and they were adopted.

Donna then became pregnant with Kerry but did not register with a doctor, nor did she attend antenatal classes. She admitted herself to hospital on the day of the birth. The midwives were worried about Donna's unplanned arrival. Kerry was born with mild opiate withdrawal symptoms (she was described as 'jittery' and admitted to a Special Care Baby Unit for several days). A meeting of the hospital's paediatrician, midwife and social worker was held to discuss the case. Donna agreed to be seen and monitored by her local health visitor and social worker, and was allowed home with Kerry.

However, she moved to another city only a few weeks after Kerry's birth. Donna soon established a pattern of leaving Kerry to be cared for by others while she disappeared, presumably to get money by one means or another to buy drugs. Kerry was left with a variety of highly unsuitable carers, including other drug-using friends and an unregistered childminder. Donna's relationship with Mikey got increasingly violent and she eventually sought safety in a women's refuge. However, she continued her drug habit. She repeatedly left Kerry with other women in the refuge while she went into the town centre. When the other women refused to help out, Donna took Kerry with her. On one of her returns, a refuge worker found a used syringe stuffed down the side of Kerry's pushchair. Social services were called, but by the time they arrived Donna had moved out and on to another town.

Donna met Ryan and they had a son, Luke, 18 months younger than Kerry. Her drug habit appeared less problematic. Considerable health and social work support were provided for a while before the case was eventually closed. Ryan was violent towards Donna. The children suffered a number of allegedly accidental injuries (bruises to the face and legs, a broken arm). An anonymous phone caller reported that Donna and Ryan, and others of their friends, had sexual intercourse in front of the children, but the parents denied this and the matter was dropped.

Donna developed a passion for playing the fruit machines at a local 'casino'. She began to leave her toddler-aged children on their own. She also locked them alone in their bedroom, which was without curtains, wallpaper or a properly assembled bed, and smelled of urine. An old, uncleaned smear of faeces covered part of one wall. There were no toys in the house. Luke was often left to sleep in his pram, parked overnight in the hall. Twice neighbours found the children wandering the streets late in the evening. On one occasion Donna went missing for five days, leaving the children in the care of Ryan. She also defaulted on clinical and hospital appointments for her children's immunisations and a minor ear problem from which Kerry was suffering.

The more needy and demanding the children, the more Donna seemed inclined to abandon them for increasingly long periods. The children were prone to accidents. For example, aged four, Kerry scalded herself while trying to make a hot drink; Luke burned himself on the cooker, swallowed cleaning fluid, and cut his head on a rusty nail sticking out of the kitchen door. The children lit a fire of paper on their bedroom floor and set fire to the curtains. Luke suffered severe nappy rash. Aged three and a half, he still did not have bowel control. The health visitor observed that he would wander aimlessly about the house: 'Donna seems oblivious of his existence and never engages with him.' Luke had never been seen to smile.

Aged five, Kerry suffered severe speech delays, developmental delays, temper tantrums, poor toilet training, regular infections, tiredness at school, and a reluctance to go home at the end of school. She was becoming increasingly aggressive with her classmates. She twice scratched and punched other children, resulting in temporary exclusion. She also began to steal food and other odd items from her peers. She was not popular, and other children said she was 'smelly' and 'a weirdo'. They told her to go away whenever she tried to play with them. There was a suspicion that she might be epileptic – she would occasionally 'blank out' and 'cut off' – but there was no medical support for this diagnosis, although the psychologist mentioned the possibility of Kerry 'dissociating' under stress.

When she was asked to draw a picture of her family by the psychologist, Kerry first depicted her mother having sex with a man, and then introduced a 'killer man' who chopped off her brother's arms and cut the dog in half. Kerry then scribbled red crayon over the picture explaining that there was blood everywhere. Donna said she could no longer control Kerry, which is why she sometimes locked her in the bedroom. On a recent occasion, Kerry turned the tables and locked her mother out of the house. Donna told the psychologist that Kerry wandered the house at night, wouldn't sleep, and made 'strange noises'. She now entertains the thought that Kerry might be

> a bit like those children you see at the movies, you know, like when they get possessed, and do weird things. I definitely see it in her eyes sometimes and it scares me. I mean, she can be a really nice kid sometimes, but I can't control her any more and I lose it with her 'cos she drives me to it. But she doesn't seem to care. She just laughs. Mind you, she doesn't laugh when Ryan's around and has a go at her. He can frighten her, and that shuts her up good and proper, the little sod.

Conclusion

Traumatic relationships, particularly attachment-related trauma, are highly predictive of poor self-organization, impaired mental health and problem behaviour. Children feel in constant danger. They even feel persecuted from within by an alien self, formed as a result of the child's interactions with a hostile/helpless caregiver. In desperate attempts to deal with this persecutory internal self, children either project this aspect of themselves onto others who are then aggressively attacked, or when they feel there is no escape, children talk of death and suicide (Fonagy et al. 2002). If we are to work well with these children and their families, we need to keep our bearings. Grounding our understanding within a developmental and attachment perspective is one way of making sense of the complexity. However, the emotional and developmental needs of both children and their parents remain extremely high, and any therapeutic progress is likely to be long and slow.

11

Drugs, Depression and Domestic Violence

Introduction

Parents who abuse drugs and alcohol, who suffer major or bipolar depression, or who are involved in domestic violence generate difficult and stressful environments for their children. Although each of these problem types of parenting might be a feature of physical abuse, psychological maltreatment, or any of the types of neglectful care we have discussed, they are considered here as examples of caregiving in which the risks of both abuse and neglect increase. As explored in the previous chapter, if children are exposed to both abuse and neglect, their attachments are likely to be insecure, and most probably disorganized/controlling. In this chapter, only the characteristics peculiar to each type of problematic caregiver and their impact on children's development will be highlighted. So although substance abuse, depression and domestic violence throw up their own distinctive features, from the child's point of the view the caregiving might be experienced as essentially abusive, neglectful, or most likely both (Dunn et al. 2002).

Substance Abuse

As drugs and alcohol are mind-altering substances, they seriously tamper with that beautiful mind-minded synchrony between parent and child that characterizes sensitive, attuned, reciprocal parenting. The more the parent becomes lost in his or her own substance-altered state of mind, the less contingently accurate or relevant is his or her behaviour with the child. From the child's point of view, it feels as if the parent is no longer able to recognize and read his or her attachment needs and emotional states. Emotional availability and understanding disappear. So not only might the parent's behaviour and manner be odd, confusing and frightening, but also the carer is unavailable to deal with that confusion and fear. The carer causes the distress, does not see it, and fails to repair the relationship that is now under growing stress. In these conditions, the young child's distress is likely to escalate and go unregulated. The child can find no behavioural strategy that increases his or her security. Her attachment behaviour is therefore likely to be disorganized. In the presence of a drunk or drugged parent, the child feels emotionally abandoned and frightened. So long as the parent remains 'out of his or her mind', the child is psychologically alone, feeling bewildered and unsafe, and unable to manage.

So if competent parenting involves minds processing and mediating care-seeking and attachment-related information in an undistorted manner, then anything which adversely affects the state of mind and information processing capacities is likely to impair the parent–child interaction. As Drummond and Fitzpatrick (2000: 136) explain:

> as an individual becomes drunk there is an interference with their coordination, judgement, verbal performance, memory and problem-solving behaviour. They might become depressed, or the disinhibiting effects of alcohol may result in aggressive behaviour.

Alcohol and drugs are substances that clearly affect the way the brain perceives, processes and responds to information, including the child's attempts to employ careseeking and attachment behaviour. In fact, the highly charged and skilful business of dealing with children at times of attachment need is likely to be particularly difficult if parents do not have all their wits and reflective capacities about them. In short, heavy use of alcohol and drugs distort, disrupt and disturb parent–child relationships.

Characteristics of the Caregiving Environment

Many substance-abusing parents say they had loveless childhoods, believing that their parents either had little time for them, or actively rejected them. Others claim indifference about their early years, adding that their childhood has had no particular effect on their personality – if anything they argue that their distant parenting has made them stronger and more independent. And yet they can convey anxiety and sadness as they reflect on their rejections and losses. Not surprisingly, therefore, there is some evidence that many substance abusers are classified as avoidant, dismissing or disorganized/unresolved in their attachments. The abuse of drugs and alcohol is seen as a way of trying to escape feeling alone and unloved, and even unlovable. This is Alan reflecting on his history and behaviour:

> Yeh, I take drugs. Not a lot, like. Not too regular. I think it's to do with that shitty childhood I had. You know. Alone. Feeling rejected. Being in so many foster homes. My mother telling me I was never going to be any good for anything, you know. It hurts thinking about it. When I'm taking, using ... you know, it's kind of

> an escape. I feel better. Not so shitty. I enjoy the feeling. It gets me out of reality.... I don't think it has affected the kids. I mean, they worry, especially Emma. But little Jez, he's a terror. Nothing frightens him. He tells me what to do, yeh, little as he is. A right little handful.

'Compared to controls, parents of abused and neglected children are much more likely to report alcohol problems, from 18 per cent to 45 per cent across controlled studies' (Wolfe 1999: 83). According to Famularo et al. (1986), over half of the serious abuse and neglect cases they studied involved a parent with a history of alcohol abuse. Furthermore, Eiden et al. (2002) found that alcoholic fathers of young children showed more irritation and aggression with their infants, especially those fathers who also suffered depression. Indeed, fathers who have serious alcohol problems tend to have higher mean levels of depression. And as risks rarely travel alone for children in adversity, partners of alcoholics also report higher levels of depression on average compared with partners of non-alcoholics. As we observe later in this chapter, depression on its own is a major risk factor for disorganized attachments and psychopathology in children, but when coupled with the distorting effects of alcohol and drugs on parental behaviour, caregiving environments can become especially confusing, distressing and difficult.

A similar story of multiple jeopardy occurs in families where one or both parents are abusing drugs. The most commonly used drugs are the opiates, cocaine, amphetamines, barbiturates, cannabis and glue. Different drugs have different effects. It is not unusual for users to be taking more than one drug, often in combination with alcohol.

As with alcohol, the effects of the drug are superimposed on the parent's underlying personality traits. In fact there is the strong suggestion that drug misusers tend to have a range of personality traits in common, which contributed to their addiction behaviour in the first place. Such traits include low frustration tolerance, impulsivity, self-centredness, emotional isolation, and feelings of inadequacy, emotional deprivation and depression (Drummond and Fitzpatrick 2000: 137).

In general, a father's alcoholism serves as a marker for increased family risk and negative parenting behaviour. However, although substance-abusing parents, particularly those who become drunk with alcohol, certainly increase the risk of children suffering some form of physical abuse, neglect is even more likely (Chaffin, Kelleher and Hollenberg 1996). Savage (cited in Iwaniec 1995: 13) found in a sample of neglectful families that alcohol abuse was present in 75 per cent of cases. In many examples, children were left to look after themselves. Food was in short supply, and young children and their clothing would go dirty and unwashed. The study also confirmed other findings that mothers' interactions with their children were few and poor in quality. Not surprisingly, both the children and their families suffered social isolation.

Substance-abusing carers tend to spend relatively little time engaged with their children, are low on supervision, and high on dissatisfaction. For example, Hurt et al. (1995 cited in Dunn et al. 2002: 1069) found that 68 per cent of cocaine-using mothers initiated less than one contact per day as measured by a visit or telephone call to the hospital for information about their sick newborn babies. And when they do interact, drug-abusing mothers are likely to engage with their children less sensitively. They are also prone to be impulsive, self-centred and irresponsible, showing a lack of empathy, or mind-mindedness (Bauman and Dougherty 1983, Bauman and Levine 1986). When researchers have taken a step back and looked at the parent's own psychological profile, they have found that drug-abusing parents have relatively low scores on intelligence tests, have impaired psychosocial development, poor levels of concentration, limited ability to persevere, and show poorer socially adaptive behaviour (Bauman and Dougherty 1983).

This package of impairments inevitably affects their parenting capacities. Not only do they find it difficult to organize and structure their own lives, they also have problems controlling and regulating their children's behaviour. This leads to a disciplinary style that switches unpredictability between hostility and distress. Helpless angry shouting, sarcasm and belittlement conceal underlying feelings of impotence.

When substance-abusing parents also have partners who abuse substances, the number of negative parental features significantly raises levels of family stress. It comes as little surprise to learn, for example, that parental alcoholism is associated with family conflict and violence (Murphy and O'Farrell 1996) and antisocial behaviour.

Substance-abusing parents can be particularly difficult to engage at the supervisory or treatment level. Even so, their children are some of the most likely to be removed, typically on the grounds of maltreatment.

Children's Behaviour, Development and Attachment

Children of substance-abusing parents are at risk even before they are born. Drinking heavily while pregnant can cause foetal alcohol syndrome (estimated to be around at least one baby for every 1,000 live births: von Knorring 1991). Children with this syndrome have low IQs, distinctive facial characteristics and a range of other physiological problems. There is some evidence that the children of mothers who have taken large amounts of alcohol while pregnant are often hyperactive.

Infants born to substance-abusing mothers are more likely to be premature and have low birth weights. In extreme cases, they might also suffer brain damage and poor motor coordination. There is certainly the strong chance that babies will be born with a drug addiction, and so suffer withdrawal symptoms over their first few weeks of life.

> Narcotics abuse is associated with obstetric complications and increased risk of stillbirth or low birth weight, and the babies are at risk of suffering drug withdrawal symptoms and fits. Many clinicians reporting withdrawal symptoms of the newborn note that the mother may herself be depressed or anxious because of the complications of labour itself or increases in her requirement of the drug brought about by the physiological changes of birth. The babies themselves tend to be irritable, have feeding difficulties, and are difficult to cuddle. The combination of the baby's and mother's irritability interferes with early mother–infant bonding and, potentially, with adequacy of attachment.
>
> (Drummond and Fitzpatrick 2000: 139–40)

It is traumatic to arrive in the world addicted to a drug, in a state of complete physiological distress. The infant's need for comfort and regulation is as high as it can get, and yet there are severe limits to what can be done to help. Moreover, if the child is in special care, the concerned, soothing attentions of a permanent, constantly available carer may not be available. We have already seen that parents of these babies are the least likely to show the degree of sensitivity and attention that these infants need.

When these infants eventually do return home to their mothers and fathers, they are in urgent need of maximum high-quality care. They are likely to make heavy demands on their parents' caregiving capacities. And yet it is the very intense nature of these attachment needs that is likely to frighten and dysregulate the parent. A vicious circle sets in. The greater the child's needs, the more helpless and hostile is the parent likely to feel, and the more likely it is that he or she will turn to drugs and alcohol, which only adds to the baby's feelings of fear and emotional abandonment. As Dunn et al. (2002) conclude, these characteristics increase the risk of babies displaying irritable, difficult and demanding behaviours, which then interact with the reduced psychological resources and low stress tolerance of the parent. The more aggressive and authoritarian is the parenting, the more disruptive, impulsive and hyperactive becomes the behaviour of the children. In these unpredictable, often alarming and generally disengaged caregiving environments, children develop a range of avoidant, disorganized and controlling attachment behaviours. For example, Eiden, Edwards and Leonard (2002: 271) found that:

> Approximately 30% of infants with problem drinking mothers and fathers displayed a disorganized pattern with mother compared with 5% in the non-alcoholic group. However, the predominant pattern of attachment displayed with the father by infants with two alcohol problem parents was the avoidant pattern.

With maturation, the children of alcohol and drug-abusing parents are likely to display a range of disorganized/controlling behaviours. Young children of parents who are frequently aggressive and hostile often develop ***compulsive compliant*** strategies in the presence of the carer. Parents who veer between helplessness and hostility present their children with a dangerous and inconsistent environment in which *aggressive controlling/punitive compulsive self-reliance* is possibly the child's best survival strategy. And children cared for by parents who appear helpless and pathetically not in control of either themselves or their children might begin to care for the carer in the form of role-reversed *compulsive caregiving*.

> Rita was regularly abused and attacked by her father when she was a girl. He said she was 'born wicked' and was 'possessed by the devil' and he intended to beat the evil out of her. Her mother said she couldn't stand the sight of her daughter, and on the day she was taken away said 'Good riddance to bad rubbish'. When she was eventually removed and placed in a children's home, Rita was scared of the dark, had sleeping difficulties and spent hours and hours washing her toys, over and over again. As a teenager, Rita was described as vulnerable, lonely and sad. When she was 18, she met Jimmy who introduced her to drugs. She became pregnant with Adie. Rita's relationship with Jimmy became increasingly violent. When Adie was ten months old, Jimmy died of a drugs overdose.
>
> Over the years, the health and welfare authorities became increasingly concerned about Adie, but failed to act. When Adie was aged eight, her class teacher referred her to the educational psychologist. The teacher said that Adie appeared anxious and tearful at school. At home, the psychologist noted that Adie was very attentive to her mother. In a later session, Adie confided that 'I am mummy and mummy is the baby'. On home visits, Rita invariably sat huddled in a large chair and smiled weakly with a helpless look on her face, saying she didn't know where she would be without Adie: 'My little ray of sunshine.... Some days I just have to hold her and kiss her a thousand times. We're very, very close, Adie and me. We know what each other's thinking. She doesn't even have to ask. She knows what I want. She's tender with me, very tender and would never hurt me. When she was born, it was like me being reborn, like someone who knew me inside out.. She makes me laugh. She dances and sings to me and I don't know where I'd be without her. I'm not sure I'd be here at all ... no ... not here at all. '

The risk of the children of substance-abusing parents suffering impaired development and later psychopathology is high. For example, children of parents who abuse drugs or alcohol are themselves at four to tenfold risk of substance abuse.

Mel and Her Son, Dylan

Mel is small, thin to the point of looking malnourished. She ties her hair severely back. She has tattoos on her upper arms and across the top of her back. Her lower arms are scarred where she has repeatedly self-harmed over many years. On several occasions, Mel has fetched up at hospital with slashed wrists.

She has a two-year-old son, Dylan. Although she tries to socialize with other young mothers, she finds it difficult and gives up.

When she was a child her mother, who was often violent toward all her children, rejected Mel. Mel finds if very difficult to talk about her childhood, and on one occasion she vomited when a psychologist asked her to reflect on family life when she was a girl. When she was three, her mother abandoned her at a petrol station. After a short period with foster carers Mel was returned to her mother, who was in a violent relationship with the father of Mel's younger half-sibling. A few months later, this man physically abused the children. Their mother left him and took the children with her. However, the children continued to deteriorate in her care. They lost weight and suffered further physical abuse. Their mother frequently left them alone for long periods in her flat. Eventually they were placed in foster care before being adopted. Five years later, Mel's adoption broke down and she went to live in a children's home. Throughout her teenage years, Mel's behaviour continued to become ever more disturbed. She was violent, took a range of drugs, began to self-harm, overdose and shoplift.

Mel has a long history of drug abuse including cocaine, speed and cannabis. When she felt depressed, she would also take heroin and alcohol. Some drugs make her aggressive and violent, and several times the police have been called.

Although Dylan is only two and a half, Mel is finding him increasingly difficult to manage. He eats very little, has very disturbed sleep patterns, and ignores all attempts by Mel to control him. When she is feeling particularly frustrated, she shouts at and smacks Dylan, who reacts by either scowling or laughing. A health visitor observed that Mel generally fails to read Dylan's signals: 'She tickles him when he's distressed, smacks him when he's grumpy, and ignores him when he wants to play. On one occasion when Mel was crying, Dylan went up to her and gave her a cuddle and then started hitting her.' He is beginning to shout at her more and more often, saying he is going to hit her. When he is with other children, Dylan seems at a loss what to do. He is aggressive and rough, going round pushing and shoving other children for no particular reason. He is usually shunned by his peers. It was at this point that Mel was referred to a child psychologist, but three weeks later she moved house leaving no forwarding address.

Depression

Becoming depressed involves an interaction between genetic susceptibility, early insensitive caregiving, life experiences and environmental stressors. Parents, particularly mothers, who try to survive on low incomes, suffer domestic violence, live in poor housing, struggle to cope with overcrowding, or experience low social support are at high risk of depression. Children and parents in these circumstances suffer multiple stressors. Although a degree of developmental risk is found for most children of depressed parents, it only becomes serious and pronounced when the depression is severe and chronic. However, the presence of a non-depressed, emotionally caring and available carer significantly reduces the developmental risks posed for children who live with a depressed parent. Both major depression and bipolar depression expose children to difficult caregiving environments, although it is suspected they sponsor different types of attachment challenge and developmental impairments. Even postnatal depression has been found to increase the risk of babies developing withdrawn, disengaged, unresponsive, anxious, insecure behaviour when they reach the age of five (Murray et al. 1999). Children seem to lack a sense of self-agency, failing to respond to other children's social initiatives. Depressed mothers have been studied much more than depressed fathers.

Characteristics of the Caregiving Environment

Depressed caregiving might result in extreme withdrawal, gross under-stimulation and disengagement. In other cases, it can produce hostile, intrusive, excited, over-stimulating, grandiose, yet inconsistent and distracted parent–child interactions. Parents who suffer bipolar depression can display both types of caregiving as they swing from manic euphoria to depressed withdrawal. Mothers with bipolar depression put infants at greatest risk of forming insecure disorganized attachments (Radke-Yarrow et al. 1985), although depression in general increases the likelihood of children being classified insecure (Cicchetti, Rogosch and Toth 1998). Underlying both types of parenting, however, is insensitivity and a lack of attunement. The caregiving lacks spontaneity. It is not child-centred or child-minded.

Although research is thin, it is suspected that many types of psychiatric illness in parents generate these unpredictable and bizarre caregiving environments. For example, in the case of schizophrenia, a parent might hallucinate and have delusional thoughts that specifically focus on the child (Hipwell et al. 2000: 159). Hipwell et al. (2000) also found:

> that severe postnatal mental illness continued to have some impact on the mother's ability to interact with her child at 12 months in a way that impaired mutually satisfying, reciprocal play. Thus, compared with their matched controls, the case group mothers were observed to be less sensitive, less appropriate, and more negative in their play.

Key features of depression include flat affect, anxiety, and a tendency, even under mild stress, to be irritable. Field et al. (1990) found that depressed mothers were angry with their infants more of the time, resulting in physical aggression or emotional disengagement – in other words they spent less time in attuned 'matched mental states' with their children. Depressed people's faces lack expression; their voices are dull. Affect mirroring, so important in children's emotional development, is largely absent (see Chapter 2). Being emotionally available to others, including one's children, is strictly limited if you are depressed. Depressed parents remain relatively unresponsive to infants' attachment behaviours, signals of distress and emotional condition. They seem uninterested in their children's internal mental states, and so fail to track or respond to their baby's signals and cues, all of which is distressing and confusing to the young mind.

Depressed mothers also report high levels of parenting stress. They find their children fussy and difficult. When asked about their own history, they describe more negative life events than controls. Although this uninterested, unresponsive, irritable caregiving upsets and dysregulates young children, the affect goes unnoticed; the parent-induced disruptions are left unacknowledged and unrepaired. Lacking much experience of parental mind-mindedness and emotional reciprocity, the child learns little about the relationship between thoughts, feelings and behaviour in both the self and others. Emotional literacy is poor. As a result, young children fail to develop good emotional self-regulation, so characteristic of secure toddlers.

Children's Behaviour, Development and Attachment

Depression, of course, is associated with flat affect. The parent's face conveys little emotional information. The voice is weary and slow. The face and the voice are two important methods of actively engaging with infant minds. If these communication channels are closed down, huge amounts of psychosocial and emotional information are denied the developing baby. There is little synchrony between the parent's and infant's mental states, which is highly distressing to the child. And yet that confusion and distress, triggered by the unresponsive parent, goes unacknowledged and unrepaired by the carer. This is yet another example of 'fear without solution' which leads to disorganized attachments.

Children of depressed mothers don't expect support, don't anticipate relief from distress and don't know how to regulate their feelings. 'Because they don't expect ruptures to be repaired, they don't turn to others. Because they have not been taught to focus on solving problems step by step, they cannot imagine solutions' (Gerhardt 2004: 131). Other than running away or escaping into alcohol/drugs despair, there is nowhere to go with their sadness and distress.

High rates of disorganized attachment have consistently been found in young children of chronically and severely depressed mothers (for example, Teti et al. 1995; van IJzendoorn, Schuengel and Bakermans-Kranenburg 1999). Teti's (1999) study of depressed mothers found that nine out of the eleven children were 'behaviourally disorganized'. Under stress they failed to display any coherent attachment strategies. 'Indeed, this group was clearly the most maladapted of all attachment groupings for both maternal and child indicators of functioning' (Teti 1999: 229). Dawson et al. (1999) found that infants of depressed mothers, unable to use their parent as a safe, secure, regulating base, were less affectionate and less likely to touch their mothers during free play. The children also seemed to find it difficult to remain calm and emotionally regulated when mildly challenged or stressed. With depressed carers, many young children appear either fretful and fussy, or emotionally flat. In fact, in a study by Field (1992), as early as three months old infants of depressed mothers also began to behave in a depressed way with both their mothers and other people.

Severe and chronic maternal depression predicts increased rates of poor self-regulation, poor peer relationships, negative self-image, behavioural problems, problems with sleep, a proneness to inactivity, weak academic performance, and mood disorders in children. Some children are socially withdrawn. Many have problems of concentration and deficits in attention. By adolescence, children of unipolar and bipolar depressed mothers show high rates of disruptive, depressed and anxious behaviour. In fact, a good predictor of disruption, depression and other affective disorders in adolescence is disruptive behaviour in the pre-school years.

A study by Graham and Easterbrooks (2000) found an association between depressive symptomatology in mothers and depression in children aged between seven and nine. Although there was no clear link between maternal depression and insecure attachments, children who were insecurely attached were at increased risk of suffering depression. Children of the most depressed mothers displayed the highest levels of depression. They were also the most likely to show disorganized/controlling attachment behaviours. Children who had depressed mothers, were insecurely attached, and lived in economic poverty and stress were most at risk of depression. As Egeland and Carlson (2004: 42) conclude, ' early childhood experiences of dysregulation have an enduring effect on depressive symptomatology ... because early experiences influence the interpretation of subsequent experiences'.

The work of Radke-Yarrow (1999) gives further insights into the effects on children's psychosocial development when they experience the complex emotional environments generated by depressed parents. The main characteristics of their parenting are:

- *Irritable, negative and angry approach to life and child rearing, with a tendency to use strong verbal, critical controls.* This style of caregiving undermines children's self-esteem and confidence that other people are interested and available at times of need. Irritable-negative parenting during the child's first three years is strongly predictive of a disruptive disorder.
- *Dependent on their children for support, self-gratification and help; over involved and enmeshed.* This pattern of parenting manipulates the child's dependency needs and ability to be autonomous. The style of caregiving tends to make

children fussy, and anxious about being self-running and independent. Enmeshed mothering during the child's first three years is also strongly predictive of later disruptive behaviour.
- Combined caregiving characteristics in which parents display both anger/irritability/negativity, and enmeshed dependency.

In Radke-Yarrow's study (1999: 133), nearly half of both unipolar and bipolar depressed mothers were rated angry/irritable. Forty per cent of the fathers were also classified as angry, with a marked tendency to become violent in some cases. As children grow older, more depressed mothers and fathers were described as irritable and negative in their outlook on life and parenting. Thus, for the majority of children of depressed parents, their environment tends to grow more bleak and harsh. A few depressed mothers showed extremely uninvolved caregiving, being unavailable and unresponsive to most of their child's needs. Radke-Yarrow (1999: 131) describes this as 'zombie-like', with some of the characteristics of depressed neglect (see Chapter 8).

As an illustration, Radke-Yarrow (1999: 48–53) describes the case of Mrs J. who suffered bipolar depression, while her husband had major depression. They had two children, Margaret and Michael. The parents separated when the children were still young:

> In the [observational] apartment, both children appeared distressed. Margaret (5 years) acted assertively and independently – but warily. Michael (3 and a half years) was very insecure and would not allow his mother out of his sight. When Mrs J. went into the bathroom, he called, 'I love you'.... Mrs J was grumpy with both children and could not get them to co-operate with her. She vented her anger on Margaret, 'You're nothing but trouble to me. I'll never bring you again.' Margaret threw a violent tantrum, after which Michael declared to his mother that he was not going to be her boy friend any more....
>
> Mother and children returned to the laboratory for the second research evaluation when Margaret was 8 and Michael was 6½.... Mrs J. told the children she wanted some peace and quiet for herself, wanted to watch a TV program. Mrs J. told them that if they didn't stay out of her way, she'd lock them in the bathroom.... Mrs J. yelled that she was going to put tape over Margaret's mouth. Margaret again got the blame at lunchtime. Her mother told her to stop talking and eat – hitting her for emphasis....
>
> Later both children were engaged in a puzzle task. 'Let Michael do it,' Mrs J. commanded. 'He's better than you. Thank God I don't have to be your teacher.' Margaret gave way to Michael. 'I'm so stupid aren't I, Mom?' Mrs J. agreed. In discussing the children, Mrs J. drew contrasting profiles.... Mrs J. reported feeling so angry at Margaret that she was afraid of losing control – 'I could beat her up. I could kill her. I tell her I'll give her to her father, but he probably wouldn't want her. I hate her'.... Mrs J. had a very different image of Michael. 'He's very likeable.... He really seems to know what I like...'.

It seems likely that different types of maternal depression lead children to develop various self-protective strategies (Crittenden and Clausen 2000: 244). Carers who feel weak, helpless, preoccupied and inattentive might trigger attention-seeking behaviours in their children. Such an ambivalent strategy, in which children hyperactivate their attachment behaviour and increase their levels of distress, also induces feelings of anxiety, anger, and desire for comfort and attention. In the case of an under-responsive carer, these raised levels of distress might just provoke a response, in which case heightening the level of displayed distress has some adaptive value for the child.

Depressed parents, including those who suffer bipolar depression and who are also irritable, sometimes to the point of being hostile, present their children with a different challenge. The fear experienced when being cared for by a helpless *and* hostile parent produces disorganized attachments. However, with maturation, the children of depressed and helpless/hostile carers typically develop controlling strategies around aggression, bossiness and reluctance to let others be in charge, that is, a *punitive controlling, compulsive self-reliant strategy*.

In contrast, parents who appear helpless and consumed by their own despair present children with a different challenge. If the carer cannot provide care and protection, the child increases parental availability by caring for and protecting the vulnerable parent. This is an example of role-reversal. Children begin to take charge of the relationship, not by being bossy, but by being attentive and solicitous. This *compulsive caregiving* strategy helps children avoid feeling that there is nothing that they can do to increase their feelings of security, but it comes at a developmental price, being a variant of an extreme avoidant strategy. Although the child develops a keen sense of what the vulnerable parent might be needing and feeling, the parent shows no interest in the child's needs and states of mind. Parentified children might be good at recognizing other people's emotional states, but they are poor at understanding their own. Their ability to regulate their own distress and arousal is therefore limited. Outside of the parent–child relationship they can be moody, tearful, aggressive and distraught.

Domestic Violence

Although for most children the family and the home is where they feel most safe, for a significant minority it is a place of tension and danger. These children find it difficult to find sanctuary. The people and the place that should be a safe bolt-hole when there is stress and a need for comfort in fact offer no such thing. The incidence of domestic violence in which a child witnesses aggression between his or her parents is estimated to be between 10 and 15 per cent. However, the figure for more extreme and serious forms of violence is likely to be lower. Matters can be further complicated when children not only witness violence between the adults in their lives but are also the victims of parental aggression and abuse themselves. Some estimates suggest that between 45 and 70 per cent of children exposed to domestic violence are also subjected to physical abuse (Margolin 1998: 60). It is these children who appear to suffer the highest levels of maladjustment and psychopathology (for example, Sternberg et al. 1993), including behaviour problems and, in girls, depression.

Characteristics of the Caregiving Environment

When the home is not a place of safety and protection, observes Margolin (1998: 58), 'the aggressor and the victim are the person with whom the child is most likely to identify and to whom the child would wish to turn for support'. This situation sets up a number of psychological dilemmas for children. Witnessing violence is frightening. Children look to their attachment figures for safety and comfort at times of fear and danger. However, when one parent is violent and attacking the other, there is no safe place to go; there is no one to comfort you. If violence erupts suddenly and without warning, unpredictable fear only adds to the cocktail of developmental difficulty. To compound matters, violence between parents rarely occurs on its own. Hostile verbal threats, conflict and heated arguments also occur. Alcohol and drug abuse can fuel further aggression.

As well as mete out physical abuse, some men also threaten to assault their partners sexually. The combinations of physical violence, sexual abuse, and aggressive and threatening language create an environment in which children experience psychological maltreatment. And men who abuse their children typically assault their partners (Farmer and Owen 1995). It also appears to be the case that mothers who are abused by their partners are more likely to abuse their child (Graham-Bermann 2002: 123).

Although all forms of domestic discord and violence are seen as potentially harmful to children's development, the more extreme the aggression, the more psychological impairment they are likely to suffer. So when assessing domestic violence, note should be made of its frequency, intensity and duration, and whether or not the children who witness the aggression are also assaulted themselves.

In most cases, woman abuse precedes child abuse. However, children who try to stop their father from attacking their mother – by intervening, calling the police, or trying to protect their siblings – become at increased risk of being assaulted themselves (Hilberman and Munson, quoted in Graham-Bermann 2002: 121).

Not surprisingly, mothers who are beaten up by their partners experience high levels of stress and mental health difficulties, often leading to further problems of alcoholism. All of this reduces the emotional availability of a parent who appears to be unable to protect herself, never mind her children. Male batterers also seem to have a high incidence of problem drinking, imprisonment, and personality problems, factors that add to the disturbed nature of the parent–child environment. As with substance abuse, mothers who are the victims of domestic violence are therefore highly likely to suffer a range of other problems including depression, anxiety, low self-esteem and social isolation. When this is added to the damage posed by witnessing marital conflict, children in families where there is violence are exposed to a number of other major developmental risks.

Children's Behaviour, Development and Attachment

Many children who observe and experience aggression develop aggressive and anxious behaviours themselves. Younger children in particular appear most vulnerable when they witness parental violence. Aggression becomes their preferred social strategy. Having observed violence between their parents at times of stress and conflict, they learn that relationship difficulties are resolved by threat and violence. As a result they tend not to be popular with peers, show poor leadership skills, are not very good at sharing, appear mean, and are liable to go into attack mode under social challenge. Their play is conflictual. It lacks empathy, mutuality, and intimacy (Salzinger et al. 1993, Parker and Herrera 1996). Children who see the violent effects of unequal power in close relationships, in which one parent physically dominates and abuses the other, fail to develop balanced, reciprocal relationships with their peers. These poor levels of social empathy and restricted social problem-solving ability lead to isolation and loneliness, particularly in cases in which mothers are also depressed. Social isolation is made worse by children's worries and fears of what might be happening at home – is their mother safe, alive and well?

Witnessing severe parental violence can cause post-traumatic stress disorder in children. They suffer nightmares, exaggerated startled responses to sudden stimuli, attention deficits and dissociative symptoms. They find their thoughts are frequently invaded by images of violence and danger. 'Consistent with this conceptualization,' suggest Henning et al. (1997: 502), 'children exposed to interpersonal violence have been shown to be highly reactive to subsequent expressions of anger … and increased psychological distress'. Whenever these children come across a situation in which there is conflict, aggression or upset, they become excited and aroused. Their inability to regulate these rising emotional tides means that they quickly lose control. They become angry and aggressive. It is also suggested that children who are the same sex as the victim of parental violence show higher levels of distress and later psychopathology. Some children are affected physiologically. They might develop eczema, lose their hair or become physically very withdrawn.

Overall, it is estimated that between 40 to 50 per cent of children who witness domestic violence are themselves the subjects of physical abuse, with boys possibly more likely to be targets than girls (Appel and Holden 1998, Jouriles and LeCompte 1991). Although abuse is typically at the hands of men, it is by no means unusual for mothers (whether they are the abused or the abusers within their sexual partnership) to assault their children.

There is also evidence that domestic violence is associated with increased rates of neglect and psychological maltreatment (McGuigan and Pratt 2001). Indeed, children who are exposed to spousal violence as babies are up to three times more likely than other children to suffer physical abuse, and twice as likely to experience neglect or psychological maltreatment before the age of five. This adds to the general picture which suggests that violent parents who frighten their children are also emotionally unavailable and unresponsive to deal with the fear which they have induced. Some parents, either as a result of feeling despair and helplessness, or because they have lost interest, provide little in the way of comfort or understanding.

In some cases, parents are absorbed and hopelessly involved in the violent relationship itself. They have no time for their children. The children's needs and the distress they experience watching so much turbulence and aggression are ignored. In general, parents who are physically violent towards their partner or who engage in mutual conflict tend to be more inconsistent, unresponsive, rejecting, negative, hostile and punitive towards their children. Thus, children who are most frightened by their parents' violent behaviour tend to have the least emotionally available and responsive carers to help them deal with their distress. Henning et al. found the young adults in their study:

> who witnessed interparental physical fighting during childhood were also more likely to have experienced other family stressors that might have a negative impact on their development. This includes being three times as likely to have been physically abused themselves, and being four times as likely to have had parent with a serious drinking problem. The young adults who witnessed physical fighting between their parents also observed one-half times as many acts of verbal aggression between their parents, had a higher parental divorce rate, and had a lower family of origin SES than the young adults who were never exposed to interparental physical conflict.
>
> (Henning et al. 1997: 510)

There is evidence that even high levels of marital discord which do not involve violence nevertheless increase the chances of children developing disorganized/controlling attachment behaviours (Owen and Cox 1997). Marital discord may also evoke role-reversing and controlling behaviours in older children, who play the role of protective carer for one of the parents. Compulsive caregiving by children of helpless mothers who are the victims of domestic violence is not unusual. These children feel anxious when they are away from their mothers, believing that their presence reduces the likelihood of male partners brutally attacking the weaker parent.

Of course, many women who are attacked seek refuge in shelters with their children. Not only are such moves stressful for mothers and children, it can also cut children off from their friends and the support of peer relationships. Bearing in mind these compounding effects, there is evidence that compared with children who have not witnessed violence, children in women's refuges and shelters are more likely to develop emotional and behavioural problems (Fantuzzo et al. 1991, cited in McCloskey and Stuewig 2001: 85).

Marital violence and conflict have been associated with increased risk of distress and maladjustment among children of all ages (Handal, Tschannen and Searight 1998; Jouriles et al. 1996; McNeal and Amato 1998). Problems can continue into adulthood, with those exposed to interparental aggression being more prone to depression, anxiety, stress, substance abuse and hostility in relationships themselves.

Domestic violence impairs children's ability to forge good-quality friendships with their peers. And the knock-on effect of this is that children who do not enjoy good social interaction with their peers are at risk of later life maladjustment and mental health problems (McCloskey and Stuewig 2001).

Interventions that aim to help children forge and maintain good quality friendships increase resilience.

> Interventions oriented to promoting important social skills, including empathy and prosocial engagement, are obviously much needed for children of battered women, and especially in shelters. In addition, interventions designed to support the mothers have been shown to be effective in reducing children's problem behaviours.
>
> (McCloskey and Stuewig 2001: 94)

Conclusion

Taken on their own, drugs, depression and domestic violent each increase the risk of children developing disorganized and controlling patterns of attachment. In practice, they are also typically associated with abuse and neglect. The combination of drugs, violence and deprivation produces wild and unpredictable caregiving environments. Little wonder that with the rise in the number of drug and alcohol-misusing parents, child health and welfare agencies are finding that more and more of their cases involve substance abuse by one or both parents. When depression and domestic violence are also present, children are at major risk of developing a range of behavioural and mental health problems.

12

Child Sexual Abuse

Introduction

It is only over the last 20 years or so that the extent of child sexual abuse has been fully recognized. Exact figures depend on how sexual abuse is being defined. Broad definitions have identified prevalence rates ranging between 10 and 30 per cent for girls.

Any sexual activity between an adult and a child, or between an older child and a younger child, might be defined as abusive:

> Contact sexual activities include penetrative acts (e.g. penile, digital, or object penetration of the vagina, mouth, or anus) and non-penetrative acts (e.g. touching or sexual kissing of sexual parts of the child's body, or through the child touching sexual parts of the abuser's body). Non-contact sexual activities include exhibitionism, involving the child in making or consuming pornographic material, or encouraging two children to have sex together.
>
> (Jones 2002: 1825)

Physical injuries to the vagina, breasts, penis or anus are often caused by sexual abuse.

Females can and do sexually abuse children. However most abuse is carried out by males, including fathers, stepfathers, mothers' partners, brothers, grandfathers, uncles, as well as friends of the family including neighbours and babysitters. Carers who are emotionally detached, violent, or who abuse alcohol or drugs increase the risk of leaving their children prey to sexual abuse (Berliner and Elliot 1996). Children between the ages of seven and 13 are most likely to be abused, although reports suggest that as many as a quarter of all cases involve children aged under five. Although girls are more likely to be sexually abused than boys, it should not be underestimated how often boys are the victims of this kind of assault (Holmes and Slap 1998). There is some evidence that boys tend to be a little older when they are first abused, and the abuser is more likely either to be a female carer or someone outside the family. According to Westcott and Jones (1999), children with a disability are at almost double the risk of sexual abuse. This risk increases further for those children with either a physical or learning disability living in some form of residential or health care provision (Sullivan and Knutson 1993, cited in Knutson 1995: 413).

Characteristics of the Caregiving Environment

Families in which children are sexually abused tend to be amongst the least cohesive and most stressful and disorganized (Egeland and Sroufe 1991; Pianta, Egeland and Erikson 1989). There is typically a lack of emotional closeness between members, although unexpressed knowledge that abuse is taking place might cause the disengagement as much as the disengagement causes the abuse. Communications between family members are poor, lacking clarity, flexibility, tolerance and emotional closeness (Berliner and Elliot 2002: 57). When emotions are expressed, they are aggressive, negative or impulsive. Anxiety, low self-esteem and uncertainty in the conduct of social relationships also seem a feature of the adults who live in sexually abusive families. In some cases this might explain why there is an attraction to children, in which the balance of control and power lies with the socially insecure and anxious adult. Children's dependence, weakness and reduced ability to evoke inadequacy and mete out ridicule increase their appeal. This is in marked contrast to the abuser's difficulties in maintaining and sustaining close relationships with other adults.

Family house moves are frequent. Both parents and partners often take drugs or get drunk on alcohol. Alcohol is a powerful reducer of inhibitions. Male partners are often physically violent with the children's mother, who typically feels depressed, helpless, confused and angry. When mothers are absorbed by their own need to protect themselves, children feel unsafe, vulnerable and frightened.

Maker, Kemmermeier and Peterson (1999) found that parents who were high on counts of criminal behaviour, stealing, arrests, violence and lying (sociopaths) predicted sexual abuse more than drug and alcohol abuse or family dysfunction, although it is recognized that sociopaths are highly likely to be substance misusers and contribute to dysfunctional caregiving environments. Other characteristics of sociopaths are a lack of shame, remorse or guilt. Sociopathic mothers, although they might be sexually abusive themselves, are also likely to be poor at providing their children with protection. Another characteristic of these chaotic, antisocial families is their willingness to let any number of risky individuals into the household, and it is these known but unrelated others who are as likely to sexually abuse the children as direct family members.

Carers who sexually abuse their children typically coerce the child, making threats if 'their' secret is broken. The frequency and intensity of the abuse tend to increase over time, with a concomitant rise in the nature of the threat, making disclosure more difficult.

Although not in the majority, biological parents who sexually abuse their children present them with a particularly difficult set of experiences in which the attachment figure as protector is also hurtful and scary.

> The abusers lack social skills and assertiveness, and show impulse-control problems, learning difficulties, and clinical depression. Their home environments are characterised by instability, family violence, and sexual problems in their parents. Parental loss or separation is common among adolescent abusers. Between 20 and 50% of abusers have a history of childhood sexual abuse themselves. Physical abuse histories are even more common, together with deprivation and periods of substitute care in childhood.
>
> (Jones 2002: 1827)

Although most people who have suffered sexual abuse in their own childhoods do not grow up to abuse, as Jones (2002) relates, a significant minority of those who do sexually abuse children have suffered physical and sexual abuse themselves when they were younger. This still suggests that perhaps a majority of adult sexual abusers were not in fact abused themselves in childhood. The most potent predictors of who is likely to commit the most serious and prolonged sexual abuse are childhood family violence, loss of a carer, and family breakdown (Skuse et al. 1998).

When sexually abusive parents who were abused themselves as children become distressed or confused or anxious, their attachment systems become activated, but as this had been associated in the past with sexual hurt and arousal, excitement, sexual arousal and feelings of submissiveness also occur. Distress and anxiety are therefore assuaged and relieved by sexually oriented (rather than attachment-oriented) behavioural responses (Smallbone and Dadds 2000). Developing this line of analysis, Bacon suggests:

> If proximity to a child, which normally activates the attachment system, is linked to distress (normally linked to the attachment system, but here linked to sexual arousal) then there may be activation of the sexual behavioural system. It may be that sexually traumatised children learn that sexual behaviour can bring relief from internal anxiety.
>
> (Bacon 2001a: 49–50)

In a further refinement, Lyons-Ruth et al. (2004) report that whereas women who have suffered sexual abuse but not physical violence tend to become emotionally and physically withdrawn when dealing with their children's attachment needs, mothers who have experienced physical abuse (with or without sexual abuse) are at risk of behaving in a more intrusive and hostile (or subtly hostile) manner with their children:

> Because clinical treatment of sexual abuse survivors clearly reveals the underlying fear and rage of those who have been victimized, we felt that both groups of

> mothers were likely to have experienced unbalanced victim or aggressor relational patterns in their families of origin. However, sexually abused mothers appeared more likely to manage their negative affects by withdrawing from interaction with their infant, whereas mother who had been exposed to violence or physical abuse appeared to handle their underlying fear by identifying with an aggressive style of interaction.
>
> (Lyons-Ruth et al. 2004: 77)

Women who have suffered sexual abuse during their childhoods appear to be at greater risk of a range of mental health and behavioural problems. These include heavy drinking and possible alcoholism, substance abuse, being the victim of domestic violence, and depression. Each of these is likely to impair parent–infant interactions. For example, a study by Buist and Janson (2001) found that amongst depressed mothers, those who also had a childhood history of sexual abuse were likely to be the most depressed, and depressed for a longer period. They also had more impaired, stressful interactions with their babies which, coupled with higher life stresses, produced a more anxious caregiving environment. The researchers had a sense that some mothers had a fear for, and continuing need to protect their toddlers from, the abuse that they had suffered as children. However, these mothers tended to offer less comfort to their distressed babies, 'perhaps because of their own ongoing need for comfort and difficulties nurturing their child when their own dependency needs had been unmet' (Buist and Janson 2001: 917).

When accused of their abuse, sexual offenders tend to (i) deny categorically that it took place, (ii) downplay its significance or harmfulness, or (iii) suggest that the child was a willing partner who sought or enjoyed the experience. These explanations and 'justifications' are all forms of cognitive distortion (Blumenthal, Gudjonsson and Burns 1999). Some fathers confuse the young child they are sexually abusing by behaving as if the abuse never took place, and persuade them that if they ever did tell anyone, they would never be believed. Macdonald (2000) neatly summarizes the main aspects of the sexual abusing adult as modelled by Finkelhor (1984), reminding us that the mind of the perpetrator remains a difficult one fully to fathom:

> [O]ffenders are conceptualised as adults who find relationships with children less threatening than those with adults ... and who enjoy children's dependent and relatively weak status. They are, for reasons not well understood, sexually attracted to children, and have difficulties in establishing and sustaining relationships with other adults. In order for these predisposing factors to lead to abuse, the taboos against sexual activity with children must be weakened or over-ruled by overcoming internal and external inhibitions. Cognitive distortions ... in which children are seen as inviting abuse, or benefiting from it (or at least not being harmed), may contribute to the breakdown of internal inhibitions, as may alcohol or substance misuse. External inhibitions may be overcome by cultivating relationships with

children, and securing a situation in which abuse can take place. Threatening or bribing a child to stay quiet constitute the 'final' piece of this particular explanatory jig-saw, or 'offending map'.

(Macdonald 2000: 96–7)

Children's Behaviour and Development

Sexual abuse is likely to be most harmful, suggests Corby (2000: 181), where the abusive act involves penetration; where the abuse has persisted for some time; where the abusive figure is a father figure; where the abuse is accompanied by force, violence or threat; and where the response of the family is negative. Although some children do disclose, many do not. Investigating sexual abuse is difficult, although children whose behaviour appears highly sexualized, either towards themselves or others, might well be the victims of sexual abuse. Children whose non-abusing carer believes them when they say they have been sexually abused and tries to protect them, appear to cope best with the abuse. Parents who neither believe nor support their children leave them to face both the aggressor and the trauma of the abuse alone. In the face of such trauma, children typically feel helpless as well as extremely frightened. Although some children, particularly those who are believed and supported, can appear relatively symptom-free, those who have suffered more extreme, prolonged and violent abuse, whether or not they are believed, are highly likely to show a range of serious psychological impairments.

Many children who suffer sexual abuse experience pain, shame, fear and confusion. Sexual abuse by carers and attachment figures poses particularly difficult problems for children. The role of adults as carers and protectors breaks down. A few adults try to cocoon the abuse with words of love. This adds a further layer of confusion in the young mind. Feeling frightened and confused in a relationship in which there is talk of care and love leaves a terrible legacy in which the maturing child has a very peculiar, distorted version of what it means to be in a loving relationship. However, threat and coercion are much more likely to be used by adults who sexually abuse children.

It is now well established that children who have been sexually abused are at risk of a range of mental health and behaviour difficulties, particularly those who are not believed or supported by their non-abusing carer. Their experience is that other people's needs are more important than theirs. They feel controlled and victimized. They experience subjugation. Fergusson, Horwood and Lynskey (1996) found that sexual abuse in childhood accounted for between 10 and 20 per cent of the risk of psychiatric disorder in young adults. Although Browne and Finkelhor (1986, cited in Corby 2000: 178) found that sexual abuse only predicted about one-fifth of adult female psychopathology, the more severe or prolonged the abuse, the more likely and serious was the psychopathology likely to be (Lange et al. 1999). However, given the alleged prevalence of sexual abuse (as high as 20 to 30 per cent in some studies of female victims, a figure 'far in excess of the base rate of the presumed adverse consequences of the event'), many abused girls appear to avoid developing serious mental health problems (Knutson 1995: 421). As we have seen, the major protective factor to help children survive sexual abuse is a carer who believes the allegation, and is able to help the child think accurately about his or her feelings and where the blame actually lies.

The risk of psychopathology also appears to increase if the sexual abuse was either suffered chronically or was acutely traumatic. Knutson, reviewing the research literature, notes that:

> sexual abuse characterized by greater force and penetration are associated with more severe outcomes. Also, more frequent abuse and longer duration abuse are associated with more adverse outcomes. The most consistent finding reflected in the sexual abuse literature has been that sexual abuse is associated with some degree of sexual maladjustment, often characterized by sexual precocities, promiscuity, or sexual aggression.
>
> (Knutson 1995: 422)

Sexual abuse can impair children's (i) physical and motor development, (ii) social and emotional development, and (iii) cognitive and academic development (Trickett and Putnam 1998). The impact on each of these developmental domains also depends on the child's age. In their review of the research literature, Trickett and Putnam (1998) highlight the following findings:

> *Pre-school children*: the major problems seems to be somatic (enuresis, stomach aches, headaches); inappropriate sexual behaviour (masturbating excessively or in public), internalizing problems (anxiety, withdrawal), and developmental delays.
>
> *Middle childhood*: Physically, some children suffer enuresis, immune dysfuntions, and genital abnormalities. Inappropriate sexual activities continue to be a possible effect. About a third of children who have been sexually abused seem at specific risk of developing sexualized behaviour and other sexual problems. Even young children might mimic sexual intercourse, insert objects into their own and other people's anus or vagina (Friedrich et al. 2001). For some children, being inappropriately sexual with other people is the only way they know about how to love and get close to people. As adolescents, some boys who have been sexually abused show an increased likelihood of exposing their genitals to women, or being sexually coercive. Some girls become sexually, and often indiscriminately very active. Anxiety, aggression and conduct disorders also are common problems shown by adolescents who have suffered sexual abuse when younger. In more traumatic cases, children may show symptoms of dissociation. Peer relationships are sometimes poor, and low self-esteem remains a high risk. Cognitive and academic development is also in danger of being impaired.

> *Adolescence and adulthood*: The findings for adolescents and adults are very similar to those found in younger children, with very low self-esteem and somatic complaints featuring across the age range. However, adolescent children are much more likely to be sexually active, delinquent, and in some cases, depressed and suicidal. A frequent finding is that seriously and chronically abused children often exhibit unusual and inappropriate sexual behaviour with their peers, siblings or new carers (Trickett 1997: 409). Sexual promiscuity can get both young boys and girls into regular social difficulties. In the case of early sexual activity amongst sexually abused girls is the risk of teenage pregnancy. The increased risk of sexual dysfunction and impaired occupational attainment is characteristic of many adults who have been abused as children.

Sexual abuse impairs children's ability to understand emotions and regulate their arousal. Severe physical and sexual abuse can traumatize children. Victims are therefore at increased risk of post-traumatic stress disorder (PTSD), and 'post-traumatic symptoms' which include hypervigilance, intrusive thoughts, sleep problems, nightmares, intrusive thoughts, feelings of helplessness, avoidance, numbing, and flashbacks of the abuse experience (Kendall-Tackett 2002: 725). Some sexually abused children become so dysregulated, they suffer depression, internalizing and externalizing behavioural problems, and peer relationship difficulties. They tend to deny feeling emotionally needy, and yet they display high levels of emotional lability, inappropriate emotional outbursts, low levels of emotional awareness, and little emotional empathy. In challenging social situations, they often seem to be psychologically disengaged and emotionally switched off. When they reach adulthood, sexually abused children are at risk of experiencing a range of psychopathologies and problem behaviours including low self-esteem, major depression, anxiety, substance abuse, self-harming behaviour, suicide, running away from home, prostitution, early pregnancy, sudden feelings of rage and fear, obsessive-compulsive disorders, and eating disorders (Berliner and Elliott 1996, Widom and Kuhns 1996, Jones 2002: 1826).

There is growing evidence that the stress of serious sexual abuse results in long-term changes in the brain's organization and chemistry, and that these effects probably underlie the symptoms of PTSD and other stress-related disorders (Bremner and Vermetten 2001). In their review of the literature, Berliner and Elliott (2002: 63) calculate that as many as 36 per cent of adult survivors suffer PTSD. The more forceful and violent the abuse, the more the individual is likely to suffer trauma. As an extension of PTSD, dissociation also appears to be a common reaction, particularly when sexual abuse is combined with physical abuse, and in cases where the victim has suffered sexual abuse by more than one person. Dissociation is an unconscious way of trying to protect the psyche from being overwhelmed by memories of the traumatic experience by keeping such thoughts out of awareness. In states of dissociation, victims feel disconnected and distant from their violated bodies. This helps the child block from awareness intense and overwhelming feelings of fear, pain and distress (Wickham and West 2002: 117). 'For victims of especially severe abuse,' observe Berliner and Elliott (2002: 63), 'the trauma may be overwhelming, making it difficult for the survivor to fully integrate the events cognitively and thus reinforce a mechanism that reduces complete awareness of the trauma.' Anderson and Alexander (1996) found that childhood sexual abuse increased the likelihood of adults developing fearful, disorganized attachments with dissociative symptoms. However, a number of studies have found that the trauma of sexual and physical abuse has to occur before the age of three or four if it is to predict dissociation (Ogawa et al. 1997: 874).

Sexually abused preschoolers, when asked to develop attachment-related stories, tend to depict themselves and their parents only somewhat negatively, but they do engage in controlling and non-responsive behaviours with the researchers that increase over time. Toth et al. (2000: 293) suggest that such controlling behaviour might be a form of 'defensive exclusion to minimize the pain or to avoid the distress associated with their caregiving experiences'.

The functionalist argument, which says that within the context of the caregiving relationship, children develop adaptive and survival strategies, reminds us that many of the emotional limitations shown by sexually abused children actually make sense when viewed in context. Suppressing anger, and not reflecting on their fear and pain when in relationship with a sexually abusing adult, help children survive both physically and psychologically. This helps prevent young minds feeling that their coping strategies are in danger of being totally overwhelmed with fear and arousal. For example, perpetrators might threaten rejection or bodily harm if the child gets upset or contemplates telling someone else about the abuse.

Nevertheless, these survival strategies impair normal psychosocial development. Shipman et al. (2000) found that sexually maltreated girls demonstrated poor levels of emotional understanding and higher levels of emotional dysregulation than their non-maltreated peers. When asked how would they respond to someone else's upset or anger, they said things such as 'I wouldn't do anything because it's their problem', in contrast to maltreated girls who had not suffered sexual abuse and who typically said, 'I'd ask them what happened and try to make them feel un-mad' (Shipman et al. 2000: 57). The *avoidant* adaptive strategies that might have marginally increased their safety with their abusers unfortunately serve them poorly when trying to make and maintain friendships. The maltreated girls were also less confident that others would respond sympathetically, particularly if they displayed anger. The authors suggest these girls had 'more difficulty accurately appraising the causes and consequences of emotionally arousing situations, fail to respond to emotional displays by others in a culturally appropriate manner, and maintain lower levels of awareness of their own emotional experience' (Shipman et al. 2000: 56–7). All of this interferes with their ability to maintain constructive relationships with family and friends. For example, there is evidence that teenage mothers who have been sexually abused are more likely to neglect, physically abuse their own children, or have partners who are a danger to their children (Boyer and Fine 1991, cited in Berliner and Elliott 2002: 60). Lyons-Ruth et al. (2003) observe that many mothers who had been sexually abused as children tended to show decreased levels of involvement with their own children.

Wickham and West (2002) give the example of George, aged seven, who showed symptoms of dissociation. He suffered neglect, and often came to school hungry, dishevelled and smelling of urine. His attendance was poor. His mother Sarah was described as 'very dysfunctional'. Sarah had experienced physical abuse for most of her life, and was suspected of having dissociative identity disorder (DID). She felt overwhelmed and could not control any of her three children. The children witnessed their father physically abusing their mother. They were also sexually abusing each other. There were suspicions that their father had sexually abused them. As a child, the father had suffered physical and sexual abuse himself.

> George ... was frequently very aggressive towards other children in his class. Following one incident, where he stabbed another child with a pencil, he was referred to the school counsellor for weekly sessions ... [in which] ... he appeared to be spaced out and did not hear her, or respond to the things she said. George seemed not to remember previous sessions with her. He described himself as a different person each day; he spoke of being a monster, a pirate, or a villain from a television show, and often talked of his 'friends' who went everywhere with him ... During a holiday break from school, George reported trying to kill himself by running into traffic. He was slightly injured.
>
> (Wickham and West: 123–4)

As we have noted, adult survivors of sexual abuse are at increased risk of a range of physical and mental health problems. These are generally mediated by poor self-concepts, unsupportive and dangerous social relationships, and unhealthy life styles including substance abuse, eating problems and sleeping difficulties. Sadly, revictimization is not uncommon. Fergusson, Horwood and Lynskey (1996) found that women with a history of sexual abuse were more likely to have been raped or physically abused by their partners. In psychiatric clinical samples, the numbers who suffer further sexual violence increase still further. In particular, female patients with borderline personality disorders appear the most likely group to have suffered both childhood and adulthood sexual abuse, including rape by partners and unknown assailants. Zanarini et al. (1999) found that five types of childhood experience seemed to predict the likelihood of adult revictimization: physical neglect by a caregiver, emotional withdrawal by a caretaker, a caretaker's failure to provide protection, sexual abuse by a non-caretaker, and any type of sexual abuse. Moreover the stress and physical danger involved in such abuse make it more likely that adult victims also suffer heart disease, depression and, of course, sexually transmitted diseases.

In a community sample of female abuse survivors, Teegan (1999) found that 93 per cent felt fearful whenever they met situations that in some way held reminders of their past abuse. Half of the women felt 'mistrusting', which gave them a negative outlook on life. In fact, on a more general note, women with histories of childhood sexual abuse are more likely than non-abused women to say that their health is poor (Moosey and Shapiro 1982, cited in Kendall-Tackett 2002: 723).

The Child's Behaviour and Mental State as an Adaptive, Coping and Survival Strategy

As we have seen throughout this book, different types of abuse have very different impacts on children's development, behaviour and mental health. In the same context, the attachment behaviours and adaptive strategies used to try to stay safe will vary as the type of abuse varies. For example, Bacon (2001b: 61), acknowledging the useful distinction made by Wyatt and Higgs, suggests that children who disclose sexual abuse are more likely to have a secure attachment with the believing, non-abusing parent. Children who have secure attachments with a believing mother are also likely to suffer fewer behavioural and developmental setbacks.

In contrast, children who suffer more violent sexual abuse and who have avoidant and disorganized attachments with unprotective carers, whether they are the abusers or not, rarely disclose. They tend to display aggressive and sexualized behaviour. Their carers are more likely to have mental health problems and to have been physically and sexually abused themselves. Moreover, in terms of the adult–child relationship, sexual abuse is not a uniform phenomenon. Crittenden (1996) speculates that the motives behind parents who sexually abuse their children may differ depending on their attachment classification. It might also be the case that the attachment behaviour and manner of caregiving of the sexually abusive adult have different adaptive challenges and developmental implications for the child victim. Alexander (1992: 189) also agrees 'that long-term effects of sexual abuse, although obviously related to the specific nature of the abuse, are better understood according to a classification of the important attachment relationships concurrent with the abuse'. The range and subtlety are many, but for the purposes of illustration, three types of sexual abuse and their impact on children's adaptive responses and psychosocial development are identified:

- Sexual abuse without physical abuse.
- Sexual abuse with physical abuse.
- Sexual abuse framed by the perpetrator as the expression of love.

Sexual Abuse Without Physical Abuse

As in other types of major maltreatment, children who are abused by their attachment figures experience fear with escape. The source of danger and confusion is the person who should normally be the one who provides safety and emotional containment. For example, in disengaged, dismissing, deactivated caregiving environments, spousal relationships might be ones of:

> distance, withdrawal and rejection. Sexual abuse might reflect a desperate attempt at a relationship … while, nevertheless, allowing the participants to remain psychologically distant and unavailable. If such a pattern exists, it would be likely that the perpetrators would highly condemn such behaviour and, like victimised children who forget the traumatising incident, the perpetrators might forget or deny their participation. To professionals, they would appear as incalcitrant, denying men who are willing to accept separation from their own families rather than admit their behaviour and accept treatment.
>
> (Crittenden 1996: 165–6)

Children who have been sexually abused in relationships in which there has been no form of physical abuse, other than the sexual abuse itself, experience fear, shame and confusion. Although no actual physical violence has taken place, the adult might issue threats about what might happen if the child reports the abuse. In such situations, children are likely to feel scared and helpless. Although the overt strategy with the adult might be one of compulsive compliance, the level of stress experienced by the child easily threatens the fragile coherence conferred by the compliant strategy.

As an attempt to maintain some kind of relationship with the non-abusing, but not-protecting parent (often the mother), some children develop role-reversed behaviours. Children comfort their helpless, unprotecting mother rather than receiving comfort themselves, while at the same time the child accommodates the sexual abuse of the father as a way of trying to keep the family together. 'The abuse remains undisclosed because the child fears that the non-abusing carer will be unable to cope' (Bacon 2001a: 46). In another variation of role-reversal, some 'children adopt the role and expectations of parents, perhaps becoming sexual partners to the parent or nurturing rather than being nurtured' (Bacon 2001a: 46). And one further twist might see a child believing that he or she is left unsafe and unprotected by the attachment figure because he/she is neither lovable nor worthy.

When coherence breaks down, the child becomes disorganized, without a strategy. At such times sexually abused children feel confusing mixtures of helplessness, anger and fear. At school, they might suddenly cry. Or they might become angry and aggressive. Since they feel powerless and ashamed, self-esteem inevitably is low. All of this is a recipe for depression. The compliant, conforming pattern of behaviour often persists into adulthood. This might partly explain why some sexually abused women continue to behave passively or in emotionally detached ways in their adult relationships, increasing their risk of further sexual abuse and debasement.

Sexual abuse, therefore, predicts increased difficulty in intimate relationship in which issues of trust and reciprocity have to be present if the relationship is to work well. The sexually abused child finds it difficult to develop mentally coherent and well-integrated representations of caring and protective relationships, and these difficulties often continue into adulthood. These 'dissociated' features of the victims of sexual abuse become even more pronounced when the relationship with their abuser contains elements of physical assault and violence.

Sexual Abuse With Physical Abuse

The combination of sexual abuse, physical abuse, threat and hostility creates an extremely difficult environment for children. Danger, shame and unpredictability undermine mental coherence. They generate frightening, threatening worlds in which the young child feels constantly vulnerable and profoundly helpless within the context of the abusive relationship, the colluding family, and the disbelieving mother. Menacingly, the abuser may threaten to drown, injure or maim the child, or do harm to the mother if the child does not do as the abuser wishes, or fails to keep the secret of what is happening.

Equally frightening, if not more so, the abuser might also tell the child that if he or she does tell anyone of the abuse, some supernatural, ever-present, ever watchful and evil force will either torture or kill them. In other words, even if the abuser himself is not present or does not hear the child disclosing, murderous powers will know and will act. There is no escape. One seven-year-old girl was told by her grandfather that 'the fairies would come after her and kill her if she didn't do what he wanted' (Bacon 2001b: 69). In these mad, terrifying, distorted worlds, it is little wonder that children comply with the abuse and keep the secret, finding it too frightening even to contemplate disclosure other than in the most indirect and coded way. Children therefore suffer a bewildering combination of secrecy and denial in which reality feels as if it is breaking down (Draijer and Langeland 1999: 383).

Family life is often characterized by violence and uncertainty. In grooming the child, the abuser creates a bewildering world in which truth, certainty and trust become utterly unreliable. Children soon lose their bearings and all confidence in themselves and others. Loss of control over what happens to you is particularly stressful and disorganizing. As we have noted several times already, the most disturbing and frightening environments are those that are both dangerous and unpredictable. Never knowing when the next assault will happen means that nowhere or no time is ever safe. The child can never relax or be off guard.

In cases of more systematic and ritual abuse, the child is further terrorized by witnessing and being made to participate in degrading and horrendously violent and sexual acts (Sinason 2002). In cases of organized and ritual violent sexual abuse, children might also be drugged, adding further to their disorientation and profound feelings of unreality. The only defence in such traumatic situations is to dissociate, to cut oneself off from all feeling and sensation. Children quickly learn to develop deeply self-protective behaviours; 'to be dumb, invisible, left alone, and not interfered with' (Steele 2003: 355). These traumatic experiences 'ultimately destroy the developing personality' (Steele 2003: 355). Rather than physical closeness with attachment figures being associated with the relief of distress, it is associated with physical and sexual abuse, starvation, torture and witnessing the bloody deaths of animals in acts of sacrifice. Although the defence of dissociation is understandable, it predicts serious psychopathology, post-traumatic stress disorder, and dissociated identity disorder.

Fear and hurt experienced during acts of unwelcome intimacy are particularly confusing. Sex, closeness, even feelings of bewildered arousal, are associated with danger and helplessness. The abusing adult, who might be an attachment figure, is experienced sometimes as hurtful and frightening, sometimes negligent, sometimes friendly and supportive. In these emotionally shifting relationships, the distressed child develops many different representations of what caregiving is like. As a result, no consistent, smoothly integrated model forms of how carers and adults 'work'. The abuser's behaviour feels unpredictable.

There is little that the child can do to increase feelings of safety. Avoidant strategies based on denial of distress and not showing need might bring some measure of protection. But generally the adult's unpredictable, hostile and sexually abusive behaviour is beyond the control of the child. At times of distress and danger, the child's attachment behaviour remains disorganized, his or her emotions profoundly dysregulated.

Sexual danger is ever present and can happen at any time, without build-up or warning. The father's footsteps on the stairs on the way up to the bedroom, the sudden and aggressive rape by an uncle, a mother's collaboration with a brother's demand for sexual contact, leave the child feeling that there is no hiding place. At times of need, carers are either not available or cannot be trusted. Parents can flip from being caring to hostile. These experiences can lead to multiple and conflicting mental representations of caregiving. In such a world, the character of other people with whom one is in close relationship feels arbitrary and confusing. All of this is stressful. Trying to survive, remaining alert, avoiding potentially dangerous situations, and diffusing fears take up most of the child's psychological energy. Little is left over for play and exploration. Mental representations of what carers mean contain all these conflicting, unintegrated elements.

As with other severely maltreated children, whenever the traumatically and sexually abused child experiences attachment-related issues, the extreme and anxious arousal triggered by the event activates one or other of these unintegrated mental representations of what to expect from a caregiver at times of need. The severely and chronically abused child one moment might be loving and seductive, the next aggressive, and later still be sad, frightened, tearful and helpless. When there is no escape, levels of attachment behaviour and stress increase further. In these emotionally escalating conditions, the child might go beyond hyperarousal and disappear into a trance-like, benumbed, dissociated state, absenting his or her psychological self from the bodily event. In these extreme conditions, mind and body disconnect. The psychologically shut-down child feels nothing. Under intolerable conditions, the extreme defence is to freeze – to absent oneself from one's own body and mind. If you are not there and you don't exist, you do not have to process the pain and fear. Under the fear and helpless distress of being physically and sexually abused, a dissociative response means that:

> (T)hinking and feeling are avoided, or become disconnected. If an abuser tells the child, 'this isn't hurting you', while at the same time the child experiences pain, the only way the child can achieve coherence is to block out either the words or the bodily sensations. Children who cannot listen to what people say, or cannot allow feelings to register, cannot effectively solve problems. They may also resort to self-harming actions when emotionally distressed, because of the anaesthetising effect will dull the pain and reduce unbearably high arousal and anxiety.
>
> (Bacon 2001a: 52)

Dissociation is a strong factor in causing the child to engage in self-destructive or self-harming behaviour in present or later life. Self-mutilation is frequently associated with the use of dissociation as a central defence mechanism, and is strongly linked with sexual abuse. It is most frequently experienced by adolescent and adult survivors, although children may also engage in related activities such as head banging, pulling out hair, engaging in risky behaviour, deliberately injuring themselves, or other forms of self-harm. The individual may behave in this way to stop flashbacks or painful affect coming into consciousness. Self-harm may be a way of feeling physical pain, as a confirmation of being alive, or of distracting awareness from intra-psychic pain to what is experienced as more tolerable, physical pain. This behaviour is also used as a way of gaining control, or self-soothing (releasing tension and anxiety) or as a powerful and disturbing way of expressing rage at oneself and others (Wickham and West 2002: 122). At the neurological level, and perhaps more plausibly, self-harm produces analgesic effects generated by the production of opiode, morphine-like substances. People who self-harm often say they feel a sense of calm relief after they have cut themselves.

Although this extreme defensive response serves its immediate purpose of protecting the child from unmanageable arousal and trauma, it leaves the child with little understanding of his/her own body, emotional make-up, or how to negotiate and survive everyday relationships. These disorganized and dissociated behaviours are likely to arise whenever sexually abused children or adults find themselves in relationships where mild stress and attachment issues are present, where need and intimacy occur, or uncertainty and confusion exists. Arousal of any kind, particularly when experienced in relationship with others, can suddenly cause feelings of fear, panic and terror; shame, disgust and despair (Bacon 2001a: 48). These feelings are likely to trigger states of dissociation in which the child's (or adult's) thoughts, movements, expressions and behaviour shift wildly and erratically and fearfully. Even minor states of anxiety, stress and arousal might lead to dissociation, allowing the child or adult to become catastrophically overwhelmed by feelings of fear and danger.

In the dissociated state, the passivity and helplessness leave the individual prey to further abuse. Such traumatic experiences, requiring massive defensive measures, consume huge amounts of psychic energy in the form of hypervigilance and dissociative responses, and leave little psychological time for play, exploration, relaxed social interaction and other important developmental experiences. The use of hypervigilance is a way of trying to increase safety and survival by being watchful, trying to anticipate and avoid or diffuse the next sexual approach.

> The abuse victim quickly learns that safety is predicated upon hypervigilance. She or he may become adept at reading the slightest nuance in the abuser's demeanour or behavior, since rapid and accurate assessment of that person's psychological or emotional state may allow the victim either to avoid an abuse episode or to placate/satisfy the perpetrator before a more aversive event transpires. The child's proficiency at meeting the needs and/or avoiding the violence of the abuser, however, exacts a psychological price – the sustained attention she or he must pay to environmental threats inevitably pulls energy and focus away from the developmental task of self-awareness. At a time when loved and well-treated children are becoming acquainted with self-celebrating a developing sense of discovery, autonomy, and fledgling impressions of self-efficacy – the abuse victim is absorbed in the daily task of psychological and physical survival. Thus the defensive requirement of other-directedness implies an equivalent lack of self-awareness. As a result, the survivor may be exquisitely attuned to the experience of others, but relatively unaware of his/her own needs, issues, or dynamics. Such individuals have a difficult time moving beyond a reactive survival mode later in life.
>
> (Briere 1989: 45–6)

Sexual Abuse Framed by the Perpetrator as the Expression of Love

In enmeshed families, often characterized by disorganized or depressed neglect, generational and emotional boundaries are typically blurred. Adults are uncertain and easily distressed, anxious about their own lovability. Coercive, pleading, anxious demands are made on others and their emotional availability. And although individuals are preoccupied about relationships and other people's love and acceptance, family and friends alike are felt to be unfair, depriving, denying, while the self is experienced as fair, put-upon and victimized.

Crittenden (1995: 165) speculates that in ambivalent, enmeshed families, sexual activity reflects a desire for affection and involvement whether with spouse or children – an 'unsoothable anxiety'. According to Crittenden, sexually abusing men in these families, whose sexual inhibitions are further lowered by drugs or alcohol, are likely to admit their abuse but claim that the child invited it and enjoyed it and that it was loving. They might even show remorse, insisting it will not happen again. For these men, the greater fear is to lose family membership.

Children sexually abused by dependent, emotionally needy and weak men experience a confused presentation of love and approval, hurt and fear. 'Sexually abused children may learn that closeness equates with sexual behaviour, pain and confusion. Sexual behaviour with the caregiver may be one way that some sexually abused children achieve closeness' (Bacon 2001a: 49). The abuser couches the abuse as an act of love. Young children might begin to feel that to like and value someone requires the relationship to be sexual. And although sexual arousal is exciting, it is mixed with feelings of uncertainty, anxiety and fear. These mixed feelings are likely to make relationships desirable, but difficult and confusing. Children whose behaviour is sexualized will be rejected by peers, adding another element of developmental risk to that already posed by the sexual abuse itself.

Conclusion

Although for a long time it was seen as an uncommon, even unlikely form of abuse, sexual abuse of children is now recognized to be widespread. With the care and support of a close, believing carer, many children manage to emerge from childhood with a degree of resilience that helps them cope with the adult world. However, a depressingly large number of children not only suffer the trauma of sexual abuse, they also have to handle it without the support of other family members. Add to this neglect and other types of abuse, it is hardly surprising that so many victims of childhood sexual assaults are at major risk of mental ill health and parenting difficulties.

Part V

Interventions, Treatment and Support

Introduction

Attachment-based support, treatments and interventions are based on the recognition that the defensive exclusion of difficult and painful feelings and memories distorts and disturbs individuals, their behaviour and their relationships with others. The adaptive strategies that children develop to survive both physically and psychologically in different caregiving environments come at some developmental cost. If emotional arousal activates the attachment system triggering attachment behaviour, the sensitivity, availability and responsiveness of carers at such times affects the way children learn to handle and regulate their emotions, particularly in the context of relationships.

As we have seen, secure children are able to access and acknowledge, and then reflect on their arousal. There is little distortion and only mild use of defences. Because their carers can contain, handle and help them understand and regulate their arousal, children begin to feel competent and clear about their own ability to handle themselves well and functionally when they feel under stress or emotionally upset. Their internal working models, their mental representations of the self, others and the way relationships work and should be handled are positive and fully conscious. They can reflect reasonably honestly, accurately and realistically about their own and other people's thoughts, feelings and behaviour.

In the case of insecure children, the availability, sensitivity and responsivity of carers at times of need is not so straightforward. Avoidant and ambivalent children have to organize their attachment behaviour to increase the availability of their carer at times of need and distress. These adaptive strategies involve downplaying or excluding some types of psychological information from conscious processing.

Avoidant children, whose carers become anxious and rejecting whenever others place emotional demands on them to do with vulnerability, dependency and strong displays of attachment behaviour, cope and adapt by excluding attachment-based feelings and behaviours from conscious processing. Although children feel safest and most accepted when they are being undemanding and emotionally self-contained, they are not helped to understand or deal with their own arousal. Strong feelings worry them. Displays of weakness, dependency, need and vulnerability in the self or others makes them anxious, avoidant and rejecting. But they might be astute observers of other people's feelings and behaviour. We saw extreme avoidant-based strategies being used by children who suffer rejection, abuse and psychological maltreatment. Here the therapeutic need is to help people access, admit, acknowledge, explore and reflect on their own feelings, especially those involving need and vulnerability.

Ambivalent children, whose carers are insensitive to and poor at recognizing other people's needs and attachment signals, cope and adapt by maximizing their distress and attachment behaviour. This way they might just get noticed. Their greatest anxiety is being ignored, abandoned and left alone with needs unmet and arousal unregulated. They live an unpredictable world, in which there seems to be no guarantee that others will be there or respond at times of need and distress. They have little confidence in their own abilities to bring about change and get the things they need. This results in a passive and fatalistic attitude to events; an anxious preoccupation with other people's inconsistent emotional availability; and an angry, dissatisfied, needy, pleading and provocative approach to relationships. There is little monitoring of one's own behaviour or emotional condition. We met more pronounced versions of this attachment strategy in some types of neglect, particularly families in which there is disorganized neglect. The therapeutic need is to help people stop and reflect, to feel valued and worthwhile, and to think through the cause and consequences of their feelings and behaviour.

The group that find it most difficult to organize an attachment strategy are children whose carers are the direct cause of their distress and fear. Attachment figures who frighten, menacingly threaten, physically and sexually abuse, or abandon their children are both the source of fear and the solution to that fear. Developmentally, children suffer more complex and profound impairments as they experience the worst elements of both avoidant and ambivalent caregiving environments: emotional withdrawal at times of great distress coupled with inconsistent care. In effect, they experience unpredictable danger over which, as infants, they have little control, and can develop no attachment strategy. Their emotions remain highly dysregulated. They fail to develop coherent models and mental representations of their own or other people's psychological make-up, and so find it difficult to regulate their own arousal or deal reflectively with their own needs. With maturation, children do manage to develop fragile and more coherent representations of themselves as less helpless or at the mercy of others. With carers who are unavailable and frightening, children begin to take control of their own safety and needs, resulting in various controlling strategies, including compulsive compliance, compulsive caregiving and compulsive self-reliance. These are very partial, incomplete and brittle strategies that quickly break down under stress leaving the child once more frightening, angry, sad and highly dysregulated. The therapeutic need for these children (and their parents) is to help them feel safe enough to recognize, acknowledge and process their emotions, at both the psychological and physiological level. They only feel safe when they are in anxious control, but this strategy denies them experiences designed to help them look at, understand and handle their own and other people's minds.

A Developmental Base for Interventions, Treatment and Support

Within this developmental perspective, in which young minds are seen to form in the context of close relationships, a model of treatment and support presents itself. Insecure attachment patterns in themselves are not pathological; rather 'psychopathology is viewed as a developmental construction, resulting from ongoing transactive processes between the evolving individual and the environment in which they find themselves' (Egeland and Carlson 2004: 45). In most normative populations between 35 and 45 per cent of people might be classified insecure. Clearly the majority of these individuals will not be presenting themselves with major mental health problems. We are considering children and adults who have endured more extreme forms of pathogenic care that carries a high risk of psychopathology.

Mental representations formed during attachment seeking behaviour establishes tendencies and expectations that influence brain neurophysiology, the ability of the individual to self-regulate emotional arousal, and hence the future conduct of relationships. Thus, continue Egeland and Carlson:

> Early developmental paths are probabilistically related to later disorder and are dependent on subsequent experiences to maintain their trajectories. Change remains possible at numerous points in development, although both theory and data suggest that such change is more readily accomplished early in the process or at least where there is a foundation of early support.
>
> (Egeland and Carlson 2004: 45)

Treatment must match the developmental level of the child, or indeed parent (Schore 2001b; Holmes 2001), a notion echoed by Macfie, Cicchetti and Toth:

> when intervening with children, it is important to assess their developmental age rather than chronological age. Early stage-salient issues, such as the achievement of a secure or at least an organized pattern of attachment with caregivers, and the development of a coherent integrated self, may need to be reworked.
>
> (Macfie, Cicchetti and Toth 2001: 250)

The regulation of emotional arousal is key to success, and therefore affect regulation must be a primary target of all interventions. Attachment-based therapies aim to develop parents' capacity for empathy, mind-mindedness and reflective function. Much help that is supportive and therapeutic allows people to get in touch with their feelings, to recognize them, consider their impact on self and others, and begin to process them in a more reflective, conscious way. Even so, some emotions are difficult to bear and it may take some time and trust before they can be examined. In effect, the worker or therapist co-constructs with the other, elements of a secure attachment in order to recognize and regulate affect. This requires the establishment of a working alliance, a safe environment in which to explore affect, and a therapeutic relationship. Practitioners must therefore be highly attuned and responsive. They have to resonate with the client's affect states. Indeed, they have to amplify what they feel and perceive in the other, in the manner of the secure parent–child relationship, to ensure as much emotional and psychological information is conveyed to the other who is not used to receiving so much interest and feedback in the context of a safe relationship.

This empathic match or affect synchrony operates both inside and outside language. In the way that carers mirror their infant's affect, so too must practitioners mirror their client's affect states using their eyes, faces, voice and body language (Schore 2001b). As with developing children, this sets up mutual and attuned monitoring. The human voice and face are powerful, non-conscious channels of communication which impact directly on the affective state of the perceiver, possibly more so than what is being said. Human beings are ultra-sensitive and responsive to what they perceive to be going on in the mind of others. We get information about these states from people's facial expressions, their tone of voice, and their body language.

Dialogue is therapy. It is mind-engaging. It provokes self-reflection and thoughts about the other. Children and adults who have been maltreated are often anxious and fearful of direct mind-to-mind communication. They have learned to stay safe by not letting other people impose and intrude their demands on them (too dangerous), and by not exploring other people's minds and perspectives (too frightening, too hurtful). The maltreated individual will avoid emotional contact and robust psychological exchanges until he or she feels safe in the relationship. Practitioners and therapists therefore have to proceed very gently, backing off if the closeness, the movement, the psychological intimacy seems to be too frightening. Fear will trigger aggression or withdrawal.

When people begin to feel safe, memories and emotions can enter consciousness and be accessed, acknowledged and processed more readily. We can put words to feelings. In fact, the more safe, contained and trusting we feel, the more we are able to allow the more painful and difficult emotions to be contemplated. And as emotions suffuse the body as well as the mind, both the client and the therapist need to understand how the strong feelings of fear and anger, shame and sadness, anxiety and distress affect us physiologically.

> The promotion of affect regulation is now seen as a common mechanism in all forms of psychotherapy. Furthermore, current developmental models clearly suggest that psychotherapeutic treatment for severe attachment disorders should begin as early in the lifespan as possible.
>
> (Schore 2001b: 245)

Experiences of sensitive, mind-engaging and secure attachments promote resilience – the individual's capacity for adapting successfully and continuing to function competently under stress and adversity (Garmezy 1997; Howe et al. 1999). Large numbers of studies have shown that most maltreated children have low resilience and as a result show greater maladaptive functioning. However, some maltreated children do appear resilient and continue to cope well and with competence.

There are many treatment and intervention implications if resilience is to be promoted in maltreated children (for example, Daniel and Wassell 2002a, 2000b; Gilligan 2001). The availability of a non-maltreating, stable carer is a protective factor and is certainly associated with increased resilience. Interestingly, the pathways to resilient adaptation seem to differ between maltreated and non-maltreated children. Again, this might have implications for interventions. Specifically, ego-resiliency, ego over control, and positive self-esteem has been found to predict competence in maltreated children (Cicchetti and Rogosch 1997). In contrast, although non-maltreated children appear to have ego-resilience, they also seem to find much of their competence and resilience from the perceived emotional availability of others at times of stress and challenge, as well as a more general ability to develop positive relationships with potentially available and helpful others (for instance, parents and teachers).

> Stated differently, it appears that relationship factors may be more critical to resilient outcomes in nonmaltreated disadvantaged children, whereas personality characteristics and self-system processes may be more important for resilient outcomes in maltreated children.
>
> (Cicchetti and Rogosch 1997: 812)

Interventions designed to promote resilience in maltreated children might, therefore, pay particular attention to improving their reserve, self-confidence, independence, self-controlling, self-efficacious and rational ways of interacting and relating. It is these behaviours that are most likely to have increased their chances of remaining safe in difficult and possibly dangerous home environments. Promoting the particular resiliencies of autonomy, mastery and self-determination might make more intuitive sense to maltreated children.

Focus of Intervention

We shall review and consider three areas of intervention, support and treatment:

- parent–infant and young child interventions
- interventions with pre-school and school-aged children
- interventions with adolescents, adults and parents.

Each has the same developmental aims: (i) to increase security, and (ii) to improve mind-mindedness, emotional intelligence and self-regulation. The two aims can only be achieved in a relationship with a sensitive, mind-minded other whose own mental state with respect to attachment is 'autonomous' or secure:

> There is evidence that just one relationship with a caregiver ... who is capable of autobiographical reflection, in other words, a caregiver who possesses a high reflective self-function, can enhance the resilience of an individual. Through just one relationship with an understanding other, trauma can be transformed and its effects neutralized or counteracted.
>
> (Fosha 2003: 223)

13

Parent–Infant and Young Child Interventions

Introduction

Early preventive interventions are essentially designed to increase infants' security of attachment by improving parental sensitivity, mind-minded, responsiveness, and involvement. This might be achieved either by changing parental behaviour as they interact with their young child, or by shifting the carers' own mental representations of attachment towards greater security and autonomy. Either way, treatment is directed at modifying the way in which parents process attachment-related information. Behaviourally informed interventions teach skills aimed to increase parental sensitivity. Representational models of therapy aim to bring about more positive internal working models that generally lead to more sensitive caregiving (Cicchetti, Toth and Rogosch 2004: 233).

Interventions seek to improve the affect-communicating capacities of mother–infant interactions. The benefits of developing a secure attachment have been well rehearsed, and include good emotional self-regulation, high social cognition, raised self-esteem and increased social competence. A growing number of more rigorous, experimental and evidence-based trials are being conducted using parent–infant treatments. The effectiveness of attachment-based interventions focusing on this dyad look very promising. The big attraction in developing treatments promoting positive parent–child interactions is the recognition that early interventions are likely to be the most effective and long-lasting in helping to improve children's socio-emotional development.

It is possible to identify four different types of intervention focus (Cohen et al. 1999; Egeland et al. 2000; Juffer, Bakermans-Kranenburg and van IJzendoorn 2003):

- enhancing parental sensitivity and responsiveness, including changing the parent's *behaviour* with their infant (behavioural change)
- changing the parents' *mental representation*/working model of attachment, including their mental representation of their relationship with their infant (cognitive change by increasing insight and reflective function)

- providing enhanced social support for parents
- improving maternal mental health and well-being.

Enhancing Parental Sensitivity and Responsiveness at the Behavioural Level

Juffer et al. (2003) usefully review a number of well-researched and evaluated parent–child interventions, covering programmes with infants at risk, parents living in adversity, babies born prematurely, clinically referred children, children with developmental disabilities, and 'children in need' placed for adoption. With young children, the focus of the intervention is the quality of the parent's interactions with the infant. Treatments are designed to help carers see, understand and respond to their child's signals, particularly their distress signals. The aim is therefore to change the carer's perceptions, understandings, behaviour and interactions with the child. Programmes can range from simple low-key support to long-term psychotherapy. However, they all attempt to improve parental sensitivity, mind-mindedness, attunement and responsiveness. For example, therapists can facilitate reflective function by commenting on interactions between parent and child that seem miscued, confusing or distressing by 'asking the parent to stop and reflect on the thoughts and feelings that accompanied the negative interaction' (Kobak and Esposito 2004: 162). Through repeated use of this 'stop-the-action' technique, parents are helped to get better at monitoring, reappraising and repairing their problematic and insensitive communications with the child.

Behaviourally oriented therapies generally attempt to guide parents as they interact with their babies (McDonough 1992, cited in Cohen et al. 1999). Videotaped parent–infant interactions are used to help the carer recognize her own positive responses and interactions. By recognizing her positive impact on the child, the mother's competence and confidence is built up. Although the infant is present, the attention is on the mother's behaviour. The therapist guides the mother 'to selected infant cues and characteristics to which she is encouraged to attend and respond' (Cohen et al. 1999: 433).

A different approach is taken by therapists who look at the infant as the potential initiator as parent and child interact. Here, the emphasis is on helping the carer follow the lead of the child. In fact, Juffer at al. (2003) recognize several levels at which parental sensitivity might be improved:

- Teaching parents' observational skills to make them 'better perceivers' of their children's signals and expression. For example, parents might be encouraged to describe their children's behaviour and feelings, note what they see down in a workbook, or 'speak for the baby', which is a way of getting parents to say aloud what they think their baby might be thinking (mind-mindedness), expressing, and doing.

- Helping parents see the value of prompt, sensitive and contingent responses to their infant's signals. This helps children recognize the character, consequences, and efficacy of their own feelings and behaviour, improving their sense of control and self-agency.
- Enhancing parents' empathy by praising and reinforcing their sensitive and responsive interactions with their child. This is best done using video feedback of a short play session between a parent and her young child.
- The practitioner might help parents understand children's development and behaviour by directly commenting on what the baby appears to be thinking and doing. Many 'at risk' parents distort and give a negative attribution to their children's behaviour and intentions, when in fact objectively nothing of the sort is taking place.

An effective, but relatively 'low-tech' intervention is described by Black and Teti (1997). The mothers who received help were all African-American teenage mothers. They were given a videotape to watch entitled *Feeding Your Baby with Love*. Compared with a control group of mothers who did not receive the video, after watching the film, the study group mothers were found to be much more involved with their babies during feeding.

Many interventions are multi-method. That is, they use a variety of techniques to improve the parent's sensitivity and responsiveness. For example, a study by Spiker, Ferguson and Brooks-Gunn (1993) employed a range of services to improve parent–infant interactions with at risk, low birth-weight, premature babies. Parents received (i) emotionally supportive home visits during which they were helped to improve their parent–infant interactional skills and knowledge, (ii) an educational training programme run at a family centre, and (iii) a parent-support group. When the babies had reached two and a half, the quality of interactions between mother and child were found to be more synchronous than those in a control group of similar parents of prematurely born babies who did not receive the intervention.

Some studies compare two types of intervention. For example, Robert-Tissot et al. (1996) examined a group of children referred to a clinic for sleep, feeding and behavioural problems, including aggression. One group of mothers was assigned to a psychodynamic-based treatment, while the other received video-assisted parent coaching. The coaching method required the mother to be video-recorded as she interacted with her young child. Competent parental behaviours were identified and commented on positively. Although both treatment groups improved maternal sensitivity, the video-based parental guidance intervention displayed greater gains in the quality of parent–child interactions, producing infants who were less behaviourally difficult, and more cooperative and emotionally positive.

Green and Goldwyn's review of the research suggests that 'interventions for disorganisation should pay more attention to the specifics of the parental state of mind (including unresolved trauma and mood state) in addition to details of developmental differences in children and parent–child interaction at different ages'. They report that Juffer has suggested:

> the incidence of parental 'frightening/frightened' behaviours may best be reduced by powerfully reinforcing parental maternal attention to the child in the present, as a competing stimulus to the internal and distracting parental preoccupations. In contrast, the patterns of mutual control identified in later childhood may best be influenced by working on mutual trust and sensitivity.
>
> (Green and Goldwyn 2002: 843)

Early Intervention in Adoptive Families: A Study by Juffer et al. (1997)

The aim of a study by Juffer et al. (1997) was to support parental sensitivity by promoting secure attachments in a group of 90 mothers who had adopted infants from another country. The mothers were divided into three equal-sized groups. One received a personal book programme on how to practise sensitive parenting, playful parenting, and holding and comforting the baby. The mothers' observational skills were enhanced by inviting them to describe and note down what their babies were doing. A second group was also given the book and advice about sensitive and responsive parents, but in addition mothers received three sessions of video feedback. Each mother was shown a short video of her interaction with her baby. Sensitive responses were noted and reinforced with positive comments, including those that seemed to have a particularly beneficial effect on the baby. The practitioner also verbalized the infant's signals and expressions to give a sense of what the baby might be thinking and feelings and doing. There was also a control group that was given just a brochure about adoption. Twelve months later, both the mothers who received the book-based programme and those who also had the video feedback showed higher levels of sensitivity and had more securely attached children than the control group.

Changing the Parent's Mental Representation/Working Model of Attachment

In the light of our relationship history, mental representations lay down expectations about how others will respond at times of need, and about how effective we feel in securing what we need from relationships. These organized mental representations of the self and others (as either positive or negative) are carried forward by individuals and used to guide behaviour in subsequent relationships. Internal working models organize appraisal processes, thought, memory and feelings with regard to attachment-saturated situations, including relationships with our children.

Some interventions aim to change the parent's representations of attachment. Carers who have suffered maltreatment or rejection in their own childhoods have their own unresolved losses and traumas activated when they become parents. The attachment behaviour of their child is dealt with defensively. This reduces the accuracy and objectivity of their perceptions, which in turn compromises their ability to be sensitive, mind-minded and responsive. Carers are wont to re-enact and repeat the caregiving behaviour of their own parents.

Therapy aims to alter these distorted representations by inviting parents to reflect on their past and present attachment and experiences. This is achieved by asking the mother to explore what she brings from her own relationship with her parents to the relationship she has with her own child. Juffer et al. (2003) note that the practitioner is required to act as a secure base during this exploratory and reflective process.

Toddler–Parent Psychotherapy

Cicchetti and his colleagues investigated a preventive intervention for toddlers with depressed mothers (Cicchetti, Toth and Rogosch 2004). The intervention is a development of similar treatments employed by Lieberman, Weston and Pawl (1991), that is, it can be viewed as a representational intervention designed to influence maternal representations of parenting by providing mothers with a corrective emotional experience. Therapists work jointly with mothers and their toddlers, generating an environment in which empathy, respect, concern and positive regard are present in high measure. By providing mothers with a much more positive representation of self and others, including their child, the hope is that they can reconstruct and internalize a less insecure and less anxious representation of themselves in relation to their toddler.

> Maternal representations that have evolved from the mother's relationship history are viewed as affecting the character of the interactions between mother and child. Furthermore, interactions and toddler behaviors also evoke maternal representations of prior relationship experiences that influence the mother's reactions to the toddler and her experience of self. As such, seemingly ordinary behaviors between mother and toddler during therapy sessions are regarded as behavioral manifestations of representational themes. Through the use of observation and empathic comments, the therapist works toward helping the mother recognize how her representations are manifested during her interactions with her toddler, thereby allowing for the clarification of distorted perceptions and alterations of how she experiences and perceives her toddler and herself.
>
> (Cicchetti, Toth and Rogosch 2004: 236)

Parallel processes go on between the therapist and the depressed mother, and the therapist and the child. Recognizing and attending to these interactions invites further reflection and insight. Toddler–parent intervention therefore sees therapeutic change arising as a result of increased maternal understanding of how past relationship experiences influence current feelings and interactions. By helping mothers recognize these links within the context of a therapeutic relationship, which provides a corrective emotional experience, the expectation is that maternal sensitivity, responsivity and attunement to the toddler will improve. The findings of this well-designed study, comparing unipolar depressed mothers who received the intervention with depressed and non-depressed mothers who did not, describe very promising positive affects. The attachment-based intervention increased parental sensitivity, which in turn improved children's security of attachment and their cognitive functioning. Although it is time-intensive, the benefits of the intervention appear to be long-lasting.

Taking a different tack, Spelz (1990) has emphasized the importance of developing negotiating skills and good-quality verbal communication between parents and their toddlers. Based on this understanding, the Seattle Approach (an attachment and cognitive-behavioural parent training approach) sees many problems arising out of breakdowns in communication, negotiation and planning (which are central to the establishment of goal-corrected partnerships) between parents and their young children. Having assessed the fluency and competency of parent–child communication and conflict-resolution skills, the intervention proper comprises 10 to 16 sessions divided into four phases. In phase 1, parents are educated about children's development, particularly the need of young children to increase their sense of control and autonomy. In phase 2, parents are encouraged to let their children lead and direct the content of play while the parent follows. Limit-setting and 'the least restraint' principle inform phase 3, so that parents can recognize when and when not to become involved with a child's demands. 'The final phase ... focuses directly on parent–child communication and negotiation. Efforts are directed at enabling the parent to structure the process of negotiation and to assist the child by "filling in" verbally during a time when a child's verbal capacities are new and limited' (Lieberman and Zeanah 1999: 568–9). The approach also helps parents to help their children self-regulate their emotions and behaviour by recognizing and labelling feelings.

Changing Parents' Behaviour *and* Mental Representations

A study of clinically referred infants by Cohen et al. (1999) compared psychodynamic psycho-therapy (PPT) with a mixed representational and behavioural approach called '*Watch, Wait and Wonder*' (WWW). In PPT – the representational approach – the therapist explored the parent's past and how it might be affecting present interactions with the infant. The aim was to help her gain insight into the assumptions and feelings that affected the parent–child interactions. WWW is an infant-led psychotherapy. WWW will be described in more detail, but we might note that although the study found both interventions reduced infant-presenting problems, WWW was more successful in shifting children to a more organized and secure attachment, with corresponding improvements in their affect regulation and cognitive competence. After 15 sessions, mothers showed a decrease in parenting stress and depression, and an improved sense of their parenting competence and satisfaction.

Watch, Wait and Wonder (Cohen et al. 1999)

This is an insight and behaviourally oriented therapy, working at both the *behavioural* and the *representational* levels. Mothers clinically presented their infants with feeding, sleeping and behavioural problems. Many parents felt depressed, feeling that the bonding and attachment process had failed. This impeded the relationship with their child. Rather than attempt to work solely with the parent, WWW gets the parent to shift focus on to the infant. The carer is encouraged to follow the infant's spontaneous and undirected play activity (watch), see what happens (wait), and reflect on what the child might be thinking, feeling and doing (wonder).

For the first half hour of the session, the parent joins her infant (typically aged between 12 and 30 months) on a floor mat on which there are a wide variety of toys and dolls. Here, she can better observe her child's self-initiated activity. The child is 'in charge' of what he or she does and how he or she 'plays', with the carer being the observer, the reflective interpreter who gains insight into her infant's inner world and relationship needs. The parent is encouraged to notice and respond to the infant's initiations, but asked not to guide, lead or take over the child's play in any way. 'At the same time, the infant himself has the therapeutic experience of negotiating his relationship with his mother, and thus begins to master his environment' (Cohen et al. 1999: 434). Just as the mother doesn't lead, nor does the therapist direct the mother's responses.

In the second half of the session, for 20 minutes the mother discusses her observations and experiences of the infant-led interaction, identifying what she has learned and understood about her child's experience and perspective:

> The therapist does not instruct, give advice, or interpret the infant's activity or play but provides a safe, supportive environment (ie a sensitive and responsive environment), so that the mother can express her own observations, thoughts, feelings, and interpretations of her infant's activity and their relationship. The mother and the therapist discuss the mother's observations of her infant activity and attempt to understand the themes and relational issues that the infant is trying to master, focussing on the inevitable problems that emerge as the mother begins to struggle with following her infant's lead. This permits the mother to examine her internal working models of herself in relation to her infant and vice versa. Through play and the mother's discussion, mother and infant are presumed to modify and revise their models to be more in line with their new mutual experiences together in therapy.
>
> (Cohen et al. 1999: 434)

Video Intervention to Promote Positive Parenting (VIPP)

The Leiden Attachment Intervention Study represents an attempt to break the intergenerational cycle of insecure attachments in a group of young mothers (Bakermans-Kranenberg, Juffer and van IJzendoorn 1998; Juffer, van IJzendoorn and Bakermans-Kranenberg 1997). The aim was to improve parental sensitivity and increase the security of the young child's attachment.

The study employed both behavioural and representational levels of interventions. The behavioural aspect used 'video intervention to promote positive parenting' (VIPP). Mothers and their young children (typically aged between seven and ten months) are videotaped at home while the parent is either playing with or bathing her baby. The practitioner examines and analyses the video-recorded parent–child interaction back at her clinic. During her next home visit, she shows the mother the tape and discusses key fragments with her. Particular attention is drawn to the baby's signals, facial expressions and body movements. This stimulates the mother's observational skills, and increases her interest in her infant's state of mind, thereby promoting empathy. On the whole negative parental responses are ignored, while positive reinforcement is given to the more sensitive examples of maternal caregiving. The parent is also given a brochure on sensitive responding. In particular, the mother is invited to discuss and articulate ('speak for the baby') on four themes, which promote the notion that the mother is the expert on her own child:

- The baby's contact-seeking (attachment), exploratory and intersubjective behaviour.
- The accurate perception of the baby's signals, facial expressions and body movements.
- The relevance of prompt and adequate responding to the baby's signals.
- Affective attunement and sharing of emotions.

The second type of intervention also employed VIPP and the brochure, but added discussions at the representational level (VIPP-R). The mother reflects on her own attachment experiences as a child, and how they might be affecting her present parenting behaviour. The discussion is aided by the mother completing a short questionnaire. Parents are also given material describing people with different types of attachment patterns, which they are asked to react to and elaborate. The discussion of representational and attachment issues during the home visits covers four themes (Juffer et al. 2003):

- Separations in the past, including when the parent was a child, and separations from her own baby now that she is a parent.
- Parenting in the past, experienced as a child, and parenting in the present experienced as a mother.

- The process of breaking away during adolescence, defining adult relationships with parents, and expectations of future relationships with her child.
- The explicit link between 'being the child of my parents' and 'being the parent of my child', focusing on which childhood experiences the mother wants to pass or not pass on to her child.

'Interestingly,' observe Juffer, Bakermans-Kranenburg and van IJzendoorn (2003):

> ... insecure dismissing mothers tended to profit most from VIPP, the intervention program with video-feedback only, whereas insecure preoccupied mothers tended to profit most from VIPP-R, the program with video feedback and attachment discussion ... A dismissing mother may profit most from an intervention with a clear focus on behaviour that provides her with helpful tips to be used in daily interaction with her child. An insecure preoccupied mother, who is still involved with her own attachment experiences, may profit most from an intervention with an additional representational approach that aims at (re-) structuring her thoughts and feelings with respect to attachment.

Cicchetti, Toth and Rogosch (2004) also wonder whether families in poverty suffering multiple stressors might benefit more from behavioural approaches than do families who do not have to struggle with material worries and might respond better to more insight-oriented approaches.

Social Support and Improving Parental Well-Being

Research highlights the powerful role that support plays in people's ability to cope with the stresses and strains of everyday life. It is no surprise, therefore, to discover that many of those who are not coping well with social relationships, suffer poor mental health and find living in disadvantaged neighbourhoods particularly stressful also lack emotional support. And contrary to much popular professional wisdom, long-term support does not make families dependent but in fact appears to increase their ability to be self-reliant. Hart, Brassard and Karlson et al. (1996) quote Seitz et al.'s 1985 conclusion of their ten-year follow-up of the effectiveness of family support programmes:

> Just as independence in children is fostered by appropriately meeting their legitimate early dependency needs, it may be that addressing the problems of troubled new parents increases the likelihood that their family will later be able to function independently as well.

Measured over the long term, support has been found to be highly cost-effective in terms of reducing the risks of children committing offences, getting pregnant in their teens, abusing or neglecting their own children, missing out on a good school experience, and failing to gain employment.

There is accumulating evidence-based research noting the positive impact on children's long-term development of providing both *practical* and *emotional* support to at-risk parents and families (for instance Barnard et al. 1988; Berry, Charlson and Dawson 2003; Gardner 2003; Gelfland et al. 1996). For example, social support is a well-recognized protective factor in both physical and mental health. Those who feel they possess high self-esteem, have a positive outlook, and enjoy good social support experience less illness and generally live longer (for example Danner, Snowden and Friesen 2001).

Practical support can include help with looking after the children, help with the shopping, being given more money, loans of money, and obtaining better housing. Emotional support describes such things as the opportunity to confide in someone, knowing that other people are available when needed, and being recognized, accepted and valued by another person. It can also include motivational features such as providing encouragement and acknowledgement.

Cohen and Syme (1985) recognize three other kinds of support. *Status recognition* helps to boost confidence and may be achieved through marriage, gaining a job, being respected by a professional or acquiring a social position say in a group or community. *Information* can be supportive; it gives people knowledge and the resources to develop some control over their experiences. Informational support can include giving advice and helping people to make decisions. *Social companionship* includes the rewards of friendship, and gaining pleasure and relaxation through shared leisure pursuits.

Community nurses and health visitors who see and support vulnerable mothers have been shown to be very effective in protecting children developmentally (Beckwith and Sigman 1995). For example, the Prenatal/Early Infancy Project in Elmira, New York involved nurses targeting their visits on mothers who were either teenagers, unmarried or poor (Olds, Henderson and Tatelbaum 1986). A nurse first visited the experimental group mothers during their pregnancy and continued to visit regularly until the at-risk child reached the age of two. During their home visits, when the nurses developed a close supportive and working relationship with the mothers, they promoted (i) good health-related behaviour during pregnancy and into the first two years of life; (ii) the care the parents provided for their child; and (iii) maternal life-course development (family planning, education achievement, participation in the workforce). The mothers were encouraged to link up with the health and other human services, and become more involved with and seek the support of family and friends. 'The program was based on theories of self-efficacy, human ecology, and human attachment' (Eckenrode et al. 2001: 879). Visits were scheduled every two weeks during pregnancy, weekly for the first six weeks postpartum, and then at a reduced rate thereafter.

The positive effects of the programme included longer gestation, higher birth weights, less reported child abuse and neglect, fewer offences, lower alcohol consumption, and mothers postponing their next pregnancy (Olds and Kitzman 1993, Olds et al. 1997).

At 15 years of age, at-risk children whose mothers had not received the service showed a range of early onset problem behaviours. The most frequent type of maltreatment suffered by the children whose mothers did not receive the support service was neglect, which, along with physical and sexual abuse, predicted antisocial behaviour during adolescence. Children in the experimental nurse home visitation preventative service were less likely to suffer maltreatment, and probably as a result, were less likely to develop antisocial and problem behaviours by the time they had reached 15. The maltreatment that did occur was detected and dealt with earlier, thus preventing early parenting difficulties from becoming chronic patterns of maltreatment.

In the United Kingdom, Sure Start is a project which aims to involve and support parents and their children at the community level by increasing the availability of childcare for all children; improving health, education and emotional development for young children; and supporting parents in their role and in developing their employment aspirations. In particular, Sure Start projects are keen to develop in disadvantaged areas. Sure Start brings together free early education and better childcare, with increased financial support through child tax credit, and increased social and emotional support provided by Children and Family Centres.

'Project Safe Care', developed for families at risk of maltreatment, focuses on three key areas relevant to young parents and children at risk of neglect: (i) home safety, (ii) infant and child health care, and (iii) bonding and stimulation (Lutzker and Bigelow 2001). The intervention is over 15 weeks, with five weeks devoted to each area. Using video, parents can practise new skills for which they receive feedback. Parents are helped to understand danger and hazards, safety and cleanliness, the need for medical attention, and how to improve their interaction with their children.

Mothers in the STEEP (Steps Towards Effective and Enjoyable Parenting) programme received practical support and advice along with some video feedback. Compared with controls, mothers increased their sensitivity and understanding of infant development (Egeland and Erickson 1993). In the United Kingdom, the United States and many other countries, the introduction of a range of community supports (family centres, day care, mother and toddler groups) has also been found to provide parents with emotional, social and practical resources to help them in their parenting tasks.

A high-frequency, low-intensity supportive service was provided to families living in a poor, disadvantaged part of New York State (*New York State Preventive Services Demonstration Project*, Jones 1985). Committed but unqualified social workers recruited from the local community regularly visited families whose children were at risk of entering public care. They provided practical and emotional support on a long-term basis. The support workers were easily accessible, and emphasis was placed on them 'being there' when needed. Compared with a similar group of families who received shorter term, task-oriented interventions by more highly trained workers; significantly fewer children from the experimental group of families who received long-term, 'low-tech' support were placed in public or foster care.

Most reviewers of *early preventive programmes* conclude that universally available home support services (for example health visitor or home nurse schemes) provided throughout the early years are particularly effective at promoting healthy development. Similar success has been achieved through providing school-based mental and physical health services, and meaningful relationship-based forms of casework conducted in the home setting. There is further evidence which suggests that allowing families to identify and work on the problems they feel are the ones most significant to them is also likely to be more effective (for example, Lutzker 1984). According to Olds and Kitzman (1993), the key components of home support and visitor programmes therefore include:

- a comprehensive, multi-problem service approach
- well-trained health visitors and home support workers
- long-term involvement
- early intervention.

However, even in these relatively effective prevention and early intervention programmes, a note of caution arises. Hart and Brassard (1991: 82) concluded that 'when psychological maltreatment of high frequency, intensity, and duration or developmental salience occurs and is predicted to produce serious harm to the child, mandatory societal intervention may be justified. This is particularly true when perpetrators resist offered help.' Many parents most at risk of seriously maltreating their children are those most likely to avoid and disengage from all types of health and welfare services and interventions. This is a reminder that in extreme cases, removal and a new family placement, with or without contact, might be the best option for children if their psychological development is not to be irretrievably impaired.

Beyond the early years, school-based services hold out the most promise. The school environment is a highly significant one for children. Children who have major psychological and social problems quickly get noticed by teachers. The presence of specially trained school-based child and family-oriented counsellors, caseworkers, psychologists, nurses and support workers can provide a focused, coordinated and intensive response to children and families in need. Services provided by schools carry fewer stigmas than those offered by social services and formal child welfare agencies. Specialists can work with children in the socially challenging environment of the school. Furthermore, there is research evidence that a caring teacher, or one who recognizes and values a child and his or her talents, can act as a powerful protective factor in a child's development, boosting self-esteem and resilience.

Conclusion

The broad conclusion reached by Egeland et al. (2000) is that early preventive interventions with multi-risk families are effective, particularly if the interventions are frequent, long-term, supportive, offer parents parent–child interaction behavioural feedback, and discuss with parents their past attachment experiences and their mental representations of attachment issues. Similar conclusions were reached by MacLeod and Nelson (2000) in their meta-analysis of 56 home-visiting and community support intervention programmes designed to promote family wellness and prevent child maltreatment. The authors speculate that proactive programmes might initiate a positive chain reaction, breaking potential negative parent–infant interactions even before they begin.

In a meta-analysis of 70 published studies, Bakermans-Kranenburg, van IJzendoorn and Juffer (2003) looked at whether improving parental sensitivity is actually accompanied by a corresponding change in infant security. Practices that were particularly effective in improving maternal sensitivity were most likely to increase children's security. However, in general, conclude the authors, 'attachment insecurity is more difficult to change than maternal sensitivity' (Bakermans-Kranenburg, van IJzendoorn and Juffer 2003: 211). What they did find though, was that interventions that focused on improving the sensitivity of maternal behaviour did improve both maternal sensitivity and infant security. Interestingly, and in contrast to Egeland et al. (2000), their analysis suggests that the most effective interventions are:

- relatively brief (under 20 contacts)
- with infants aged at least six months
- with a *behavioural* focus (rather than a focus on trying to change the parent's mental representations by improving insight).

However, common to all approaches are a number of key ingredients. Support and availability reduce parental stress. Less stressed carers invest more time and energy in their babies. Interventions that help parents become interested in what their babies might be thinking and feeling, and how thought and feeling affect behaviour, not only increase attachment security, but also promote healthy psychosocial development and improve children's ability to self-regulate. Parents who collaborate with their children's attempts to make sense of themselves and those around them, help in the formation of coherent, fully integrated young minds.

14

Interventions with Pre-School and School-Age Children

Introduction

Interventions with this age group are much more likely to work jointly with both carer and child. Although children towards the older end of middle childhood might be worked with independently, the practice principles identified when working with infants still apply. Maltreated children have experienced little in the way of being cared for by mind-minded, sensitive, emotionally attuned, mentalizing parents. These are the children who have suffered the highest levels of emotional arousal and distress, and the least sensitive and containing caregiving. They have been left in highly unregulated states for long periods. Attachment-based therapies with children displaying severe attachment difficulties therefore aim to introduce the child, maybe for the first time, to the basic elements of good enough parent–infant bonding. However, the catch-22 for these children is that developmentally they need to establish a close, mind-engaging relationship with their primary carers but they only feel safe when they are emotionally distant, independent and in fierce self-control. Their trauma interferes with their ability to enter a healing relationship (Allen 2001: 298).

Typically, therapists seek to engage children through all their senses, using a range of developmentally informed techniques including play, eye contact, movement, affect mirroring, humour, nurturing, structure and emotional containment. There is an emphasis on right-brain functioning, that is, socio-emotional growth is addressed through activity, art and play. However, within this, left-brain functioning also has to be engaged. Emotions when felt and expressed are named and described at the subjective and physiological level. Language is used to help children gain some cognitive recognition and control of previously 'felt' but not fully understood mental states, and what might be causing them.

As we have seen, children who suffer severe stress and trauma find it difficult to achieve good social cognition. Their ability to reflect fully on their own and other people's mental states, and thereby regulate their own and other people's arousal, is strictly limited. The feeling that the world is dangerous, uninterested and unpredictable is frightening. Not to have a strong sense of control over events makes both children and adults feel helpless. Depression easily sets in. Feeling helpless is also shameful and disturbing. Desperate and ultimately dysfunctional ways of dealing with fear, anxiety and distress arise. Survival strategies are based on switches between aggression and hostility, withdrawal and helplessness. Even under low social stress, many children and adults who have suffered abuse, neglect and rejection feel out of control and overwhelmed by their own arousal. This is a recipe for poor peer relationships, weak educational performance, anti-social behaviour, and problems of addiction, depression, low self-esteem and incompetent parenting.

However, unlike the infant, the slightly older child is beginning to establish a range of psychological defences to deal with emotional arousal and the strong feelings triggered by attachment-related events. Different defences produce different attachment strategies, each of which denies the individual full and rounded knowledge about the mental state of the self and the other. The most extreme defence segregates or dissociates particular attachment-related mental representations in the unconscious so that no coherent sense of the self or the other is possible. This is an uncomfortable, fearful psychological state in which to be, and it is strongly associated with a range of major psychopathologies including depression, personality disorder, violent aggression and conduct disorder. The use of defensive controlling strategies (compulsive caregiving, compulsive compliance, compulsive self-reliance) allows children to reduce their feelings of confusion and helplessness. But they also prevent carers (including foster carers, adoptive parents, and therapists as well as biological parents) from making meaningful and reflective psychological contact with the child. If severely maltreated children are to be helped, they need to feel safe as they relate and engage with the mind of a safe, sensitive and attuned other. Once that channel of communication is opened, new psychological information and experiences can begin to enter the child's (or adult's) conscious mental processes, producing more integrated and coherent psychological states.

For example, the work of Dozier and colleagues (2002) recommends that foster carers consciously resist being drawn into the avoidant, self-reliant and controlling dynamic of the maltreated child. Their intervention model 'helps foster parents behave in nurturing ways to their children, even when children send out the message that they do not want nurturance' (Dozier et al. 2003: 256). The care is not meted out intrusively, and may amount to no more than a gesture or brief pat on the back and smile, but it might be enough to generate a 'disconfirming' model of caregiving which enables the defended child to let go and trust the carer. Dozier and colleagues found that insecure children placed with foster carers who had autonomous states of mind gradually developed secure attachments (cited in Dozier and Bates 2004: 178). Beek and Schofield (2004) expand on this insight. They describe in fascinating detail how foster carers provide a secure base and promote reflective capacity, self-esteem and autonomy for children whose pre-placement histories were ones of neglect, hurt and rejection.

Development Age and Chronological Age

The more severe and earlier the onset of the maltreatment, the more immature will be the child's emotional processing and regulating abilities. Many severely abused and neglected children suffer core developmental impairments in their social cognition. Chronological age is therefore not a guide to the child's socio-emotional developmental age. Interventions and therapy have to be pitched at the child's developmental age if they are to be effective.

Thus, we have three notions to help us think how best to help parents and maltreated children increase their feelings of safety and security, regulate their emotions, and improve their relationships and behaviour:

- If sensitive, attuned and mind-minded parenting increases a child's security and psychosocial development, how can we promote it in carers?
- Even if such sensitive caregiving is available, maltreated children have developed coping and survival strategies that work by keeping dangerous and negligent carers 'out of their minds'. This then generalizes to all carers and those in a therapeutic role. Children need to let go of the fearful controlling behaviours that have actually served them well in environments of fear and danger, and instead begin to trust, value and enjoy open communication with a sensitive, mind-minded carer. This 'letting go' and learning to feel safe when others get psychologically close can be a therapeutic aim in its own right.
- Children's chronological age is not necessarily a good indicator of their developmental age. Although children can show some flexibility in their emotional maturity, the more severe the maltreatment, the more likely it is that the child has missed out on all the wonderful, reciprocal, parent–child intersubjectivity which helps shape growing minds into fully integrated, coherent processors of complex psychological, emotional and interpersonal information. Treatment and support of both children and their parents need to bear in mind the developmental level at which they function when under relational stress and whenever attachment issues arise.

We have already noted that parent–infant interventions have been the most rigorously researched group, in part because infants are particularly responsive to changes in caregiving, and in part because helping parents get it right at this early stage is likely to have a long-lasting impact on children's psychosocial development. Although there are fewer good-quality intervention studies tackling parents and their toddlers, a small number of promising treatments are emerging. However, beyond toddlerhood, the number of high-quality intervention studies thins out. This is not to say that there is not a lot of high-quality clinical activity going on with pre-school and school-age children. Rather, it has attracted less research attention and less money. The reasons for this are to do with the more complex nature of children's problems in this age group, and the difficulty of generating good-quality research designs in these more challenging cases. Of course there is a good deal of clinical experience on which to draw, but it lacks the authority of trialled and evidence-based practice. Attachment theory with this age group is more often used as an assessment rather than a therapeutic tool. This is somewhat frustrating as it is older children who present with the greatest needs and the most demanding behaviours for biological parents, foster carers, adopters and residential workers. Nevertheless, some of the main practice features identified when working with this group will be described, and examples given.

The Circle of Security Project (COS) (Marvin et al. 2002)

The Circle of Security intervention takes its inspiration from Bowlby's observation that parenting provides a secure base from which the child:

> can make sorties into the outside world and to which he can return knowing for sure that he will be welcomed when he gets there, nourished physically and emotionally, comforted if distressed, reassured if frightened.
>
> (Bowlby 1988: 11)

The protocol takes particular note of:

> the ideas of emotion regulation; interactive synchrony; states of mind regarding attachments and intimate relationships; shared states of consciousness, affect, and perspectives; and reflective functioning.
>
> (Marvin et al. 2002: 108)

The intervention has been developed for high-risk toddlers and pre-school children and their carers. A small number of at risk children (aged one to four) and their primary caregivers meet as a group with a psychotherapist for 75 minutes each week for 20 weeks. Parents are introduced to Ainsworth's idea of a 'secure base and a haven of safety' (Ainsworth et al. 1978), using very user-friendly pictures based on a circle to illustrate what is meant. Essentially, the pictures convey the idea that when relaxed and feeling safe, children will explore their environment. Secure children have an internal working model of the carer as available if needed at any time. Children expect their carers to have them in mind, whatever they are doing, and generally to monitor and watch over them in case they need protection and regulation. When the child does return to 'base', for example when his or her attachment system is activated, the carer offers safety, care and reassuring comfort. Parents are taught that children like and need to explore, but they can only do this if they know and feel that should they find themselves in difficulty or danger, their caregiver will be available to protect, contain and regulate them, helping them understand and learn from the emotionally arousing experience.

Parents are helped to understand that the smooth running of the parent–child relationship inevitably breaks down from time to time – parents unavoidably let children down, upset them or fail to be immediately available. However, secure carers are quick to spot and acknowledge the damage and are able to 'repair' the disruption. From this, the child learns that the carer is in principle available and responsive, and can help the child make sense of the feelings that arise at moments of upset and distress. In order for these 'repairs' to be successful, both parent(s) and child must feel able to communicate and be confident in the regulatory value of their exchanges. Parent(s) and child must send out clear, undistorted signals and clues about what they are thinking and feeling.

Signals become distorted and disturbed when the child's needs (attachment signals) trigger anxiety in the parent, which he or she deals with defensively. For example, a dismissing carer might reduce the distress she feels whenever her child makes a demand on her availability by defensively encouraging the child to be independent, not make a fuss, carry on playing, and not be always bothering 'mummy'. If the child learns not to make demands at times of need, the parent need not activate her caregiving behaviour. In effect, under stress, both parent and child learn to miscue each other about their actual needs and mental states. The avoidant child downplays his distress, continues to play at a distance, and at such times avoids physical and emotional proximity with his parent. The dismissing mother signals that she is not available when most needed.

In contrast, preoccupied, ambivalent mothers discourage their child's independence and exploratory behaviour because it increases their anxiety and feelings of abandonment. They encourage dependence in their children, and promote anxiety whenever the child becomes too distant and exploratory. Ambivalent children begin to feel anxious and unsafe whenever they are at a distance, socially disengaged, and not involved with their carer.

Disorganized/controlling children and their parents have major problems at all points in the 'circle of security', with confused messages about who is in control, whether to approach or not at times of need, and who should care for whom (with controlling, role-reversed children either taking aggressive charge of their own safety or even worrying more about their carer's distress than their own).

Parents are helped to recognize how their own feeling states affect children's attempt to balance their need to explore on the one hand, and the appropriateness of displaying attachment behaviour and sending out distress signals at times of need on the other. Through observation, the therapists work out the particular character of each parent–child attachment relationship in the group.

Intervention goals are constructed depending on the parent–child attachment classification For example:

> Dismissing caregivers are usually assigned the following treatment goals: increased appreciation of how much their children need them; increased skill at reading and

registering their children's subtle distress signals; and decreased miscuing under circumstances in which a child's attachment behavior is activated.

(Marvin et al. 2002: 115)

The focus is mainly on helping the carer to become more aware, perceptive, available and skilful in reading her child's signals, and to become more appropriately responsive. The therapists create a safe, holding environment for the parents from which they can explore their own caregiving. During the course of the 20-week programme, the parents follow a set programme. Much use is made of video material of parent–child interaction, in which the child is observed moving from play and exploration to proximity-seeking and back to exploration, and the therapy looks at how the parent responds to these behaviours, and how the child reacts in return.

In the group, the parents collectively are encouraged 'to figure out what is happening'. This helps parents build up and improve their observational skills. Other video vignettes are used to help parents recognize and understand how their own anxieties and defences affect the child's attachment-exploratory balance, and how the insecure child begins to miscue the parent about his/her feelings and needs. 'A miscue is the defensive denial of a genuine need' (Marvin et al. 2002: 121). Positive aspects of the parent's behaviour are also identified and encouraged.

Preliminary results are very encouraging, with a significant number of children shifting from insecure/disordered patterns to more secure/ordered patterns of attachment. Marvin et al. (2002: 122) conclude, 'Given the group format, we are optimistic that the Circle of Security protocol will prove to be a successful model for a cost-effective, university-community therapeutic partnership.'

Attachment Problems and Types of Treatment

Minde (2003: 294) suggests a helpful way of thinking about and analysing attachment disorders at four different levels:

1 Children whose attachments are disorganized and disordered experience strong activation of attachment behaviour. This behaviour goes unterminated because of the emotional unavailability of the caregiver (hostile, helpless, absent). The child is therefore left in states of high, unregulated arousal, which is extremely distressing and disturbing.
2 In terms of their social cognitions and belief systems, these children have an expectation (a mental model or representation) that at times of need and distress, others are unavailable. Indeed, adults who attempt to get both emotionally and physically close to these children might make matters worse.

3 Carers, whether old or new, will also have expectations, interpretations and defences affecting their dealing with the child, which may be open to revision.
4 Ecological factors outside, but affecting the attachment relationship, also play a part. For example, environmental stress is likely to mean that carers will be functioning less optimally; peers or teachers might provide an alternative source of support and valorisation. For example, 'children who experience sensitive and responsive teachers form secure attachment relationships with them.... One recent study finds that child–teacher attachment relationships experiences can serve as compensatory relationship experiences for children who have experienced difficult life circumstances' (Howes and Ritchie 1999: 252).

Treatment, says Minde, involves modifying one or more of these levels. Removal of environmental stress, and improving the quality of the child's (and carer's) social and interpersonal day-to-day life is generally the best place to begin. Carers' views, understanding and expectations might then be improved. The needs and behaviour of children who have suffered abuse and neglect might need to be explained in simple adaptive and attachment terms. The carer is helped to gain realistic and age-appropriate expectations of children in general, and maltreated children in particular.

> In addition, such children may be exposed to a cognitively tailored treatment approach where they initially learn the day-to-day behaviours that make life with them a more positive experience for others. This may mean concentrating on managing frustration, on building social skills, understanding natural consequences etc. Once such positive social cognitions are developed, one may gradually also affect the attachment level, i.e., help the child see that living with and caring about others is also more satisfying – although this last goal may not be totally achievable for children who have shown a complete absence of attachment in early years.
>
> (Minde 2003: 294)

As a broad approach, this is sound advice that will certainly impact positively on some children. Minde's confidence in this treatment is based on his analysis of the outcome of children who had suffered traumatic separations, and multiple short-term and poor care while in Second World War concentration camps. After several years of trauma, loss and extremely impoverished care, these motherless children ended up living in a well-run, caring residential home. They arrived hypersensitive, restless, aggressive towards adults and very difficult to handle. Freud and Dann (1961, cited in Minde 2003: 293) thought one of the helpful therapeutic factors was that such children 'should not be "forced to be close to adults" but given ample time to learn closeness and be accepted even if they do need more distance from others'. Although not all the children followed a successful developmental trajectory, many reached adulthood in reasonably good psychological health. This is a reminder that many maltreated children seem able to extract remarkable amounts of good-quality experience when it is provided as part of a broadly warm, caring, supportive and interested caregiving environment. However, achieving these happy outcomes remains problematic for large numbers of abused and neglected children.

Psychological and Affectively Attuned Interventions

Many children who have suffered maltreatment are removed from their biological families and placed with either long-term foster carers or adoptive parents. Given their experiences of early trauma, significant numbers of these children develop a variety of disorders of attachment. In response to the needs of these children, a range of 'attachment therapies' has been developed. Although these interventions are much sought after by adopters, to date there has been little scientific evaluation of their effectiveness. By their nature, the treatments available tend to be lengthy and very relationship-based. In that sense, it is difficult to capture their subtlety and richness. The reader is therefore referred to the source texts for a fuller picture of the practices associated with these therapies.

Most of the therapies recognize that maltreated children have missed out on early 'affective mentalization' and good quality, secure parent–child intersubjectivity. The children's understanding of their own and other people's emotions is very poor, and their ability to regulate their arousal is limited. Thus, a basic aim of many of these treatments is to help the child emotionally 'connect' with the mind of his or her adopter or foster carer. By improving the quality of the relationship between parent and child, including the introduction of open and coherent communication, it is possible to revise the child's internal working model of attachment relationships from disorganized insecure, anxious and controlling, to organized insecure, or even secure.

Hughes (2002), for example, is developing a treatment that he describes as 'dyadic developmental psychotherapy'. The key intervention principle requires both the therapist and caregiver to observe, recognize and become attuned to the child's subjective experiences and affective states, and *contingently* reflect them back to the child. When relationships are affectively attuned, parent and child not only experience the same affect, they begin to recognize how it is affecting each of them. This repeats much of what should have happened in infancy. It is during these periods of affective attunement that the child feels connected to the carer and learns how to recognize, co-regulate and then individually regulate his or her arousal. It also provides the child with opportunities to construct a coherent autobiographical narrative. A secure base is created during treatment, by the carer and therapist being playful, loving, accepting, curious and empathic. Within the safety of the therapeutic relationship, children can explore and seek to resolve their past losses and traumas.

The self-reliant, aggressive controlling strategies used by many of these children have encouraged some practitioners to develop 'holding therapy' as a way of keeping the extremely avoidant and anxious child physically and psychologically engaged with a warm, accepting carer so that the child learns that it is safe to 'let go' of being fearfully in control. The nature of the 'holding' seems to vary from physical restraint, which is incompatible with attachment theory, ethically unacceptable and potentially dangerous, to gentler forms of physical holding and eye-contact maintenance, practised without restraint or coercion and conducted with the child's permission (nurturing holding).

Holding therapies of whatever type remain controversial (see the special issue of the journal *Attachment and Human Development* Vol. 5, No. 3, 2003 for a fuller discussion), and they will not be considered further. However, many therapists who have practised the non-restraining, gentler, voluntary types of 'holding' have, along with many others who work with school-age children, simultaneously developed further interventions based on attachment theory, affect attunement and improved mentalisation. A brief distillation of the main features of these aspects of treatment is given, but again the reader is encouraged to visit the source texts for a much fuller picture (Atkinson and Goldberg 2004; Bannister 2004; Fearnley 2000; Hughes 1997, 1998; Kagan 2004; Keck and Kupecky 1995; Levy and Orlans 1998; van Gulden and Bartels-Rabb 1995; Archer and Burnell 2003; Cairns 2002; Schofield and Beek forthcoming).

Through the medium of a secure attachment, therapists working with children's carers seek to introduce the full range of developmental experiences that a child might normally expect to enjoy if he or she is to become mentally healthy and behaviourally unproblematic. Within the context of a warm, safe, reciprocal and attuned relationship, the child can develop affectively, cognitively, behaviourally and socially. Using a developmental approach to attachment and mental health means that interventions need to arrive in the right developmental order. For example, children's ability to respond to cognitive and rational approaches depends on their having achieved a clear understanding of how they themselves 'work' emotionally. The order of therapeutic play, conducted with some flexibility and latitude, is as follows.

1. Develop a Trusting, Secure Attachment with Primary Carers

Carers themselves must present their children with a secure, autonomous state of mind before they become actively and directly involved in therapy. In particular, carers with unresolved attachment issues will continue to distress and dysregulate their children whenever attachment behaviour is manifest (for example, Steele et al. 2003). Unresolved issues must be identified and explored before the parent becomes fully involved in treatment.

2. Establishing Intersubjectivity and Mind-Mindedness

In the manner discussed under parent–infant interactions in the previous chapter:

> (T)he caregiver and therapist need to assume an active, intersubjective stance in which their experience of the child's subjective experience is made clear and becomes a bridge to help the child eventually regulate and construct meaning regarding his inner life.
>
> (Hughes 2003: 274)

In particular, the therapist and caregiver need to be highly attuned to the child's affective states, for it is these states that the child finds hard to recognize, understand, communicate and manage. Maltreated and traumatized children react impulsively and unreflectively when they become unduly aroused. Developmentally they have experienced little affective feedback about their mental states. Affect mirroring and mentalization of the child's psychological condition therefore become important elements of treatment. Secure children are helped to 'see' their inner life by mind-minded parents. Having missed out on much of this sensitive intersubjectivity, maltreated children need to develop their own emotional intelligence and social cognition in relationship with a highly attuned and responsive carer or therapist. Here is an example of an adoptive parent interacting along these lines with her angry, destructive seven-year-old daughter:

> Zoe, I can see you're angry and feeling all hot and bothered. I am really sorry that you feel that way. I know when you feel angry it often gets you into trouble, but I want to help you keep out of trouble.

Note that the parent is feeding back affective information to the child about the child's emotional state at both the psychological and somatic level. Much of what takes place, both inside and outside therapy, is similar to that which occurs between parents and their young children. Although chronologically it might seem strange to interact with a nine-year-old in the manner of an infant or toddler, developmentally this is both appropriate and effective. Until the child has been helped to recognize and process emotional and interpersonal information, he or she is likely to find affect regulation difficult. Just as mothers of young babies do, therapist and carer might therefore exaggerate their emotional expressions, voice tone and rhythm as they respond to a child's feeling states. Body language might also be emphasized to convey understanding, acceptance and protection. Gestures, voice, gaze, and facial expressions need to be synchronized and coordinated. As eye contact is often difficult for maltreated children, carers might have to be sensitively alert and respond quickly to the child making any kind of visual or psychological connection. Reciprocal gazing, so typical of parent–infant interaction, has to be introduced and slowly developed with traumatized children. Eye-to-eye contact is a powerful channel of communication. It is therefore important to help the child feel that it is safe and worthwhile to connect with the non-maltreating carer's mind.

Two things begin to emerge in this process: attachment security and increased intersubjectivity. There are no short cuts to these achievements. Carers have to begin to feel comfortable with these basic and early-stage interactions, remembering that developmentally their child is relatively immature. In extreme cases, this developmental delay might even apply to the child's physiological development. Emotions are experienced both psychologically and somatically. All sensory stimuli provide infants with information about their environment, including signs of danger. Therefore, the body and how it feels is as important as how the mind feels whenever affect is aroused and needs to be regulated.

Again, sensitive caregiving helps children learn about and understand how their bodies and senses work. 'Your tummy's full that's why you feel sleepy.' 'You're cold, that's why your are shivering and feeling unhappy, so I'm going to put on your nice, warm jacket and then you'll feel better.' Children who miss out on routine information and feedback of this kind find it difficult to make sense of their bodies. Parents who cause their children traumatic physical distress, by punching them, starving them, burning them, create extreme feelings of pain and physical arousal *and* fail to help the child deal with it. Safe carers, as well as acting as regulators of children's psychological affect, also act as 'psychobiological' regulators of their physiological arousal.

Children who are denied this second type of regulation experience a kind of sensory deprivation. As a result, severely maltreated children's sensory development is often impaired, particularly those who have suffered severe neglect. They are clumsy and accident-prone. They become easily confused and distressed to the point of trauma if they experience a body sensation that suddenly reminds them, unconsciously, of earlier abuse and neglect. A cold, spilled drink over the legs, a loud noise, or even the appearance of a male in the case of sexually abused children, might precipitate a catastrophic, alarm response. Every day sensory stimuli can be experienced as threatening. The brain never switches off from being in survival mode. All of this information is being processed in parts of the brain (the limbic system) that are developmentally prior to and more primitive than the conscious, thinking areas (the cortex).

Under threat, both our mind and body respond adaptively. Perry (1999) observes that we move along an arousal continuum from calm to alarm to fear to terror. Under low arousal and stress, the conscious, rational thinking part of our brain is likely to be in charge. But the more threatening and dangerous the situation, the more likely it is that the more 'primitive' emotional and behavioural centres of the brain that lie outside consciousness will be activated.

> When a traumatized child is in a state of alarm (because they are thinking about the trauma, for example) they will be less capable of concentrating, they will be more anxious and they will pay more attention to 'non-verbal' cues such as tone of voice, body posture and facial expression. This has important implications for understanding the way the child is processing, learning and reacting in a given situation.
>
> (Perry 1999: 1)

The emotions are to do with fast, non-reflective responses, particularly in situations of danger. In this sense, they always out-trump reflective thought, at least over the short term. Children who suffer early and severe trauma never fully integrate these powerful experiences into working consciousness. This is why they remain vulnerable in the face of arousal.

> Neurophysiological hyperarousal has survival value. It is highly adaptive in the face of threat. The human response to threat is a regression into the survival mode of fright, flight, fight and freeze. When threat is ever present in early childhood, the survival response may become permanent. A temporary state of high arousal becomes a more or less permanent trait of personality. Children who have been traumatised in early childhood when the brain is still developing tend to develop survival responses that are characterised by either hyperarousal or dissociation. When faced with sensory stimuli, they are unable to process it cortically. Instead the stimulus is processed sub-cortically within the limbic system.... Children who are traumatised appear to re-activate an already activated 'fear system' in the brain.
>
> (Gogarty 2000: 63–4)

Building on this insight, Gogarty has developed therapeutic practices with maltreated children in foster care that address these fundamental physiological and developmental issues. Along with colleagues, she has turned to the work of Ayers (1979, 1989) and Kranowitz (1998) on 'sensory integration', first developed with children suffering neurological disabilities. Gogarty (2000) has incorporated these types of practice within an attachment perspective. Many maltreated children also suffer sensory integration dysfunctions. They have difficulty processing and regulating sensory information, whether it is sight, sound, touch, taste, smell, balance and body awareness, or temperature. They can react in very distressed and dysregulated ways whenever they experience strong or confusing sensory information with which a secure child would have no difficulty. Developmentally, children have to learn to recognize and handle sensory information before they can establish secure attachments. Traumatized children read danger into much of their own physiological arousal. Until these children can regulate and process such stimulation, they cannot regulate their emotions. Developmentally speaking, this leaves them in a very immature condition. For example:

> Children who feel insecure in space cannot let go emotionally. Children who cannot plan their movements are unable to organise a coherent attachment strategy ... it is difficult to 'think' one's way out of fear which is played out as fight, flight or freeze – everyday experiences for many maltreated children.
>
> (Gogarty 2000: 253)

Using 'sensory integration' techniques, children are helped to feel calm and relaxed in multi-sensory and stimulating environments. Children are helped to recognize, control and discriminate between whole ranges of sensations. Only then can they move on to regulate themselves at higher levels of emotional processing, behaviour and cognition. Physical integration precedes emotional integration. By organizing sensation, infants gain control over their emotions (Ayers 1989). This helps prepare children for the next developmental level of emotional regulation, which is best developed using techniques such as 'sandplay' (see below). Beginning with cognitive-behavioural techniques is unlikely to have much impact on traumatized children. Cognitive-behavioural approaches presume that the cortex can deal with the emotional limbic system. Under the challenge, arousal and threat of prematurely delivered cognitive therapies, traumatized children are once more likely to go into survival mode – flight, fight or freeze – and therapy halts.

Along with 'sensory integration', which is best used for children who have suffered very early trauma, 'sandplay' (for example, Bradway 1997; Lowenfield 1991) is another highly favoured therapeutic technique in this field. It combines a psychological and physiological approach in which children symbolically but tangibly play out and reorganize their internal working models using a wide range of realistic play figures. For example, using a sand tray and water, a child might repeatedly enact a kitten getting into danger or being attacked by a monster, and then being rescued by some benign and protective figure. By allowing the rescue to happen repeatedly, children begin to allow themselves to represent new attachment figures as available and responsive at times of need. They become freed up to take advantage of their new carer's love and availability. Symbolic sandplay can be both powerful and therapeutic, facilitating attachments and allowing the child to experience affect feedback, intersubjectivity, and all the benefits of engaging with the mind of a mind-minded and sensitive carer. This non-verbal, non-rational form of therapy operates at a neurologically primitive, pre-verbal level.

Building on this way of thinking, Bhreathnach and Gogarty (2000) suggest an overall therapeutic order based on children's normal development from very basic physiological regulation right through to cognitive and reflective-based regulation characteristic of securely attached children. They call it an *integrative model of self-regulation*:

Cognitive, language based therapies and teaching approaches
↑
Sensory-emotional discrimination:
Sensory Integration; story telling; symbolic, pre-sand and sand play
↑
Sensory-emotional modulation:
Sensory Integration, Sensory stimulation
↑
Autonomic functioning:
Medication, homeopathy, aromatherapy,
massage to facilitate physiological regulation

This developmental 'bottom-up' approach is echoed by many attachment-oriented therapists, including Fosha:

> Emotional experience is accessed through language and logic.... Therapies dealing with disorders that are fundamentally emotional in nature need to be able to reliably access sensory, motoric, and somatic experiences to engage them in a dyadic process of affect regulation and eventual transformation. This requires the bottom-up processing approach of experiential therapies, rather than the top-down approach of most cognitive and insight-focused therapies. There is a premium on activating right-brain mediated emotional processes through techniques that focus on sensory, somatic, and motoric experience, and that involve reliving and picturing, rather than narrating, interpreting, and analyzing.... Powerful negative emotions need to be integrated into the individual's autobiographical narrative, making it increasingly coherent and cohesive.
>
> (Fosha 2003: 229–30)

Working mainly with maltreated children placed for adoption, van Gulden's therapeutic approach is also developmental in character. van Gulden and Bartels-Rabb (1995) use a combination of attachment theory and object relations theory. Abused and neglected children have problems feeling that their carers and their selves *continue to exist* across space, time and different emotional states (object permanence). Infants need to understand that carers, particularly new carers, are permanent and 'here to stay.' Games such as peek-a-boo and hide-and-seek should therefore be encouraged. Similarly, many children have difficulty experiencing the self and the other as *remaining psychologically coherent and whole* across space, time and different emotional states (object constancy). With new carers (or treated and supported birth parents), these children have to be helped to understand that parents continue to love them even when they are being told off (object permanence). An angry mother and a loving mother are still the same mother. Traumatized children develop separate mental representations of their helpless and hostile carers (dissociation). They need to feel that other people, and their own selves, actually continue to be the same psychologically whole entities whether they happen to be feeling angry, tense, anxious, happy, disapproving or disapproved of (object constancy).

van Gulden and Bartels-Rabb (1995) believe that much of maltreated children's behaviour is stuck at the age of development when they experienced the loss or trauma. Problematic behaviours are seen as symptomatic of these earlier needs and experiences. But more importantly, if the age that the troubling behaviour normally occurs in development can be recognized, it provides a powerful guide how best to respond and treat children and their behaviour. This is another reminder that developmental attachment therapists deal with the child's psycho-emotional age and not his or her chronological age.

For example, most children aged around three tend to lie when caught doing something they shouldn't. Parents rarely call their toddler a liar. They react warmly but knowingly, even with a smile: 'You cheeky boy! You did eat the cake. You're telling fibs, that is what you're doing!' Little children are told not to 'tell tales'. They are encouraged to 'tell the truth' and 'own up'. When they do admit their wrongdoings, they might even be told that they are good. However, when a ten-year-old tells lies, most parents react with much less tolerance, which is fine for children whose development has been normal. But for maltreated children whose perspective-taking and social development has been impaired, rather like the toddler, their sense of where the boundaries lie between truth and falsehood are not good. When dealing with such children, van Gulden and Bartels-Rabb advise trying to deal with the ten-year-old more in the manner of the three-year-old. In the face of strong emotions, traumatized children find it difficult to tell fantasy from reality. They resort to immature defences. The trick the carer has to make is to help the child understand that although the carer is not condoning the misdemeanour, the child is still secure, loved and valued for him/herself.

This way of thinking and reacting can be used for a whole range of 'immature' behaviours displayed by older children. The carer has to learn to perceive and deal with the older child at his or her emotional and developmental age, which is not always easy, but can be surprisingly effective if conducted sensitively and if the child feels like accepting it. This is particularly true when dealing with the emotions. We tend to interact very differently with angry infants and angry eight-year-olds. And yet if the assessment suggests that in many areas, the maltreated older child is developmentally very infant-like, the more therapeutic response might be to deal with the emotion as you might handle it with a baby. Affect-mirroring would come into play. Strong, exaggerated and repeated verbal descriptions might be offered: 'Good heavens, I can see you are feeling very angry. That's a very angry face you've got on. What do you think has caused that? Let's see if we can sort it out. Come on....'.

Praise and encouragement are equally important. We tend to be very applauding, repetitious and confirming when infants and toddlers do something well, but less exaggeratedly positive when an older child achieves something similar: bakes a cake, submits a good piece of homework, and remembers to turn off the TV. And, suggests Lieberman, parents also:

> need to over-emphasize their responses to the child's muted signs of need, marking separations with unambiguous demonstrations of sadness and assurances of a prompt reunion, and underlining reunions with clear demonstrations of joy.
>
> (Lieberman 2003: 282)

van Gulden counsels:

> Think how you would react to and manage behavior if the child was chronologically the age that the behavior usually occurs. Using your perceptions and interpretation of the behavior when it presents at the 'normal' age begin to identify ways to meet the child's needs and teach the missing skills while respecting the child's chronological age. Try to identify and connect with the child as soon as possible. These children need your love most when their behaviors are most 'unlovable'!
>
> (van Gulden 2000)

By taking children through all these developmental stages, the maltreated or adopted child is, in effect, being 're-parented' in order to achieve trust and a secure attachment.

3. Dealing with Conflicts and Repairing Disruptions

It is inevitable that from time to time carer and child will fall into conflict. Attunement breaks down. This happens in secure as well as insecure attachments. However, what characterizes secure relationships is that the carer acknowledges what has happened, recognizes how it is affecting the mental state of the child, intersubjectively represents this understanding to the child, and so repairs the disruption and regulates the arousal. When traumatized children feel out of control or helpless, shame is felt which is a pervasive and highly debilitating emotion. Even routine discipline and frustration can cause feelings of shame. Hughes recommends:

> Frequently then in therapy and at home, the child will benefit from empathy, acceptance, curiosity and reassurance over routine conflict, memories, and stress in his life that is experienced by him as being shameful, rejecting, and abusive. The distressing affects of shame and fear need to be co-regulated by the therapist and caregiver before continuing the interactions.
>
> (Hughes 2003: 275)

The parent must contain, hold and regulate the child's distress and disorganization, allowing the child to feel his or her their emotions are containable and manageable; that they need not overwhelm the child or his/her carer.

4. Cognitive-Behavioural Strategies

Only when the child begins to develop a more coherent mental representation of the self and others, and is beginning to understand and reflect on his or her own affective make-up, should more explicitly cognitive and behavioural interventions be introduced. 'The use of these strategies follows, and does not precede, the intersubjective states of attunement, interpersonal motivation, and meaning-making which are crucial for facilitating the secure base necessary to utilize these strategies' (Hughes 2003: 276).

Scott (2003) argues that so long as parents' *behaviour* with their child is adequately sensitive, their mental representation of attachment issues is less important. For example, 'social learning theory', based on cognitive behavioural techniques, when used by parents has been found to be effective for a range of anti-social behaviours. Webster-Stratton's (1999) work on helping parents praise desired behaviour, ignore negative behaviour, set clear limits, and impose swift and explicit consequences for rule breaking, all in the context of a warm and accepting relationship, is now widely used by many childcare workers. Carers are encouraged to try out and rehearse a range of well-tried and effective parenting skills. These parenting techniques are certainly effective with many children, but the evidence is less solid when treating maltreated and traumatized children. Green and Goldwyn (2002) have also explored the benefits of cognitively based treatments for older children, as our understanding of the cognitive aspects of disorganized attachment representations has increased.

> They focus on the relationship of mood, arousal and cognition in treatment in a way that is increasingly convergent with attachment theory. They provide a model for the generation of new forms of cognitively oriented individual treatments for children, focusing on modifying strategies for disorganised cognitive representations of relationships and associated emotional dysregulation.
>
> (Green and Goldwyn 2002: 843)

Treatments Based on Affect Attunement and Corrective Emotional Experiences

Therapies recognize that treatment needs to replicate the characteristics of a secure caregiving environment, albeit with a child who deeply mistrusts being looked after, cared for, protected and benignly regulated by his or her 'attachment figures'. Considerable emphasis is placed on helping children develop their 'mentalizing' and 'reflective' capacities, thus improving their ability to understand themselves and other people as psychological and intentional beings, and how feelings affect behaviour, and behaviour affects other people (Fonagy and Target 1997). Children have to recognize, understand and learn to regulate their emotions within the context of close relationships. It is within the intensity of close relationships that emotional information is expressed and processed as both parent and child share it. 'Helping young children acquire self-regulation through reciprocal management of affects with an emotionally available therapist,' write Osofsky and her colleagues (1995: 605), can help children 'return to a healthy developmental pathway'.

Later stages of treatment address issues of grief, loss, sadness and depression associated with past experiences and traumatic events. Children are helped to understand the difference between wants and needs, and differentiate between feelings and behaviours. Later stages look at how feelings can be handled and discharged appropriately. Cognitive techniques therefore tend to be introduced once the child is more adept at recognizing and processing emotional and attachment-related information.

Close relationships are the one thing that controlling (compulsively self-reliant, compulsively compliant, and compulsively caregiving) and traumatized children avoid. Their developmental agenda is to control and not emotionally engage people. This denies them exposure to the very experiences they need. So long as they remain unable to relinquish control and relate fully and accurately with their carers and therapists, the children make little emotional or developmental progress.

The intensity of the relationship between the maltreating parent and the child, although damaging, was nevertheless experienced as intense. 'One goal of therapy, then, is to approximate to the healthy bonding cycle, thus reworking the process that was so traumatically interrupted early in the child's life' (Keck and Kupecky 1995: 152).

Educating the child about his or her early attachment experiences and psychosocial difficulties gives the message, 'We understand how you got to be this way and can help you.' Further, this positive reframing gives another message that 'It was not your fault that you were maltreated. We also understand that in the past you needed to use your defences and be in control in order to protect yourself and survive, but those defences are now preventing you from learning to love and trust' (Fearnley 2000, Keck and Kupecky 1995, Levy and Orlans 1998).

Treatment generally comprises two broad elements:

1 Cognitive restructuring of emotional experiences and 'disconfirmation' of negative, insecure working models of the self and others.
2 This is done by experiencing an intense, close, sensitive, mind-minded, caring, containing, and affectively alert therapeutic relationship.

As we have seen, many attachment-disordered children remain at very early stages of their biopsycho-social development. They therefore may need to create many touch, sensory, emotional and verbal exchanges with their carers that they have not previously experienced. It is key that children learn to feel safe in the care of their carers (new or old), trusting their emotional availability and willingness to respond at times of fear and need, anger and sadness. In essence, the treatment helps both children and parents interact in an emotionally synchronized and regulated way, so that the child feels mentally understood by a fully 'mind-minded' carer. This helps the child develop a secure, safe attachment within which normal psychological development; reflective function and mental integration can begin to take place.

Therapeutic goals include (Fearnley 2000; Levy and Orlans 1998):

- to contain and reduce acting-out behaviour
- to identify and express emotions verbally
- to experience a safe, caring, nurturing, interested relationship with significant adults
- to facilitate descriptions of past traumas and the feelings associated with them, including fear, anger and sadness.

This stage of treatment seeks to recreate feelings of infant security. It allows children to release control, develop trust and express strong feelings in a safe environment. Therapy aims to create a 'corrective emotional experience' that approximates to what should have occurred in the child's formative years. The intense introduction of safe and non-abusive bonding helps initiate more secure attachment behaviours. Children's carers should be involved and informed at all stages of the therapeutic process. The growing attachment relationship is systematically transferred to the carers. Children often self-stimulate in the early stages of treatment. Many find eye contact very difficult. Eye contact aids communication, bonding, and the recognition of internal mental states, in both the child and the carer. It is integral to the formation of close, trusting relationships in which socio-emotional learning takes place. Therapists therefore have to be extremely alert and responsive if they are going to open up channels of communication with children. The more that these children feel understood and are helped to understand, the safer they will feel. The safer the children feel, the less reliant they will be on their defences, including self-stimulation, avoidance of eye contact, compulsive self-reliance and aggressively trying to be in control.

In a relationship with either the therapist or the carer, children slowly begin to experience what it feels like to be dependent and yet safe, exposed but understood. In the therapeutic relationship, attachment-related experiences rise rapidly to the surface. Under such conditions, disorganized children typically react with confused anger, fear and feelings of distress linked to their earlier experiences of abandonment and abuse, trauma and neglect. Distress activates both controlling behaviour and dissociated states of mind.

The therapeutic relationship increases emotional arousal and provokes responses that are unlikely to occur in less demanding treatments, in which children simply avoid or deflect attempts at psychological connection. The skill of the therapist lies in creating a relationship in which children recognize that it is safe to have strong feelings. Children begin to sense that their emotions, including anger, can be contained; that they do not always lead to destruction (of the self as well as others) or abandonment. In short, therapy at this stage seeks to generate an experience that replicates the qualities of 'good enough' early care – nurturing, trust, safety and security. Once children begin to experience these, they can then allow themselves to be understood, influenced and guided by a trusted, loving parent – the starting point for sound socio-emotional development.

Perry (1999) captures much of the same therapeutic territory when he recommends the following behaviours for carers of traumatized and maltreated children:

- Do not be afraid to talk about the traumatic event if the child brings it up on his or her own.
- Provide a consistent, predictable pattern for the day and make sure the child knows and can expect this pattern. If the day is likely to include doing something different or out of the ordinary, this will need to be carefully explained. Traumatised children feel anxious about change and the unexpected. They also like to feel that caring, safe adults are in control of events.
- Be nurturing, comforting and affectionate in the appropriate context. Intimacy, particularly for sexually abused children, can be frightening and confusing. Provide cuddles, hugs and kisses when the child seeks them. Never demand a kiss or a hug. Abused children associate commands with power in others and helplessness (and therefore danger).
- Discuss your expectations of behaviour and your style of 'discipline' with the child. Make sure rules and expectations are clear, and what the consequences will be if they are broken. Be consistent.
- Talk with the child, giving them age-appropriate information so that they have as much knowledge about present and future situations as possible. Don't be afraid of repetition. Traumatised children need clear and full explanations. It is uncertainty that distresses them. Honesty and openness help children develop trust.
- Protect the child. Cut short activities that are upsetting or re-traumatising for the child.
- Give the child 'choices' and some sense of control. It is lack of control that makes traumatised children feel that the situation is dangerous, and may cause them to behave in a wild, frightened and uncontrolled way. Giving the child choices (chosen by the parent) makes them feel safer. ('You can either choose to do what I have asked or you can carry on being noisy and miss out on watching your favourite video. You can choose.')

Once a safe and sensitive relationship has been established, cognitive restructuring of the self and others can begin to take place. This is achieved by building positive and accurate emotional understanding and affect regulation.

The intense and physically close nature of therapy allows both child and caregiver (or therapist) to access feelings not always verbally expressed. Treatment not only helps children release and demonstrate feelings, it aims to help children recognize, label and understand them. Not until children can distinguish between despair, anger, guilt, happiness, shame, rage and fear can they begin to regulate their own affect and understand the nature and origin of other people's feelings and behaviour. Indeed, because of the close connection developmentally between the body and the emotions, many children find it difficult to differentiate feelings associated with their basic senses, including those of touch, smell, taste, sound and sight. Bodily signals, such as pain or hunger or needing to urinate, are easily misread and can lead to inappropriate behaviours (putting a winter coat on for a hot summer's day; wanting to eat when they are already full). Experience and recognition of feelings is a first important step helping children get in touch with themselves. It helps them access and deal with their early experiences of loss and abuse and to recognize their true origins.

The deep anxiety felt by 'controlling' children is that by 'letting go', danger, abandonment and feelings of fear and rage will overwhelm and destroy them. By identifying, labelling and differentiating strong feelings and understanding some of their origins in abusive, rejecting and neglecting early caregiving relationships, children can begin to 'disconfirm' their current insecure internal working models. The self can be experienced as worthy of care and protection rather than as unlovable, bad and deserving of abuse. Other people can be represented as available and caring, and not as unavailable and unpredictable, helpless and hostile. Children need to stay in the psychological present, and articulate what has actually happened to them.

These particular kinds of treatments are long. Progress is very slow during the first six to nine months, as children remain 'stuck' in their old, familiar 'controlling' mode. Towards the end of the first year, therapists typically see a surge as children begin to realize that carers can care for them without destroying them. It begins to feel safe to be parented. During the final 12 months, children often take two steps forward and one step back. Progress is punctuated by outbursts of regressive behaviour. However, by the end of two years, children begin to trust new carers, and relax as they learn to let go of their controlling, defensive behaviours. Social and emotional exploration begins to take place at an increasingly rapid pace, helping the children develop mind-mindedness and improved reflective function.

Chloe (based on a case discussed in Howe and Fearnley 2003)

Chloe's father is a Schedule 1 offender, although this was not known when she was born. He had convictions for sexual assaults against young girls. When

Chloe was just over a year old her sister was born. Their father also had a major drink problem. There was extensive domestic violence between the children's parents. Their mother was isolated and had no family or social supports. From a very young age, the children were often left alone for long periods. They suffered severe neglect. When social services were eventually alerted to the case, Chloe's body was covered in sores, her hair was matted and falling out, she was seriously underweight and dirty, and a rash covered her mouth and cheek as a result of bottle-propped feeding. Initially social services tried to put in a range of support services, but they found the parents uncooperative.

The children continued to be neglected. They were finally removed when Chloe was 21 months old and her sister six months old. They were placed together in foster care. However, the carer found Chloe unmanageable. She screamed, was very aggressive towards her baby sister whom she would drag to the floor in a violent manner, and she would go rigid and arch her back whenever the carer tried to control or calm her down. Her demands for attention and food, and the need to get her own way, seemed unending. Chloe also slept poorly, and would often wake up several times in the night. After three months the foster carer said she could no longer cope and asked for Chloe to be removed.

Chloe remained in her second foster home for two years. Contact was arranged between the two sisters. Her birth mother was also allowed contact but she often failed to turn up. Social services were granted a 'Care Order', and the plan was to have the sisters adopted without parental contact.

In her second foster home, Chloe continued to show difficult and disturbed behaviours. Again, she would scream for long periods, lash out at anyone and everyone, angrily throw her toys across the room, resist being nurtured and cared for, and refuse to do anyone's bidding. Although Chloe was aggressive and violent, her little frame threatened no one in the home. The carer, who was experienced, felt she could cope, knowing that Chloe would soon be moving to a permanent placement. It was at this time that social services learned that Chloe's father was a Schedule 1 offender and that his violence against his wife had been regular and severe. Chloe would sometimes talk about how she had seen her daddy beat up her mummy and that this had frightened her.

In spite of Chloe's earlier aggression towards her younger sister and her continued highly disturbed state, social services placed both children (four and three years old) with the same couple with a view to adoption. There were no other children of the new family. A year into the placement, the adoptive mother said she was at the end of her tether with Chloe. Reluctantly, she said that although she could manage Chloe's sister and had grown very fond of her, she felt unable to cope with Chloe. The adoptive mother felt that Chloe did not want her. She resisted being cared for and loved. Often, when her adoptive mother tried to get close (to cuddle, control, wash, reprimand, nurture), Chloe would freeze and her eyes would glaze over, behaviours typical of children in a dissociated state. Other times, Chloe would scream in a high-pitched cry for long periods. 'Whenever I tried to get her attention in some way,' said her adoptive mother, 'it was as if she had disappeared somewhere. I couldn't get near her. It was as if I was holding a cold, empty shell. A physical presence, yes, but no Chloe.'

In her hyperaroused states, Chloe would scream at the top of her voice, 'Don't strangle me! Get off me! You're hurting me! Take it out! Take it out! Don't do it!' These exclamations bore no relation to the adoptive mother's behaviour or her attempts to engage Chloe's attention. It was as if Chloe was in a different reality, somewhere in the past, which for her was very real and frightening. However, for her adoptive mother, Chloe and her behaviours were both puzzling and alarming.

It became clear that Chloe had either experienced some form of sexual abuse or witnessed her mother being sexually abused and degraded by her father. The traumatic nature of these experiences could be triggered and re-experienced by any number of ordinary, everyday parent–child interactions which in Chloe's mind were associated with danger and the need for fearfully aggressive acts of self-preservation. Chloe's thoughts and language were often described as 'weird' and bizarre. Typical of children suffering major disorders of attachment, her world was populated with dark and menacing forces that could emerge at any time to hurt and destroy both her and her imagined protagonists ('My mummy [birth mother] is in that cupboard and she's going to jump out and get you!').

Much of this was enacted by Chloe during play therapy. Mummy, daddy and little girl dolls would beat each other up; fingers would be poked up the dolls' bottoms with cries of 'That hurts! Take it out!' One doll would attempt to strangle another. However, whenever Chloe's adoptive mother was invited to join a session, the little girl refused to play. Although the therapist continued to help Chloe enact these violent and frightening experiences, she felt unable to move her on. Chloe appeared therapeutically stuck in a world that was out of control, violent and very frightening. A play therapist had suggested that the adoptive mother try 'babying' Chloe, but this only made matters 'ten times worse', with increased spitting, pulling, biting, punching, and screaming that would go on for an hour or more.

With support and encouragement from social services, Chloe's adoptive mother referred her daughter (then aged six) to an attachment therapist. A comprehensive assessment established that in terms of relating to her carer, Chloe was stuck in a relationship that she was experiencing and mentally representing as frightening, neglectful, potentially dangerous and without protection. Every time her carer spoke to her, Chloe immediately went into an excited and violent state. The adoptive mother felt exhausted: 'I don't know if I can continue looking after Chloe. I can't even speak to her any more.'

During the initial 'intensive' phase of therapy it became clear that Chloe rejected all caregiver figures – people who 'do mum-like things', who attempt to provide care and protection. The therapist who seemed to Chloe to behave most like a caregiver was also aggressively rejected. This gave the therapist a diagnostic insight into Chloe's state of mind whenever the young girl felt frightened, angry or hostile. Chloe's experiences of caregivers is that they hurt you, abandon you at times of greatest need, and leave you frightened and feeling helpless. Children in relationship with helpless-hostile carers also begin to adopt helpless-hostile 'controlling' behaviours (Solomon and George 1999).

Chloe's adoptive mother was prepared to become involved in the treatment. It was important for her to understand why Chloe treated her as she did; that Chloe was not actually relating to her as her true self, but rather as representative of Chloe's idea and past experiences of what mothers imply and entail.

A turning point was reached some months into therapy. Feeling particularly anxious in one session, Chloe was in a state of fearful aggression, most of which was directed at one of the therapists who was being treated as if she was the birth mother, the part-author of Chloe's original trauma. In contrast, Chloe treated the other therapist as a potential source of comfort and safety and characterized her as her adoptive mother. Chloe had managed, for the first time, to separate in her mind that some 'mummies' harm you and others protect you, and that each implies a different experience and warrants a different type of relationship. Up until that point, all mummies, in spite of her experience with her adoptive mother as a loving and safe carer, were treated as if they were frightening and hostile. It was therefore a breakthrough for Chloe to relate to each therapist as a separate individual, one being a 'bad mummy' and the other 'a good, safe mummy'. It was the 'good mummy', the one whom she was seeing as her adoptive mother, that Chloe began to turn to at times of distress. She began to perceive her adoptive mother as a secure base. It was not long after this achievement that Chloe began to ask for her real adoptive mother when she felt anxious; no one else would do.

Up until this point, Chloe could never relax with her adoptive mother; she remained alert, highly aroused, and self-protectively hostile. Her eyes would stay wide open and hypervigilant. However, after the breakthrough, for the first time Chloe could curl up on her adoptive mother's lap, relax, trust and close her eyes. Progress now became more rapid. Chloe began to talk a lot more objectively and retrospectively about her birth mother, saying things like 'It hurt with that mummy.'

Many of these early memories were pre-verbal and were being experienced emotionally and somatically. Therapy at this stage needs to help children experience, recognize and understand the complex but important psychological relationship between feelings, emotions and behaviour, both in their own minds and other people's. Once Chloe could distinguish between her mental representations of mummies who hurt you and mummies who don't, cognitive work could also be added to the therapeutic repertoire to help her interpret, accurately appraise and make sense of her contrasting relationships and experiences. Her journey of normal psychosocial development could now begin.

After two years of therapy, Chloe was formally adopted. Although Chloe can still lose her temper and be difficult, she deals with her adoptive mother as her adoptive mother in the objective present, and not as her birth mother in some re-experienced past trauma. Under stress, she is more likely to remain in the 'here and now' rather than in some past dissociated state. She no longer uses bizarre words, has flashbacks or dissociates. Social services remained supportive throughout and put in place a package of respite care with a foster parent who knows and gets on well with the adoptive family. Further therapy has also been made available if required.

Attachment Theory and Family Therapy

Although John Bowlby was always clear that attachment theory and family systems were intimately bound – indeed he wrote a paper in 1949 on group tensions in the family – the two fields have largely run in parallel but separate lines over the last 40 years. However, the two systems of thought are now being more formally integrated. One common theme examines the role that affect regulation plays in the context of family relationships, and how one member's mental representations of the self, the other and relationships play differently with each member of the rest of the family.

Attachment behaviours serve as stimuli to all other family members, signalling their emotional availability. Attachment-based family therapists aim to promote secure individuals with autonomous, reflective states of mind. Other family members can be either an asset or a liability. The therapeutic trick is to use both other family members and the therapeutic relationship to explore, recognize, understand and change insecure and anxious mental representations of both the self and the other. The aim is to help people develop a coherent narrative of their own emotional and relationship experiences, and how these have affected and continue to affect current thoughts, feelings and behaviour. Other people, and their support and willingness to communicate accurately, honestly and collaboratively, are the greatest resource in this endeavour.

> [A]lthough [internal working models] affect both the choice of one's partner and the interaction with one's family of creation, these cognitive models are also modified by one's partner and one's family of creation. Attachment theory and family systems theory are thus most valid when considered in conjunction.
>
> (Marotta 2003: 247)

Byng-Hall (1991, 1995, 1999) was among the first to apply an attachment perspective to treatment in family therapy. Families themselves can act as a 'secure base', one which provides 'a reliable and readily available network of attachment relationships, and appropriate caregivers, from which all members of the family are able to feel sufficiently secure to explore their potential' (Byng-Hall 1997: 27, cited in Byng-Hall 1999: 627). Within secure and functional families, caregivers collaboratively and in concert. By their behaviour, they illustrate the benefits of open communication, joint problem solving and mutuality. Armed with the concept of the family itself as a secure base, therapists can look at what currently supports or undermines security.

Classifications of family organizations (Minuchin 1974) developed by family therapists map neatly onto attachment classifications. 'Adaptive' families have all the features of secure and autonomous individuals. 'Enmeshed' families look like ambivalent and preoccupied patterns. 'Disengaged' families mimic avoidant and dismissing individuals. And 'chaotic' families show some conceptual overlaps with the disorganized category. For example, the prevalence in therapy of parents of whom one is ambivalent/preoccupied and the other avoidant/dismissing can be understood in terms of the highly conflictual relationship this combination generates. The preoccupied partner tends to express most of the discontent, feeling deprived, undervalued and emotionally abandoned. The dismissing partner on the other hand sees the other's discontent as the problem, adopting a contemptuous attitude to his or her neediness and proneness to cling. 'As the preoccupied partner escalates the appeal to have dependency needs met, this escalates the dismissing partner's defensive response of distancing, which lead to subsequent pursuer-distancer escalation' (Byng-Hall 1999: 629).

The therapy itself triggers attachment behaviours in all family members. Such behaviours are exhibited within the safe and 'secure base' created by the therapist, allowing family members to 'explore', examine and reflect on difficult feelings and attachment-related issues. 'Family therapists have an opportunity to work on the communications about attachment needs as they occur in the room' (Byng-Hall 1991: 213). Byng-Hall believes the availability of the therapist before, during and after treatment is regarded as important. Links are made between the parents' own attachment histories and their current patterns of interaction; that is, families are helped to become self-reflective and create a 'coherent story'.

An example of a family-based approached to treating a parentified child's burden is given by Byng-Hall (2002), in which he sees the 'family script' as one in which there are expectations that a parental role is performed by a child within the family, based on shared internal working models of who seeks care and who gives it. The compilation edited by Erdman and Caffrey (2003), which usefully brings together a range of papers written by leading experts on the theory and practice of attachment theory and family systems thinking, also outlines a number of approaches which offer a way of thinking about individual development beyond the parent–child dyad.

Conclusion

Working therapeutically with traumatized older children is extremely demanding. Given their histories of abuse and neglect, many are removed from their genetic parents and placed residentially, or with foster carers or adopters. The policy and practice implications of placing more and more maltreated children with new carers, many needing considerable support, have yet to be fully appreciated in terms of resource requirements, moral dilemmas and political responsibilities. Whereas parent–infant interventions can be relatively short-term and effective, therapeutic work with traumatized older children requires long-term and much more costly professional inputs. As many maltreated children have learned to survive by developing avoidant, defended and controlling strategies, the key therapeutic challenge is to help them feel safe in the presence of sensitive and responsive carers. Not until they learn to 'let go' and connect, mind to mind, with an open and attuned caregiver can they begin to explore their own and other people's mental states. This is the road to self-regulation and good mental health, but the older the child and the more profound the trauma, the longer and more difficult the journey.

15

Interventions with Adolescents, Adults and Parents

Introduction

We briefly consider two levels of attachment-based support and intervention when working with adults. One is the specialized practice of adult psychotherapy in which the therapist explores 'defences against love' (Schwartz and Pollard 2004: 115). The other is much more low-tech, but nevertheless uses many of the basic principles of attachment-related adult psychotherapy. It is much more relevant to those, including health and social workers, who work with maltreating parents and their families in the community and home setting. Professionals working with parents also have to remember that the supportive nature of their involvement will activate old unconscious childhood experiences of being cared for. This will affect how parents behave with professionals. For example, Hill et al. observe that experience of low care in childhood leads mothers who find themselves 'in a vulnerable situation to expect or elicit low support, or to have a reduced capacity to make use of the support that is provided' (Hill et al. 2004: 28).

Both approaches recognize the importance of 'minds connecting', particularly at the emotional level. Many theorists and practitioners, noting the way that the brain 'hard-wires' itself as psychological information is exchanged in close social interaction, appreciate 'the power of relationships to nurture and heal the mind' (Siegel 2003: 3). Psychotherapy, explains Cozolino (2002), provides a rich environment, designed to encourage the growth and integration of neural networks, which regulate memory, cognition, emotion and attachment. If the brain is built and shaped by early relationship experiences, then psychotherapy creates an interpersonal exchange in which it can grow and regrow, in which cognition, emotions and behaviour become integrated at the neurological, psychological and conscious levels. Those who can access and process the full range of their thoughts, feelings and behaviour not only do not need to employ defences, they also have the widest range of options in complex socio-emotional situations.

Anticipating this way of thinking about therapy, Bowlby (1980) believed that mental health required individuals with histories of loss and trauma consciously to reorganize their negative attachment-related experiences. In short, they had to integrate the memory of the experience with the accompanying affect (George and West 1999: 295). Painful, normally defensively excluded material had to be accessed, recognized, contained, understood and coupled with reflection and thought. For example, Allen (2001: 18, 293) believes trauma results when overwhelming arousal cannot be contained and processed. Traumatized clients, who are highly sensitized to all social interaction, try to deal with their unbearably painful emotional states by retreat (for example depression, isolation, dissociation), self-destructive acts (such as substance abuse, self-harm, suicidal ideation), and destructive acts (for instance aggression, rage). Therapists have to help clients contain and 'stay with' their painful feelings in order to learn how to recognize, contain, process and regulate them.

Most attachment therapists believe that those they wish to help should understand the basis of treatment: that is, they should be introduced to the basic ideas of attachment relationships and the part they play in helping us to regulate our emotions. Fonagy et al. (1995) found that individuals' capacity to represent their own and other people's mental states ('reflective function') was significantly associated with improved mental health. Most treatments aim to help us 'enhance consciousness of our own mental life' (Holmes 2001: 4). According to Brisch (1999), it is the therapist's central task to provide a secure base and a 'corrective emotional experience' for clients who have disordered social relationships. This requires great sensitivity and social cognition.

One of the characteristics of children and adults who have been severely abused, neglected and traumatized is their inability to deal flexibly and fluidly with situations. They fail to adapt to and cope with change, whether in their own feeling states or external relationships. The extreme arousal experienced during early traumatic episodes results in the brain being flooded with direct and very intense negative emotions that completely bypass the reflective, rational, language parts of the brain. This limits the ability of the individual to process and regulate the strong emotions experienced in most attachment-related situations, including parenting, feeling vulnerable, being dependent, and entering a romantic relationship. In effect, the brain lacks complexity. It operates in a relatively rigid, compartmentalized way, lacking integration between many of its key social, cognitive and emotional operations.

In contrast, secure individuals have very 'open' minds in which the emotional, language, somatic, rational and cognitive parts of the brain communicate and exchange maximum information, allowing the individual to access different types of memory and consider a range of behavioural options. Secure brains are complex. They are both highly differentiated and well integrated. In effect, they are coherent information processing systems (Siegel 2003). Psychotherapy, using an attuned and responsive relationship, therefore attempts to supply new information and provoke contact between those parts of the brain that have not had a chance to communicate because of previous trauma.

Analysing psychotherapy at the neurological level, Cozolino (2002) argues that a moderate amount of arousal and stress is necessary to trigger neural change. In most therapies, clients are exposed to their unintegrated and dysregulating thoughts and feelings in the context of a safe, nurturing, containing relationship that promotes understanding, linkage and integration between thoughts and feelings, memories and behaviour. 'As in development,' suggests Cozolino (2002: 33), 'the repeated exposure to stress in the supportive interpersonal context of psychotherapy results in the ability to tolerate increasing levels of arousal. This process reflects the building and integration of cortical circuits and their increasing ability to inhibit and regulate subcortical activation': which is to say that conscious, reflective thought begins to recognize, monitor and control emotional arousal and the associated memories, experiences and behaviours.

Whether in early childhood or adult psychotherapy, positive brain development, mental health and integrated states of mind are achieved in relationship with another who is emotionally attuned, and can mentalize and help regulate affect, and co-construct explanations and narratives which use words and therefore link and engage the rational and language centres of the brain. The combination of emotional attunement and language in the form of affect recognition and narrative construction runs throughout therapy. Affect regulation probably underpins most therapies as it allows defences to be dropped and integration to take place between affect and cognition.

Too much stress results in trauma, but 'the controlled exposure to stress during therapy is a way in which therapists have attempted to harness the interaction of stress and learning to change the brain in a manner promoting mental health' (Cozolino 2002: 24). Those who have suffered abuse, neglect and trauma experience dissociated states of mind in which they cannot make reflective links between the emotional, behavioural and cognitive centres of the brain. By recognizing or even stimulating important and difficult emotional experiences, therapists seek to help people integrate and access the full range of their psychological make-up; to recognize, stay with, and make links between previously unintegrated thoughts and feelings. Neural growth and integration are enhanced by (Cozolino 2002: 27):

1. The establishment of a safe and trusting relationship.
2. Gaining new information and experiences across the domains of cognition, emotion, sensation, and behaviour.
3. The simultaneous or alternating activation of neural networks that are inadequately integrated or dissociated.
4. Moderate levels of stress or emotional arousal alternating with periods of calm and safety.
5. The integration of conceptual knowledge with emotional and bodily experience through narratives that are co-constructed with the therapist.
6. Developing a method of processing and organizing new experiences so as to continue ongoing growth and integration outside of therapy.

Therapists should attempt to provide a secure base from which the client or patient feels a degree of increased safety in exploring his or her own and other minds and how these affect relationships. Therapists, according to Sable (2004: 11), by offering a trusting relationship, allow clients to examine their emotional experiences, and investigate and re-experience various aspects of their lives that have been locked away, 'some of which would be too painful to think about without a reliable and "trusted companion"' (Bowlby 1988). Lyons-Ruth et al. (2004: 84) suggest a number of ways in which those who work with insecure parents and others might provide a secure base:

1 Listen to the parent.
2 Express approval and positive regard for the parent.
3 Encourage communication about all kinds of affects.
4 Respond to hostility with increased attention, openness to listening, and problem-solving. In attachment literature, anger and distress are understood as attachment behaviours....
5 Join with the parent empathically around the complexities of parenting....
6 Encourage a patient but hopeful problem-solving approach....
7 Maintain an active, balanced, collaborative dialogue with the parent.

Making Emotional Contact

During treatment, therapists communicate their presence, that they are *thinking* about and have in mind the client's thoughts and feelings. There is emotional and empathic attunement within a safe but structured relationship. They are interested in how clients tell their story; what they can allow themselves to know and feel, remember and tell (Slade 1999: 582). For example, dismissing clients typically disavow the affect that emotions have on them and tell rigid stories suggesting rejection during childhood. In contrast, suggests Slade (1999: 582), preoccupied clients convey a sense of chaos, helplessness and being overwhelmed indicating the need for structure and containment. Clients who have unresolved states of mind with respect to loss and trauma cannot offer a coherent story; they can find no narrative structure 'strong enough to contact their traumatic pain' (Slade 1999: 585). Traumatized clients are ultra-sensitive to feeling abandoned (and being left alone with their fears), and therapists have to be extra-aware of this reaction to even the most innocuous of absences.

Clients are helped to recognize their anxieties and fears, tolerate them, explore them, understand them, before finally learning to regulate and control them as the cortex begins slowly to gain control over the brain's emotional centres. Feeling safe and secure comes from being sensitively understood: However:

> This will inevitably involve struggle. Patients are often trying not to think about their pain, or to project it into others who will act on it rather than re-present it to

> them. To be thought about is both relieving and terrifying. The therapist has to be able doggedly to carry on with the thinking task without persecuting the patient with his thoughts. Thus at times he is a quiet presence, at others actively engaging the patient in debate about the nature of the patient's own thoughts.
>
> (Holmes 2001: 19)

Siegel (2003: 6) talks about sailing the 'Cs' of psychotherapy, each of which promote contact and communication between therapist and client. For example, therapists need to employ warmth, empathy, *compassion* and *congruence*; they need to convey interest, acceptance and a desire to understand, and achieve *connection*. The client finds his or her mind in the mind of the mind-minded therapist. The individual begins to experience the self more consciously and explicitly.

Just as *contingent responsiveness* is extremely important in early parent–infant interactions, it is crucial that the therapist's responses, both verbal and non-verbal, are related to and contingent upon the other's signals, both verbal and non-verbal. This requires high levels of alertness and sensitivity. Having made sense of what has been observed, accurate and swift feedback is the essence of mind-mindedness, whether it is practised in parent–child interactions or psychotherapy. Contingent communication is therefore central to the development of a coherent, reflective, regulated, mentally healthy self. Just as in parent–infant interactions, therapy involves:

- perception of the other's signals, including their timing and intensity
- making sense of the words, eye contact, facial expressions, voice tone, and body language, and how they might be being experienced
- a timely, contingent and effective response.

The other then feels 'felt' and understood by the therapist, who seems to have the client and his or her mental state in mind. Interpersonal contingency promotes coherence. When we offer here-and-now contingency, clients 'develop a sense of here-and-now consciousness that is cohesive' (Siegel 2003: 45):

> For individuals with unresolved trauma, this therapeutic attachment relationship enables the patient's mind to enter terrifying states that can then process information which before may have led to excessively restrictive or chaotic patterns in the flow of energy and information. These rigidly constrained or disorganized states, at the core of unresolved trauma, can then have the opportunity within this interpersonal communicative experience to be dramatically – and permanently altered. Note that the essential feature is not that all of the details of the trauma be related with words, but rather that the patient be given a sense of safety that such traumatic states can be re-experienced, communicated if possible, and altered into more adaptive patterns in the future.
>
> (Siegel 2003: 45)

Even when the therapist 'gets it wrong', so long as the rupture in communication is recognized and repaired, the other feels an increasing sense of connectedness and *continuity*. And as the therapist recognizes and responds to the other's different, unconnected and unintegrated bits of memory, arousal and mental representations of the self and others, the client's associated feelings can be explored and linked, all within the context of the safe psychotherapeutic relationships (for example Heard and Lake 1997, Heard 2003, Marrone 1998). The self begins to knit together experiences and emotions that previously crashed into consciousness without warning or understanding. A sense of personal coherence emerges as stronger information pathways begin to develop between different parts of the brain and across a range of memories.

Again, mirroring parent–infant interaction, *co-construction* of experience is a key element of therapeutic success. Over time, the psychotherapist and client begin explicitly to try to make sense of both past and present experiences. They co-construct the meaning of their shared experiences. Narratives help us make sense of experience. For example, the more parents are able to make sense of their own childhood experiences, the more attuned and mind-minded are their parent–child interactions, and the more secure their children. Siegel (2003: 38) discusses the value of 'reflective dialogue' in which the therapist tunes into and reflects back the mental state of the other, which exists beneath the words and external behaviour. This is yet another example of the importance of displaying mind-mindedness, in which the therapist perceives the subjective experience of both the other and him or herself. The therapist may feedback, or invite reflection on what the other is thinking, feeling (sensations both in the body and the mind), perceiving, remembering, imagining, believing and intending. This encourages linkage between the non-verbal, body-focused, affect-laden, visual/imagistic and emotional processing parts of the brain (the right hemisphere), and the logical, cause-and-effect, cognitive, analytic and reflective parts of the brain (the left hemisphere). The patient can begin to link non-verbal affective experiences of the right hemisphere with the language (naming) and more consciously reflective processing centres of the left hemisphere.

Hyperarousal and trauma flood the emotional centres of the brain. They operate 'beneath' and are disconnected from the more language-based and analytic parts of the brain. In such conditions, traumatized individuals are driven and dominated by the lower regions of the brain, which deal with emotions and behaviour, but without linkage or reference to the reflective, analytic, more advanced parts of the brain found in the cortex. This is why those who have suffered trauma, particularly in early life, find it so difficult to articulate their feelings, or understand why certain situations suddenly trigger flashbacks, fear and panic (LeDoux 1998). Thus, during the activation of a traumatic memory, the brain is:

> 'having' its experience. The person may feel, see, or hear the sensory elements of the traumatic experience, but he or she may be physiologically prevented from

> being able to translate this experience into communicable language. When they are having their traumatic recall, victims may suffer from speechless terror in which they may be literally 'out of touch with their feelings' ... Particularly when a person experiences depersonalization and derealization they cannot 'own' what is happening, and thus cannot take steps to do anything about it.
>
> (van der Kolk 2003: 187)

Strong feelings, rageful behaviours, or frightening flashbacks can become activated without any sense of what has caused them or what is being recalled. The highly dysregulated and distressed state just seems to happen. Memories are somatic, sensory and emotional and stored sub-cortically, that is, they are nonverbal and outside conscious memory, and when activated give the feeling that the non-conscious remembered experience is actually taking place in the present. Treatment has to help the traumatized person begin to name and allow these feelings into more explicit consciousness. It involves the simultaneous activation of cognition and affect, words and feelings, the left hemisphere and the limbic system in which traumatic memories are stored.

Integration (which normally takes place in the orbitofrontal cortex) is probably the central process that enables self-regulation to occur. It allows more complex and realistic mental representations of the self and others to be accessed, linked and reflected upon. Emotions therefore have to be processed at both the sensori-motor level (in the body) and increasingly at the cognitive, reflective level of symbolic mental representations, accessible to conscious reflection, control and regulation. Integration between areas of the brain that have remained dissociated because of past stress and trauma can be achieved through the simultaneous or alternate activation of both the verbal/language centres of the brain (left cortex and hemisphere) and the emotional and unconscious centres (right hemisphere and limbic system). According to Cozolino (2002), therapists facilitate this integration by supplying a range of challenges to enhance awareness, and possible conscious linkage, between dysregulated emotions, memories, thoughts and behaviour.

> Some suggest that the ... factual elements of memory are stored predominantly in the left hemisphere, whereas the autobiographical (the sense of self in the past, not merely the knowledge of such an experience) representations are stored in the right hemisphere ... flashbacks appear to involve the intense activation of the right hemisphere (visual cortex) in the setting of left hemisphere (speech area) deactivation. In this manner, focusing attention on verbal and nonverbal dimensions of memory may 'force' the activation of both hemispheres in the therapeutic process of integrating autobiographical and semantic representations or traumatic events.
>
> (Siegel 2003: 49)

Feeling safe, and with improved feelings of connectedness, trust, and openness of communication, the individual can acknowledge, accept and process more and more information. The brain becomes less rigid and defended, and more complex and free-flowing. The origin of feelings is recognized. Their power and impact is understood. Once understood, previously dysregulating affect can be regulated. And with a self that feels more together and more under control, individuals begin to feel more connected with those around them. The more they can avail themselves of relationships and engage the mind of others, the more people feel they belong.

Mentalized Affectivity

The emotions, their understanding and regulation are seen as central to sound psychological development. Attachment-based therapists regularly import this idea into treatment. The communication, recognition and naming of emotions underpin much of therapy. Clients say and do things. Therapists react contingently and with sensitivity. They observe and comment on the other's affective state using reflective dialogue. They track the other's emotional state as conveyed in the body, the voice and the face. Fonagy et al. (2002) describe this as 'mentalised affectivity', something rather like the affect mirroring that takes place between mothers and babies discussed in Chapter 2. Mentalized affectivity is present when the individual recognizes the way one's own and other people's affective states affect both parties' feelings, thoughts and behaviour. It is a sophisticated kind of affect regulation. Therapists must foster the capacity for mentalization, replicating many of the features that help bring it about in secure attachments. Mental states, particularly emotional states, have to be recognized and then explicated. To regulate affect, one must first learn to tolerate it; and 'conversely to be able to tolerate affect, one must have the confidence in being able to regulate it' (Allen 2001: 313). In maintaining an attuned, reflective stance, the therapist:

> ultimately enables the client to find himself or herself in the therapist's mind and to integrate this image as part of his or her self-representation. In successful therapy, the client gradually comes to accept that feelings can safely be felt and ideas may be safely thought about.
>
> (Fonagy 1998 cited in Allen 2001: 310)

When employed therapeutically, the other's emotional, mental and physiological states are recognized, named and mirrored back verbally, facially, in gesture and body posture. Attachment-focused treatments aim to help develop more adaptive strategies of affect regulation by providing attuned, sensitive, alert and collaborative feedback with clients as they repeatedly experience affect-laden material during the course of therapy. This is the adult version of the way some therapists work with abused and neglected children (see previous chapter). The maltreated, traumatized child or adult has missed out on affective feedback in the context of a safe, trusted relationship. Mentalized affectivity therefore feeds the incoherent, unintegrated mind with powerful and valuable information about its own state:

> An important aim of psychotherapy, then, if not its central aim, is the extension of mentalization. With some patients ... the therapist's task may be considered to be similar to that of the parent who intuitively engages with the child world of psychic equivalence to emphasize its representational character ... The aim of psychotherapy for these individuals is to regenerate the connection between the consciousness of an affect state and its experience at the constitutional level. We have labeled this 'mentalized affectivity' – a term intended to indicate the capacity to connect to the meaning of one's emotions.
>
> (Fonagy et al. 2002: 14–15)

> (I)t is our belief that the relatively safe (secure base) attachment relationship with the therapist provides a relational context in which it is safe to explore the mind of the other in order to find one's own mind represented within it.
>
> (Bateman and Fonagy 2004: 143)

Along with Bateman and Fonagy (2004), Holmes (2004) also believes that such an approach – termed 'Mentalisation-Based Treatment' or MBT by Bateman and Fonagy – is particularly appropriate when working with those who suffer borderline personality disorder (BPD), most of who have suffered loss, rejection, abuse and neglect as children. They place great demands on mental health and welfare services, easily inducing feelings of helplessness, anger, exasperation, pity, the need to rescue, avoidance and rejection in professionals. The children of parents with BPD are at high risk of being classified disorganized/controlling, and likely to display a range of emotional and behavioural problems. It is therefore imperative that such parents are helped to develop a degree of mentalizing capacity:

> PD patients find it difficult to sustain a stable sense of the self and other as having beliefs, desires, and intentions. This puts them at grave disadvantage in interpersonal relationships, and may influence their problematic relationships with care-giving institutions. It has been suggested that such people as children lacked a care-giver who could ... validate their internal world, and see them as autonomous and sentient. One of the functions of therapy with people suffering from BPD is to offer a 'thinking mind' which can plan, intervene, and take a perspective on them as persons, in which meta-cognitive monitoring is a central component. We hope this 'holding in mind' function may eventually be internalised by the PD sufferer as self-reflexive capacity which in turn will enhance their interpersonal life.
>
> (Holmes 2004: 189)

The naming of emotions is important. Some people characteristically tread quickly and lightly over emotional ground. Others are confused about what they are feeling. Some express a feeling that is not entirely congruent with what is actually being experienced internally. And yet others feel overwhelmed and not in control of their emotions. In all these cases, not only do individuals need to gain a purchase on their feelings and their possible origin, they also need help to stay with, recognize, understand and learn to handle their arousal. Sometimes this might result in the appropriate external expression of emotions, sometimes in their containment by learning to express them inwardly. Expressed emotions, all too frequently displayed without regard to others, need to take account of their impact within the context of the relationship. 'Communicating affects,' believe Fonagy et al. (2002: 440) 'means that the expression is offered with the expectation of how it will be received by others. One wants the other person(s) not just to know what one feels, but also to understand and perhaps respond to this feeling.'

There will be times within treatment when the therapist upsets, misunderstands or fails to notice a key aspect of the other's state. At this point contingent communication is ruptured, and distress and abandonment are felt. The sensitive therapist, like the sensitive mind-minded parent, should recognize that something has gone wrong or has been missed. The ***rupture*** has to be recognized ('I think I ignored how you felt then, and I can see on your face that you feel annoyed'), and then ***repaired*** ('I got it wrong. Sorry. I guess you were trying to tell me that you felt sad about missing so much in your childhood, and me ignoring you felt like yet another rejection. Is that what happened just then?'). This response recognizes what is happening and how it felt, seeks to repair the rupture, and models sensitive, mind-minded interaction.

The contingent, mentalized affectivity offered by the therapist allows previously segregated representational states and processes to become simultaneously activated. Fear of abandonment might be recognized as leading to confused feelings of sadness and aggression, which end up shutting other people out. Being helped to recognize these powerful feelings in a safe, containing relationship allows conscious exploration, reflection and the gradual integration of old memories, current triggers and here-and-now thoughts, feelings and behaviours.

In effect, what the sensitively attuned therapist does is allow the client to keep in focus and hold in present, short-term working memory all those thoughts, emotions and psychological feelings, body sensations, memories, beliefs and behavioural intents just long enough to sense how they might be linked. Normally, the feelings generated by any one of these old unresolved triggers cascade uncontrollably through the mind, leading to highly dysregulated and out-of-control behaviour. Individuals with unresolved losses and traumas need emotionally to re-experience the event without feeling helpless. In the context of a safe relationship, the client is helped to realize that 'remembering the trauma is not equivalent to experiencing it again … that the experience had a beginning, middle, and an end, and that the event now belongs to one's personal history' (van der Kolk 2003: 189).

The safety of a containing and mind-engaging therapeutic relationship should allow the client to 'stay with', recognize and name his or her feelings of fear, terror, discomfort, anxiety, anger, sadness and confusion in conscious working memory, and so explore and reflect on what has happened and what is happening. Relaxation techniques can also be introduced to help the client focus attention on these distressing experiences while at the same time experiencing a calmer state of mind. In this way, old, unresolved, dysregulating emotions become associated with feelings of calm and safety. Staying with these strong feelings and fragmentary bits of uncontrollable mental representations gradually helps the client come together in consciousness. This is the beginning of integrated mental systems in which the individual can hold multiple, sometimes contradictory representations of the self and others in mind at the same time, and so recognize that all of us behave in complex, not always consistent ways and yet remain the same individual. It is our emotional states that drive our various behaviours, and it is as well to know this if we are to make sense of others as well as our selves (Fosha 2000).

Secure individuals find no difficulty holding in mind multiple representations of other people:

> Julie is being grumpy with me today because she isn't being allowed to drive her mother's car, but I don't experience this as a rejection of me. Rather it tells me that most of us when denied something we want tend to behave in an annoyed, hostile manner and take it out on other people, just to make the point. I know that when Julie is in a good mood, we'll still have fun together, so maybe I ought to react by suggesting we go shopping for clothes together. I know that always perks her up.

Once new linkages are formed, the individual's subjective experience of the self and others begin to alter. Benign circles set in, which feedback further into the disconfirmation of paranoid, defensive and distressed internal working models. Old, previously unresolved attachment issues become 're-encoded' in the context of the safe, less distressed environment of therapeutic 'mentalized affectivity'. A more positive (or at least less distressed) emotional charge then becomes associated with the 're-constructed' memory representation (Siegel 2003: 48). Repeatedly revisiting old unresolved losses and traumas in the safe context of therapy helps revise and reconfigure memories so that they become less distressing and more tolerable:

- Therapy activates old unresolved memories and the feeling and body states that go with them.
- Sensitive, attuned, mind-minded 'mentalized affectivity' gradually allows the client to stay with and focus on the memories and sensations.

- The safe, non-distressing, collaborative, co-constructing therapeutic environment facilitates a re-encoding of the mental processes and psychic information both verbally and, perhaps more importantly, non-verbally at the affective level of intersubjectivity.
- This cycle will be repeated many times in therapy, but each reactivation will be experienced more consciously, explicitly and coherently.
- The result will be a gradual modification of the material and the associated memories so that they are recognized and experienced as more tolerable and understandable. They can be integrated, and ideally 'resolved'. Thus, old, highly defended, dissociated material enters and disorganizes current consciousness and behaviour before it is re-organized into more secure, reflective, autonomous patterns.

In short, 'effective psychotherapy can be seen fundamentally as an emotionally engaging and transformative experience that enables new levels of representational integration to occur. Emotion is inherently integrative' (Siegel 2003: 47). But as well as taking place in the context of formal treatment, opportunistic versions of 'mentalized affectivity' can take place between any health, mental health, social, care, welfare or educational worker and the parents of an abused, neglected, rejected or traumatized child, whether the encounter takes place in the home, the clinic, the family centre or the office.

Attachment Type and Therapeutic Matching

To help deal with the 'processing' biases of each attachment type, Tyrell et al. (1999) found that avoidant/dismissing people (who are not comfortable with the emotional and psychological content of situations) respond best to practices (and practitioners) which are explicitly and actively engaged in the psycho-emotional aspect of relationships, including parent–child interactions. Similarly, ambivalent/preoccupied parents (who are not comfortable with being independent and thinking systematically about stressful situations), respond well to practices (and practitioners) which promote a systematic and problem-solving approach.

Holmes (2001) suggests similar therapeutic tactics. Whereas avoidant types remain distant and theoretical about their experiences, the ambivalent types need to develop a bit of distance, systematic thought and objectification of their own and other people's behaviour. The therapist models ego-control. 'The avoidant person is all container and no feelings; the ambivalent person is overwhelmed with feelings, but with nowhere to contain them. Avoidant people use their objects to do their feeling for them; ambivalent sufferers use others to do the holding, which they cannot sustain themselves' (Holmes 2001: 40).

Many avoidant/dismissing patients bring a well-rehearsed script about their own experiences and behaviour to treatment. The narrative lacks emotional content or depth. The self is presented as self-sufficient and unaffected by emotion or challenge. Individuals with dismissing states of mind tend to have difficulty asking for help, or indeed even acknowledging that they need help (Dozier and Bates 2004: 171). Therapy has to help the individual recognize and acknowledge the dismissed emotional content; that maybe the patient does feel anxious in relationships, does feel alone and rejected and that this is painful. 'Tell me a bit more about your mother. Describe her and how you felt about her in more detail. Give me an example.' The dismissing person has to be helped to recognize, express and stay with their feelings. 'I thought I heard you say were feeling a bit depressed but you went on to something else. Tell me a bit more about what it feels like for you when you're depressed.' And Holmes (2001: 86) reminds us of the importance of the somatic side of learning how to be emotionally intelligent: 'Whereabouts in your body do you experience your unhappiness?'

In contrast, ambivalent personality types lack structure in their presentation of self. The emotionally laden story, in which the self appears needy and deprived, floods out, with very little monitoring of its content or effect. There is no dialogue, just an emotional outpouring. Therapy has to provide structure and a practical focus. It has to introduce shape, punctuation and form to the story and the uncontained emotion: 'OK, what you've said about your child is important but let's just stop a moment and think about what you're saying about your feelings right now. Let's get the order right and see what triggers what. OK with you?'

The Opportunistic, Low-Intensity Route to Mentalized Affectivity

Many practitioners work with parents and families outside the formal clinical and psychotherapeutic arena. Nevertheless, they tend to be involved for long periods, typically in the immediacy of the home setting. They meet clients as they face the day-to-day demands of relationships, the stress of setbacks, the pressure of needs. Under these stresses, parents show distress, display attachment behaviour, become emotionally dysregulated, and occasionally enjoy success, pleasure and happiness. These moments of heightened arousal are all opportunities for the field practitioner to show sensitivity, understanding and mind-mindedness – to offer a secure, containing, attuned relationship in which the client feels his or her mental state is recognized, understood and mirrored back. Practitioners might comment on what they think the other is feeling by interpreting their facial expression or body language. Just as parents might react with exaggerated 'affect mirroring' as they reflect the infant's emotional state, social workers, health visitors and other community-based professionals might make a point of describing what they think their client is feeling and how it appears to be affecting them. The worker shows a deep interest and concern in the other's mental state. The exploration of these states is offered sensitively, with a view to collaboration and understanding.

For many maltreating parents, experiences of such 'mentalized affectivity', whether as a child or adult, have been few and far between. It is, of course, what secure children routinely get from their carers, and it helps brings about emotional intelligence, social cognition and interpersonal competence. With adults, opportunities for such interaction have to be seized whenever they arise. In themselves, each episode of intense and emotionally demanding communication might not appear to achieve much, but the cumulative effect of providing an attuned, mind-engaging relationship helps build a more coherent, integrated mind. It also helps disconfirm mental representations that at times of need and anxiety others will be unavailable, punish you, reject you or abandon you. 'Being there', interested and responsive, should never be underestimated by community-based field workers.

The attempt to make sense of other people's feelings and behaviour is both an intellectual event and a way of emotionally connecting with them. Rather than feel exasperated or confused with difficult and demanding users and clients, practitioners who try to understand what is happening are more likely to show patience and develop humane practices. Being emotionally available and staying with people when they are anxious or frightened or aggressive strips away the fear that when the self feels helpless or out of control, no one can contain or help regulate you and your profoundly distressed state. Disorganized and unresolved clients feel powerfully destructive and alone. To experience someone who is prepared to 'stay in there', wanting to understand what is happening, conveys the hint that what is being experienced might be manageable, might be understood, might not be a hopelessly destructive force with which no one can live.

Conclusion: Turning Points

We began this book by looking at how, as Schore succinctly put it, young minds form in the context of close relationships. We have seen that carers who, because of their own histories, experience distress and confusion when dealing with the emotional needs of their children, create stressful, mis-attuned relationships in which the young minds that form are inadequately equipped to deal with either their own or other people's emotional demands. Abuse and neglect, trauma and rejection leave disfiguring scars on children's young and developing psychological selves. Unless they meet a fresh mind in a new relationship, one which is open, available, and well versed in the language of the emotions, the risk is that when these children become parents themselves they too will injure their babies, reject their infants, neglect their families and emotionally hurt their children.

The mark of a caring society is to ensure that children who might otherwise become lost along tortured pathways of increasing developmental despair encounter others who can understand, value and contain them.

Strong minds keep you safe. Wise ones teach you how to understand the world and play your part in it. Only when children feel secure can they go on to explore – their own feelings, the reactions of others, and how their own behaviour affects those around them. Encounters with minds that are stronger and wiser often act as a turning point for maltreated children. In many cases, these therapeutic relationships have not been planned. They crop up serendipitously. A teacher recognizes and takes an encouraging interest in a girl's talent for drama or sport. A foster carer sees through the anger, and senses an unhappy, frightened boy.

However, in many cases planned help also allows children to let down their defences, trust the goodwill of carers, and feel safe exploring their affective make-up. Therapy, adoption by an attuned parent, or the deliberate promotion of identified skills and talents designed to boost self-esteem might also act as turning points. As we have seen, working with the child's biological parents in order to improve their sensitivity and responsiveness certainly has the capacity to improve children's security of attachment. The social benefits of improving parents' emotional competence and availability, and increasing children's ability to self-regulate, are immense. Attachment theory and research have advanced hugely over the last two decades. And attachment-based interventions, perhaps too long in the slow lane, are now picking up speed and offering practitioners an increasing number of well-evidenced therapies and support strategies.

Epilogue

Modern developmental sciences, including attachment theory and the neurosciences, are opening up a fascinating account of how minds grow, how psychological selves form in the context of close relationships, and how different social and cultural outsides get into the mental insides of human experience and understanding. In human development, we see the wonderful interplay between nature and nurture. Riddley (2003) describes it as 'nature via nurture', recognizing that 'nature needs nurture' and that 'nature is designed for nurture'. Programmed to make sense of experience, the infant needs experience of which to make sense. In this way, children become exquisitely adapted to the world in which they happen to find themselves and will have to survive and function. All of this is fine if that world is benign, but not so good if it is hostile, indifferent or confused. Children who suffer abuse and neglect will still develop adaptive strategies to help them cope, but their survival, as we have seen, comes at a developmental price and a heavy mental health cost.

However, as well as helping us to understand children's psychosocial development under both favourable and adverse conditions, developmental attachment theory is guiding us towards effective interventions in cases where children's development has been seriously impaired by abuse and neglect. By understanding how competent, integrated, emotionally literate minds are built, professionals can help maltreated children and their carers capture these same constructive ingredients, facilitating healthy development and aiding recovery. The extraordinary story that is beginning to unfold around the nature of being human and the emergence of the psychological self is offering hope to all children whose lives have been blighted by abuse, neglect and trauma.

Developmental attachment theory's willingness to evolve and be influenced by findings from the full range of the biological, neurological, psychological and social sciences ensures its continued relevance to the understanding of children's psychosocial development. This has been especially true in the case of attachment theory's determination to make sense of some of the more profound and disturbing features of maltreated children's behaviour and development, and how their extreme experiences place them in real danger of repeating the cycles of abuse and neglect when they become parents.

It was Bowlby (1998a: 413, originally published in 1973) who used the metaphor of branching railway lines to explain the many alternative developmental routes individuals might take through life as they meet, negotiate and try to adapt to environmental events (turning points) peculiar to their journey. The more hazardous the events to be negotiated, the more the individual is diverted from the main lines of sound psychosocial progress. The accumulation of risks over time can send children into very difficult psychological landscapes, so that in the case of older maltreated children, the lengths they have to travel to find themselves back in safer country can be considerable. This is why early interventions with younger children hold out the prospect of the shortest, speediest and greatest recovery. Developmentally speaking, they are likely to have suffered fewer diversions. The therapeutic distance they have to travel to regain psychological integrity might not be too great. And although older children and more traumatized infants might require more time, more thought and more effort, we are learning that even in these cases, change and recovery, at least to a degree, is possible. Those who can stay with and touch these children, emotionally and psychologically, have the capacity to heal young minds. If relationships are where things developmental can go wrong, then relationships are where they are most likely to be put right.

Bibliography

Aber, J. and Zigler, D. (1981) Developmental considerations in the definition of child maltreatment. In R. Rizley and D. Cicchetti (eds), *New Directions in Child Development*. San Francisco: Jossey Bass, pp. 1–29.

Ainsworth, M., Blehar, M., Waters, E. and Wall, S. (1978) *Patterns of Attachment: Psychological study of the strange situation*. Hillsdale, NJ: Erlbaum.

Alexander, P. (1992) Application of attachment theory to the study of sexual abuse. *Journal of Consulting and Clinical Psychology* 60, pp. 185–95.

Allen, J. (2001) *Traumatic Relationships and Serious Mental Disorders*. Chichester: Wiley.

Anderson, C. and Alexander, P. (1996) The relationship between attachment and dissociation in adult survivors of incest. *Psychiatry* 59, pp. 213–39.

Appel, A. and Holden, G. (1998) Spouse and physical child abuse: a review and appraisal. *Journal of Family Psychology* 12 (4), pp. 578–99.

Archer, C. and Burnell, A. (eds) (2003) *Trauma, Attachment and Family Permanence: Fear can stop you loving*. London: Jessica Kingsley.

Armstrong, K. and Wood, D. (1991) Can infant death from abuse be prevented? *Medical Journal of Australia* 155, pp. 593–6.

Atkinson, L. and Goldberg, S. (eds), (2004) *Attachment Issues in Psychopathology and Interventions*. Mahwah, NJ: Lawrence Erlbaum Associates.

Atkinson, L. and Goldberg, S. (2004) Applications of attachment: the integration of developmental and clinical traditions. In L. Atkinson and S. Goldberg (eds), *Attachment Issues in Psychopathology and Interventions*. Mahwah, NJ: Lawrence Erlbaum Associates, pp. 3–25.

Ayers, R. (1979) *Sensory Integration and the Child*. Los Angeles: Western Psychological Press.

Ayers, R. (1989) *Sensory Integration and Praxis Tests*. Los Angeles: Western Psychological Press.

Bacon, H. (2001a) Attachment, trauma and sexual abuse. In S. Richardson and H. Bacon (eds), *Creative Responses to Child Sexual Abuse: Challenges and dilemmas*. London: Jessica Kingsley, pp. 44–59.

Bacon, H. (2001b) Telling the baby crocodile story: attachment and the continuum of disclosure. In S. Richardson and H. Bacon (eds), *Creative Responses to Child Sexual Abuse: Challenges and dilemmas*. London: Jessica Kingsley, pp. 60–84.

Bakersmans-Kranenberg, M., Juffer, F. and van IJzendoorn, M. (1998) Interventions with video feedback and attachment discussions: does type of maternal insecurity make a difference? *Infant Mental Health Journal* 19, pp. 202–19.

Bakermans-Kranenburg, M., van IJzendoorn, M. and Juffer, F. (2003) Less is more: meta-analysis of sensitivity and attachment interventions in early childhood. *Psychological Bulletin* 129(2), pp. 195–215.

Balbernie, R. (2001) Circuits and circumstances: the early neurobiological consequences of early relationship experiences and how they shape later behaviour. *Journal of Child Psychotherapy* 27(3), pp. 237–55.

Bannister, A. (2004) *Creative Therapies with Traumatised Children.* London: Jessica Kingsley.

Barnard, K., Magyary, D., Summer, G., Booth, C., Mitchell, S. and Spieker, S. (1988) Prevention of parenting alterations for women with low social support. *Psychiatry* 51, pp. 248–53.

Barnett, B. and Parker, G. (1998) The parentified child: early competence or childhood deprivation? *Child Psychology and Psychiatry Review* 3(4), pp. 146–55.

Barnett, D., Manly, J. and Cicchetti, D. (1993) Defining child maltreatment: the interface between policy and research. In D. Cicchetti and S. Toth (eds), *Child Abuse, Child Development, and Social Policy.* Vol. 8. Norwood, NJ: Ablex, pp. 392–412.

Baron-Cohen, S. (2003) *The Essential Difference.* London: Penguin Books.

Baron-Cohen, S., Ring, H., Bullmore, E., Wheelwright, S., Ashwin, C. and Williams, S. (2000) The amygdala theory of autism. *Neuroscience and Behavioral Reviews* 24, pp. 355–64.

Batchelor, J. (1999) *Failure to Thrive in Young Children: Research and practice evaluated.* London: Children's Society.

Bateman, A. and Fonagy, P. (2004) *Psychotherapy for Borderline Personality Disorder.* Oxford: Oxford University Press.

Bauman, P. and Dougherty, F. (1983) Drug-addicted mothers' parenting and their children's development. *The International Journal of the Addictions* 18(3), pp. 291–302.

Bauman, P. and Levine, S. (1986) The development of children of drug addicts. *International Journal of the Addictions* 21(8), pp. 849–63.

Beck, A. (1976) *Cognitive Therapy and Emotional Disorders* New York: International University Press.

Becker-Lausen, E. and Mallon-Kraft, S. (1997) Pandemic outcomes: the intimacy variable. In G. Kantor and J. Jasinski (eds), *Out of Darkness: Current perspectives on family violence.* Newbury Park: Sage, pp. 49–57.

Beckwith, L. and Sigman, M. (1995) Preventive interventions in infancy. *Child and Adolescent Psychiatric Clinics of North America* 4(3), pp. 683–700.

Beeghly, M. and Cicchetti, D. (1994) Child maltreatment, attachment and the self system: emergence of an internal state lexicon in toddlers at high social risk. *Developmental Psychopathology* 6, pp. 5–30.

Beek, M. and Schofield, G. (2004) *Providing a Secure Base in Long-term Foster Care.* London: BAAF.

Berliner, L. and Elliott, D. (1996) Sexual abuse of children. In J. Briere,

L. Berliner, J. Bulkley, C. Jenny and T. Reid (eds), *The APSAC Handbook on Child Maltreatment*, 2nd edn. London: Sage, pp. 51–71.

Berliner, L. and Elliott, D. (2002) Sexual abuse of children. In J. Myers, L. Berliner, J. Briere, C.T. Hendrix, J. Carole and T. Reid (eds), *The APSAC Handbook on Maltreatment*, 2nd edn. Thousand Oaks: Sage, pp. 55–78.

Berry, M., Charlson, R. and Dawson, K. (2003) Promising practices in understanding and treating child neglect. *Child and Family Social Work* 8(1), pp. 13–24.

Bhreathnach, E. and Gogarty, H. (2000) An introduction to the Integrative Model of Self Regulation: a sensory attachment perspective (personal communication).

Bifulco, A., Brown, G., Neubauer, A., Moran, P. and Harris, T. (1994) *Childhood Experience of Care and Abuse (CECA) Training Manual.* London: Royal Holloway.

Bifulco, A. and Moran, P. (1998) *Wednesday's Child: Research into women's experiences of neglect and abuse in childhood, and adult depression.* London: Routledge.

Black, M. and Teti, L. (1997) Promoting mealtime communication between adolescent mothers and their infants through videotape. *Pediatrics* 99, pp. 432–7.

Blumenthal, S., Gudjonsson, G. and Burns, J. (1999) Cognitive distortions and blame attribution in sex offenders against adults and children. *Child Abuse and Neglect* 23(2), pp. 129–44.

Bradway, K. (1997) *Sandplay: Silent Workshop of the Psyche.* New York: Routledge.

Bowlby, J. (1944) Forty-four juvenile thieves: their characters and home life. *International Journal of Psychoanalysis* 25, pp. 19–52, 107–27.

Bowlby, J. (1969) *Attachment and Loss: Volume I: Attachment.* London: Hogarth Press.

Bowlby, J. (1979) *The Making and Breaking of Affectional Bonds.* London: Tavistock.

Bowlby, J. (1980) *Attachment and Loss: Volume 3: Loss.* London: Hogarth Press.

Bowlby, J. (1988) *A Secure Base: Parent–child attachment and healthy human development.* New York: Basic Books.

Bowlby, J. (1998a edition/originally 1973) *Attachment and Loss Volume 2: Separation, anger and anxiety.* London: Pimlico.

Bowlby, J. (1998b edition/originally 1980) *Attachment and Loss Volume 3: Loss, sadness and depression.* London: Pimlico.

Bremner, J. D. and Vermetten, E. (2001) Stress and development: behavioral and biological consequences. *Development and Psychopathology* 13, pp. 473–89.

Briere, J. (1989) *Therapy for Adults Molested as Children: Beyond survival.* New York: Springer.

Briere J. and Elliot, D. (1994) Immediate and long-term impacts of child sexual abuse. *The Future of Children* 4, pp. 54–69.

Brisch, K. (1999) *Treating Attachment Disorders.* New York: Guilford Press.

Buist, A. and Janson, H. (2001) Childhood sexual abuse, parenting and post-partum depression: a 3-year follow-up study. *Child Abuse and Neglect* 25, pp. 909–21.

Byng-Hall, J. (1991) The application of attachment theory to understanding and treatment in family therapy. In C. Parkes, J. Stevenson-Hinde and P. Marris (eds), *Attachment Across the Life Cycle.* London: Tavistock, pp. 199–215.

Byng-Hall, J. (1995) Creating a secure base: some applications of attachment theory for family therapy. *Family Process* 34, pp. 45–58.

Byng-Hall, J. (1999) Family and couple therapy. In J. Cassidy and P. Shaver, *Handbook of Attachment.* New York: Guilford Press, pp. 625–45.

Byng-Hall, J. (2002) Relieving parentified children's burdens in families with insecure attachment patterns. *Family Process* 41(3), pp. 375–88.

Cairns, K. (2002) *Attachment, Trauma and Resilience: Therapeutic caring for children.* London: BAAF.

Calam, R., Bolton, C., Barrowclough, C. and Roberts, J. (2002) Maternal expressed emotion and clinician ratings of emotional maltreatment potential. *Child Abuse and Neglect* 26(10), pp. 1101–6.

Caspi, A., McClay, J., Moffit, T., Mill, J., Martin, J., Craig, I., Taylor, A. and Poulton, R. (2002) Role of genotype in the cycle of violence in maltreated children. *Science* 297, pp. 851–4.

Cassidy, J. and Shaver, P. (1999) *Handbook of Attachment.* New York: Guilford Press.

Chaffin, M., Kelleher, K. and Hollenberg, J. (1996) Onset of physical abuse and neglect: psychiatric, substance abuse, and social risk factors from prospective community data. *Child Abuse and Neglect* 20, pp. 191–203.

Chisholm, K. (1998) A three-year follow-up of attachment and indiscriminate friendliness in children adopted from Romanian orphanages. *Child Development* 69, pp. 1092–106.

Chisholm, K. (2000) Attachment in children adopted from Romanian orphanages: two case studies. In P. Crittenden and A. Claussen (eds), *The Organization of Attachment Relationships: Maturation, culture and context.* Cambridge: Cambridge University Press, pp. 171–89.

Cicchetti, D. (1989) How research on child maltreatment has informed the study of child development. In D. Cicchetti and V. Carlson (eds), *Child Maltreatment: Theory and research on the causes and consequences of child abuse and neglect.* New York: Cambridge University Press, pp. 377–431.

Cicchetti, D. and Lynch, M. (1993) Toward an ecological/transactional model of community violence and child maltreatment. *Psychiatry* 56: pp. 96–118.

Cicchetti, D. and Rogosch, F. (1997) The role of self-organization in the promotion of resilience in maltreated children. *Development and Psychopathology* 9, pp. 797–815.

Cicchetti, D., Rogosch, F. and Toth, S. (1998) Maternal depressive disorder and contextual risk: contributions to the development of attachment insecurity and behavior problems in childhood. *Development and Psychopathology* 10, pp. 283–300.

Cicchetti, D., Toth, S. L. and Hennessey, K. (1989) Research on the consequences of child maltreatment and its application to educational settings. *Topics in Early Childhood Special Education* 9, pp. 33–5.

Cicchetti, D., Toth, S. L. and Hennessey, K. (1993) Child maltreatment and school adaptation: problems and promises. In D. Cicchetti and S. Toth (eds), *Child Abuse, Child Development and Social Policy.* Norwood, NJ: Ablex, pp. 301–29.

Cicchetti, D., Toth, S. and Rogosch, F. (2004) Toddler–parent psychotherapy for depressed mothers and their offspring: implications for attachment theory. In L. Atkinson and S. Goldberg (eds), *Attachment Issues in Psychopathology and Interventions.* Mahwah, NJ: Lawrence Erlbaum Associates, pp. 229–75.

Claussen, A. and Crittenden, P. (1991) Physical and psychological maltreatment: relations among types of maltreatment. *Child Abuse and Neglect* 15, pp. 5–18.

Claussen, A., Mundy, P., Mallik, S. and Willoughby, J. (2002) Joint attention and disorganized attachment status in infants at risk. *Development and Psychopathology* 14, pp. 279–91.

Cohen, N., Muir, E., Parker, C., Brown, M., Lojkasek, M., Muir, R. and Barwick, M. (1999) Watch, Wait and Wonder: testing the effectiveness of a new approach to mother-infant psychotherapy. *Infant Mental Health Journal* 20(4), pp. 429–51.

Cohen, S. and Syme, S. (1985) *Social Support and Health.* New York: Academic Press.

Coohey, C. and Braun, N. (1997) Toward an integrated framework for understanding child physical abuse. *Child Abuse and Neglect* 21(11), pp. 1081–94.

Corby, B. (2000) *Child Abuse: Towards a knowledge base.* Buckingham: Open University Press.

Cozolino, L. (2002) *The Neuroscience of Psychotherapy: Building and rebuilding the human brain.* New York: W.W. Norton.

Crimmins, S., Langley, S., Brownstein, H. and Spunt, B. (1997) Convicted women who have killed their children: a self-psychology perspective. *Journal of Interpersonal Violence* 12, pp. 49–69.

Crittenden, P. (1992) Children's strategies for coping with adverse home environments: an interpretation using attachment theory. *Child Abuse and Neglect* 16(3), pp. 329–43.

Crittenden, P. (1993) An information-processing perspective on the behaviour of neglectful parents. *Criminal Justice Behavior* 20, pp. 27–48.

Crittenden, P. (1995) Attachment and psychopathology. In S. Goldberg, R. Muir and J. Kerr *Attachment Theory: Social, developmental, and clinical perspectives.* Hillsdale, NJ: Analytic Press, pp. 367–406.

Crittenden, P. (1996) Research on Maltreating Families. In J. Briere et al. (eds), *The APSAC Handbook on Child Maltreatment.* Thousand Oaks: Sage, pp. 158–74.

Crittenden, P. (1997a) Truth, error, omission, distortion, and deception: the application of attachment theory to the assessment and treatment of psychological disorder. In S. Dollinger and L. DiLalla (eds), *Assessment and Intervention Issues Across the Life Span.* Mahweh, NJ: Lawrence Erlbaum, pp. 35–76.

Crittenden, P. (1997b) Patterns of attachment and sexual behaviour: risk of dysfunction versus opportunity for creative integration. In L. Atkinson and K. Zucker (eds), *Attachment and Psychopathology.* New York: Guilford Press, pp. 47–93.

Crittenden, P. (1998) Dangerous behaviour and dangerous contexts: a 35-year perspective on research on the developmental effects of child physical abuse. In P. Trickett and C. Schellenbach (eds), *Violence Against Children in the Family and Community.* Washington, DC: American Psychological Association, pp. 11–38.

Crittenden, P. (1999a) Child neglect: causes and contributors. In H. Dubowitz (ed.), *Neglected Children: Research, practice and policy.* Thousand Oaks: Sage, pp. 47–68.

Crittenden, P. (1999b) Danger and development: the organization of self-protective strategies. In J. Vondra and D. Barnett (eds), *Atypical Attachment in Infancy and Early Childhood among Children at Developmental Risk.* Monographs of the Society for Research in Child Development Series no. 258, Vol. 64(3), pp. 145–71.

Crittenden, P. (2002) If I knew then what I know now: integrity and fragmentation in the treatment of child abuse and neglect. In K. Browne, H. Hanks, P. Stratton and C. Hamilton (eds), *Early Prediction and Prevention of Child Abuse: A handbook.* Chichester: Wiley, pp. 111–26.

Crittenden, P. and Ainsworth, M. (1989) Child maltreatment and attachment theory. In D. Cicchetti and V. Carlson (eds), *Child Maltreatment: Theory and research on the causes and consequences of child abuse and neglect.* New York: Cambridge University Press, pp. 432–63.

Crittenden, P. and Claussen, A. (2000) Adaptations to varied environments. In P. Crittenden and A. Claussen (eds), *The Organization of Attachment Relationships: Maturation, culture and context.* Cambridge: Cambridge University Press, pp. 234–50.

Crittenden, P., Claussen, A. and Sugarman, D. (1994) Physical and psychological maltreatment in middle childhood and adolescence. *Development and Psychopathology* 6, pp. 145–64.

Crittenden, P. and DiLalla, D. (1988) Compulsive compliance: the development of an inhibitory coping strategy in infancy. *Journal of Abnormal Child Psychology* 16, pp. 585–99.

Dadds, M., Mullins, M., McAllister, R. and Atkinson, E. (2003) Attributions, affect, and behavior in abuse-risk mothers: a laboratory study. *Child Abuse and Neglect* 27(1), pp. 21–45.

Daniel, B. and Wassell, S. (2002a) *Assessing and Promoting Resilience in Vulnerable Children: Early years.* London: Jessica Kingsley.

Daniel, B. and Wassell, S. (2002b) *Assessing and Promoting Resilience in Vulnerable Children: Adolescence.* London: Jessica Kingsley.

Danner, R., Snowden, D. and Friesen, W. (2001) Positive emotions in early life and longevity. *Journal of Personality and Social Psychology* 80, pp. 804–13.

Dawson, G., Frey, K., Self, J., Panagiotides, H., Hessl, D., Yamada, E. and Rinaldi, J. (1999) Frontal electrical brain activity in infants of depressed mothers. *Development and Psychopathology* 11, pp. 589–605.

De Bellis, M. (2001) Developmental traumatology: the psychobiological development of maltreated children and its implications for research, treatment, and policy. *Development and Psychopathology* 13, pp. 539–64.

Dennett, D. (1987) *The Intentional Stance.* Cambridge, Mass.: MIT Press.

Department of Health (2000) *Working Together to Safeguard Children: A guide to inter-agency working to safeguard and promote the welfare of children.* London: The Stationery Office.

Dozier, M. (2003) Attachment-based treatment for vulnerable children *Attachment and Human Development* 5(3), pp. 253–7.

Dozier, M. and Bates, B. (2004) Attachment state of mind and the treatment relationship. In L. Atkinson and S. Goldberg (eds), *Attachment Issues in Psychopathology and Interventions.* Mahwah, NJ: Lawrence Erlbaum Associates, pp. 167–80.

Dozier, M., Higley, E., Albus, K. and Nutter, A. (2002) Intervening with foster infants' caregivers. *Infant Mental Health Journal* 25, pp. 541–54.

Draijer, N. and Langeland, W. (1999) Childhood trauma and perceived parental dysfunction in the etiology of dissociative symptoms in psychiatric inpatients. *American Journal of Psychiatry* 156 (3), pp. 379–85.

Drummond, D. C. and Fitzpatrick, G. (2000) Children of substance-misusing parents. In P. Peder, M. McClure and A. Jolley (eds), *Family Matters: Interfaces between child and adult mental health.* London: Routledge, pp. 135–49.

Dunn, M., Tarter, R., Mezzich, A., Vanyukov, M., Kirisci, L. and Kirillova, G. (2002) Origins and consequences of child neglect in substance abuse families. *Clinical Psychology Review* 22, pp. 1063–90.

Eckenrode, J., Zielinski, D., Smith, E., Marcynyszyn, L., Henderson, C., Kitzman, H., Cole, R., Powers, J. and Olds, D. (2001) Child Maltreatment and the early onset of problem behaviours: can a program of nurse home visitation break the link? *Development and Psychopathology* 13, pp. 873–90.

Egeland, B. (1991) From data to definition. *Development and Psychopathology* 3, pp. 37–43.

Egeland, B. and Carlson, E. (2004) Attachment and psychopathology. In L. Atkinson and S. Goldberg (eds), *Attachment Issues in Psychopathology and Interventions.* Mahwah, NJ: Lawrence Erlbaum Associates, pp. 27–48.

Egeland, B. and Erickson, M. (1993) Attachment theory and findings: implications for prevention and intervention. In S. Kramer and H. Parens (eds), *Prevention in Mental Health.* Northvale, NJ: Jason Aronson.

Egeland, B., Jacobvitz, D. and Papatola, K. (1987) Intergenerational continuity of abuse. In R. Gelles and J. Lancaster (eds), *Child Abuse and Neglect: Biosocial dimensions.* New York: Aldine de Gruyter, pp. 255–76.

Egeland, B. and Sroufe, A. (1991) Attachment and early maltreatment. *Child Development* 52, pp. 44–52.

Egeland, B., Weinfield, N., Bosquet, M. and Cheng, V. (2000) Remembering, repeating, and working through: lessons from attachment-based interventions. In J. Osofsky and H. Fitzgerald (eds), *Handbook of Infant Mental Health Volume 4: Infant mental health in groups at high risk.* New York: Wiley, pp. 35–89.

Eiden, R., Cahvez, F. and Leonard, K. (1999) Parent–infant interactions in alcoholic and control families. *Development and Psychopathology* 11, pp. 745–62.

Eiden, R., Edwards, P. and Leonard, K. (2002) Mother–infant and father–infant attachment among alcoholic families. *Development and Psychopathology* 14, pp. 252–78.

Eliot, L. (2001) *Early Intelligence: How the brain and mind develop in the first years.* London: Penguin.

Erdman, P. and Caffrey, T. (eds) (2003) *Attachment and Family Systems: Conceptual, empirical and therapeutic relatedness.* New York: Brunner/Routledge.

Erickson, M. and Egeland, B. (2002) Child neglect. In J. Myers, L. Berliner, J. Briere, C.T. Hendrix, J. C. Reid and T. Reid (eds), *The APSAC Handbook on Maltreatment,* 2nd edn. Thousand Oaks: Sage, pp. 3–20.

Erikson, M., Egeland, B. and Pianta, R. (1989) The effects of maltreatment on the development of young children. In D. Cicchetti and V. Carlson (eds), *Child Maltreatment: Theory and research on the causes and consequences of child abuse and neglect.* New York: Cambridge University Press, pp. 647–84.

Famularo, R., Stone, K., Barnum, R. and Wharton, R. (1986) Alcoholism and severe child maltreatment. *American Journal of Orthopsychiatry* 56, pp. 481–5.

Farmer, E. and Owen, M. (1995) *Child Protection Practice: Private risks and public remedies.* London: HMSO.

Fearnley, S. (2000) *The Extra Dimension: Making sense of attachments – both positive and negative.* Rawtenstall: Keys Child Care Consultancy.

Feldman, R., Greenbaum, C., Yirmaya, N. and Mayes, L. (1996) Relations between cyclicity and regulation in mother-infant interaction at 3 and 9 months and cognition as 2 years. *Journal of Applied Developmental Psychology* 17, pp. 347–65.

Fergusson, D., Horwood, L. and Lynskey, M. (1996) Childhood sexual abuse and psychiatric disorder in young adulthood: II. Psychiatric outcomes of childhood sexual abuse. *Journal of the American Academy of Child and Adolescent Psychiatry* 34, pp. 1365–74.

Field, T. (1992) Infants of depressed mothers. *Development and Psychopathology* 4, pp. 49–66.

Field, T., Healy, B., Goldstein, S. and Guthertz, M. (1990) Behavior-state matching and synchrony in mother–infant interactions of nondepressed vs depressed dyads. *Developmental Psychopathology* 26(1), pp. 7–14.

Finkelhor, D. (1984) *Child Sexual Abuse: New theory and research.* New York: Free Press.

Fischer-Mamblona, H. (2000) On the evolution of attachment-disordered behaviour. *Attachment and Human Development* 2(1), pp. 8–22.

Flisher, A., Kramer, R., Hoven, C., Greenwald, S., Bird, H., Canino, G., Connell, R. and Moore, R. (1997) Psychosocial characteristics of physically abused children and adolescents. *Journal of American Academy of Child and Adolescent Psychiatry* 36(1), pp. 123–31.

Fonagy, P. (2000) Attachment in infancy and the problem of conduct disorders in adolescence: the role of reflective function. Plenary address to the International Association of Adolescent Psychiatry, San Francisco, January.

Fonagy, P. (2001) Foreword. In J. Allen, *Traumatic Relationships and Serious Mental Disorders.* Chichester: John Wiley, pp. xv–xvii.

Fonagy, P., Gergely, G., Jurist, E. and Target, M. (2002) *Affect Regulation, Mentalization and the Development of the Self.* New York: Other Press.

Fonagy, P., Steele, M., Steele, H., Leigh, T., Kennedy, R., Mattoon, G. and Target, M. (1995) Attachment, the reflective self, and borderline states. In S. Goldberg, R. Muir and J. Kerr (eds), *Attachment Theory: Social, developmental, and clinical perspectives.* Hillsdale, NJ: Analytic Press, pp. 233–78.

Fonagy, P., Steele, H., Steele, M., Moran, G., and Higgit, A. (1991) The capacity to understand mental states: the reflective self in parent and child and its significance in security of attachment. *Infant Mental Health Journal* 12(3), pp. 210–18.

Fonagy, P. and Target, M. (1997) Attachment and reflective function: their role in self-organization. *Development and Psychopathology* 9, pp. 679–700.

Fosha, D. (2000) *The Transforming Power of Affect.* New York: Basic Books.

Fosha, D. (2003) Dyadic regulation and experiential work with emotion and relatedness in trauma and disorganized attachment. In M. Solomon and D. Siegel (eds), *Healing Trauma: Attachment, Mind, body and brain.* New York: W.W. Norton, pp. 221–81.

Friedrich, W., Dittner, C., Action, R., Berliner, L., Butler, J., Damon, L., Davies, W., Gray, A. and Wright, J. (2001) Child sexual behaviour inventory. *Child Maltreatment* 6, pp. 37–49.

Frodi, A. and Lamb, M. (1980) Child abusers' responses to infant smiles and cries. *Child Development* 51, pp. 238–41.

Garbarino, J. and Collins, C. (1999) Child Neglect: the family with a hole in the middle. In H. Dubowitz (ed.), *Neglected Children: Research, practice and policy*. Thousand Oaks: Sage, pp. 1–23.

Gardner, R. (2003) *Supporting Families: Child protection in the community*. Chichester: Wiley.

Garmezy, N. (1997) Reflections and commentary on risk, resiliency, and development. In R. Haggerty et al. (eds), *Stress, Risk and Resilience in Children and Adolescence: Processes, mechanisms and interventions*. Cambridge: Cambridge University Press, pp. 1–18.

Gauthier, L., Stollack, G., Messe, L. and Gosnell, B. (1996) Recall of childhood neglect and physical abuse as differential predictors of current psychological functioning. *Child Abuse and Neglect* 20, pp. 549–59.

Gelfland, D., Teti, D., Seiner, S., and Jameson, P. (1996) Helping mothers fight depression: evaluation of a home-based intervention program for depressed mothers and their infants. *Journal of Clinical Child Psychology* 25, pp. 406–22.

George, C. (1996) A representational perspective of child abuse and prevention: internal working models of attachment and caregiving. *Child Abuse and Neglect* 20(5), pp. 411–24.

George, C. and Solomon, J. (1996) Representational models of relationships: links between caregiving and attachment. *Infant Mental Health Journal* 17(3), 198–216.

George, C. and Solomon, J. (1999) Attachment and caregiving: the caregiving behavioural system. In J. Cassidy and P. Shaver (eds), *Handbook of Attachment*. New York: Guilford Press, pp. 649–70.

George, C. and West, M. (1999) Developmental vs. social personality models of adult attachment and mental ill health. *British Journal of Medical Psychology*, 72, pp. 285–303.

George, C., West, M. and Pettem, O. (1999) The adult attachment projective. In J. Solomon and C. George (eds), *Attachment Disorganization*. New York: Guilford Press, pp. 318–46.

Gerhardt, Sue (2004) *Why Love Matters: How affection shapes a baby's brain*. Hove and New York: Brunner-Routledge.

Gilligan, R. (2001) *Promoting Resilience: A resource guide on working with children in the care system*. London: BAAF.

Gladstone, G., Parker, G., Wilhelm, K. and Mitchel, P. (1999) Characteristics of depressed patients who report childhood sexual abuse. *American Journal of Psychiatry* 156, pp. 431–7.

Glaser, D. (1993) Emotional abuse. In C. Hobbs and J. Wynne (eds), *Child Abuse*. London: Balliere Tindall, pp. 251–67.

Glaser, D. (2002) Emotional abuse and neglect (psychological maltreatment), a conceptual framework. *Child Abuse and Neglect* 26, pp. 697–714.

Gogarty, H. (2000) *The Triad of Attachment in the Care Experience.* Unpublished doctoral thesis. Derry: University of Ulster.

Goldberg, S. (1999) *Attachment and Development.* London: Arnold.

Goldberg, S., Benoit, D., Blokland, K. and Madigan, S. (2003) Atypical maternal behavior, maternal representations, and infant disorganized attachment. *Development and Psychopathology* 15, pp. 239–57.

Goleman, D. (1996) *Emotional Intelligence.* London: Bloomsbury.

Gomez, R., Gomez, A., DeMello, L. and Tallent, R. (2001) Perceived maternal control and support: effects on hostile biased social information processing and aggression among clinic-referred children with high aggression. *Journal of Child Psychology and Psychiatry* 42(4), pp. 513–22.

Graham, C. and Easterbrooks, M. A. (2000) School-aged children's vulnerability to depressive symptomatology: the role of attachment security, maternal depressive symptomatology, and economic risk. *Development and Psychopathology* 12(2), pp. 201–14.

Graham-Bermann, S. (2002) Child abuse in the context of domestic violence. In J. Myers, L. Berliner, J. Briere, C.T. Hendrix, J. Carole, and T. Reid (eds), *The APSAC Handbook on Maltreatment,* 2nd edn. Thousand Oaks: Sage, pp. 119–29.

Green, J. and Goldwyn, R. (2002) Annotation: attachment disorganisation and psychopathology: new findings in attachment research and their potential implications for development of psychopathology in childhood. *Journal of Child Psychology and Psychiatry* 43(7), pp. 835–46.

Gunnar, M., Morison, S., Chisholm, K. and Schuder, M. (2001) Salivary cortisol levels in children adopted from Romanian orphanages. *Development and Psychopathology* 13, pp. 611–28.

Handal, P., Tschannen, T. and Searight, H. (1998) The relationship of child adjustment to husbands' and wives' marital distress, perceived family conflict, and mothers' occupational status. *Child Psychiatry and Human Development* 29, pp. 113–26.

Harris, J. (1999) Individual differences in understanding emotion: the role of attachment status and psychological discourse. *Attachment and Human Development* 1(3), pp. 325–42.

Hart, S. and Brassard, M. (1991) Psychological maltreatment: progress achieved. *Developmental and Psychopathology* 3, pp. 61–70.

Hart, S., Brassard, M., Binggeli, N. and Davidson, H. (2002) Psychological maltreatment. In J. Myers, L. Berliner, J. Briere, C.T. Hendrix, J. Carole and T. Reid (eds), *The APSAC Handbook on Maltreatment,* 2nd edn. Thousand Oaks: Sage, pp. 79–103.

Hart, S., Brassard, M. and Karlson, H. (1996) Psychological maltreatment. In J. Briere et al. (eds), *The APSAC Handbook on Child Maltreatment.* Thousand Oaks: Sage, pp. 72–89.

Hartt, J. and Waller, G. (2002) Child abuse, dissociation, and core beliefs in bulimic disorders. *Child Abuse and Neglect* 26, pp. 923–38.

Haskett, M., Scott, S., Grant, R., Ward, C. and Robinson, C. (2003) Child-related cognitions and affective functioning of physically abusive and comparison parents. *Child Abuse and Neglect* 27, pp. 663–86.

Heard, D. (2003) Using extended attachment theory as an evidence-based guide when working with families. In M. Bell and K. Wilson (eds), *The Practitioner's Guide to Working with Families.* London: Palgrave/Macmillan, pp. 85–102.

Heard, D. and Lake, B. (1997) *The Challenge of Attachment for Caregiving.* London: Routledge.

Hegelson, V. and Fritz, H. (1999) Unmitigated agency and unmitigated communion. *Journal of Research in Personality* 33, pp. 131–58.

Henning, K., Leitenberg, H., Coffey, P., Bennett, T. and Jankowski, M. (1997) Long-term psychological adjustment to witnessing interparental physical conflict during childhood. *Child Abuse and Neglect* 6, pp. 501–15.

Hilburn-Cobb, C. (2004) Adolescent psychopathology in terms of multiple behavioral systems: the role of attachment and controlling strategies and frankly disorganized behavior. In L. Atkinson and S. Goldberg (eds), *Attachment Issues in Psychopathology and Interventions.* Mahwah, NJ: Lawrence Erlbaum Associates, pp. 95–135.

Hildyard, K. and Wolfe, D. (2002) Child neglect: developmental issues and outcomes. *Child Abuse and Neglect* 29, pp. 679–95.

Hill, J., Murray, L., Woodall, P., Parmar, B. and Hentges, F. (2004) Recalled relationships with parents and perceptions of professional support in mothers of infants treated for cleft lip. *Attachment and Human Development* 6(1), pp. 21–30.

Hipwell, A., Goossens, F., Melhuish, E. and Kumar, R. (2000) Severe maternal psychopathology and infant-mother attachment. *Development and Psychopathology* 12(2), pp. 157–76.

Hobson, P. (2002) *The Cradle of Thought: Exploring the origins of thinking.* London: Macmillan.

Holmes, J. (2001) *The Search for the Secure Base: Attachment theory and psychotherapy.* London: Bruner/Routledge.

Holmes, J. (2004) Disorganized attachment and Borderline Personality Disorder: a clinical perspective. *Attachment and Human Development* 6(2), pp. 181–90.

Holmes, W. and Slap, G. (1998) Sexual abuse of boys: definition, prevalence, correlates, sequelae, and management. *Journal of American Medical Association* 280(21), pp. 1855–62.

Howe, D. (1998) *Patterns of Adoption: Nature, nurture and psychosocial development.* Oxford: Blackwell.

Howe, D., Brandon, M., Hinings, D. and Schofield, G. (1999) *Attachment Theory, Child Maltreatment and Family Support: A practice and assessment model.* London: Palgrave Macmillan.

Howe, D. and Fearnley, S. (2003) Disorder of attachment in adopted and fostered children: recognition and treatment. *Clinical Child Psychology and Psychiatry* 8(3), pp. 369–87.

Howes, C. and Ritchie, S. (1999) Attachment organization in children with difficult life circumstances. *Development and Psychopathology* 11, pp. 251–68.

Hughes, D. (1997) *Facilitating Developmental Attachment.* New Jersey: Jason Aronson.

Hughes, D. (1998) *Building the Bonds of Attachment.* New Jersey: Jason Aronson.

Hughes, D. (2002) The psychological treatment of children with PTSD and attachment disorganization: Dyadic Developmental Psychotherapy. http://danielahughes.homestead.com/Model.html

Hughes, D. (2003) Psychological interventions for the spectrum of attachment disorders and intrafamilial trauma. *Attachment and Human Development* 5(3), pp. 271–7.

Iwaniec, D. (1995) *The Emotionally Abused and Neglected Child: Identification, assessment and intervention.* Chichester: Wiley.

Iwaniec, D., Herbert, M. and McNeish, A. (1985) Social work with failure-to-thrive children and their families, Part I: Psychosocial factors. *British Journal of Social Work* 15, pp. 243–59.

Jacobvitz, D. and Hazen, N. (1999) Developmental pathways from infant disorganization to childhood peer relationships. In J. Solomon and C. George (eds), *Attachment Disorganization.* New York: Guilford Press, pp. 127–59.

Johnson, D. (2000) The impact of orphanage rearing on growth and development. In C. Nelson (ed.), *Minnesota Symposia in Child Psychology: Volume 31: The effects of adversity on neurobehavioral development.* Mahweh, NJ: Erlbaum, pp. 113–62.

Jones, D.P.H. (2002) Situations affecting child mental health. In M. Rutter and Taylor (eds), *Child and Adolescent Psychiatry.* Oxford: Blackwell Science.

Jones, D. and Bools, C. (1999) Factitious illness by proxy. In T. David (ed.) *Recent Advances in Paediatrics.* Edinburgh: Churchill, pp. 57–71.

Jones, M.A. (1985) *A Second Chance for Families: Five years later.* New York: Child Welfare League of America.

Joseph, R. (1999) The neurology of traumatic 'dissociative' amnesia. *Child Abuse and Neglect* 23(8), pp. 715–27.

Jouriles, E. and LeCompte, S. (1991) Husbands' aggression towards wives and mothers' and fathers' aggression towards children. *Journal of Consulting and Clinical Psychology* 59, pp. 190–2.

Jouriles, E., Norwood, W., McDonald, R., Vincent, J. and Mahoney, A. (1996) Physical violence and other forms of marital aggression: links with children's behavior problems. *Journal of Family Psychology* 10, pp. 223–34.

Juffer, F., Bakermans-Kranenburg, M. and van IJzendoorn, M. (2003) Enhancing children's socio-emotional development: a review of intervention studies. In D. Teti (ed.), *Handbook of Research Methods in Developmental Psychology.* Oxford: Blackwell.

Juffer, F., van IJzendoorn, M. and Bakermans-Kranenberg, M. (1997) Intervention in transmission of insecure attachment: a case study. *Psychological Reports* 80, pp. 531–43.

Juffer, F., Hoksbergen, R., Riksen-Walraven, J. and Kohnstamm, G. (1997) Early intervention in adoptive families: supporting maternal sensitive responsiveness, infant-mother attachment, and infant competence. *Journal of Child Psychology and Psychiatry* 38, pp. 1039–50.

Kagan, R. (2004) *Rebuilding Attachments with Traumatised Children: Healing from losses, violence, abuse, and neglect.* New York: Haworth Press.

Kasl, C. (1989) *Women, Sex and Addiction.* New York: Mandarin.

Kaufman, J. and Charney, D. (2001) Effects of early stress on brain structure and function: implications for understanding the relationship between child maltreatment and depression. *Development and Psychopathology* 13, pp. 451–71.

Keck, G. and Kupecky, R. (1995) *Adopting the Hurt Child.* Colorado Springs, CO: Pinon Press.

Kempe, C., Silverman, F., Steele, B., Droegemueller, W. and Silver, H. (1962) The battered child syndrome. *Journal of the American Medical Association* 181, pp. 17–24.

Kendall-Tackett, K. (2002) The health effects of childhood abuse: four pathways by which abuse can influence health. *Child Abuse and Neglect* 26(6), pp. 715–29.

Klimes-Dougan, B. and Kistner, J. (1990) Physically abused preschoolers responses to peers' distress. *Developmental Psychopathology* 26, pp. 599–602.

Knutson, J. (1995) Psychological characteristics of maltreated children: putative risk factors and consequences. *Psychology* 46, pp. 401–31.

Kobak, R. and Esposito, A. (2004) Levels of processing in parent-child relationships: implications for clinical assessment and treatment. In L. Atkinson and S. Goldberg (eds), *Attachment Issues in Psychopathology and Interventions.* Mahwah, NJ: Lawrence Erlbaum Associates, pp. 139–66.

Kolko, D. (1996) Child physical abuse. In J. Briere et al. (eds), *The APSAC Handbook on Child Maltreatment.* Thousand Oaks: Sage, pp. 21–50.

Kraemer, G. and Clarke, A. (1996) Social attachment, brain function, and aggression. *Annals of the New York Academy of Sciences* 794, pp. 121–35.

Kranowitz, M. (1998) *The Out-of-Sync Child: Recognising and coping with sensory integration dysfunction.* New York: Berkley.

Krugman, R. (1985) Fatal child abuse: analysis of 24 cases. *Pediatrician* 12, pp. 68–72.

Lange, A., De Beurs, E., Dolan, C., Lachnit, T., Sjollema, S. and Hanewald, G.

(1999) Long-term effects of childhood sexual abuse: objective and subjective characteristics of the abuse and psychopathology in later life. *Journal of Nervous and Mental Diseases* 187(3), pp. 150–8.

Lazarus, R. and Folkman, S. (1984) *Stress, Appraisal and Coping*. New York: Springer.

LeDoux, J. (1998) *The Emotional Brain*. London: Weidenfeld and Nicolson.

Levy, T. and Orlans, M. (1998) *Attachment, Trauma and Healing: Understanding and treating attachment disorder in children and families*. Washington DC: CWLA.

Lieberman, A. (2003) The treatment of attachment disorder in infancy and early childhood: reflections form clinical intervention with later-adopted foster care children. *Attachment and Human Development* 5(3), pp. 279–82.

Lieberman, A., Weston, D. and Pawl, J. (1991) Preventive intervention and outcome with anxiously attached dyads. *Child Development* 62, pp. 199–209.

Lieberman, A. and Zeanah, C. (1999) Contributions of attachment theory to infant-parent psychotherapy and other interventions with infants and young children. In J. Cassidy and P. Shaver (eds), *Handbook of Attachment*. New York: Guilford Press, pp. 555–74.

Lieberman, F. and Pawl, J. (1988) Clinical applications of attachment theory. In J. Belsky and T. Nezworski (eds) *Clinical Applications of Attachment*. Hillsdale, NJ: Lawrence Erlbaum, pp. 327–51.

Liotti, G. (1999) Disorganization of attachment as a model for understanding dissociative psychopathology. In J. Solomon and C. George (eds), *Attachment Disorganization*. New York: Guilford Press, pp. 291–317.

Lowenfeld, M. (1991) *Play in Childhood*. Oxford: Blackwell Science.

Lundy, M., Pfohl, B. and Kuperman, S. (1993) Adult criminality among formerly hospitalized child psychiatric patients. *Journal of the American Academy of Child and Adolescent Psychiatry* 32, pp. 569–76.

Luthar, S., Cushing, G., Meriskangas, K. and Rounsaville (1998) Multiple jeopardy: risk/protective factors among addicted mothers' offspring. *Development and Psychopathology* 10, pp. 117–36.

Luthar, S. and Suchman, N. (2000) Relational Psychotherapy Mothers' Group: a developmentally informed intervention for at-risk mothers. *Development and Psychopathology* 12(2), pp. 235–53.

Lutzker, J. (1985). Project 12-way: treating child abuse and neglect from an eco-behavioral perspective. In R. Dangel and R. Polster (eds), *Parent Training*. New York: Guilford Press, pp. 260–97.

Lutzker, J. and Bigelow, K. (2001) *Reducing Child Maltreatment: A guidebook for parent services*. New York: Guilford Press.

Lyons-Ruth, K. (1996) Attachment relationships among children with aggressive behavior problems: the role of disorganised early attachment patterns. *Journal of Consulting and Clinical Psychology* 64, pp. 64–73.

Lyons-Ruth, K. and Block, D. (1996) The disturbed caregiving system: relations among childhood trauma, maternal caregiving, and infant affect and attachment. *Infant Mental Health Journal* 17, pp. 257–75.

Lyons-Ruth, K., Bronfman, E. and Atwood, G. (1999) A relational diathesis model of hostile-helpless states of mind: expressions in mother-infant interaction. In J. Solomon and C. George (eds), *Attachment Disorganization.* New York: Guilford Press, pp. 33–70.

Lyons-Ruth, K., Bronfman, E. and Parsons, E. (1999). Maternal disrupted affective communication, maternal frightened or frightening behavior, and disorganised infant strategies. In J. Vondra and D. Barnett (eds), *Atypical Patterns of Infant Attachment*, Monographs of the Society for Research in Child Development 64 (3), pp. 67–96.

Lyons-Ruth, K., Melnick, S., Bronfman, E., Sherry, S. and Llanas, L. (2004) Hostile-helpless relational models and disorganized attachment patterns between parents and their young children: review of research and implications for clinical work. In L. Atkinson and S. Goldberg (eds), *Attachment Issues in Psychopathology and Interventions.* Mahwah, NJ: Lawrence Erlbaum Associates, pp. 65–94.

Lyons-Ruth, K., Yellin, C., Melnick, S. and Atwood, G. (2003) Childhood experiences of trauma and loss have different relations to maternal unresolved and hostile-helpless states of mind on the AAI. *Attachment and Human Development* 5(4), pp. 330–52.

Lyons-Ruth, K., Zoll, D., Connell, D. and Grunebaum, H. (1989) Family deviance and parental loss in childhood: associations with maternal behavior and infant maltreatment during the first two years of life. *Development and Psychopathology* 1, pp. 219–36.

Macdonald, G. (2000) *Effective Interventions for Child Abuse and Neglect: An evidence-based approach to planning and evaluating interventions.* Chichester: Wiley.

Macfie, J., Cicchetti, D. and Toth, S. (2001) The development of dissociation in maltreated children preschool-aged children. *Development and Psychopathology* 13, pp. 233–54.

Macfie, J., Toth, S., Rogosch, F., Robinson, J., Emde, R. and Cicchetti, D. (1999) Effect of maltreatment on preschoolers' narrative representations of responses to relieve distress and of role reversal. *Developmental Psychology* 35(2), pp. 460–5.

MacLeod, J. and Nelson, G. (2000) Programs for the promotion of family wellness and the prevention of child maltreatment: a meta-analytic review. *Child Abuse and Neglect* 24(9), pp. 1127–49.

Main, M. and Cassidy, J. Categories of response to reunion with the parent at age 6. *Developmental Psychology* 24, pp. 415–26.

Main, M. and Goldwyn, R. (1984) Predicting rejection of her infant from mothers' representation of her own experience, *Child Abuse and Neglect* 8, pp. 203–17.

Main, M. and Hesse, E. (1990) Parents' unresolved traumatic experiences are related to infants' disorganized attachment status: Is frightened and/or frightening parental behavior the linking mechanism? In M. Greenberg, D. Cicchetti and E. Cummings (eds), *Attachment in the Pre-School Years.* Chicago: University of Chicago Press, pp. 161–82.

Main, M. (1990) Cross cultural studies of attachment organization: recent studies of changing methodologies, and the concept of conditional strategies. *Human Development* 33, pp. 48–71.

Main, M. and Hesse, E. (1990) Parents' unresolved traumatic experiences are related to infant disorganized attachment status. In M. Greenberg, D. Cicchetti and E. Cummings (eds), *Attachment in the Preschool Years: Theory, research and intervention.* Chicago: University of Chicago Press, pp. 161–82.

Main, M. and George, C. (1985) Responses of abused and disadvantaged toddlers to distress in agemates. *Developmental Psychology* 21, pp. 407–12.

Main, M. and Solomon, J. (1986) Discovery of an insecure-disorganized/disoriented attachment pattern. In T. B. Brazelton and M. W. Yogman (eds), *Affective Development in Infancy.* Norwood, NJ: Ablex, pp. 95–124.

Main, M. and Solomon, J. (1990) Procedures for identifying infants as disorganized/disoriented during the Ainsworth Strange Situation. In M. Greenberg, D. Cicchetti and E. M. Cummings (eds), *Attachment During the Preschool Years: Theory, research and intervention.* Chicago: University of Chicago Press, pp. 121–60.

Maker, A., Kemmermeier, M. and Peterson, C. (1999) Parental sociopathy as a predictor of childhood sexual abuse. *Journal of Family Violence* 14(1), pp. 47–59.

Margolin, G. (1998) Effects of domestic violence on children. In P. Trickett and C. Schellenbach (eds), *Violence Against Children in the Family and the Community.* Washington DC: American Psychological Association, pp. 57–101.

Marotta, S. (2003) Integrative systemic approaches to attachment-related trauma. In P. Erdman and T. Caffrey (eds), *Attachment and Family Systems: Conceptual, empirical and therapeutic relatedness.* New York: Brunner/Routledge, pp. 225–40.

Marrone, M. (1998) *Attachment and Interaction.* London: Jessica Kingsley.

Marvin, R., Cooper, G., Hoffman, K. and Powell, B. (2002) The Circle of Security project: attachment-based intervention with caregiver-pre-school child dyads. *Attachment and Human Development* 4(1), pp. 107–24.

Mattinson, J. (1975) *The Reflective Process in Casework Supervision.* London: Institute of Marital Studies.

Maxfield, M. and Widom, C. (1996) The cycle of violence: revisited six years later. *Archives of Pediatrics and Adolescent Medicine* 150, pp. 390–5.

McCloskey, L. and Stuewig, J. (2001) The quality of peer relationships among children exposed to domestic violence. *Development and Psychopathology* 13, pp. 83–96.

McDonough, S. (1992) *Interactional Guidance Manual.* Unpublished manuscript. East Providence, RI: Brown University.

McGuigan, W. and Pratt, C. (2001) The predictive impact of domestic violence on three types of child maltreatment. *Child Abuse and Neglect* 25, pp. 869–83.

McNeal, C. and Amato, P. (1998) Parents' marital violence: long-term consequences for children. *Journal of Family Issues* 19, pp. 123–39.

Meins, E. (1997) *Security of Attachment and the Social Development of Cognition.* Hove: Psychology Press.

Meins, E. (1999) Sensitivity, security and internal working models: bridging the transmission gap. *Attachment and Human Development* 1(3), pp. 325–42.

Meins, E., Fernyhough, C., Fradley, E. and Tuckey, M. (2001) Rethinking maternal sensitivity: mothers' comments on infants' mental processes predict security of attachment at 12 months. *Journal of Child Psychology and Psychiatry* 42, pp. 637–48.

Meins, E., Fernyhough, C., Wainwright, R., Gupta, M., Fradley, E. and Tuckey, M. (2002) Maternal mind-mindedness and attachment security as predictors of Theory of Mind understanding. *Child Development* 73(6), pp. 1715–26.

Miller-Perrin, C. and Perrin, R. (1999) *Child Maltreatment: An introduction.* Thousand Oaks: Sage.

Milling Kinard, E. (1980) Emotional development in physically abused children. *American Journal of Orthopsychiatry* 50(4), pp. 686–96.

Milner, J. (2003) Social information processing in high-risk and physically abusive parents. *Child Abuse and Neglect* 27, pp. 7–20.

Minde, K. (2003) Attachment problems as a spectrum disorder: implications for diagnosis and treatment. *Attachment and Human Development* 5(3), pp. 289–96.

Minuchin, S. (1974) *Families and Family Therapy.* Cambridge, MA: Harvard University Press.

Moss, E., St.Laurent, D. and Parent, S. (1999) Disorganized attachment and developmental risk at school age. In J. Solomon and C. George (eds), *Attachment Disorganization.* New York: Guilford Press pp. 160–86.

Murphy, C. and O'Farrell, P. (1996) Marital violence among alcoholics. *Current Directions in Psychological Science* 5, pp. 183–6.

Murray, L., Sinclair, D., Cooper, P., Ducournau, P and Turner, P. (1999) The Socioemotional development of 5-year old children of postnatally depressed mothers. *Journal of Child Psychology and Psychiatry* 40(8), pp. 1259–71.

Myers, J., Berliner, L., Briere, J., Hendrix, C.T., Carole, J. and Reid, T. (eds)

(2002) *The APSAC Handbook on Maltreatment*, 2nd edn. Thousand Oaks: Sage.

Ney, P. Fung, T. and Wickett, A. (1994) The worst combination of child abuse and neglect. *Child Abuse and Neglect* 18, pp. 705–14.

Norwood, R. (1985) *Women who Love Too Much*. New York: Arrow Books.

Oates, R. (1996) *The Spectrum of Child Abuse: Assessment, treatment, and prevention*. New York: Brunner/Mazel.

Oatley, K. and Jenkins, J. (1996) *Understanding Emotions*. Oxford: Blackwell.

O'Connor, T. (2002) Attachment disorders of infancy and childhood. In M. Rutter and E. Taylor (eds), *Child and Adolescent Psychiatry: Modern approaches*, 4th edn. Oxford: Blackwell Scientific, pp. 776–92.

O'Connor, T. and the ERA study team (1999) Attachment disturbances and disorders in children exposed to early deprivation. *Infant Mental Health Journal* 20, pp. 10–29.

O'Connor, T., Marvin, R., Rutter, M., Olrick, J., Britner, P. and the ERA Study Team (2003) Child-parent attachment following early institutional deprivation. *Development and Psychopathology* 15, pp. 19–38.

O'Connor, T., Rutter, M. and the ERA study team (2000) Attachment disorder behavior following early severe deprivation: extension and longitudinal follow-up. *Journal of the American Academy of Child Adolescent Psychiatry* 39(6), pp. 703–12.

Ogawa, J., Sroufe, A., Weinfield, N., Carlson, E. and Egeland, B. (1997) Development and the fragmented self: longitudinal study of dissociative symptomatology in a nonclinical sample. *Development and Psychopathology* 9, pp. 855–79.

Olds, D., Eckenrode, J., Henderson, C., Kitzman, H., Powers, J., Cole, R., Sidora, K., Morris, P., Pettiee, L. and Luckey, D. (1997) Long-term effects of home visitation on maternal life course and child abuse and neglect: 15-year follow-up of a randomized trial. *Journal of the American Medical Association* 278, pp. 637–43.

Olds, D., Henderson, C. and Tatelbaum, D. (1986) Preventing child abuse and neglect: a randomized trial of nurse home visitation. *Pediatrics* 78, pp. 65–78.

Olds, D. and Kitzman, H. (1993) Review of research on home visiting for pregnant women and parents of young children. *The Future of Children: Home Visiting* 3(3), pp. 53–92.

Osofsky, J. Cohen, G. and Drell, M. (1995) The effects of trauma on young children: a case of 2 year old twins. *International Journal of Psycho-Analysis* 76(3), pp. 595–607.

Owen, M. and Cox, M. (1997) Marital conflict and the development of infant parent attachment relationships. *Journal of Family Psychology* 11, pp. 152–64.

Parker, J. and Herrera, C. (1996) Interpersonal processes in friendship. *Developmental Psychology* 29, pp. 611–21.

Perry, B. (1997) Incubated in error: neurodevelopmental factors in the 'cycle of violence'. In J. Osofsky (ed.), *Children in a Violent Society.* New York: Guilford Press.

Perry, B. (1999) http://www.bcm.tmc.edu/civitas/principles

Perry, B., Pollard, R., Blakley, T., Baker, W. and Vigilante, D. (1995) Childhood trauma, the neurobiology of adaptation, and 'use dependent' development of the brain: how 'states' become 'traits'. *Infant Mental Health Journal* 16(4), pp. 271–91.

Pianta, R., Egeland, B. and Erikson, M. (1989) The antecedents of maltreatment: results of the Mother-Child Interaction Project. In D. Cicchetti and V. Carlson (eds), *Child Maltreatment: Theory and research on the causes of and consequences of child abuse and neglect.* New York: Cambridge University Press, pp. 158–74.

Polansky, N., Chalmers, M., Buttenwieser, E. and Williams, D. (1981) *Damaged Parents: An anatomy of child neglect.* Chicago: University of Chicago Press.

Polledri, P. (1996) Munchausen Syndrome by Proxy and perversion of the maternal instinct. *Journal of Forensic Psychiatry* 7, pp. 551–62

Precey, G. (1998) Assessing issues in working with mothers who induce illness in their children. *Child and Family Social Work* 3(4), pp. 227–37.

Radke-Yarrow, M. (1999) *Children of Depressed Mothers: From early childhood to maturity.* Cambridge: Cambridge University Press.

Radke-Yarrow, M., Cummings, E., Kuczynski, L., and Chapmen, M. (1985) Patterns of attachment in two- and three-year olds in normal families and families with parental depression. *Child Development* 56, pp. 591–615.

Reder, P., Duncan, S. and Gray, M. (1993) *Beyond Blame: Child abuse tragedies revisited.* London: Routledge.

Reder, P. and Duncan, S. (1999) *Lost Innocents: A follow up study of fatal child abuse.* London: Routledge.

Reder, P. and Duncan, S. (2000) Abuse then and now. In P. Peder, M. McClure and A. Jolley (eds), *Family Matters: Interfaces between child and adult mental health.* London: Routledge, pp. 38–54.

Riddley, M. (2003) *Nature via Nurture: Genes, experience and what makes us human.* London: Fourth Estate.

Robert-Tissot, C., Cramer, B., Stern, D., Serpa, S., Bachman, J., Palacio-Espasa, F., Knauer, D., de Muralt, M., Berney, C. and Mendiguren, G. (1996) Outcome evaluation in brief mother-infant psychotherapies: report on 75 cases. *Infant Mental Health Journal* 17, pp. 97–114.

Roberts, J. (1988) Why are some families more vulnerable to child abuse? In K. Browne, C. Davies and P. Stratton (eds), *Early Prediction and Prevention of Child Abuse.* Chichester: Wiley, pp 58–78.

Roy, P., Rutter, M. and Pickles, A. (2000) Institutional care: risk from family background or pattern of rearing? *Journal of Child Psychology and Psychiatry* 41(2), pp. 139–49.

Rutter, M. (1979) Protective factors in children's responses to stress and disadvantage. In M. W. Kent and J. Rolf (eds), *Primary Prevention of Psychopathology: Vol 3: Social competence in children.* Hanover, NH: University Press of New England, pp. 49–74.

Rutter, M., Anderson-Wood, L., Beckett, C., Bredenkamp, D., Castle, J., Groothues, C., Kreppner, J., Keaveney, L., Lord, C. and O'Connor (1999) Quasi-autistic patterns following severe early global privation. *Journal of Child Psychology and Psychiatry* 40, pp. 537–49.

Sable, P. (2004) Attachment, ethology and adult psychotherapy. *Attachment and Human Development* 6(1), pp. 3–19.

Saltaris, C. (2002) Psychopathy in juvenile offenders: can temperament and attachment be considered as robust developmental precursors? *Clinical Psychology Review* 22, pp. 729–52.

Salzinger, S., Feldman, R., Hammer, M. and Rosario, M. (1993) The effects of physical abuse on children's social relationships. *Child Development* 64, pp. 169–87.

Schofield, G. and Beek, M. (forthcoming) *Providing a Secure Base: A handbook of attachment theory for fostering and adoption.* London: BAAF.

Schore, A. (1994) *Affect Regulation and the Origins of the Self: The neurobiology of emotional development.* Hillsdale, NJ: Erlbaum.

Schore, A. (1996) The experience-dependent maturation of a regulatory system in the orbital prefrontal cortex and the origin of developmental psychopathology. *Development and Psychopathology* 8, pp. 59–87.

Schore, A. (2001a) Effects of a secure attachment relationship on right brain development, affect regulation, and infant mental health. *Infant Mental Health Journal* 22(1–2), pp. 7–66.

Schore, A. (2001b) The effects of early relational trauma on right brain development, affect regulation, and infant mental health. *Infant Mental Health Journal* 22(1–2), pp. 201–69.

Schuengel, C., van IJzendoorn, M. and Bakerman-Kranenberg, M. (1999) Frightening maternal behaviour linking unresolved loss and disorganised infant attachment. *Journal of Consulting and Clinical Psychology* 67, pp. 54–63.

Schwartz, J. and Pollard, J. (2004) Introduction to the special issue: attachment-based psychoanalytic psychotherapy. *Attachment and Human Development* 6(2), pp. 113–16.

Scott, S. (2003) Integrating attachment theory with other approaches to developmental psychology. *Attachment and Human Development* 5(3), pp. 307–12

Siegel, D. (1999) *The Developing Mind: Toward a neurobiology of interpersonal experience.* New York: Guilford Press.

Siegel, D. (2003) An interpersonal neurobiology of psychotherapy: the developing mind and the resolution of trauma. In M. Solomon and D. Siegel (eds), *Healing Trauma: Attachment, mind, body and brain.* New York: W.W. Norton, pp.1–56.

Shapiro, F. (1995) *Eye Movement Desensitization and Reprocessing: Basic principles, protocols and procedures.* New York: Guilford Press.

Shapiro, F. and Maxfield, L. (2003) EMDR and information processing in psychotherapy treatment. In M. Solomon and D. Siegel (eds), *Healing Trauma: Attachment, mind, body and brain.* New York: W.W. Norton, pp. 196–220.

Shaw, D., Owens, E., Vondra, J., Keenan, K. and Winslow, E. (1997) Early risk factors and pathways in the development of early disruptive behavior problems. *Development and Psychopathology* 8, pp. 679–700.

Shipman, K., Zeman, J., Penza, S. and Champion, K. (2000) Emotion management skills in sexually maltreated and nonmaltreated girls: a developmental psychopathology perspective. *Development and Psychopathology* 12(1), pp. 47–62.

Sidebotham, P. Heron, J. and the ALSPAC Team (2003) Child maltreatment in the 'children of the nineties': the role of the child. *Child Abuse and Neglect* 27(3), pp. 337–52.

Sinason, V. (ed.) (2002) *Attachment, Trauma and Multiplicity: Working with dissociative identity disorder.* London: Routledge.

Skuse, D., Bentovim, A., Hodges, J., Stevenson, J., Andreou, C., Lanyado, M., New, M., Williams, B. and McMillan, D. (1998) Risk factors for development of sexually abusive behaviour in sexually victimised adolescent boys: cross sectional study. *British Medical Journal* 317, pp. 175–9.

Slade, A. (1999) Attachment theory and research: implications for the theory and practice of individual psychotherapy with adults. In J. Cassidy and P. Shaver (eds), *Handbook of Attachment.* New York: Guilford Press, pp. 575–94.

Slade, A. (2004) Two therapies: attachment organization and the clinical process. In L. Atkinson, and S. Goldberg (eds), *Attachment Issues in Psychopathology and Interventions.* Mahwah, NJ: Lawrence Erlbaum Associates, pp. 181–206.

Smallbone, S. and Dadds, M. (2000) Attachment and coercive sexual behavior. *Sexual Abuse* 12(1).

Solomon, J. and George, C. (1996) Defining the caregiving system: toward a theory of caregiving. *Infant Mental Health Journal* 17(3), pp. 447–64.

Solomon, J, and George, C. (1999a) The place of disorganization in attachment theory: linking classic observations with contemporary findings. In J. Solomon and C. George (eds), *Attachment Disorganization.* New York: Guilford Press, pp. 3–32.

Solomon, J. and George, C. (1999) (eds), *Attachment Disorganization.* New York: Guilford Press.

Spelz, M. (1990) The treatment of preschool conduct problems: an integration of behavioral and attachment concepts. In M. Greenberg, D. Cicchetti and M. Cummings (eds), *Attachment in the Preschool Years: Theory, research and intervention.* Chicago: University of Chicago Press, pp. 399–426.

Spiker, D., Ferguson, J. and Brooks-Gunn, J. (1993) Enhancing maternal interactive behaviour and child social competence in low birth weight, premature children. *Child Development* 64, pp. 754–68.

Sroufe, J. (2003) Commentary: comprehending the incomprehensible. *Attachment and Human Development* 5(4), pp. 409–14.

Sroufe, L.A., Carlson, E., Levy, A. and Egeland, B. (1999) Implications of attachment theory for developmental psychopathology. *Development and Psychopathology* 11(1), pp. 1–14.

Steele, B. (1986) Notes on the lasting effects of early child abuse throughout the life cycle. *Child Abuse and Neglect* 10, pp. 283–91.

Steele, H. (2003) Unrelenting catastrophic trauma within the family: when every secure base is abusive. *Attachment and Human Development* 5(4), pp. 353–66.

Steele, M., Hodges, J., Kaniuk, J., Hillman, S. and Henderson, K. (2003) Attachment representations and adoption: associations between maternal states of mind and emotion narratives in previously maltreated children. *Journal of Child Psychotherapy* 29(2), pp. 187–205.

Stern, D. (1987) *The Interpersonal World of the Infant.* New York: Basic Books.

Sternberg, K., Lamb, M., Greenbaum, C., Cicchetti, D., Dawud, S., Cortes, R., Krispin, O., and Lorey, F. (1993) Effects of domestic violence in children's behaviour problems and depression. *Developmental Psychology* 29, pp. 44–52.

Stevenson, O. (1998) *Neglected Children: Issues and dilemmas.* Oxford: Blackwell Science.

Sulloway, F. (1996) *Born to Rebel.* New York: Pantheon.

Taylor, G., Bagby, R. M., Parker, J. (1997) *Disorders of Affect Regulation: Alexithymia in medical and psychiatric illness.* Cambridge: Cambridge University Press.

Teegan, F. (1999) Childhood sexual abuse and long-term sequelae. In A. Maercker, M. Schutzwohl, and Z. Solomon (eds), *Post-Traumatic Stress Disorder.* Seattle, WA: Hogrefe and Huber, pp. 97–112.

Teti, D. (1999) Conceptualizations of disorganisation in the preschool years. In J. Solomon and C. George (eds), *Attachment Disorganization.* New York: Guilford Press, pp. 213–42.

Teti, D., Gelfand, D., Messinger, D. and Isabella, R. (1995) Maternal depression and the quality of early attunement. *Developmental Psychology* 31, pp. 364–76.

Toth, S., Cicchetti, D., Macfie, J. and Emde, R. (1997) Representations of self and other in the narratives of neglected, physically abused, and sexually abused preschoolers. *Development and Psychopathology* 9, pp. 781–96.

Toth, S., Cicchetti, D., Macfie, J., Maughan, A. and Vanmeenen, K. (2000) Narrative representations of caregivers and self in maltreated pre-schoolers. *Attachment and Human Development* 2(3), pp. 271–305.

Trevarthen, C. and Aitkin, K. (2001) Infant intersubjectivity: research, theory, and clinical applications. *Journal of Child Psychology and Psychiatry* 42(1), pp. 3–48.

Trevarthen, C. and Hubley, P. (1978) Secondary intersubjectivity: confidence, confiding and acts of meaning in the first year. In A. Lock (ed.), *Action Gesture and Symbol*. London: Academic Press, pp. 183–229.

Trickett, P. (1997) Sexual and physical abuse and the development of social competence. In S. Luthar, J. Burack, D. Cicchetti and J. Weisz (eds), *Developmental Psychopathology: Perspectives on adjustment, risk and disorder.* New York: Cambridge University Press, pp. 67–92.

Trickett, P. and McBride-Chang, C. (1995) The developmental impact of different forms of child abuse and neglect. *Developmental Review* 15, pp. 311–37.

Trickett, P. and Putnam, F. (1998) Developmental consequences of child sexual abuse. In P. Trickett and C. Schellenbach (eds), *Violence Against Children in the Family and the Community.* Washington DC: American Psychological Association, pp. 39–56.

Tronick, E. and Weinberg, M. (1997) Depressed mothers and infants: failure to form dyadic states of consciousness. In L. Murray and P. Cooper (eds), *Post-partum Depression in Child Development.* New York: Guilford Press, pp. 54–81.

Tyrell, C., Dozier, M., Teague, G. and Fallot, R. (1999) Effective treatment relationships for persons with serious psychiatric disorders: the importance of attachment states of mind. *Journal of Consulting and Clinical Psychology* 67, pp. 725–33.

van der Kolk, B. (2003) Post traumatic stress disorder and the nature of trauma. In M. Solomon and D. Siegel (eds), *Healing Trauma: Attachment, mind, body and brain.* New York: W.W. Norton, pp. 168–195.

van Gulden, H. and Bartels-Rabb, L. (1995) *Real Parents, Real Children: Parenting the adopted child.* New York: Crossroad.

van IJzendoorn, M., Schuengel, C. and Bakermans-Kranenburg, M. (1999) Disorganized attachment in early childhood: meta-analysis of precursors, concomitants, and sequelae. *Development and Psychopathology* 11, pp. 225–49.

von Knorring, A. (1991) Children and alcoholics. *Journal of Child Psychology and Psychiatry* 23(3), pp. 411–21.

Walsh, C., MacMillan, H. and Jamieson, E. (2002) The relationship between parental psychiatric disorder and child physical and sexual abuse. *Child Abuse and Neglect* 26, pp. 11–22.

Waters, E. and Valenzuela, M. (1999) Explaining attachment: clues from research on mild-to-moderately undernourished children in Chile. In J. Solomon and C. George (eds), *Attachment Disorganization.* New York: Guilford Press, pp. 265–87.

Webster-Stratton, C. (1999) *How to Promote Children's Social and Emotional Competence*. London: Sage.

West, M. and George, C. (1999) Abuse and violence in intimate adult relationships: new perspectives from attachment theory. *Attachment and Human Development* 1(2), pp. 137–56.

West, M. and George, C. (2002) Attachment and dysthymia: the contributions of preoccupied attachment and agency of self to depression in women. *Attachment and Human Development* 4(3), pp. 278–93.

Westcott, H. and Jones, D. (1999) Annotation: the abuse of disabled children *Journal of Child Psychology and Psychiatry* 40, pp. 497–506.

Wickham, R. Easton and West, J. (2002) *Therapeutic Work with Sexually Abused Children*. London: Sage.

Widom, C. and Kuhns, J. (1996) Childhood victimization and subsequent risk for promiscuity, prostitution, and teenage pregnancy: a prospective study. *American Journal of Public Health* 86, pp. 1607–12.

Wilson, K. and James, A. (2001) *The Child Protection Handbook*. Bailliere Tindall.

Wilt, S. and Olsen, S. (1996) Prevalence of domestic violence in the United States. *Journal of the American Women's Association* 51, pp. 77–82.

Winnicott, D. (1960) The theory of the parent–infant relationship. In *The Maturational Process and the Facilitating Environment*. New York: International Universities Press, pp. 37–55.

Winnicott, D. (1967) Mirror-role of mother and family in child development. In P. Lomas (ed.), *The Predicament of the Family*. London: Hogarth Press.

Winnicott, D. (1971) *Playing and Reality*. New York: Basic Books.

Wolfe, D. (1999) *Child Abuse: Implications for child development and psychopathology*. Thousand Oaks: Sage.

Young, J. (1994) *Cognitive Therapy for Personality Disorders: A schema-focused approach*, 2nd edn. Sarasota: Professional Resource Press.

Zanarini, M., Frakenburg, F., Bradford Reich, D., Marino, M., Haynes, M. and Gunderson, J. (1999) Violence in the lives of adult borderline patients. *Journal of Nervous and Mental Disease* 187, pp. 65–71.

Zeanah, C. (1996) Beyond insecurity: a reconceptualization of attachment disorders of infancy. *Journal of Consulting and Clinical Psychology* 64, pp. 42–52.

Zimmermann, P. (1999) Structure and functions of internal working models of attachment and their role for emotion regulation. *Attachment and Human Development* 1(3), pp. 291–306.

Author Index

Subject Index